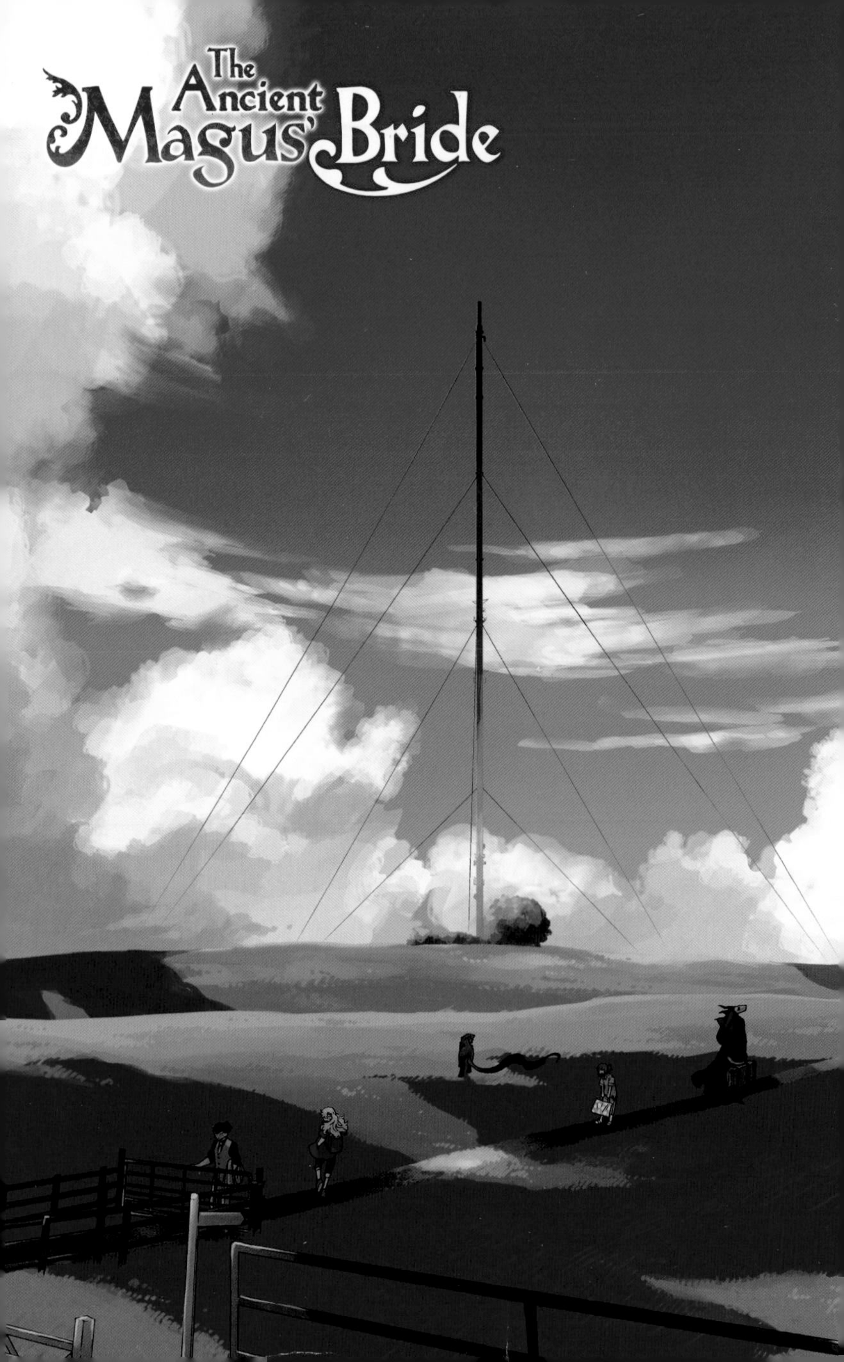
The Ancient Magus' Bride

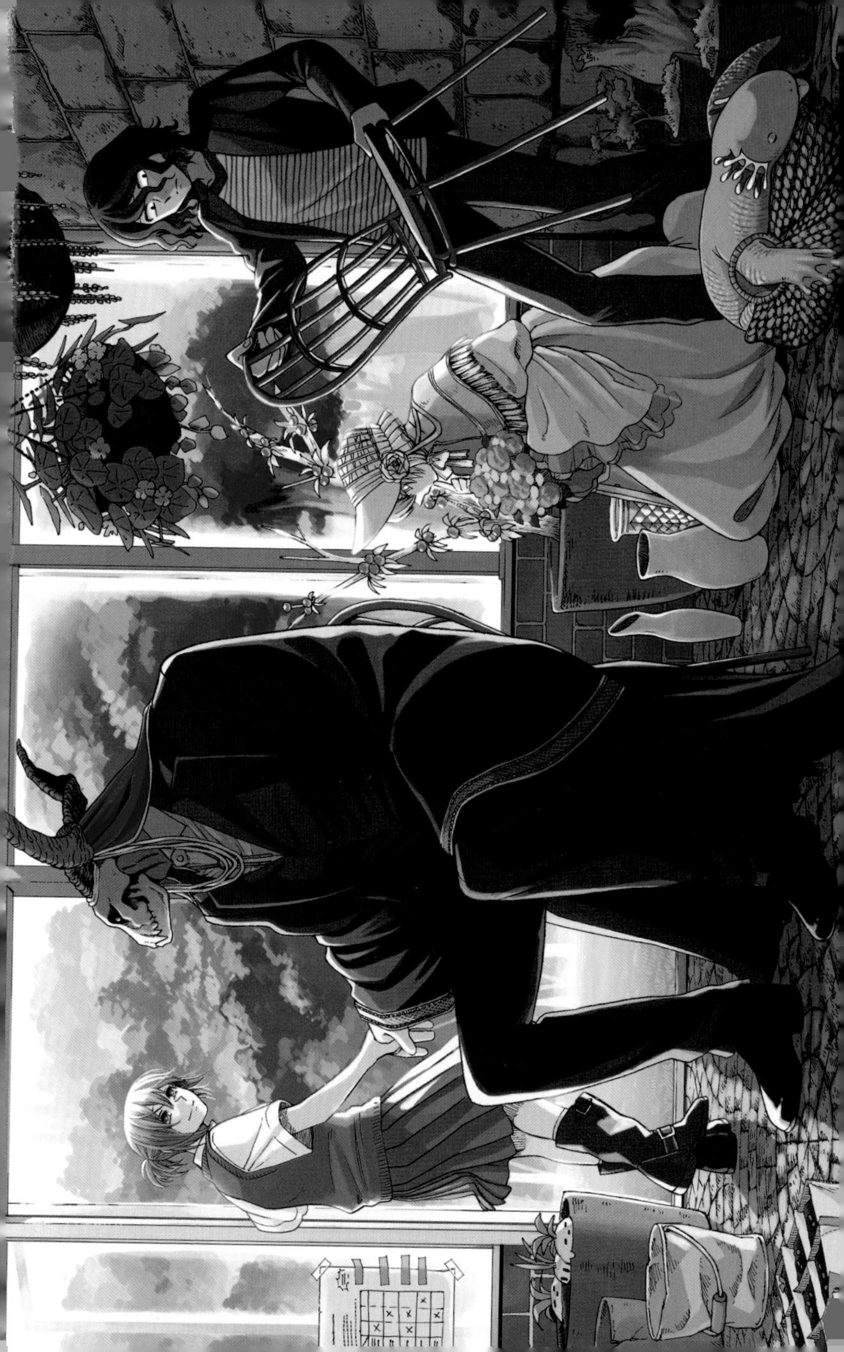

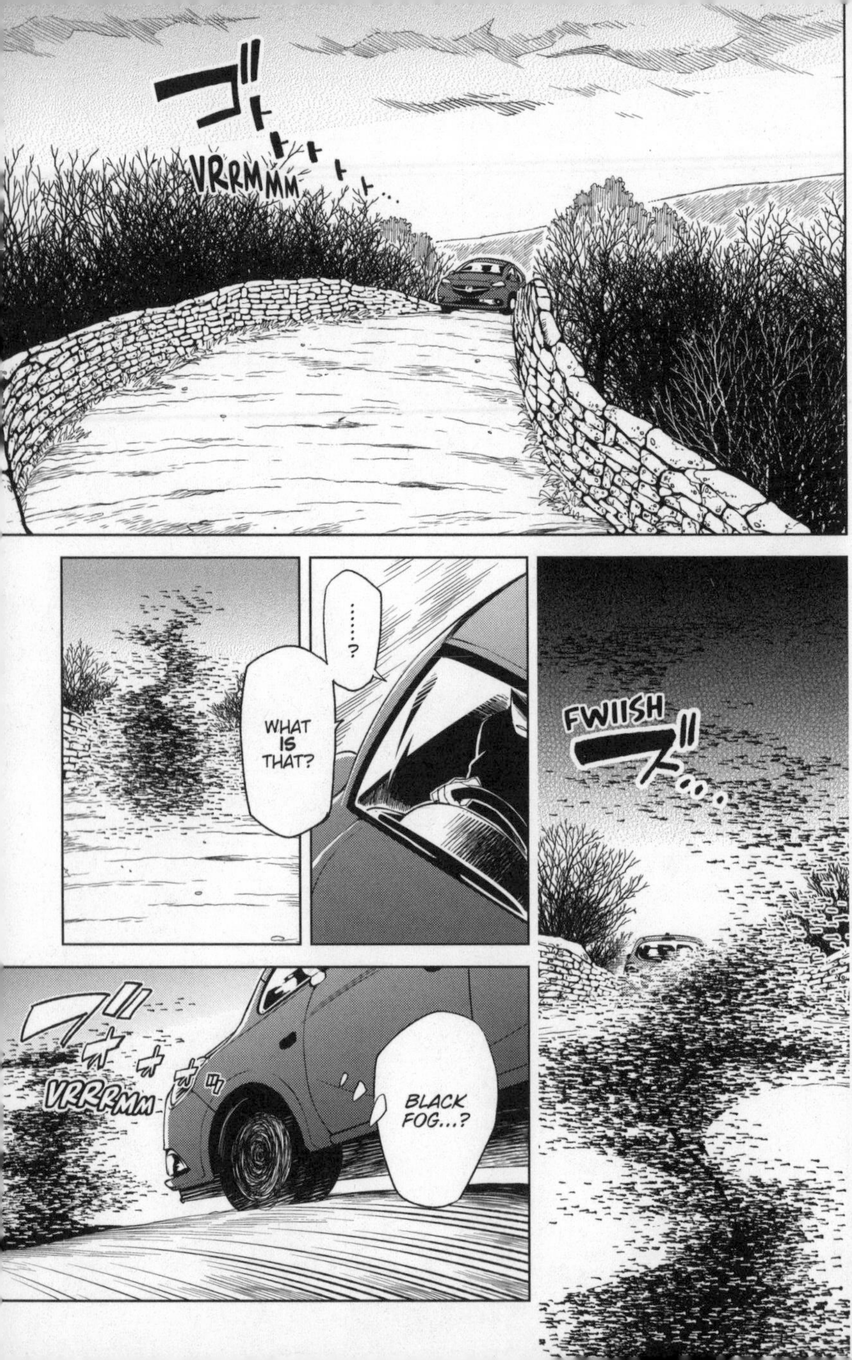
VRRMMM
FWIISH
......?
WHAT IS THAT?
BLACK FOG...?
VRRRMM

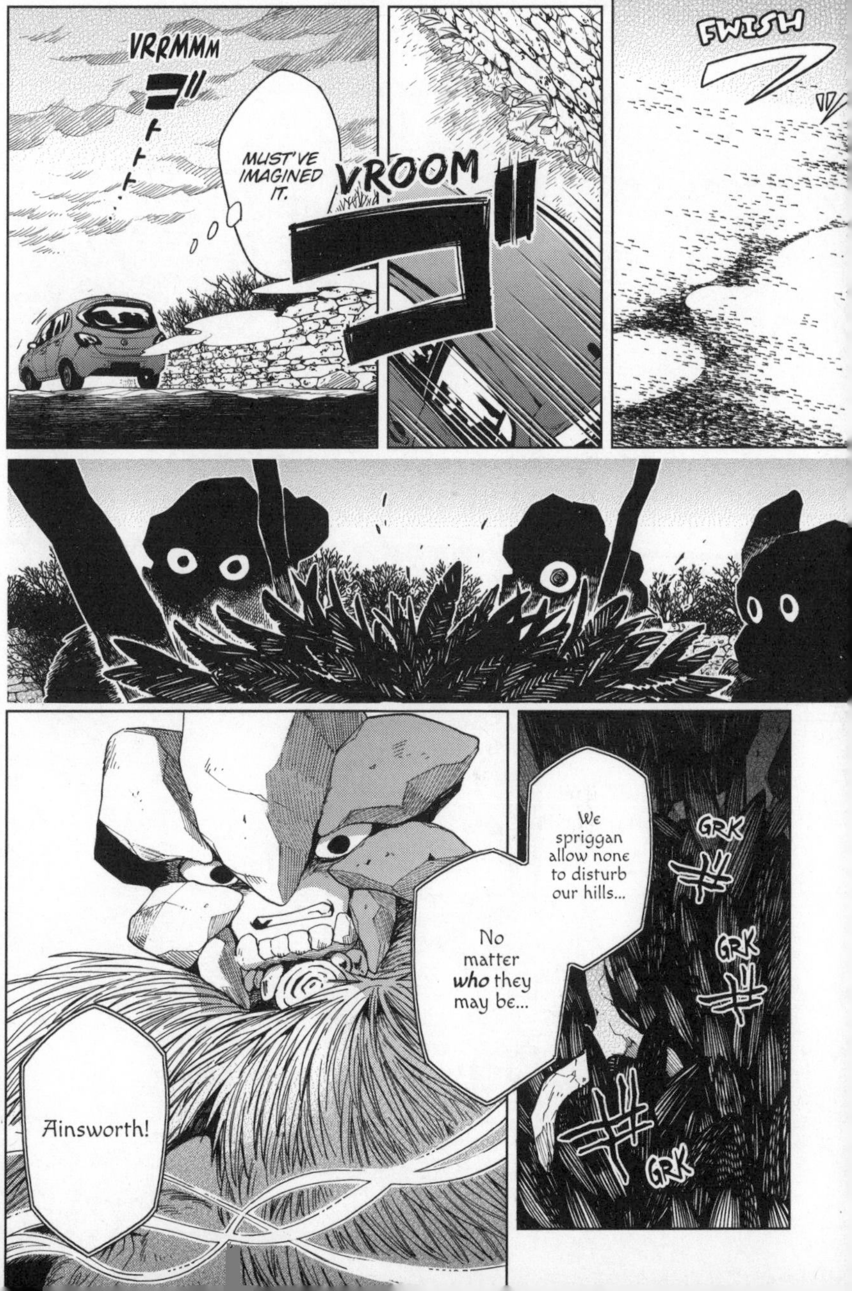
FWISH
VROOM
VRRMMM
MUST'VE IMAGINED IT.
We spriggan allow none to disturb our hills...
GRK
GRK
GRK
No matter **who** they may be...
Ainsworth!

Chapter 41: As you sow, so you shall reap.

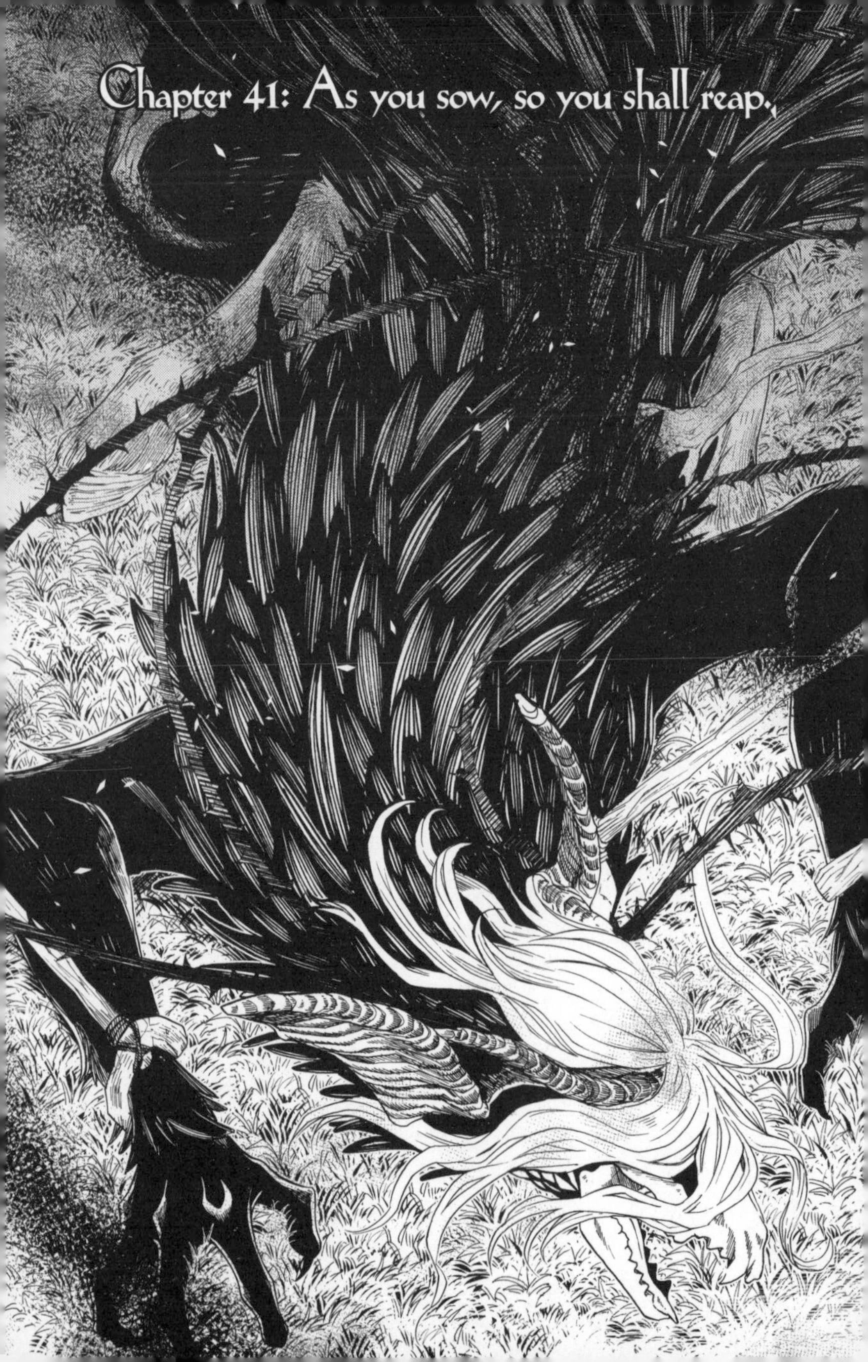

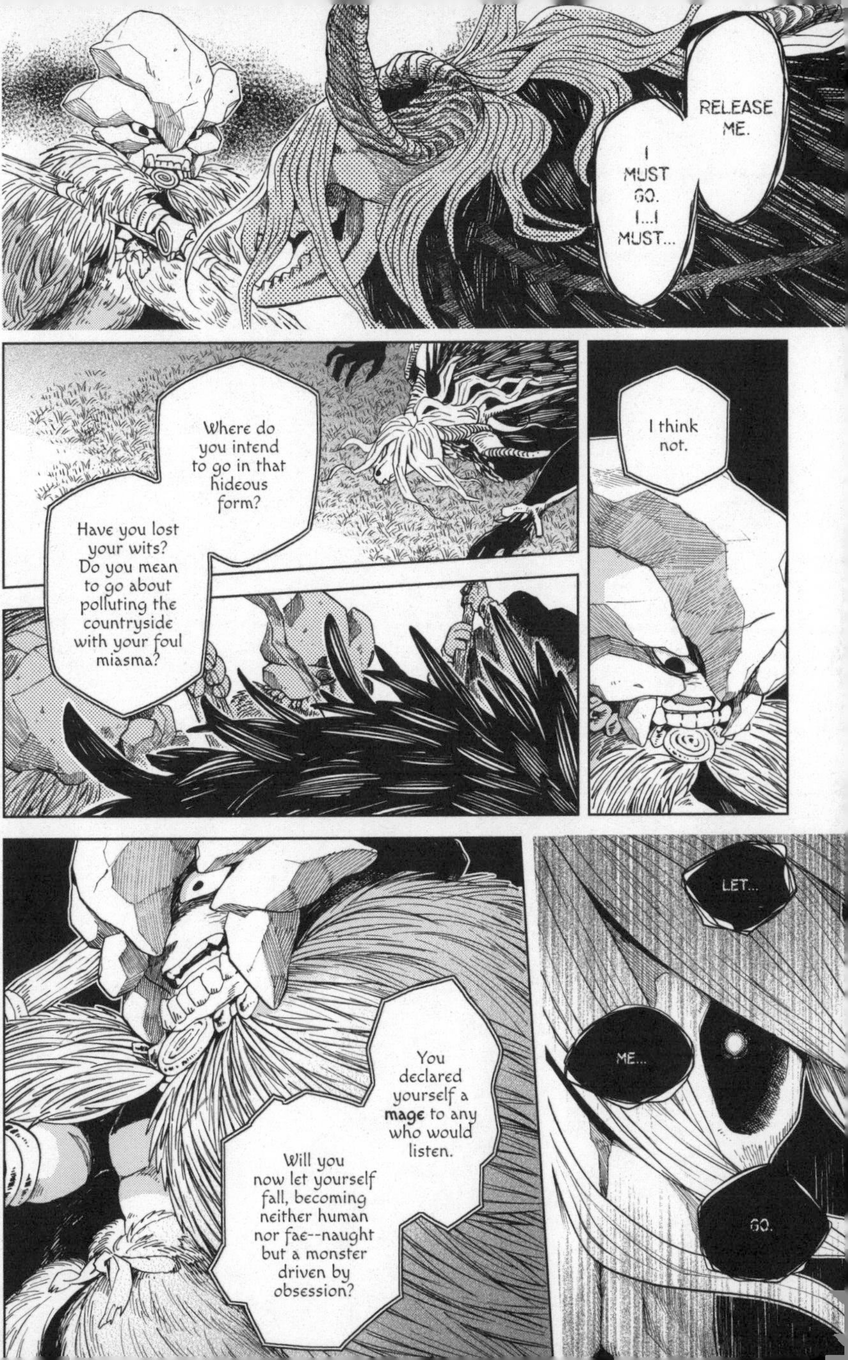
RELEASE ME.
I MUST GO. I...I MUST...
I think not.
Where do you intend to go in that hideous form?
Have you lost your wits? Do you mean to go about polluting the countryside with your foul miasma?
LET...
ME...
GO.
You declared yourself a **mage** to any who would listen.
Will you now let yourself fall, becoming neither human nor fae--naught but a monster driven by obsession?

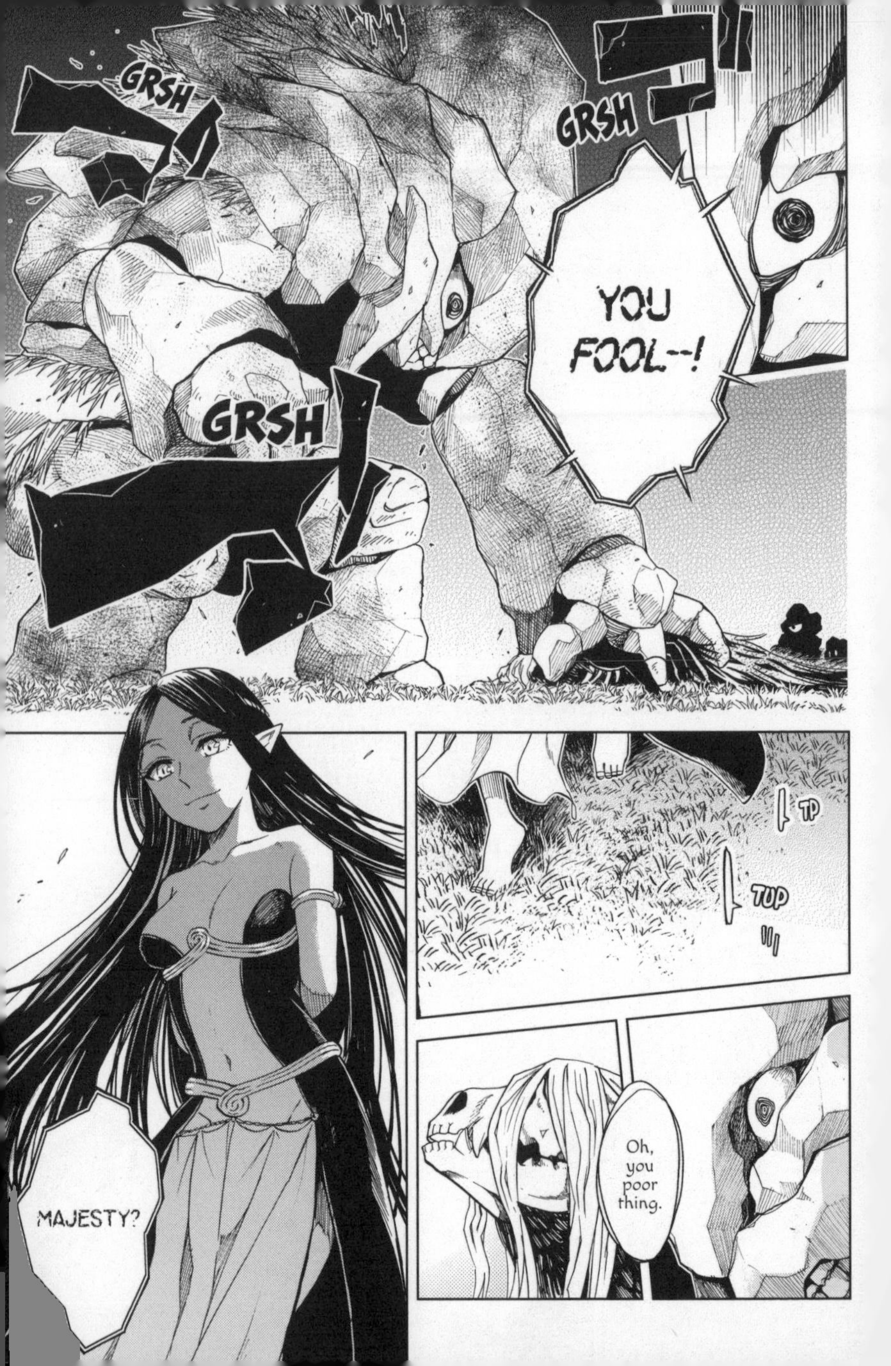
GRSH
YOU FOOL--!
GRSH
GRSH
TP
TUP
Oh, you poor thing.
MAJESTY?

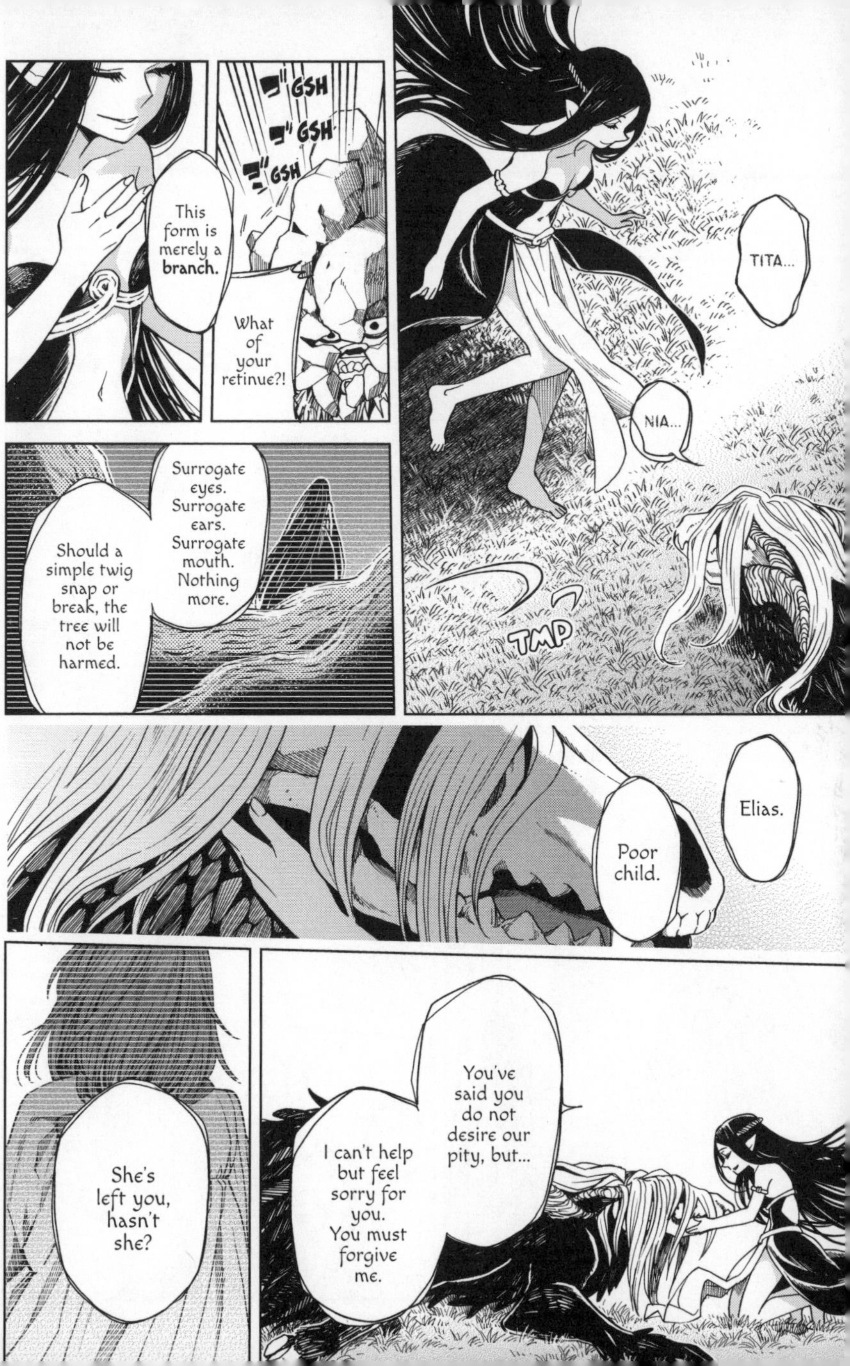
TITA...
NIA...
TMP
GSH
GSH
GSH
What of your retinue?!
This form is merely a branch.
Surrogate eyes. Surrogate ears. Surrogate mouth. Nothing more.
Should a simple twig snap or break, the tree will not be harmed.
Elias.
Poor child.
You've said you do not desire our pity, but...
I can't help but feel sorry for you. You must forgive me.
She's left you, hasn't she?

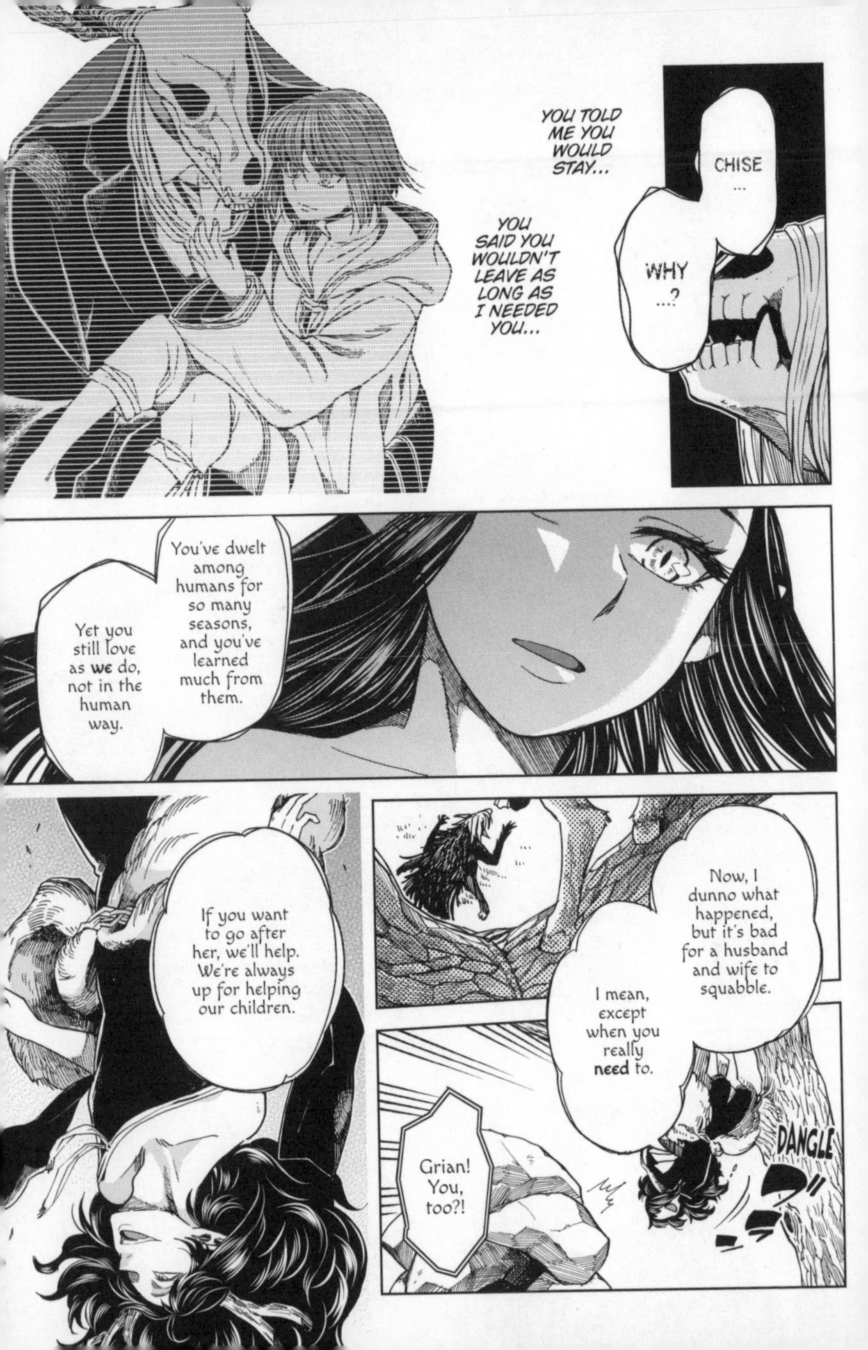
CHISE ...
WHY ...?
YOU TOLD ME YOU WOULD STAY...
YOU SAID YOU WOULDN'T LEAVE AS LONG AS I NEEDED YOU...
You've dwelt among humans for so many seasons, and you've learned much from them.
Yet you still love as **we** do, not in the human way.
Now, I dunno what happened, but it's bad for a husband and wife to squabble.
I mean, except when you really **need** to.
DANGLE
Grian! You, too?!
If you want to go after her, we'll help. We're always up for helping our children.

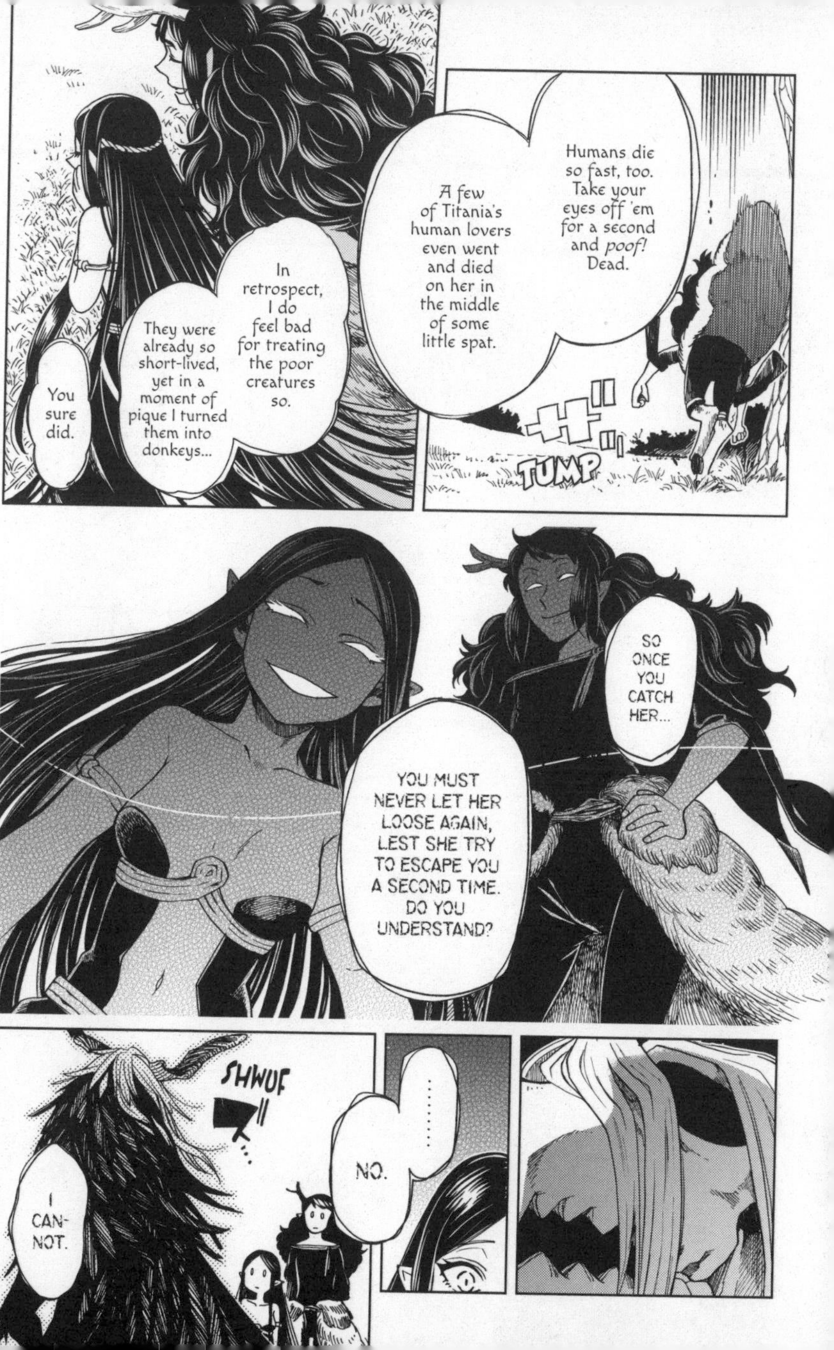
Humans die so fast, too. Take your eyes off 'em for a second and *poof!* Dead.
A few of Titania's human lovers even went and died on her in the middle of some little spat.
TUMP
In retrospect, I do feel bad for treating the poor creatures so.
They were already so short-lived, yet in a moment of pique I turned them into donkeys...
You sure did.
SO ONCE YOU CATCH HER...
YOU MUST NEVER LET HER LOOSE AGAIN, LEST SHE TRY TO ESCAPE YOU A SECOND TIME. DO YOU UNDERSTAND?
......
NO.
SHWUF
I CAN-NOT.

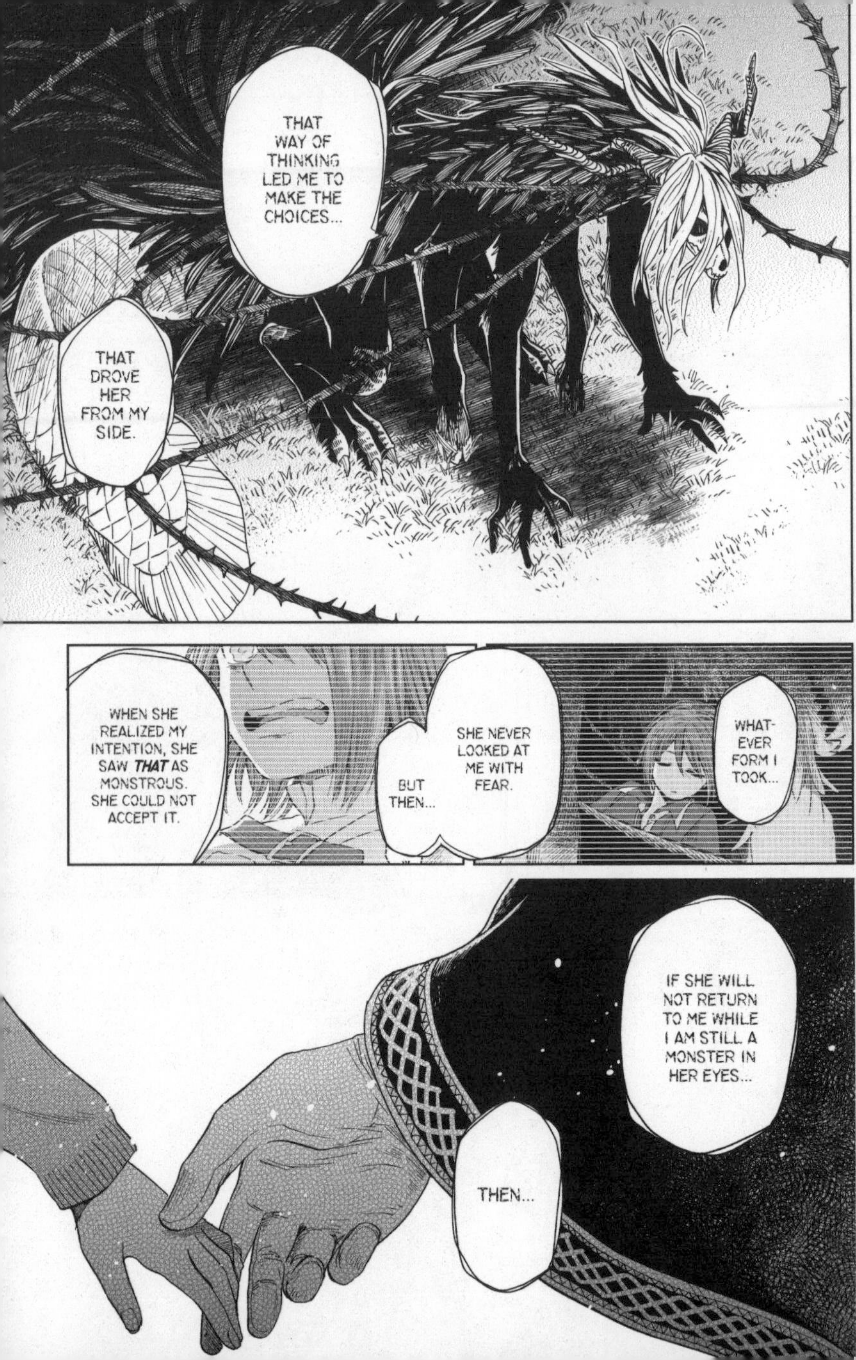
THAT WAY OF THINKING LED ME TO MAKE THE CHOICES...
THAT DROVE HER FROM MY SIDE.
WHAT-EVER FORM I TOOK...
SHE NEVER LOOKED AT ME WITH FEAR.
BUT THEN...
WHEN SHE REALIZED MY INTENTION, SHE SAW *THAT* AS MONSTROUS. SHE COULD NOT ACCEPT IT.
IF SHE WILL NOT RETURN TO ME WHILE I AM STILL A MONSTER IN HER EYES...
THEN...

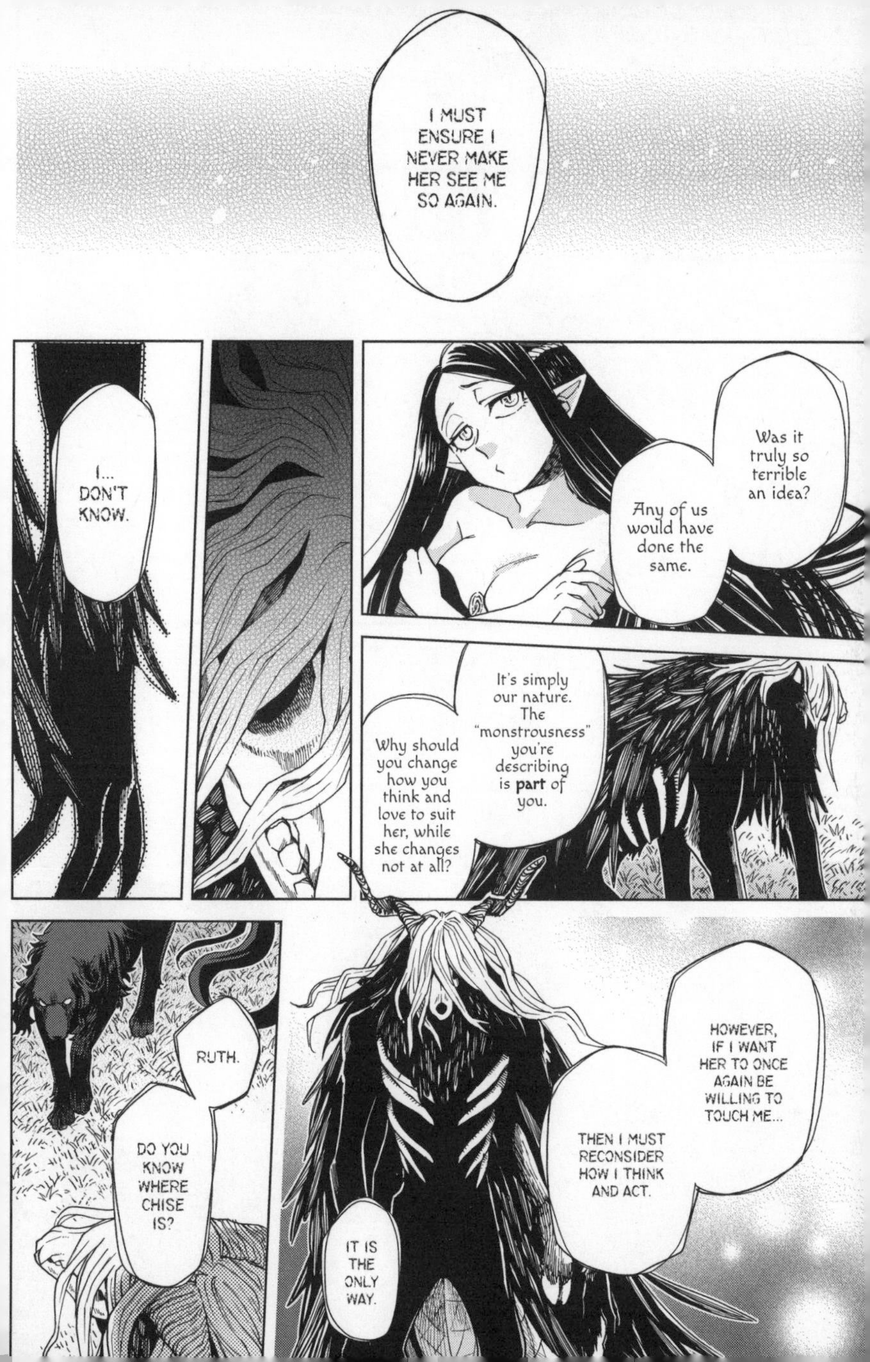
I MUST ENSURE I NEVER MAKE HER SEE ME SO AGAIN.
Was it truly so terrible an idea?
Any of us would have done the same.
It's simply our nature. The "monstrousness" you're describing is **part** of you.
Why should you change how you think and love to suit her, while she changes not at all?
I... DON'T KNOW.
HOWEVER, IF I WANT HER TO ONCE AGAIN BE WILLING TO TOUCH ME...
THEN I MUST RECONSIDER HOW I THINK AND ACT.
IT IS THE ONLY WAY.
RUTH.
DO YOU KNOW WHERE CHISE IS?

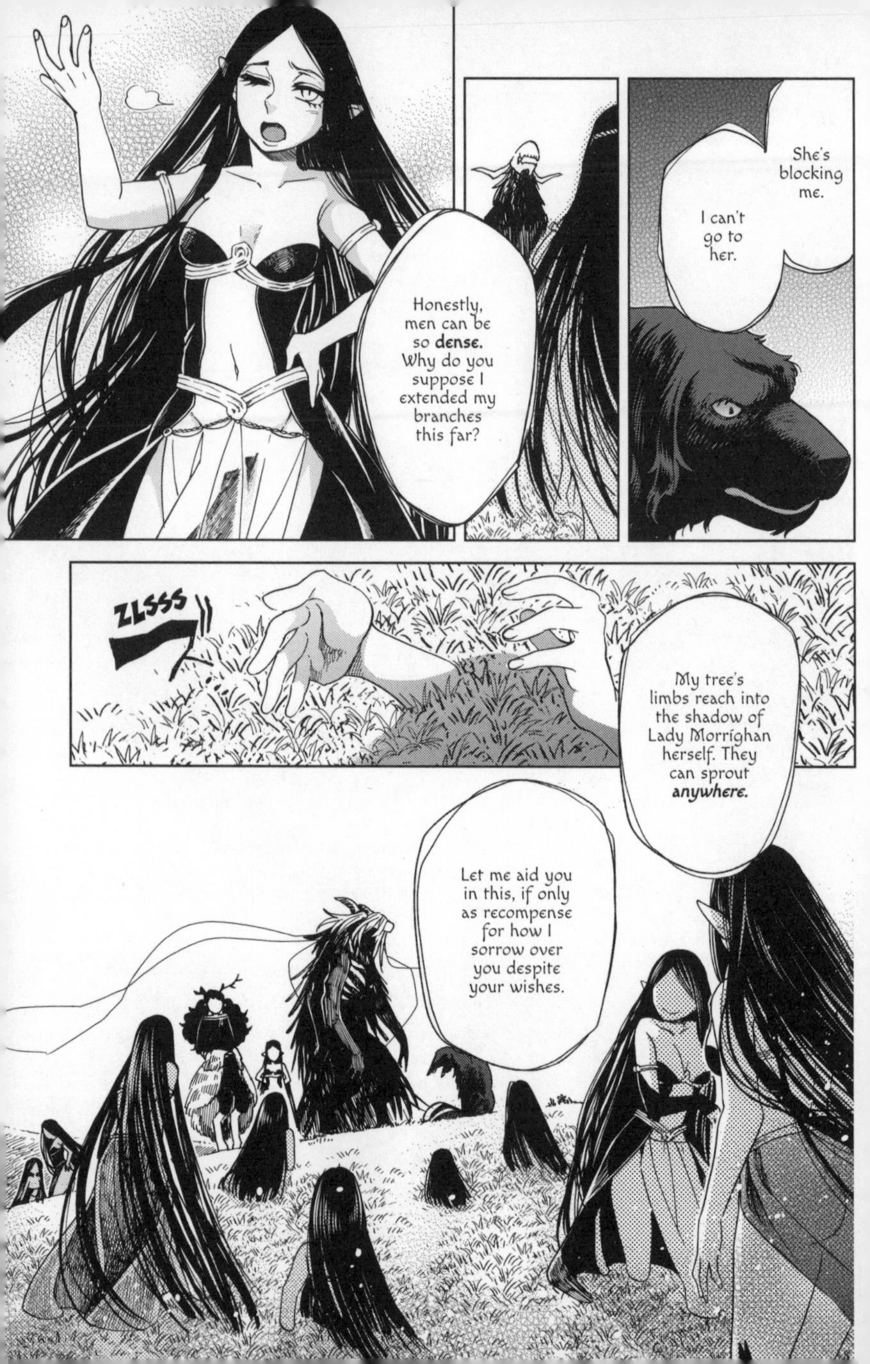
She's blocking me.
I can't go to her.
Honestly, men can be so **dense.** Why do you suppose I extended my branches this far?
My tree's limbs reach into the shadow of Lady Morrighan herself. They can sprout ***anywhere.***
ZLSSS
Let me aid you in this, if only as recompense for how I sorrow over you despite your wishes.

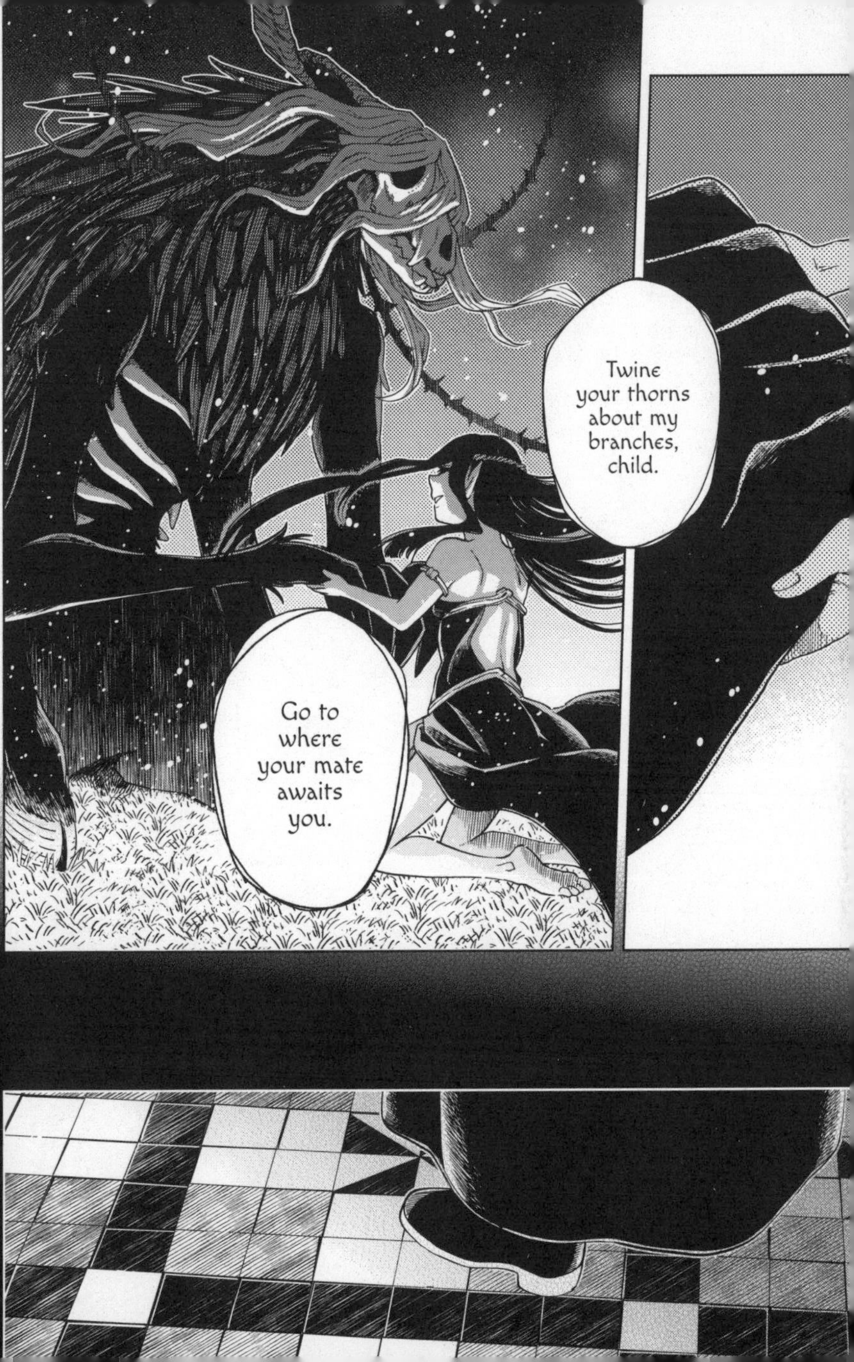
Twine your thorns about my branches, child.
Go to where your mate awaits you.

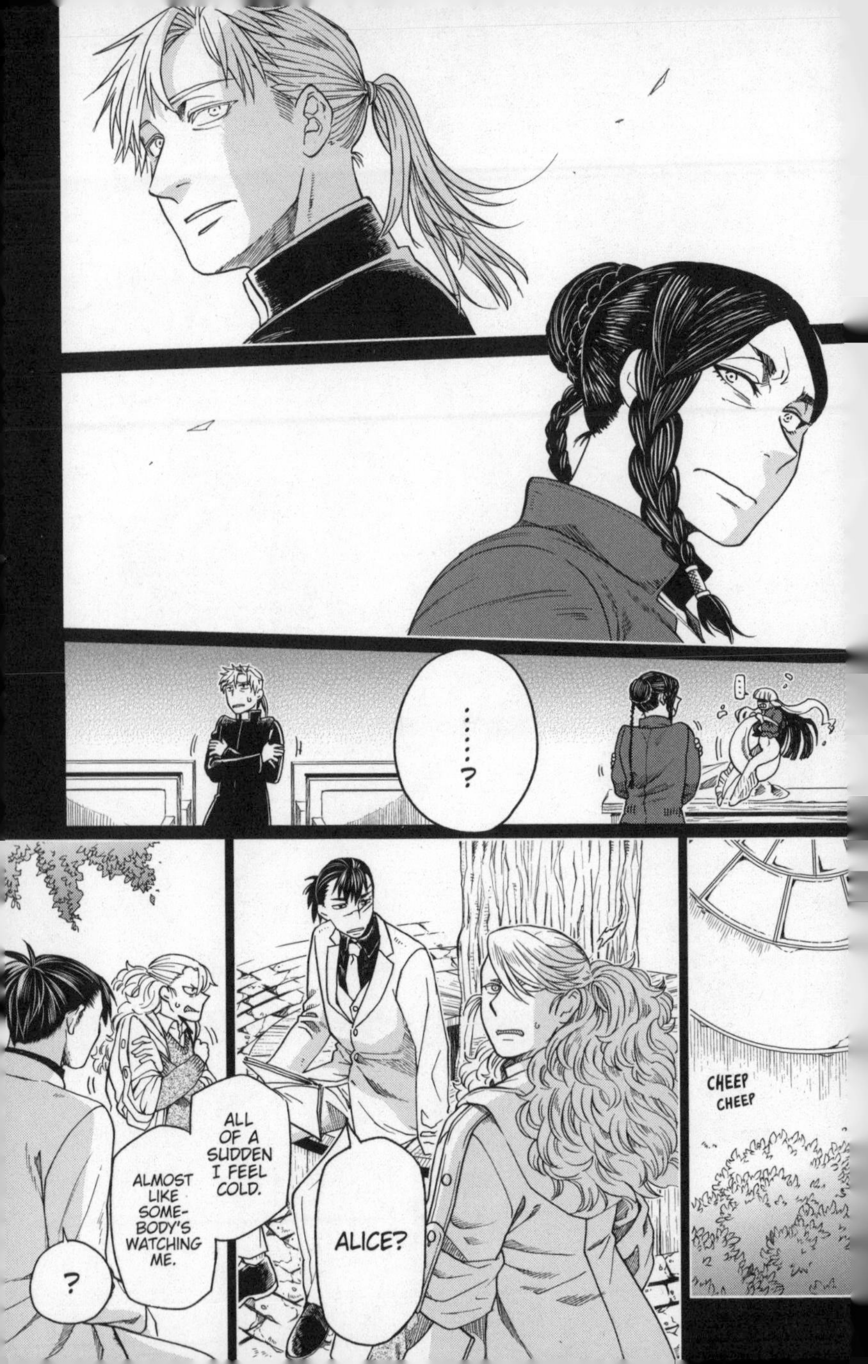

......?
...
CHEEP
CHEEP
ALICE?
ALL OF A SUDDEN I FEEL COLD.
ALMOST LIKE SOME-BODY'S WATCHING ME.
?

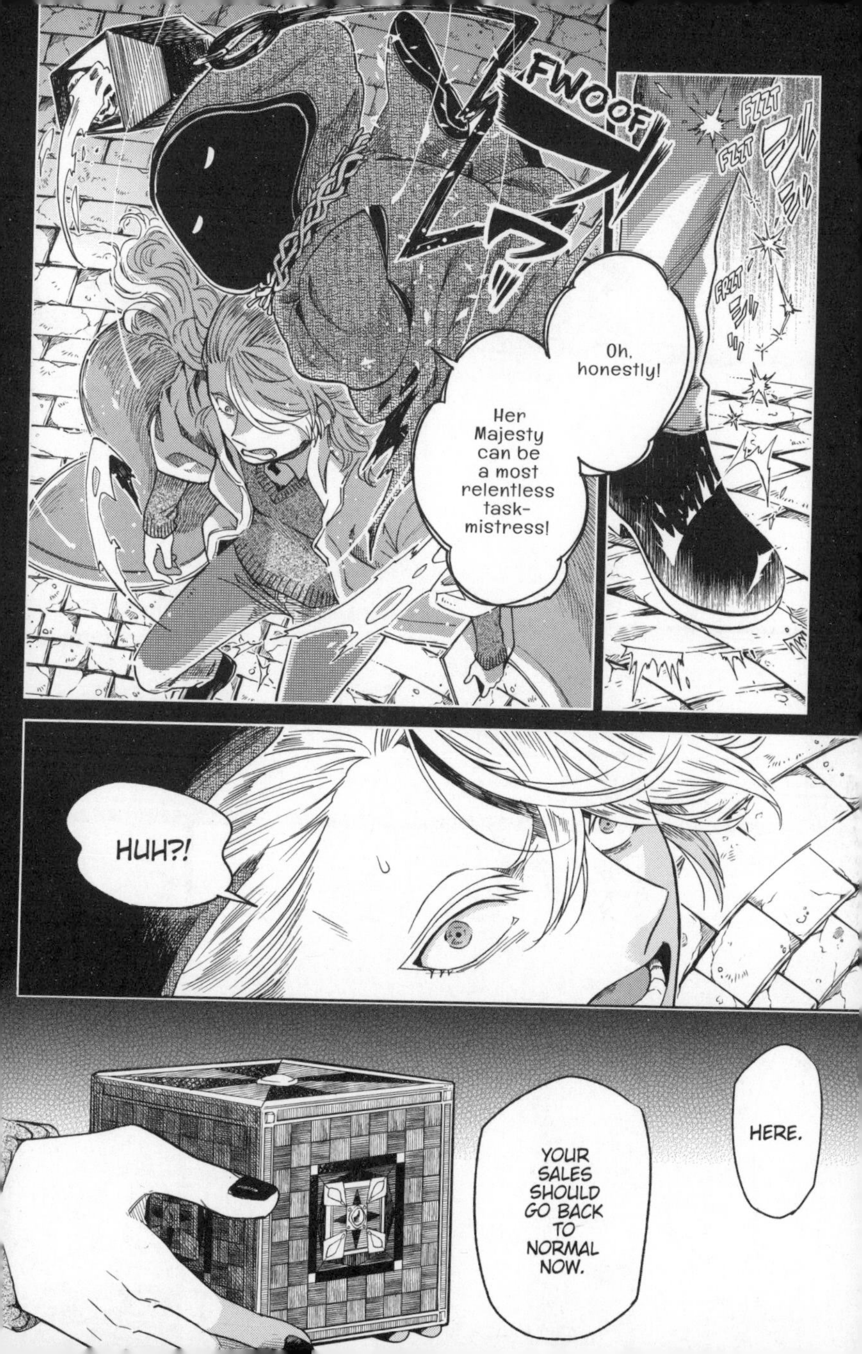
FZZT
FZZT
FRZT
FWOOF
Oh, honestly!
Her Majesty can be a most relentless task-mistress!
HUH?!
HERE.
YOUR SALES SHOULD GO BACK TO NORMAL NOW.

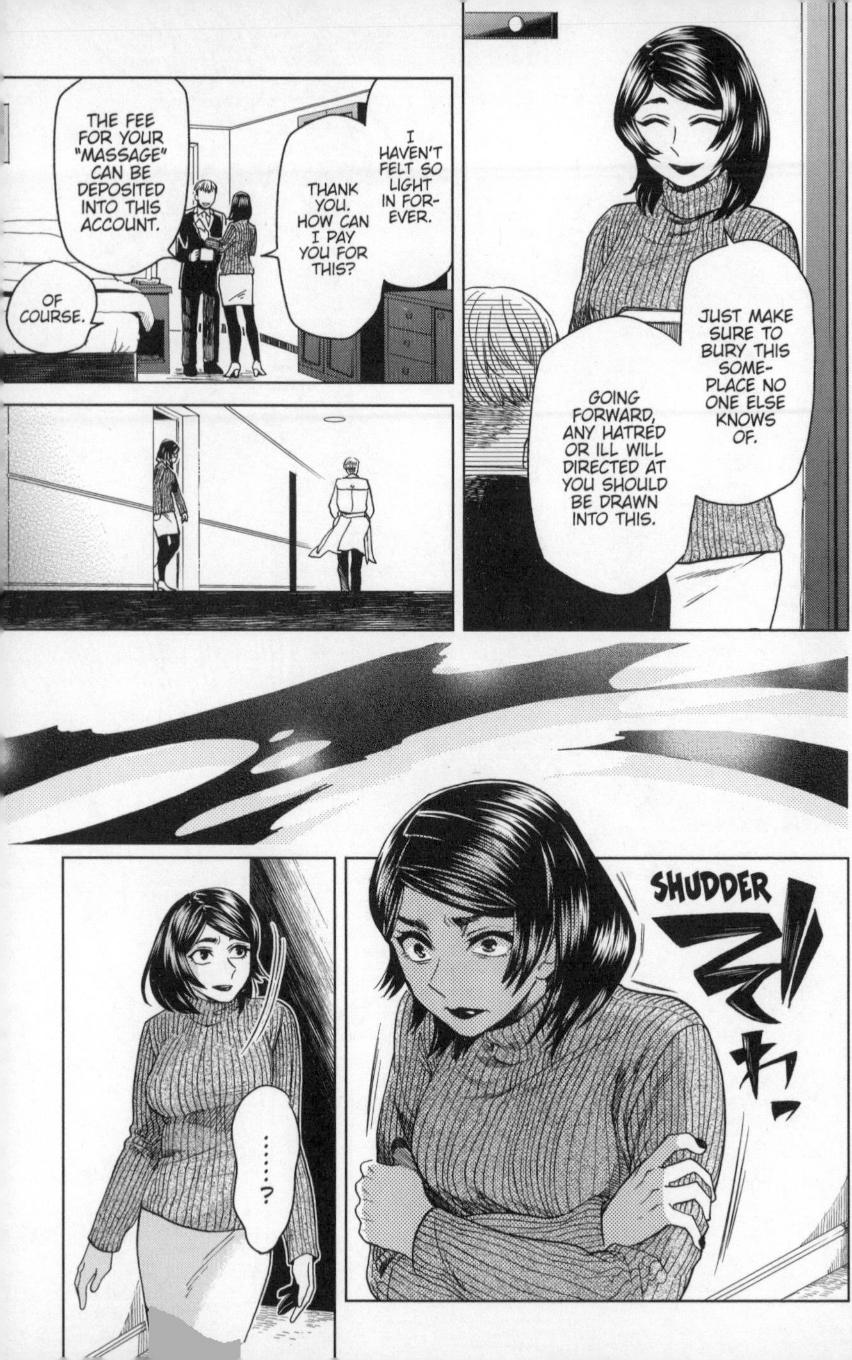
JUST MAKE SURE TO BURY THIS SOME-PLACE NO ONE ELSE KNOWS OF.
GOING FORWARD, ANY HATRED OR ILL WILL DIRECTED AT YOU SHOULD BE DRAWN INTO THIS.
I HAVEN'T FELT SO LIGHT IN FOR-EVER.
THANK YOU. HOW CAN I PAY YOU FOR THIS?
THE FEE FOR YOUR "MASSAGE" CAN BE DEPOSITED INTO THIS ACCOUNT.
OF COURSE.
SHUDDER
......?

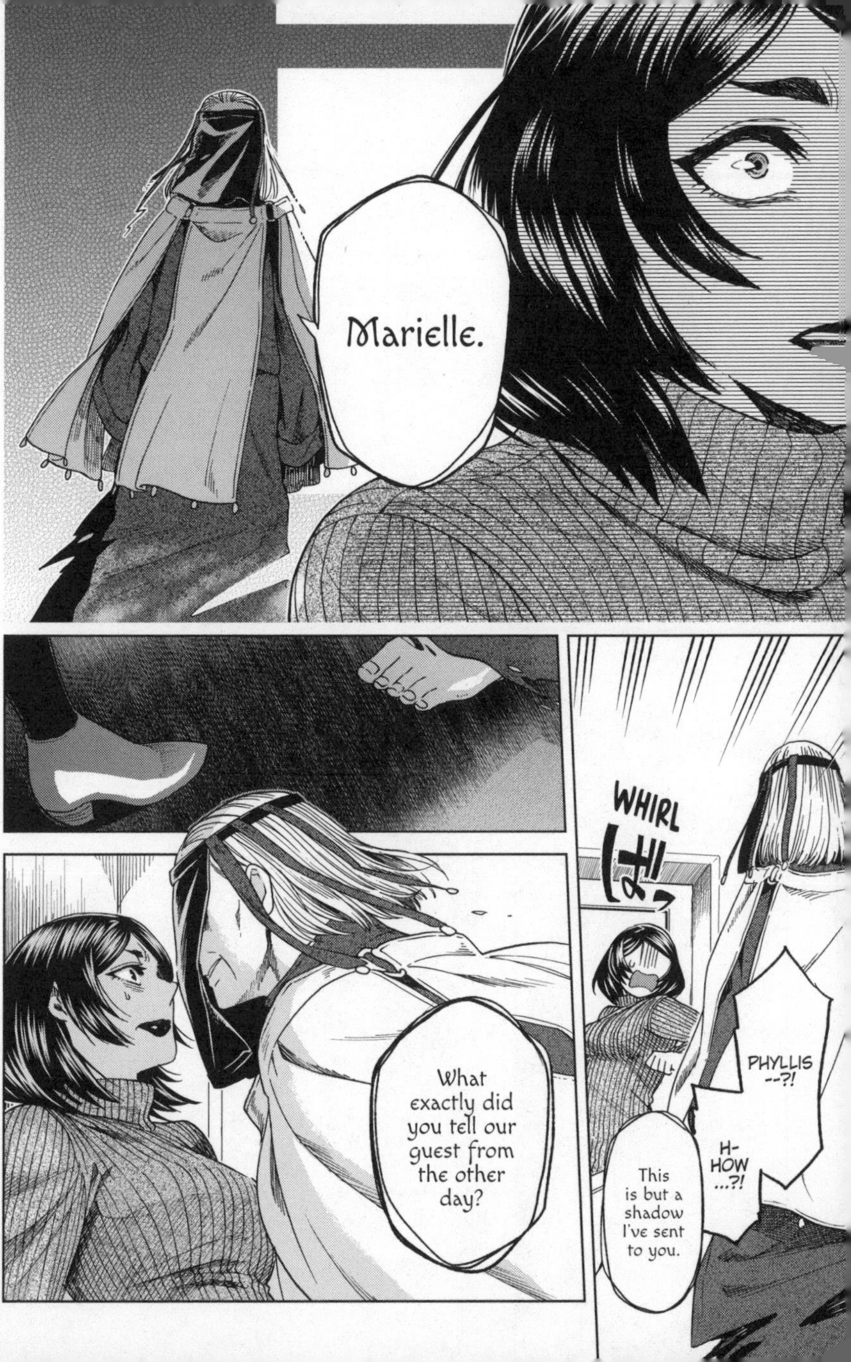

Marielle.
WHIRL
ばっ
PHYLLIS --?!
H-HOW ...?!
This is but a shadow I've sent to you.
What exactly did you tell our guest from the other day?

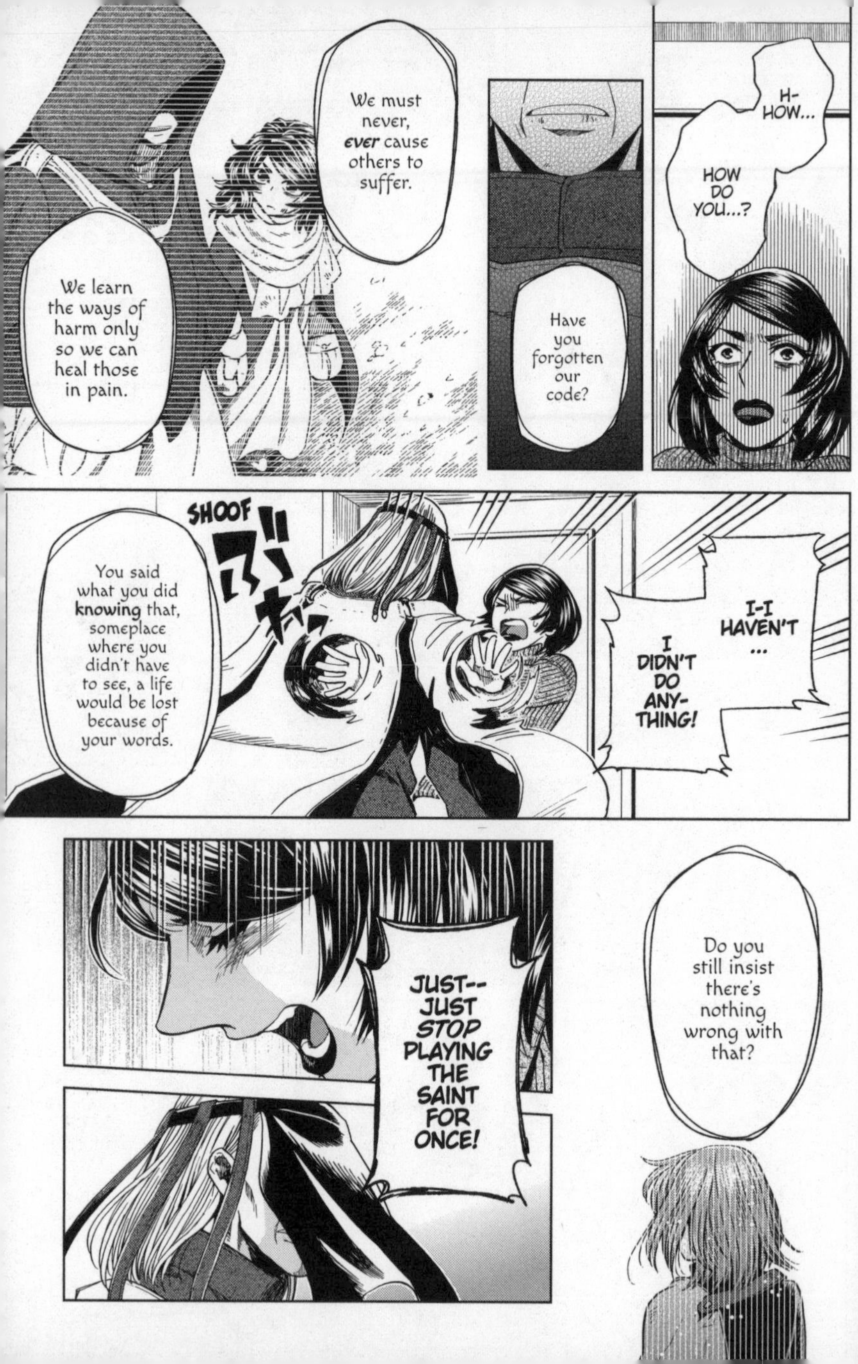
H- HOW...
HOW DO YOU...?
Have you forgotten our code?
We must never, ***ever*** cause others to suffer.
We learn the ways of harm only so we can heal those in pain.
I-I HAVEN'T ...
I DIDN'T DO ANYTHING!
SHOOF
You said what you did **knowing** that, someplace where you didn't have to see, a life would be lost because of your words.
Do you still insist there's nothing wrong with that?
JUST-- JUST *STOP* PLAYING THE SAINT FOR ONCE!

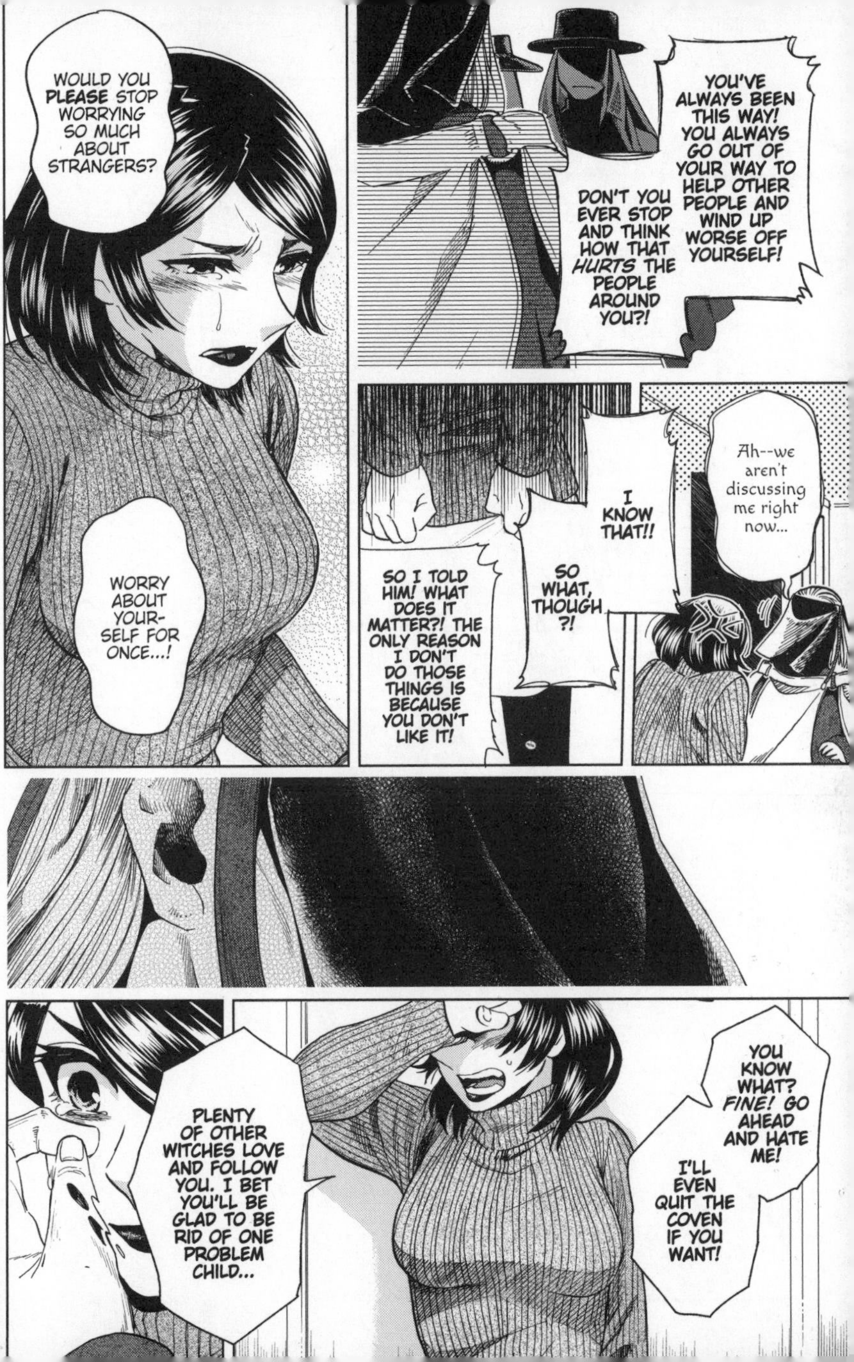
YOU'VE ALWAYS BEEN THIS WAY! YOU ALWAYS GO OUT OF YOUR WAY TO HELP OTHER PEOPLE AND WIND UP WORSE OFF YOURSELF!
DON'T YOU EVER STOP AND THINK HOW THAT *HURTS* THE PEOPLE AROUND YOU?!
Ah--we aren't discussing me right now...
I KNOW THAT!!
SO WHAT, THOUGH?!
SO I TOLD HIM! WHAT DOES IT MATTER?! THE ONLY REASON I DON'T DO THOSE THINGS IS BECAUSE YOU DON'T LIKE IT!
WOULD YOU **PLEASE** STOP WORRYING SO MUCH ABOUT STRANGERS?
WORRY ABOUT YOUR-SELF FOR ONCE...!
YOU KNOW WHAT? *FINE!* GO AHEAD AND HATE ME!
I'LL EVEN QUIT THE COVEN IF YOU WANT!
PLENTY OF OTHER WITCHES LOVE AND FOLLOW YOU. I BET YOU'LL BE GLAD TO BE RID OF ONE PROBLEM CHILD...

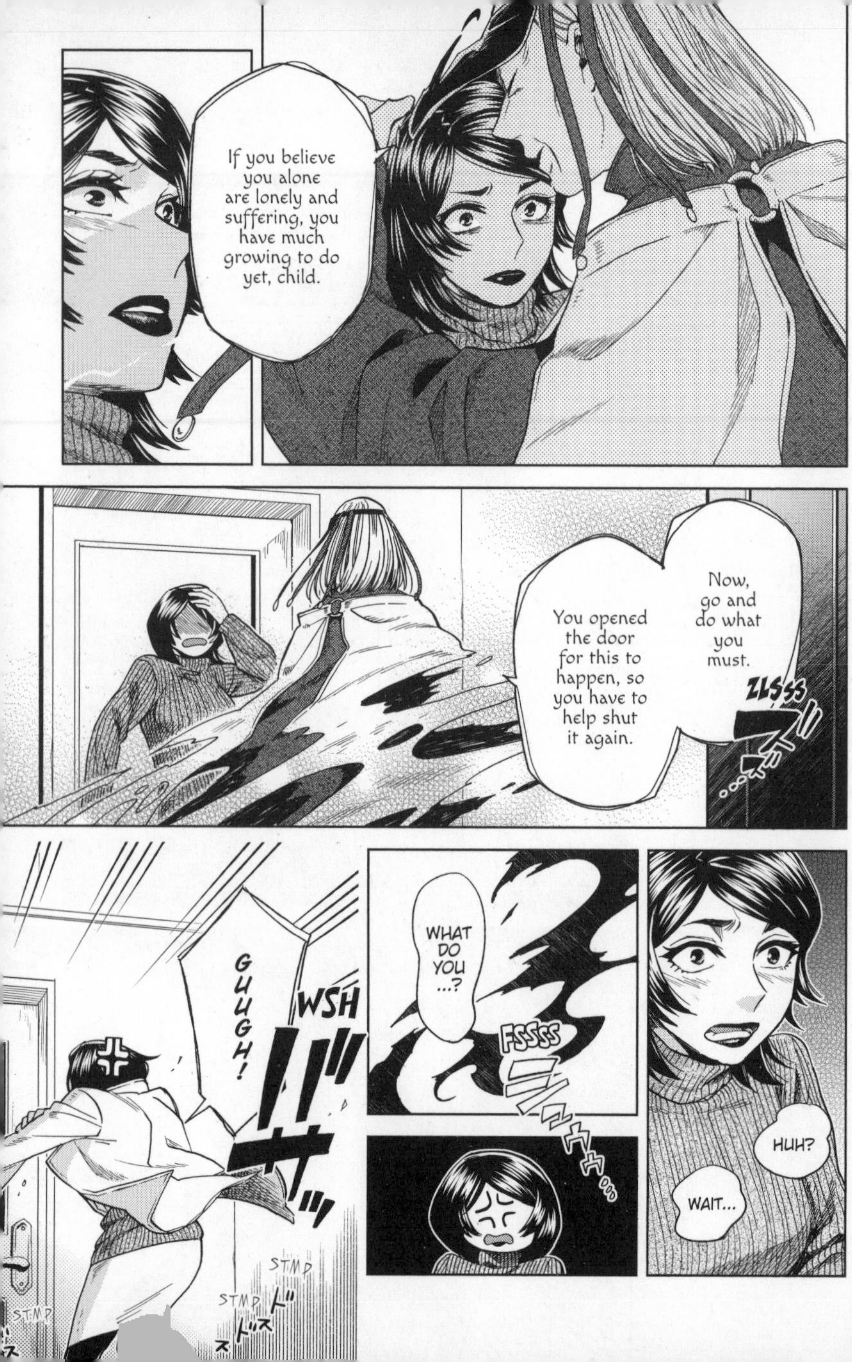
If you believe you alone are lonely and suffering, you have much growing to do yet, child.
Now, go and do what you must.
You opened the door for this to happen, so you have to help shut it again.
ZLSSS
HUH?
WAIT...
WHAT DO YOU ...?
FSSSS
GUUGH!
WSH
STMP
STMP
STMP

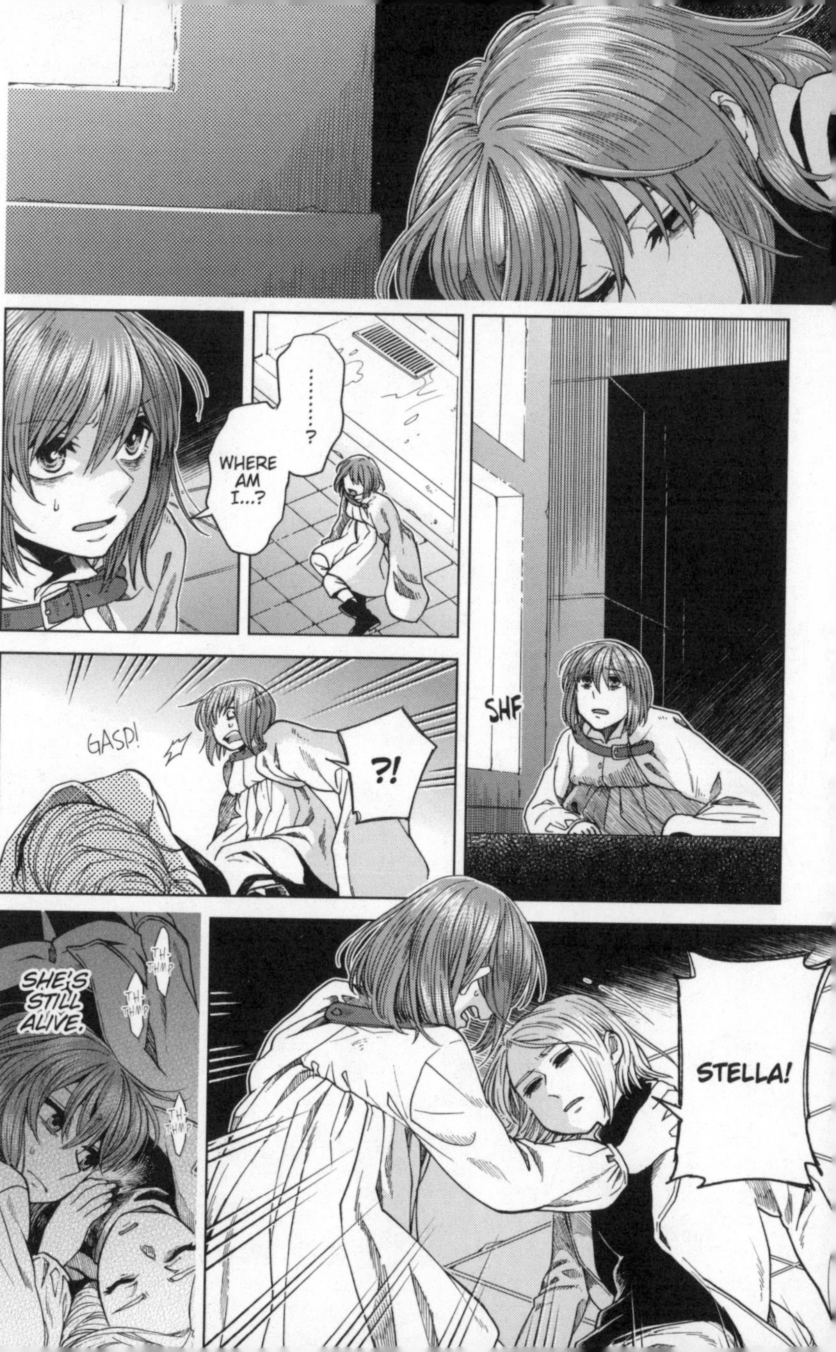
SHF
......?
WHERE AM I...?
?!
GASP!
STELLA!
TH-THMP
SHE'S STILL ALIVE.
TH-THMP
TH-THMP

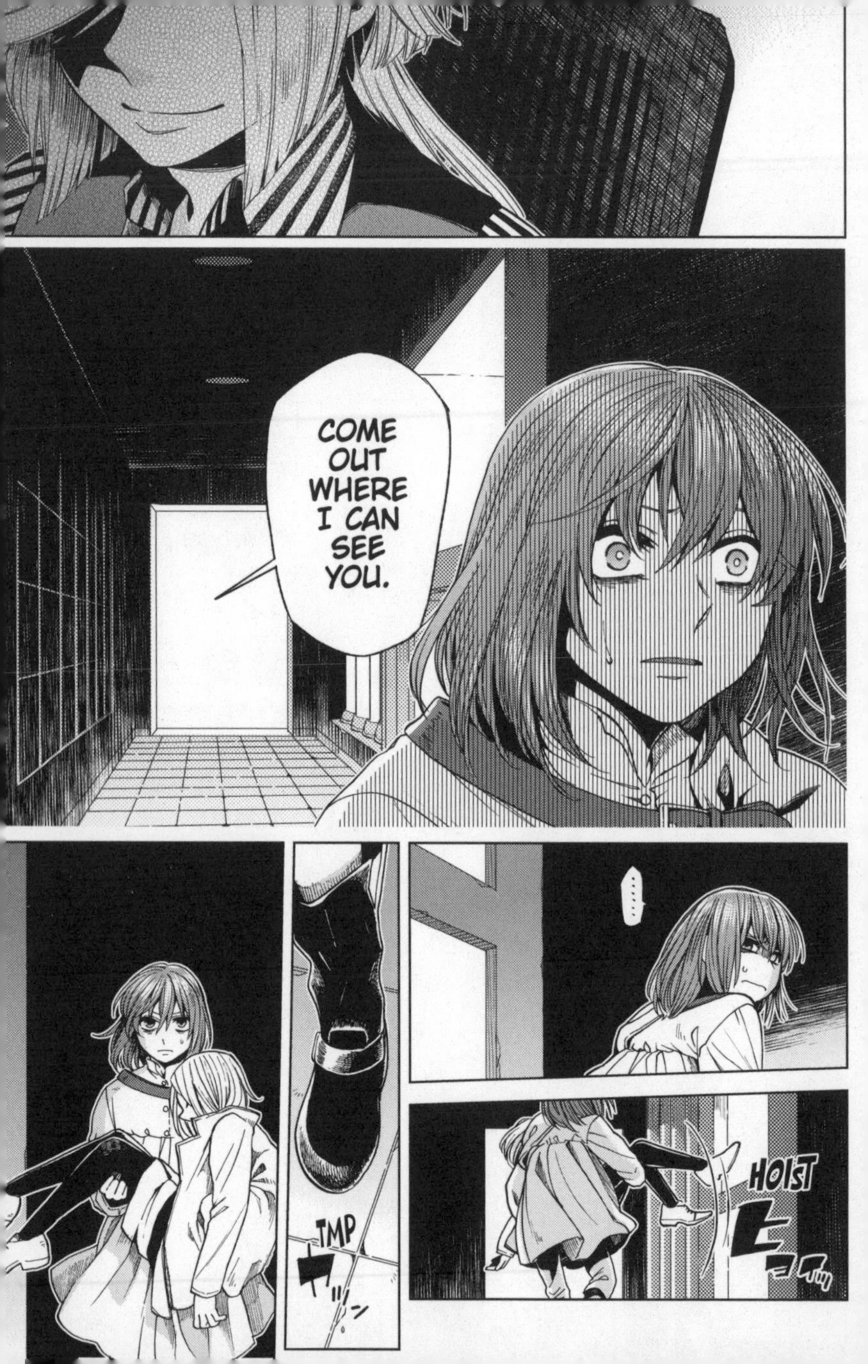
COME OUT WHERE I CAN SEE YOU.
......
HOIST
TMP

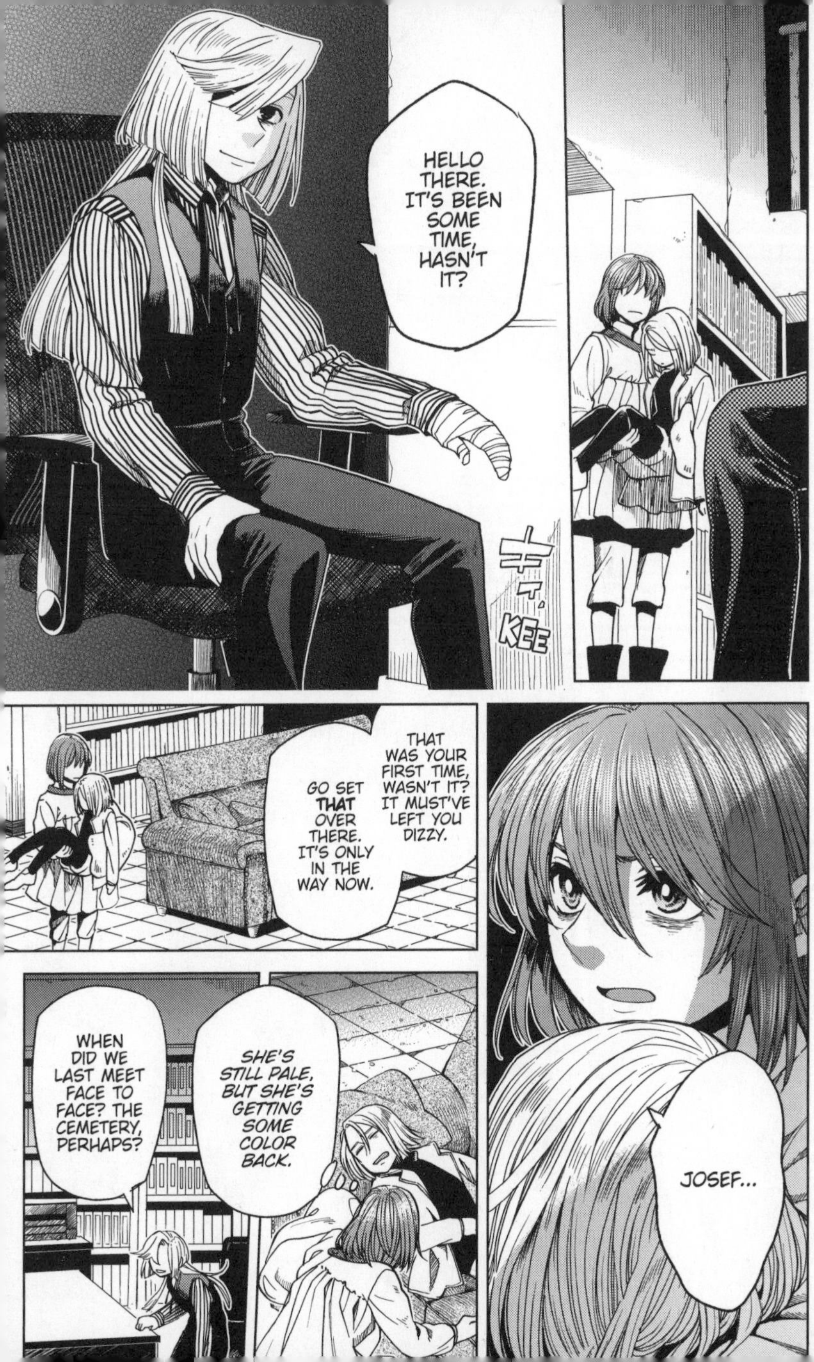
KEE
HELLO THERE. IT'S BEEN SOME TIME, HASN'T IT?
JOSEF...
THAT WAS YOUR FIRST TIME, WASN'T IT? IT MUST'VE LEFT YOU DIZZY.
GO SET **THAT** OVER THERE. IT'S ONLY IN THE WAY NOW.
SHE'S STILL PALE, BUT SHE'S GETTING SOME COLOR BACK.
WHEN DID WE LAST MEET FACE TO FACE? THE CEMETERY, PERHAPS?

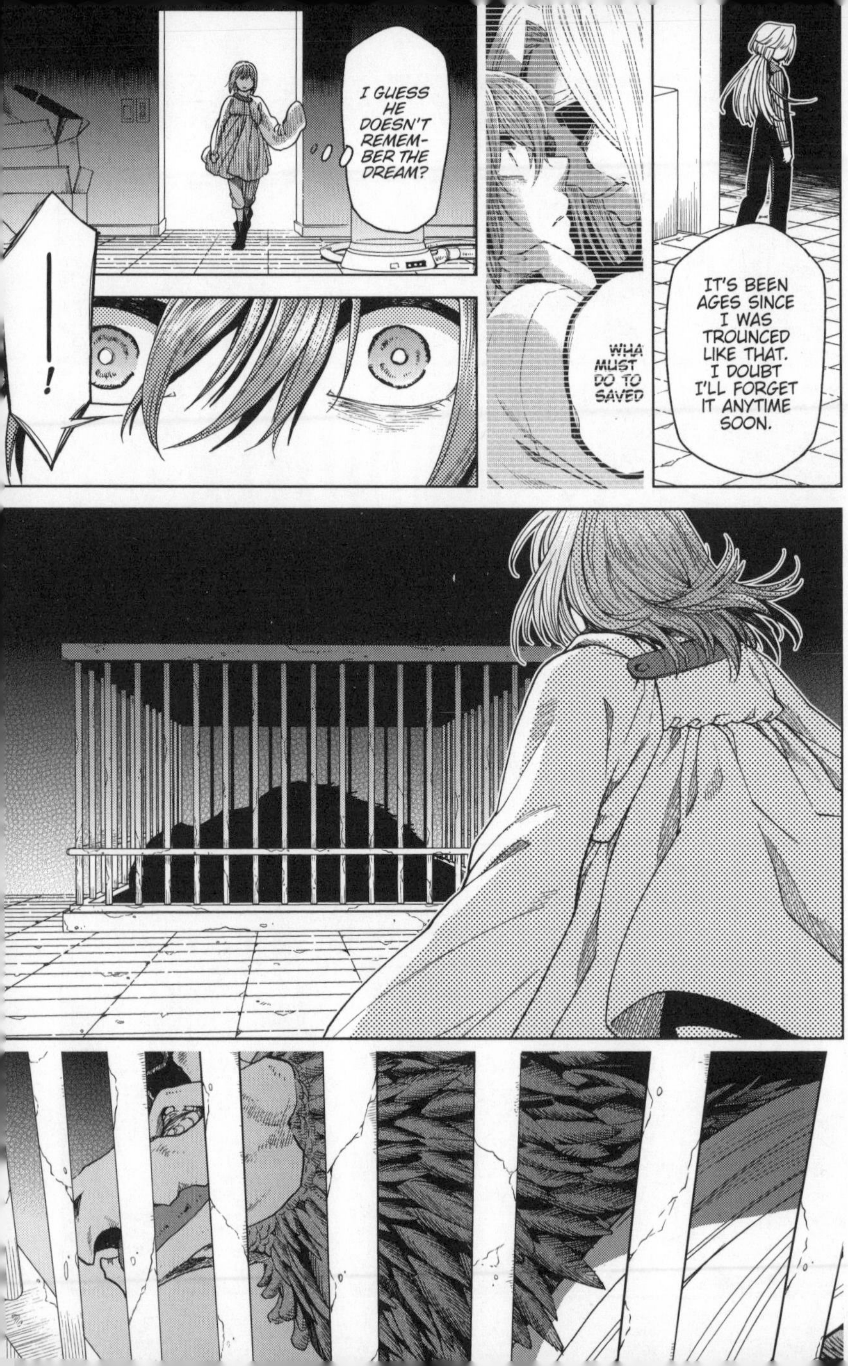
IT'S BEEN AGES SINCE I WAS TROUNCED LIKE THAT. I DOUBT I'LL FORGET IT ANYTIME SOON.
WHA MUST DO TO SAVED
I GUESS HE DOESN'T REMEMBER THE DREAM?
—!

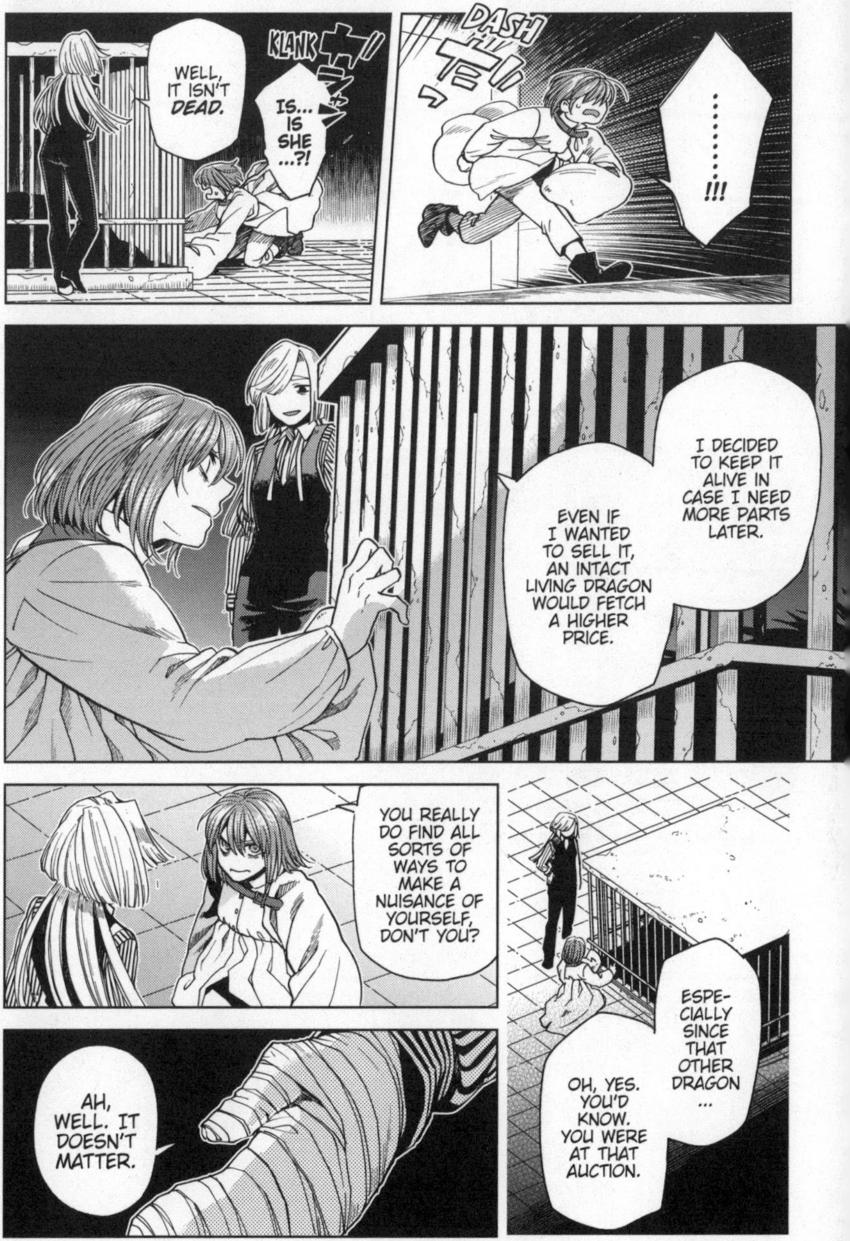
DASH
......!!!
KLANK
IS... IS SHE ...?!
WELL, IT ISN'T DEAD.
I DECIDED TO KEEP IT ALIVE IN CASE I NEED MORE PARTS LATER.
EVEN IF I WANTED TO SELL IT, AN INTACT LIVING DRAGON WOULD FETCH A HIGHER PRICE.
ESPE-CIALLY SINCE THAT OTHER DRAGON ...
OH, YES. YOU'D KNOW. YOU WERE AT THAT AUCTION.
YOU REALLY DO FIND ALL SORTS OF WAYS TO MAKE A NUISANCE OF YOURSELF, DON'T YOU?
AH, WELL. IT DOESN'T MATTER.

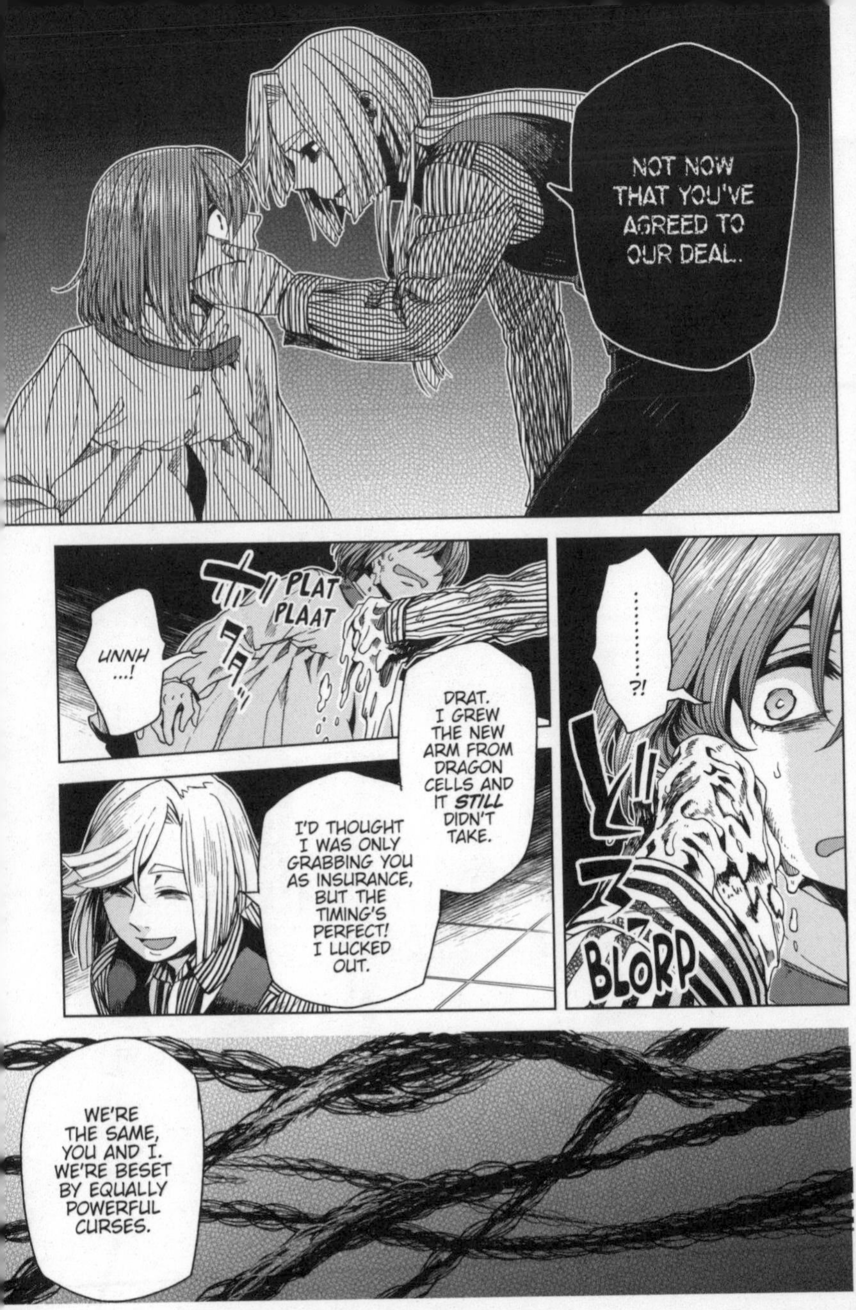
NOT NOW THAT YOU'VE AGREED TO OUR DEAL.
.........?!
BLORP
PLAT
PLAAT
UNNH ...!
DRAT. I GREW THE NEW ARM FROM DRAGON CELLS AND IT *STILL* DIDN'T TAKE.
I'D THOUGHT I WAS ONLY GRABBING YOU AS INSURANCE, BUT THE TIMING'S PERFECT! I LUCKED OUT.
WE'RE THE SAME, YOU AND I. WE'RE BESET BY EQUALLY POWERFUL CURSES.

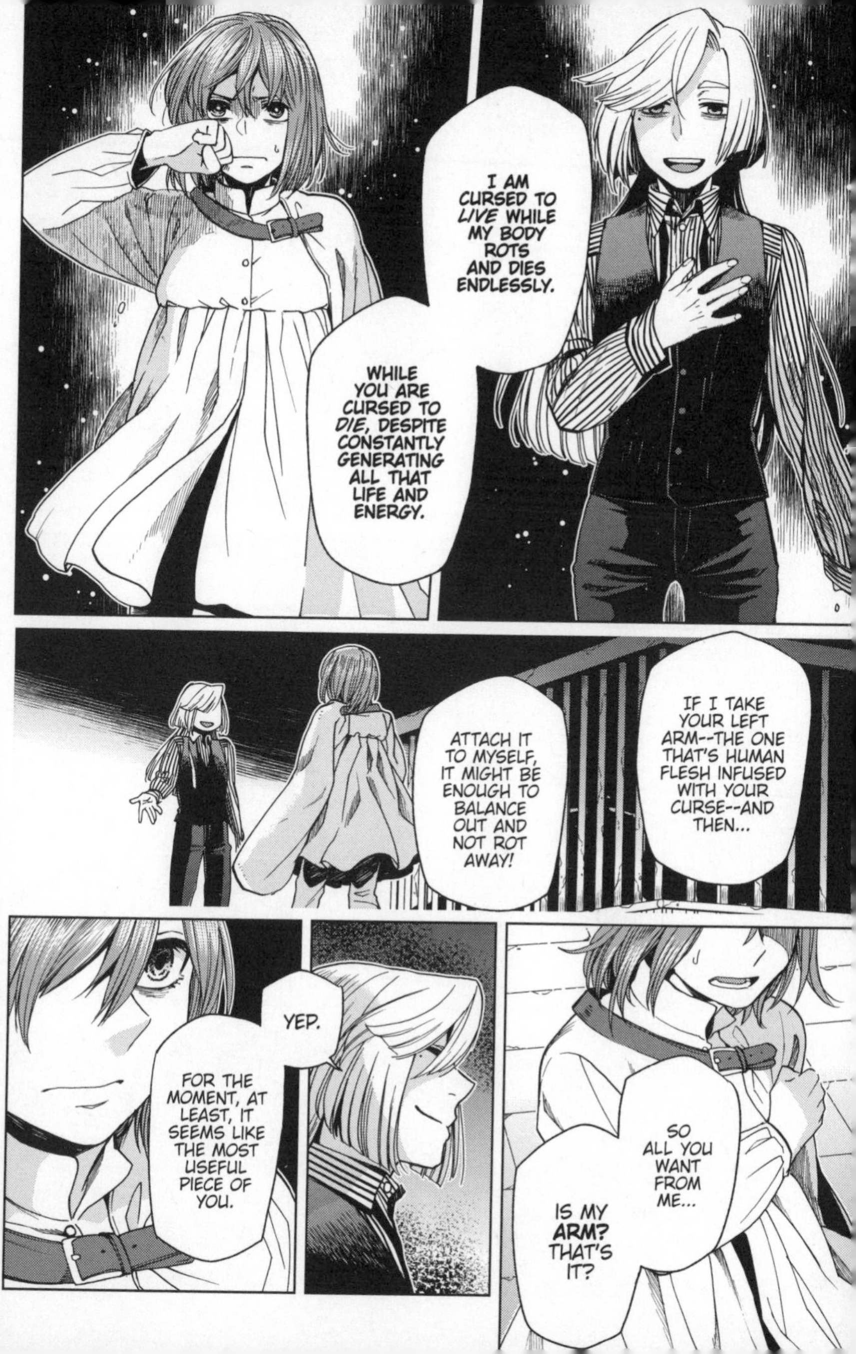
I AM CURSED TO *LIVE* WHILE MY BODY ROTS AND DIES ENDLESSLY.
WHILE YOU ARE CURSED TO *DIE*, DESPITE CONSTANTLY GENERATING ALL THAT LIFE AND ENERGY.
IF I TAKE YOUR LEFT ARM--THE ONE THAT'S HUMAN FLESH INFUSED WITH YOUR CURSE--AND THEN...
ATTACH IT TO MYSELF, IT MIGHT BE ENOUGH TO BALANCE OUT AND NOT ROT AWAY!
SO ALL YOU WANT FROM ME...
IS MY **ARM?** THAT'S IT?
YEP.
FOR THE MOMENT, AT LEAST, IT SEEMS LIKE THE MOST USEFUL PIECE OF YOU.

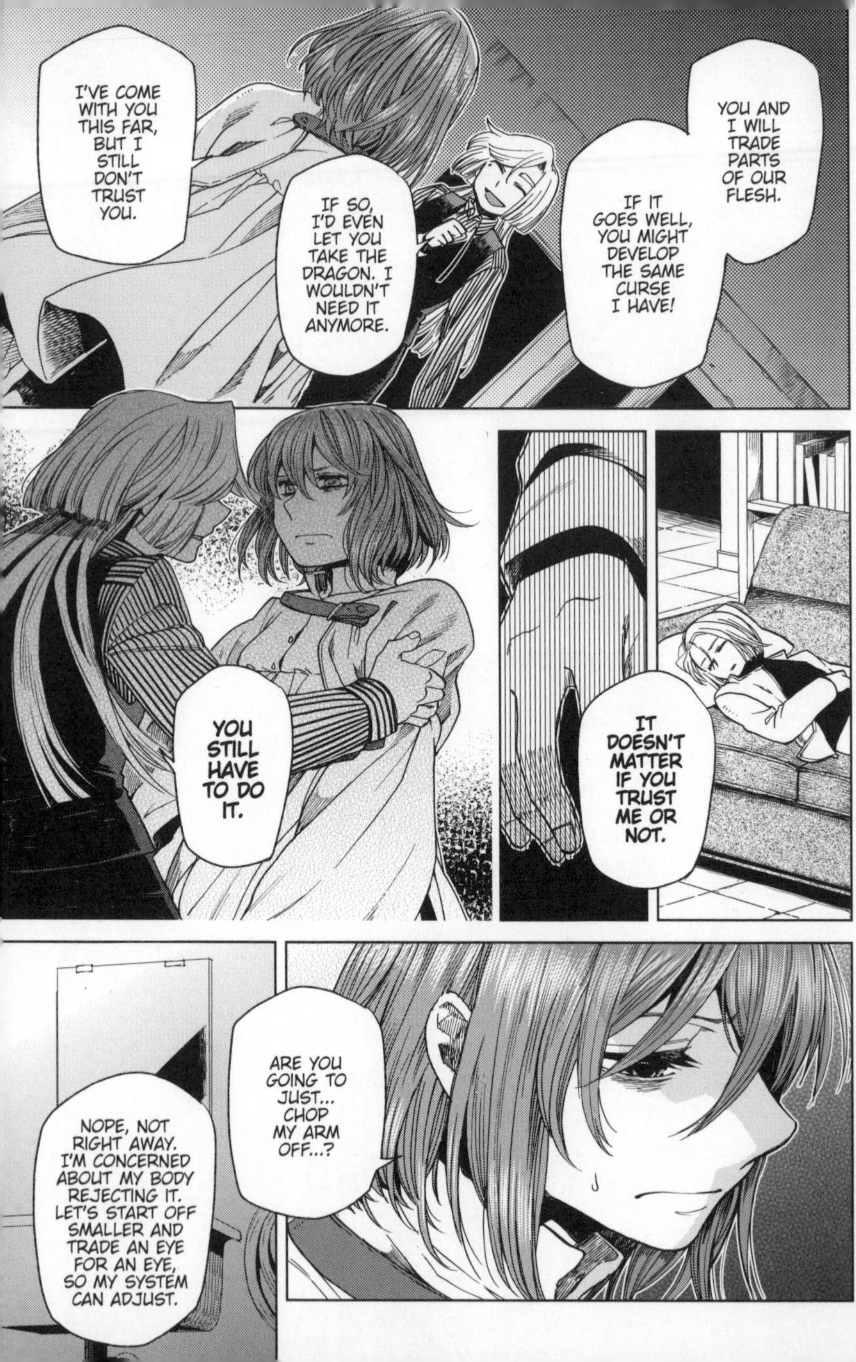
YOU AND I WILL TRADE PARTS OF OUR FLESH.
IF IT GOES WELL, YOU MIGHT DEVELOP THE SAME CURSE I HAVE!
IF SO, I'D EVEN LET YOU TAKE THE DRAGON. I WOULDN'T NEED IT ANYMORE.
I'VE COME WITH YOU THIS FAR, BUT I STILL DON'T TRUST YOU.
IT DOESN'T MATTER IF YOU TRUST ME OR NOT.
YOU STILL HAVE TO DO IT.
ARE YOU GOING TO JUST... CHOP MY ARM OFF...?
NOPE, NOT RIGHT AWAY. I'M CONCERNED ABOUT MY BODY REJECTING IT. LET'S START OFF SMALLER AND TRADE AN EYE FOR AN EYE, SO MY SYSTEM CAN ADJUST.

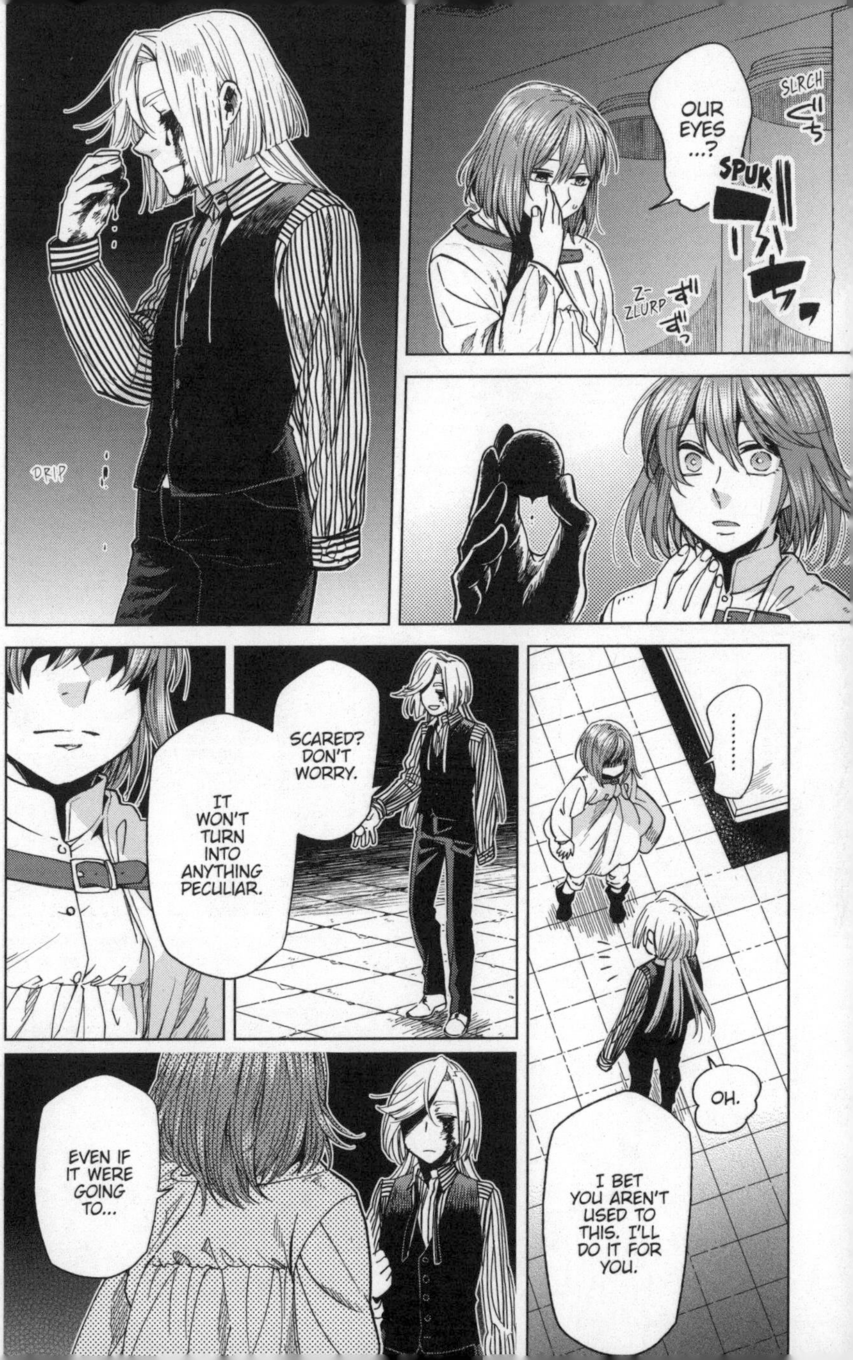
OUR EYES ...?
SLRCH
ぐち
SPUK
Z-ZLURP
ずずっ
DRIP
......
OH.
I BET YOU AREN'T USED TO THIS. I'LL DO IT FOR YOU.
SCARED? DON'T WORRY.
IT WON'T TURN INTO ANYTHING PECULIAR.
EVEN IF IT WERE GOING TO...

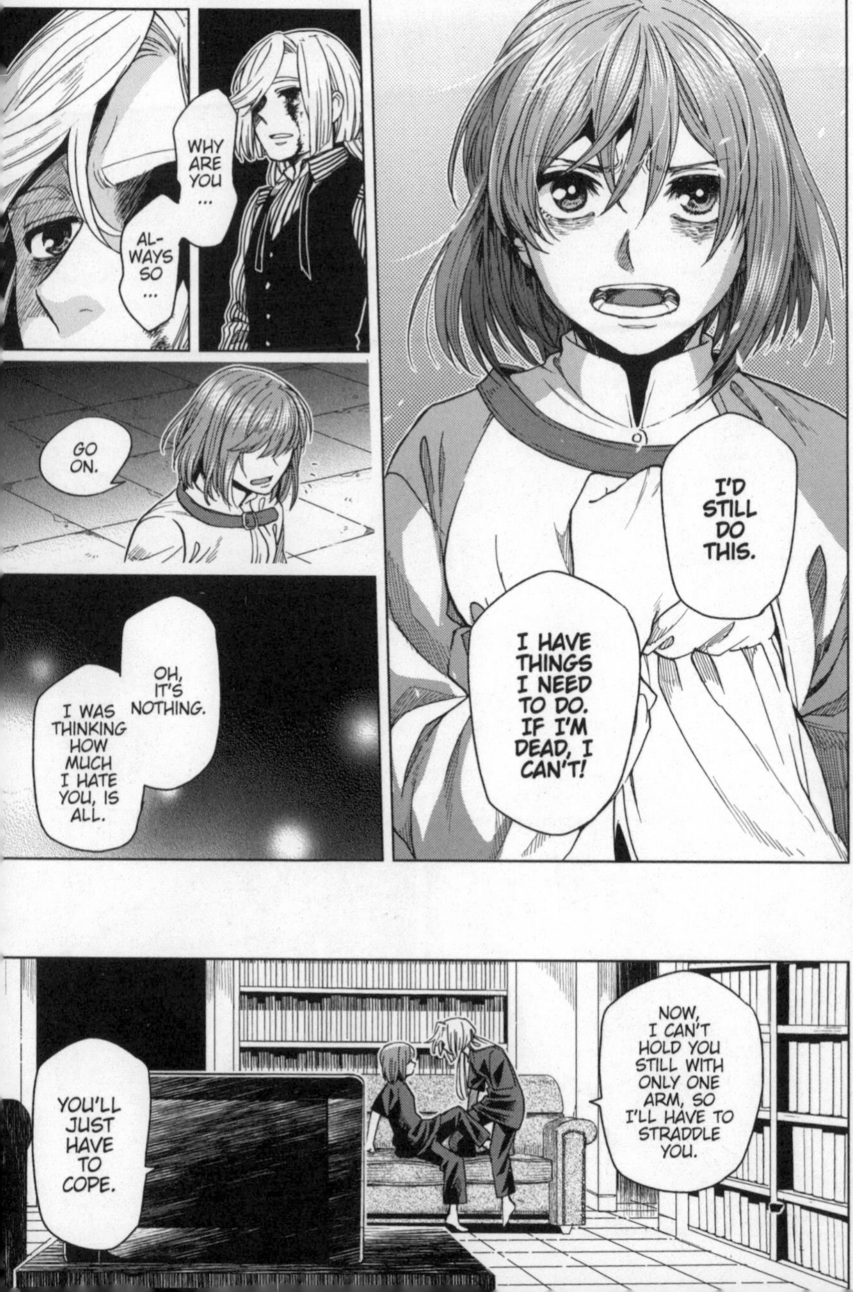
I'D STILL DO THIS.
I HAVE THINGS I NEED TO DO. IF I'M DEAD, I CAN'T!
WHY ARE YOU...
ALWAYS SO...
GO ON.
OH, IT'S NOTHING.
I WAS THINKING HOW MUCH I HATE YOU, IS ALL.
NOW, I CAN'T HOLD YOU STILL WITH ONLY ONE ARM, SO I'LL HAVE TO STRADDLE YOU.
YOU'LL JUST HAVE TO COPE.

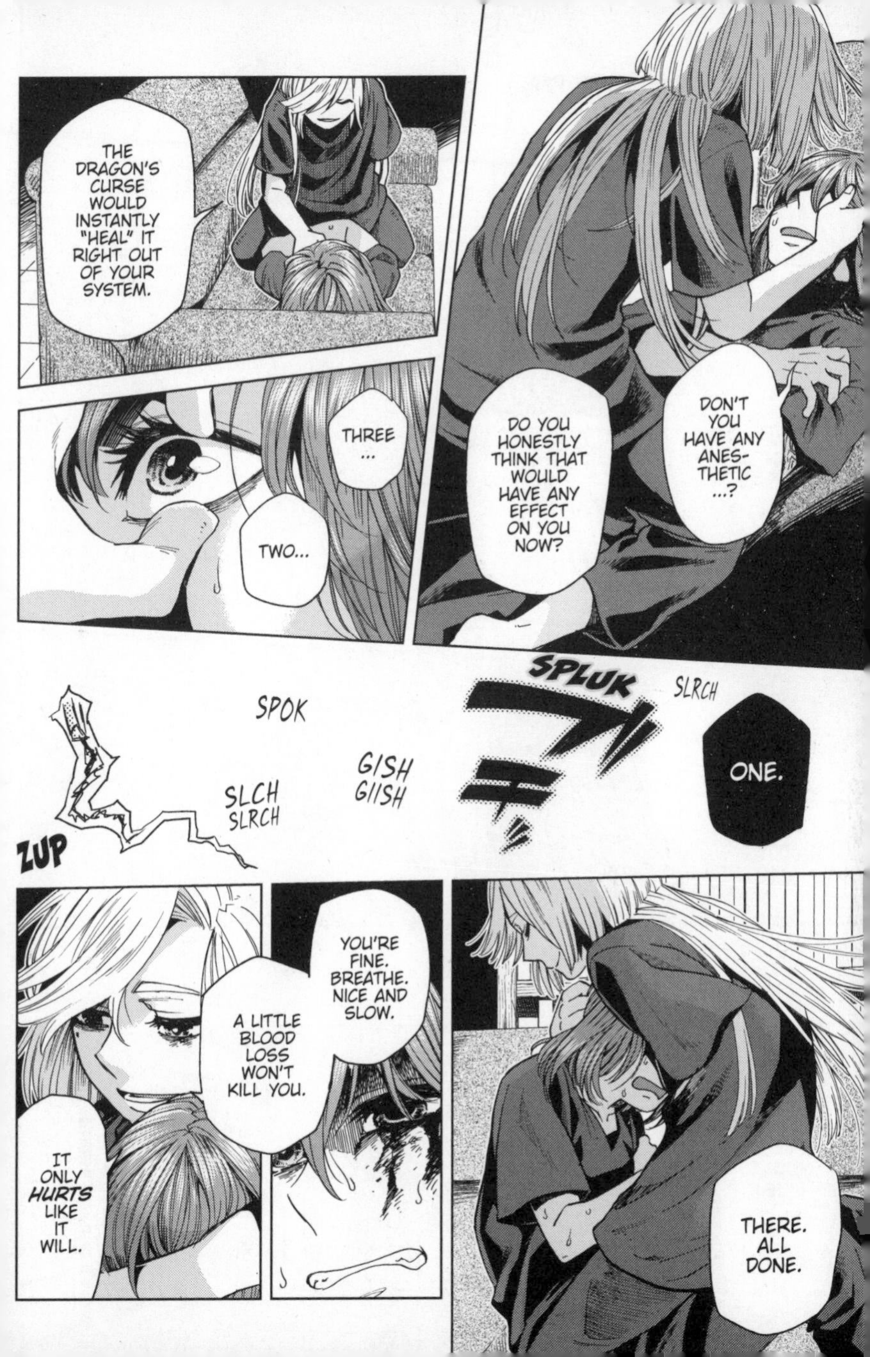
DON'T YOU HAVE ANY ANES- THETIC ...?
DO YOU HONESTLY THINK THAT WOULD HAVE ANY EFFECT ON YOU NOW?
THE DRAGON'S CURSE WOULD INSTANTLY "HEAL" IT RIGHT OUT OF YOUR SYSTEM.
THREE ...
TWO...
ONE.
SLRCH
SPLUK
GISH GIISH
SPOK
SLCH SLRCH
ZUP
THERE. ALL DONE.
YOU'RE FINE. BREATHE. NICE AND SLOW.
A LITTLE BLOOD LOSS WON'T KILL YOU.
IT ONLY **HURTS** LIKE IT WILL.

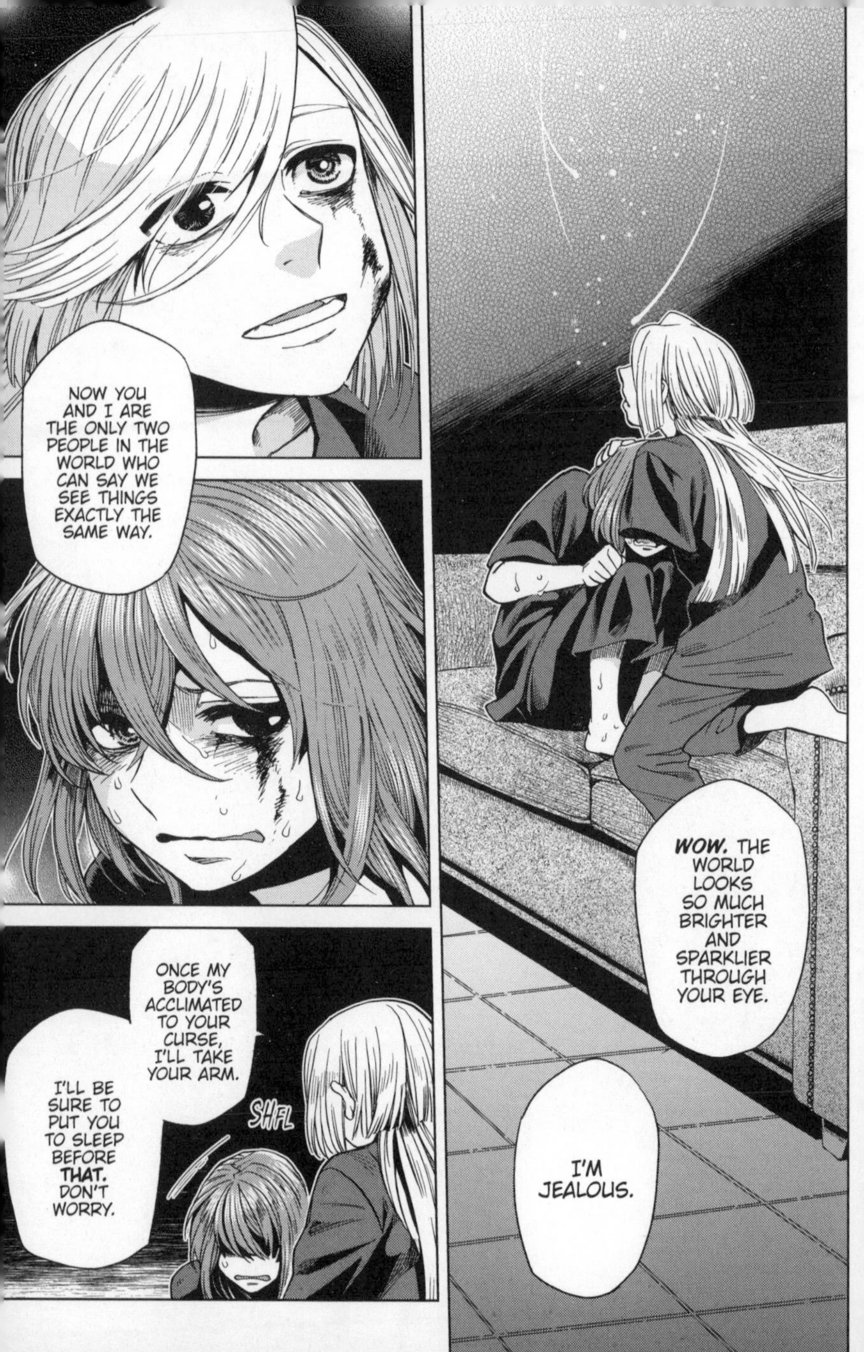
WOW. THE WORLD LOOKS SO MUCH BRIGHTER AND SPARKLIER THROUGH YOUR EYE.
I'M JEALOUS.
NOW YOU AND I ARE THE ONLY TWO PEOPLE IN THE WORLD WHO CAN SAY WE SEE THINGS EXACTLY THE SAME WAY.
ONCE MY BODY'S ACCLIMATED TO YOUR CURSE, I'LL TAKE YOUR ARM.
I'LL BE SURE TO PUT YOU TO SLEEP BEFORE **THAT.** DON'T WORRY.
SHFL

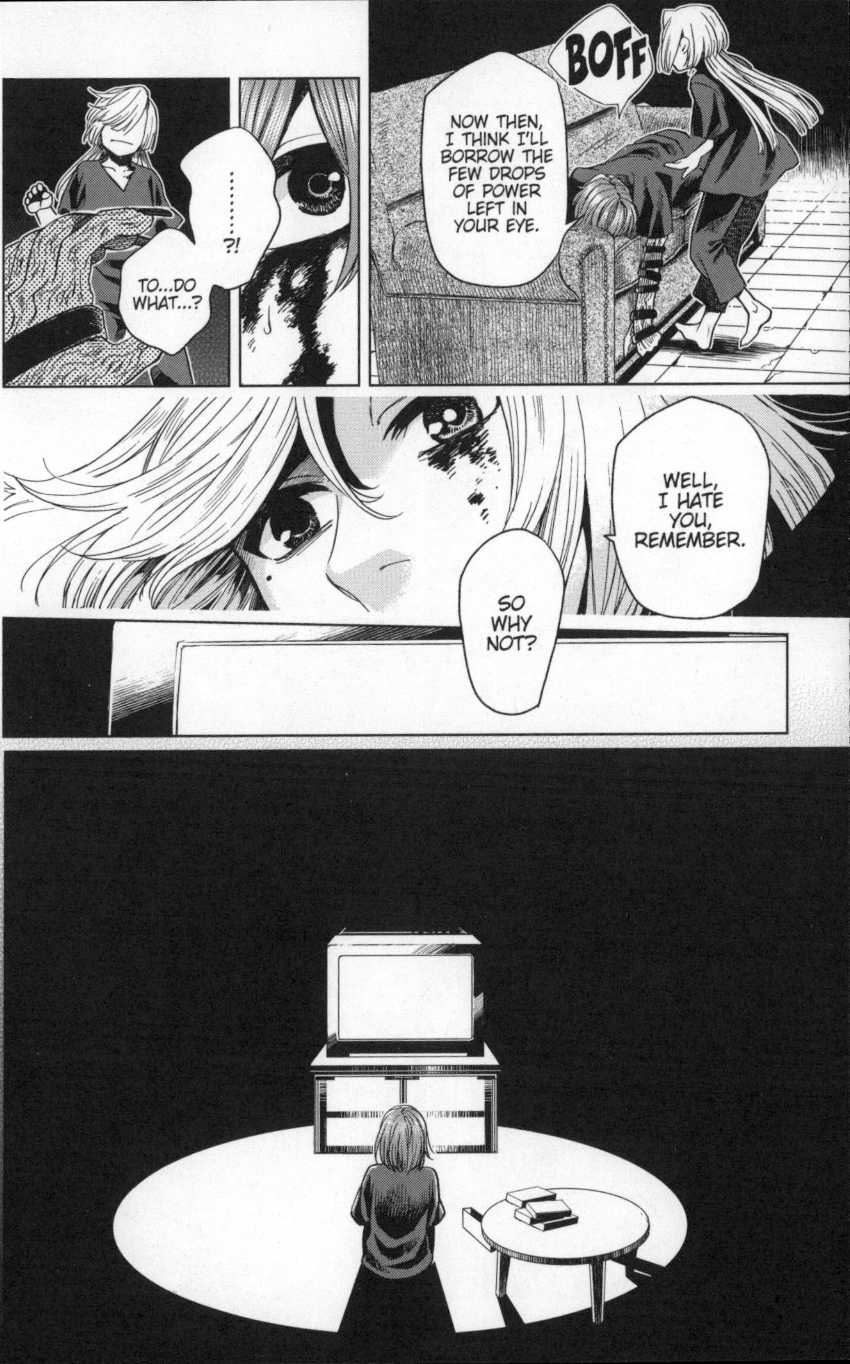
BOFF
NOW THEN, I THINK I'LL BORROW THE FEW DROPS OF POWER LEFT IN YOUR EYE.
......
?!
TO...DO WHAT...?
WELL, I HATE YOU, REMEMBER.
SO WHY NOT?

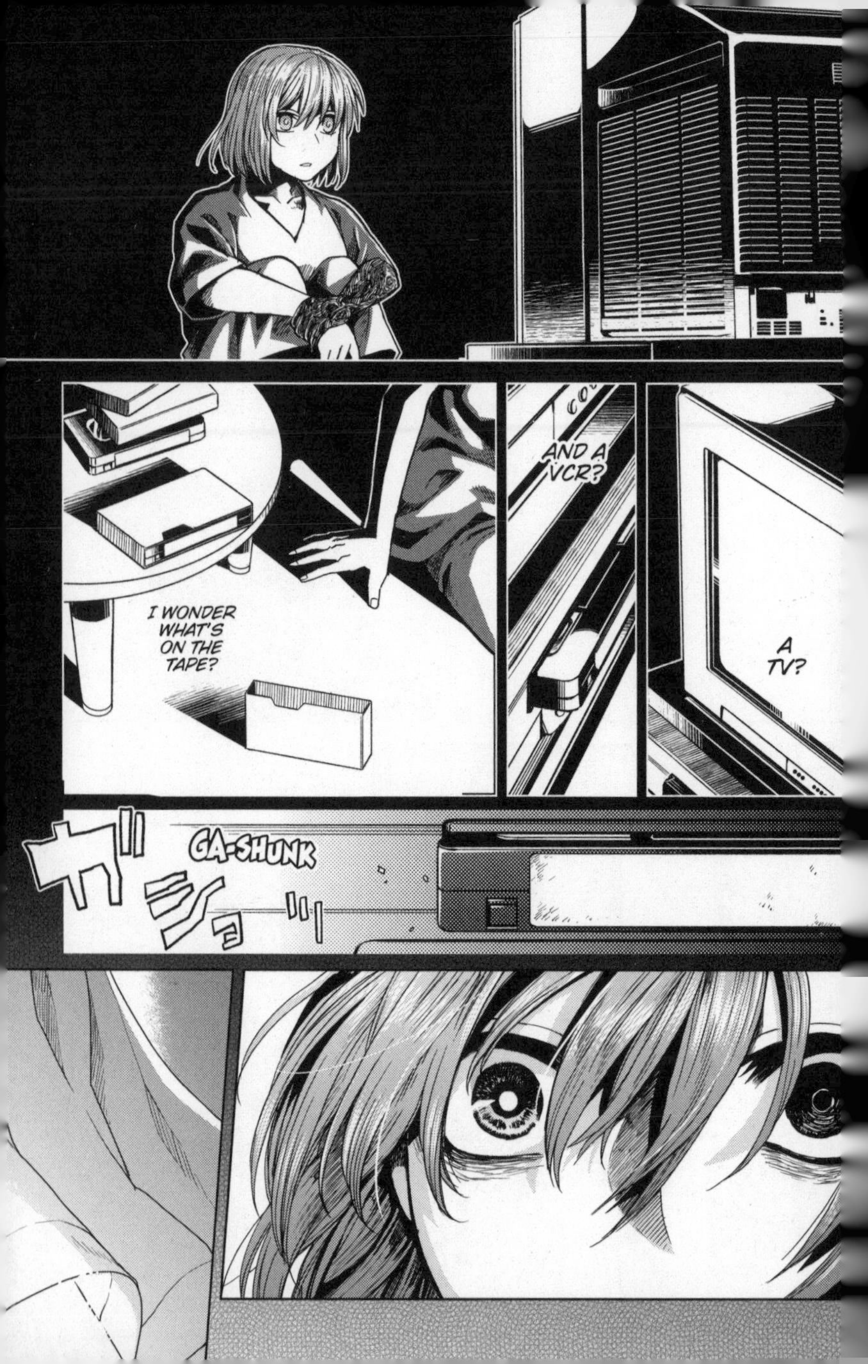
A TV?
AND A VCR?
I WONDER WHAT'S ON THE TAPE?
GA-SHUNK

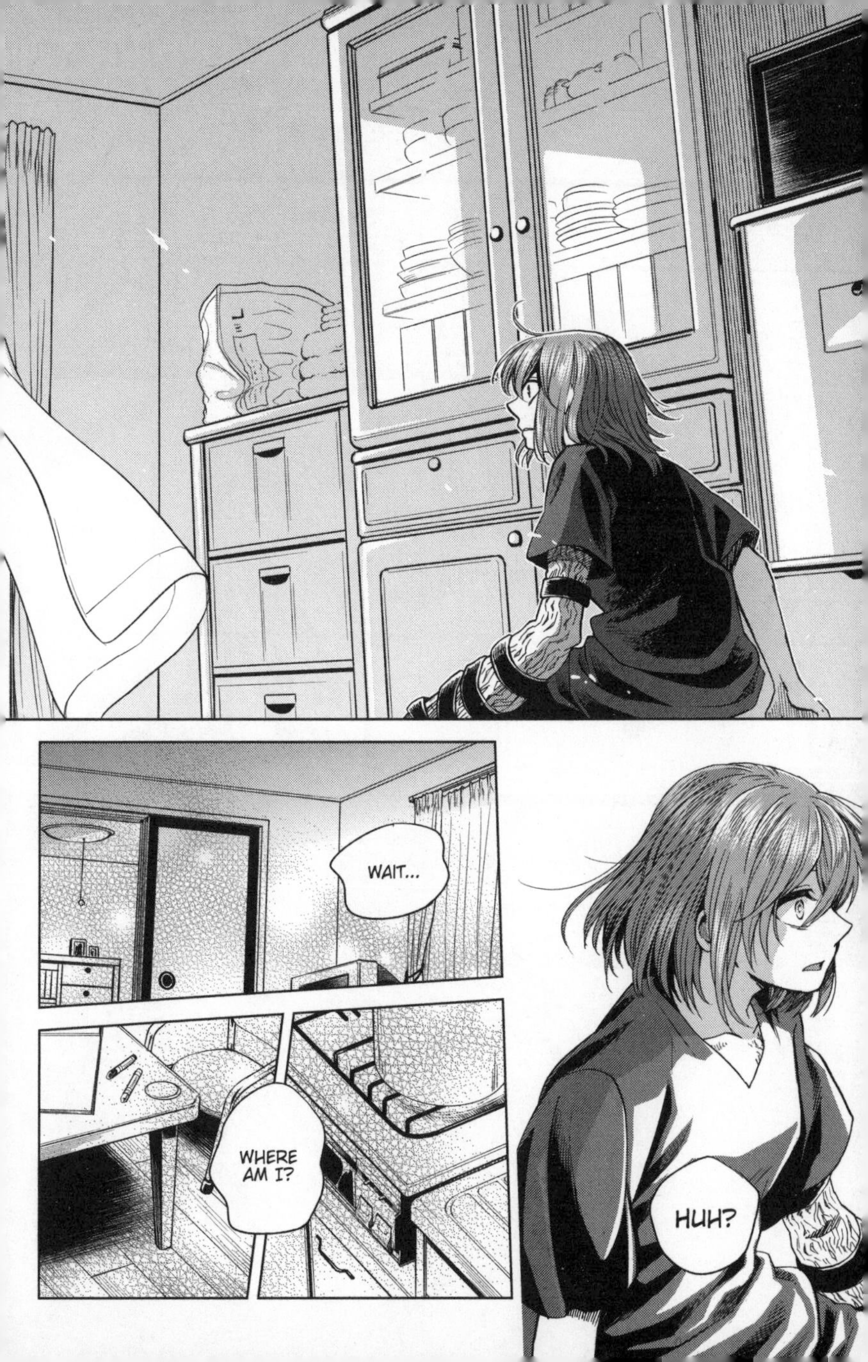
HUH?
WAIT...
WHERE AM I?

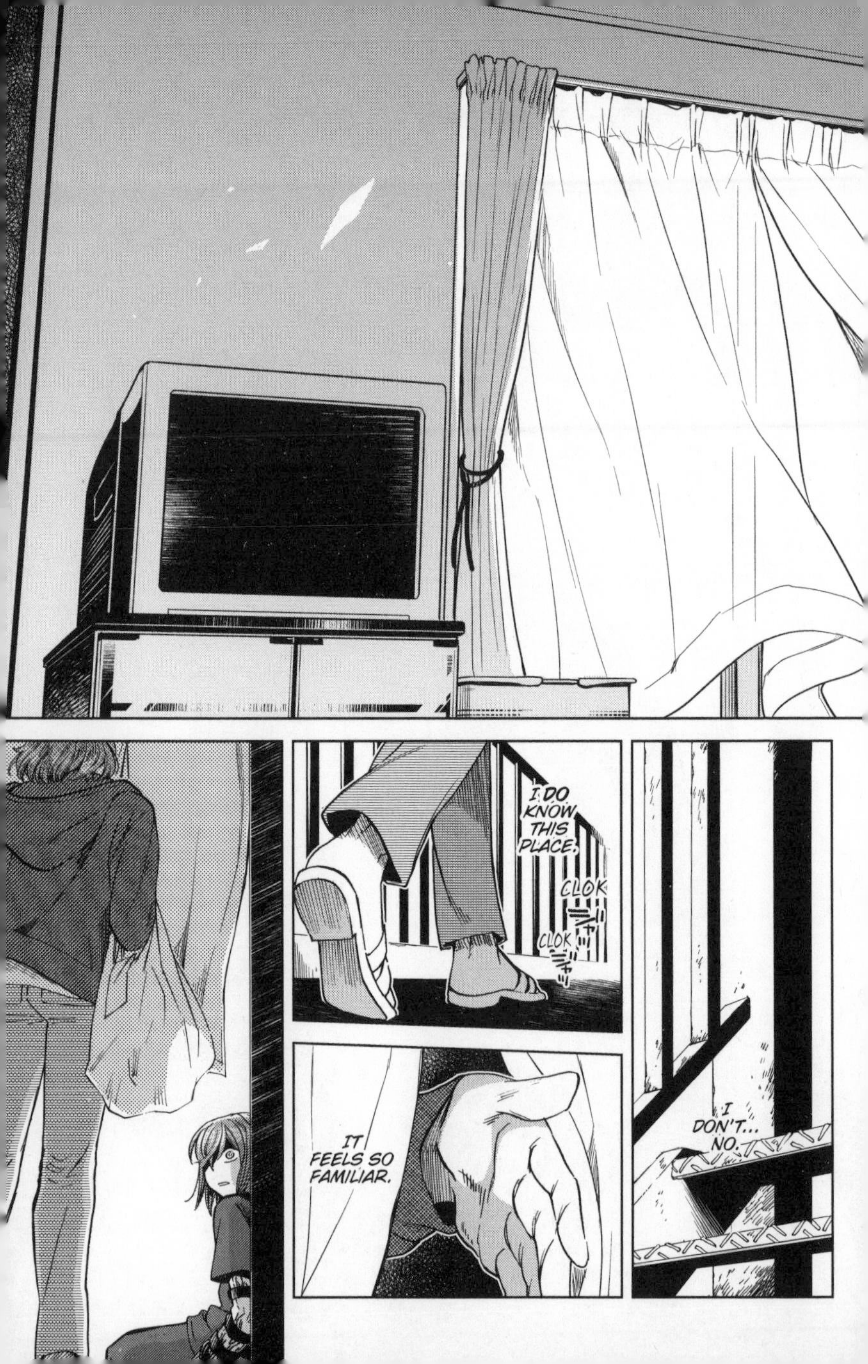
I DON'T... NO.
I DO KNOW THIS PLACE.
CLOK
CLOK
IT FEELS SO FAMILIAR.

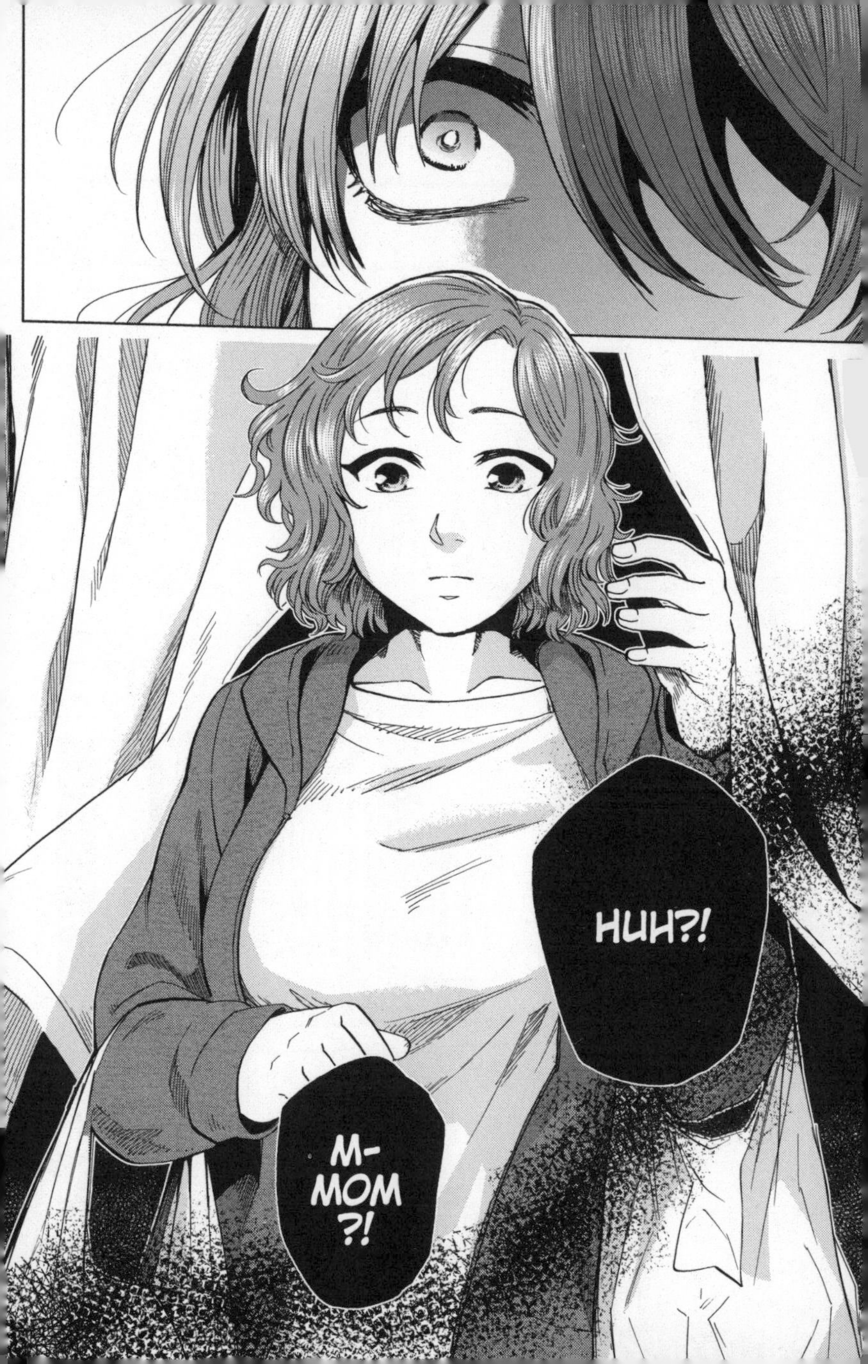
HUH?!
M-MOM?!

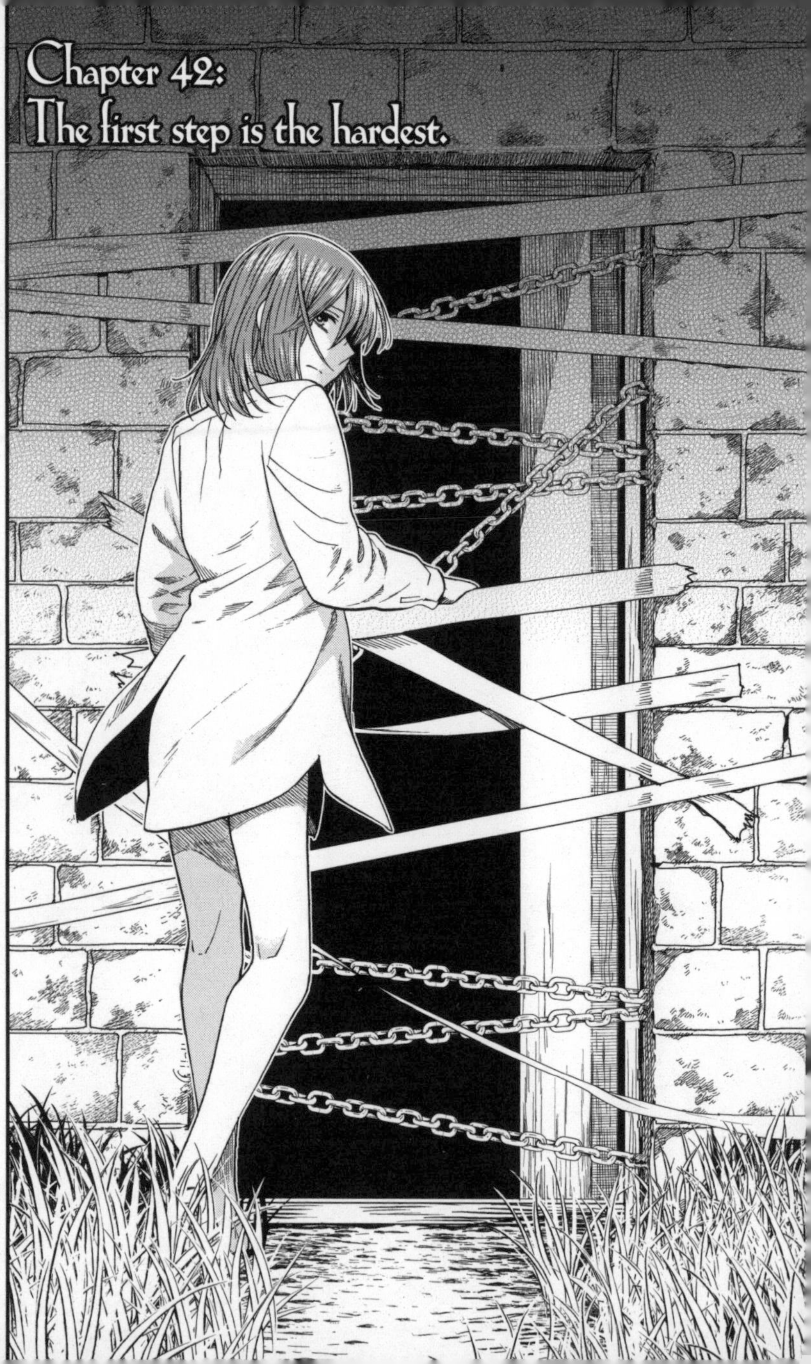
Chapter 42:
The first step is the hardest.

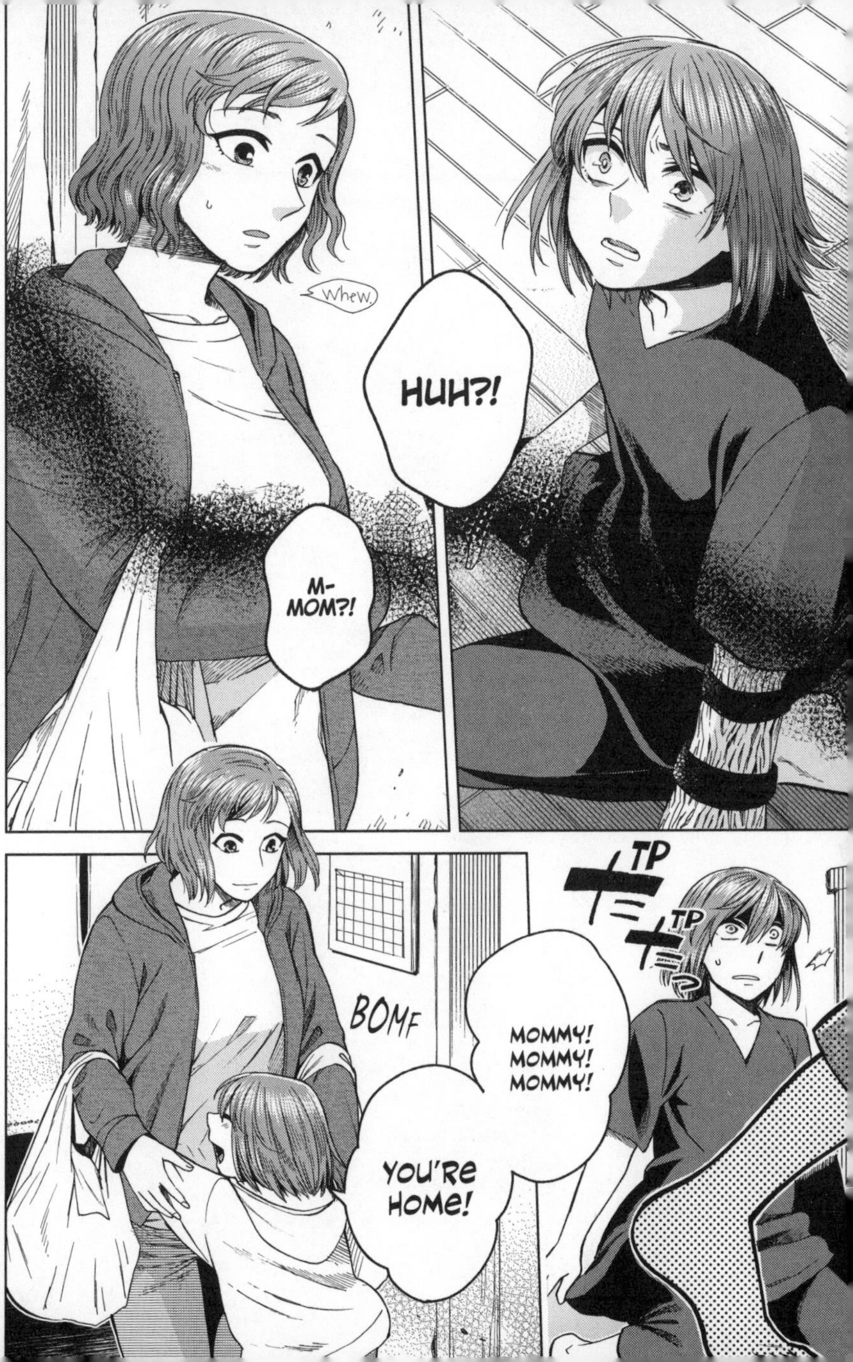
HUH?!
Whew.
M-MOM?!
TP
TP
MOMMY! MOMMY! MOMMY!
YOU'RE HOME!
BOMF

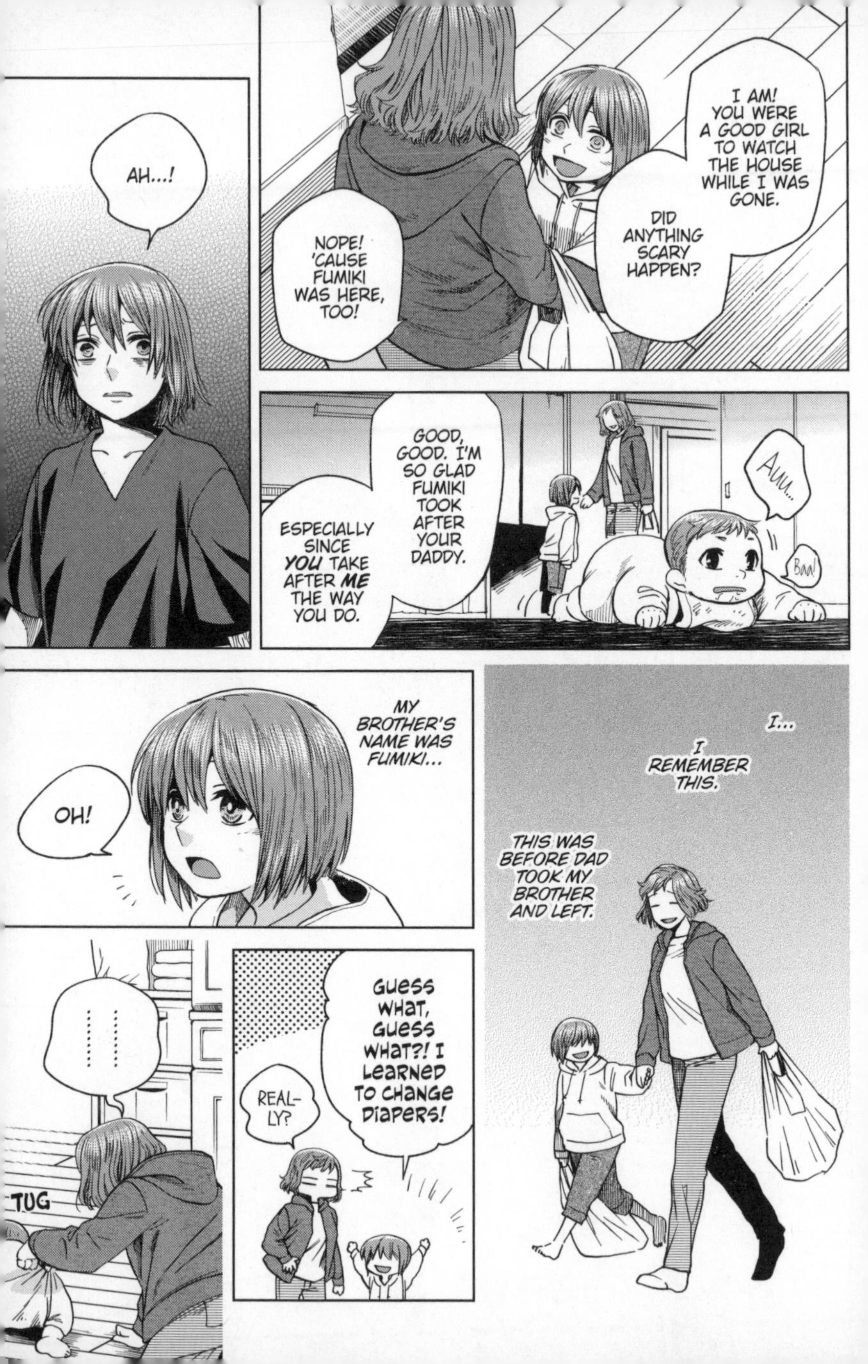
I AM! YOU WERE A GOOD GIRL TO WATCH THE HOUSE WHILE I WAS GONE.
DID ANYTHING SCARY HAPPEN?
NOPE! 'CAUSE FUMIKI WAS HERE, TOO!
GOOD, GOOD. I'M SO GLAD FUMIKI TOOK AFTER YOUR DADDY.
ESPECIALLY SINCE *YOU* TAKE AFTER *ME* THE WAY YOU DO.
Auu...
Baa!
AH...!
I...
I REMEMBER THIS.
THIS WAS BEFORE DAD TOOK MY BROTHER AND LEFT.
MY BROTHER'S NAME WAS FUMIKI...
OH!
GUESS WHAT, GUESS WHAT?! I LEARNED TO CHANGE DIAPERS!
REAL-LY?
......
TUG

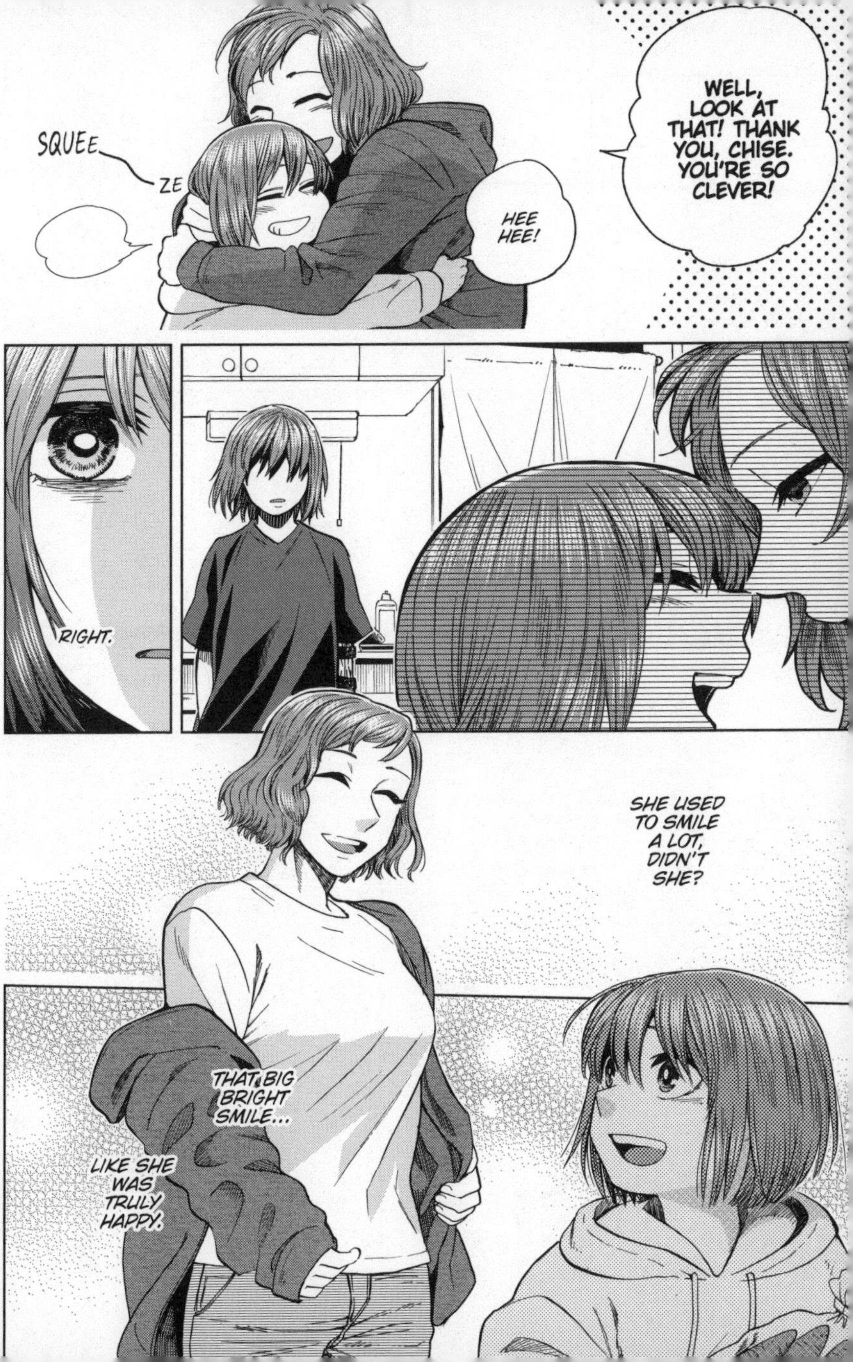

WELL, LOOK AT THAT! THANK YOU, CHISE. YOU'RE SO CLEVER!
HEE HEE!
SQUEEZE
RIGHT.
SHE USED TO SMILE A LOT, DIDN'T SHE?
THAT BIG BRIGHT SMILE...
LIKE SHE WAS TRULY HAPPY.

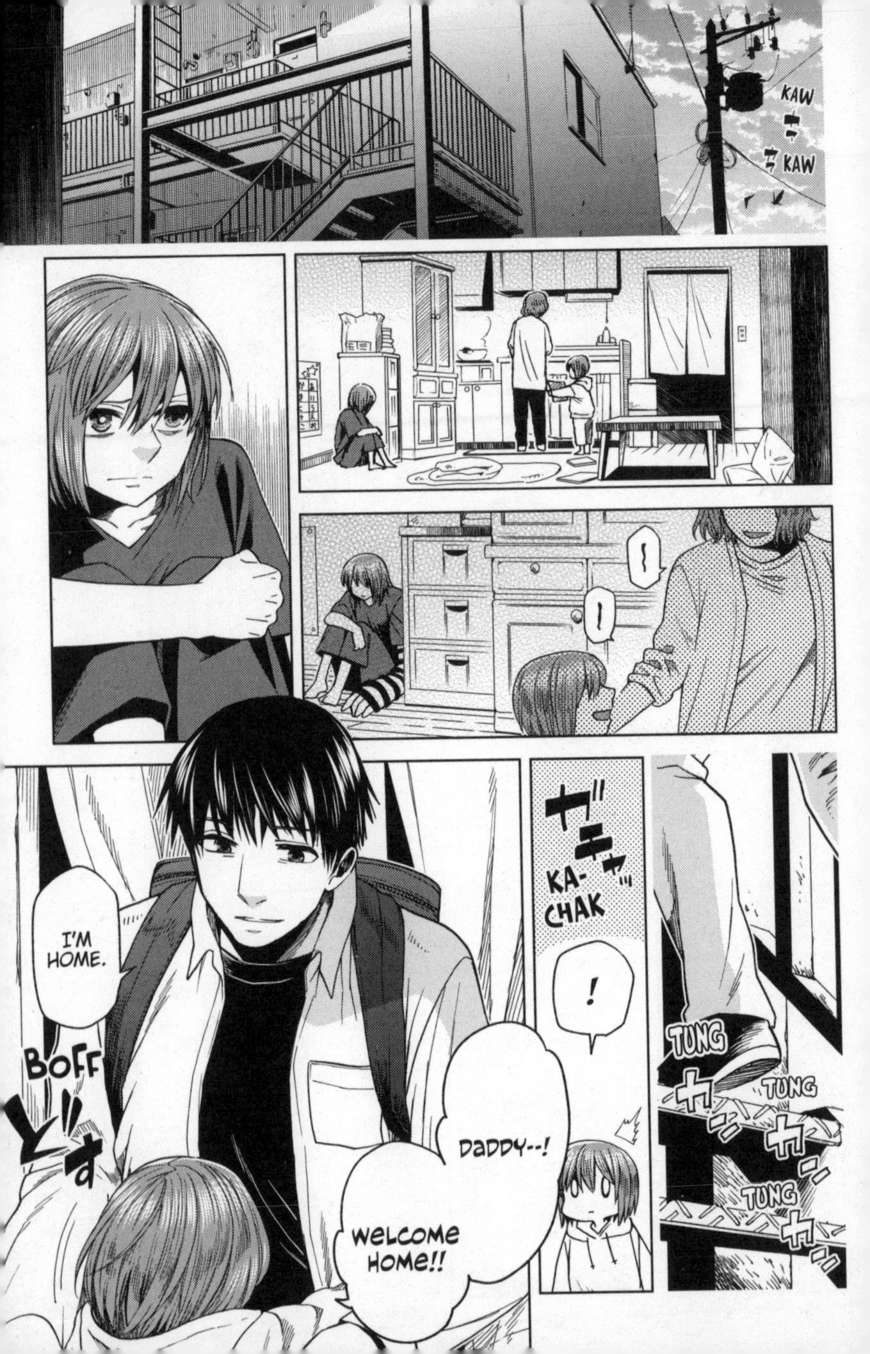
KAW
KAW
!
!
TUNG
TUNG
TUNG
KA-CHAK
!
I'M HOME.
BOFF
DADDY--!
WELCOME HOME!!

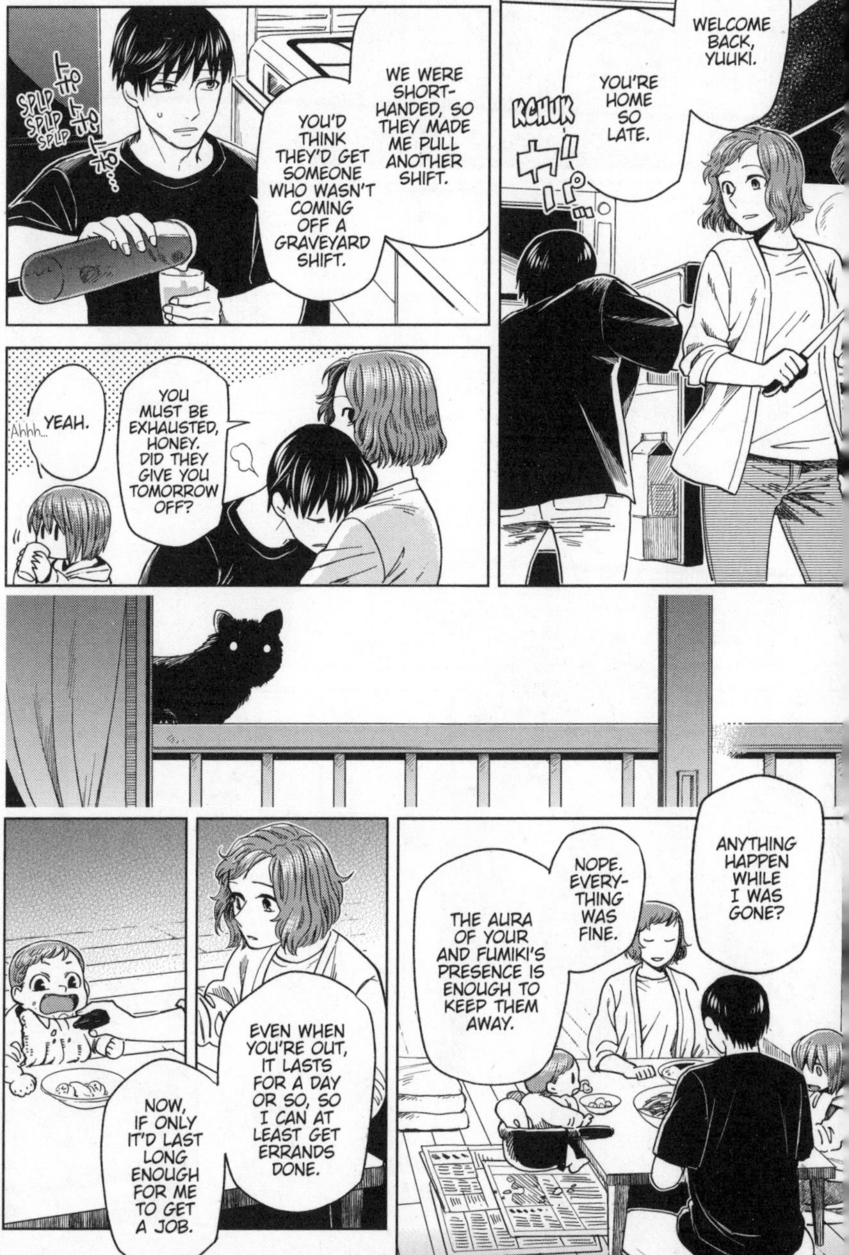
WELCOME BACK, YUUKI.
YOU'RE HOME SO LATE.
KCHUK
WE WERE SHORT-HANDED, SO THEY MADE ME PULL ANOTHER SHIFT.
YOU'D THINK THEY'D GET SOMEONE WHO WASN'T COMING OFF A GRAVEYARD SHIFT.
SPLP SPLP SPLP
YOU MUST BE EXHAUSTED, HONEY. DID THEY GIVE YOU TOMORROW OFF?
YEAH.
Ahhh...
ANYTHING HAPPEN WHILE I WAS GONE?
NOPE. EVERYTHING WAS FINE.
THE AURA OF YOUR AND FUMIKI'S PRESENCE IS ENOUGH TO KEEP THEM AWAY.
EVEN WHEN YOU'RE OUT, IT LASTS FOR A DAY OR SO, SO I CAN AT LEAST GET ERRANDS DONE.
NOW, IF ONLY IT'D LAST LONG ENOUGH FOR ME TO GET A JOB.

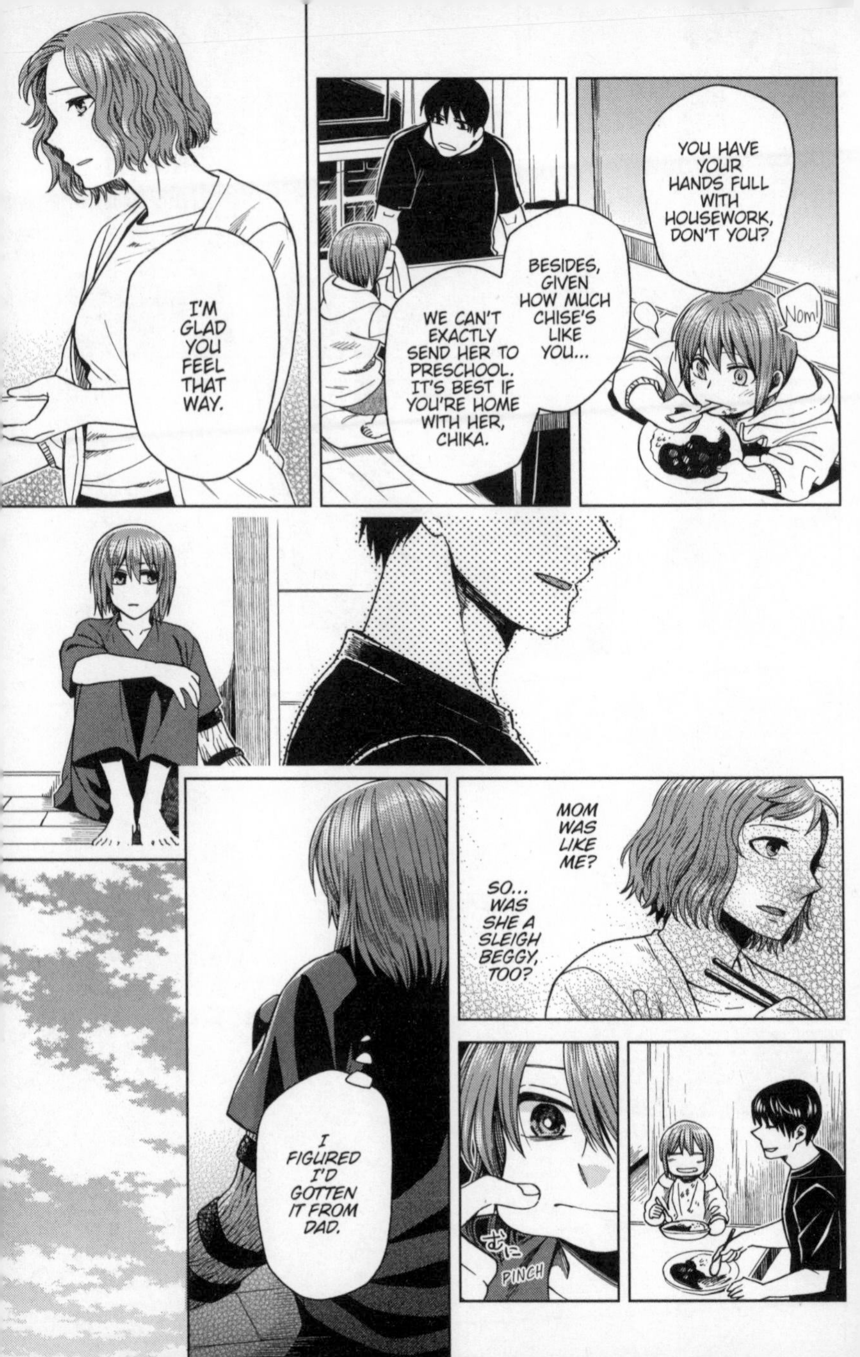
YOU HAVE YOUR HANDS FULL WITH HOUSEWORK, DON'T YOU?
Nom!
BESIDES, GIVEN HOW MUCH CHISE'S LIKE YOU...
WE CAN'T EXACTLY SEND HER TO PRESCHOOL. IT'S BEST IF YOU'RE HOME WITH HER, CHIKA.
I'M GLAD YOU FEEL THAT WAY.
MOM WAS LIKE ME?
SO... WAS SHE A SLEIGH BEGGY, TOO?
むに
PINCH
I FIGURED I'D GOTTEN IT FROM DAD.

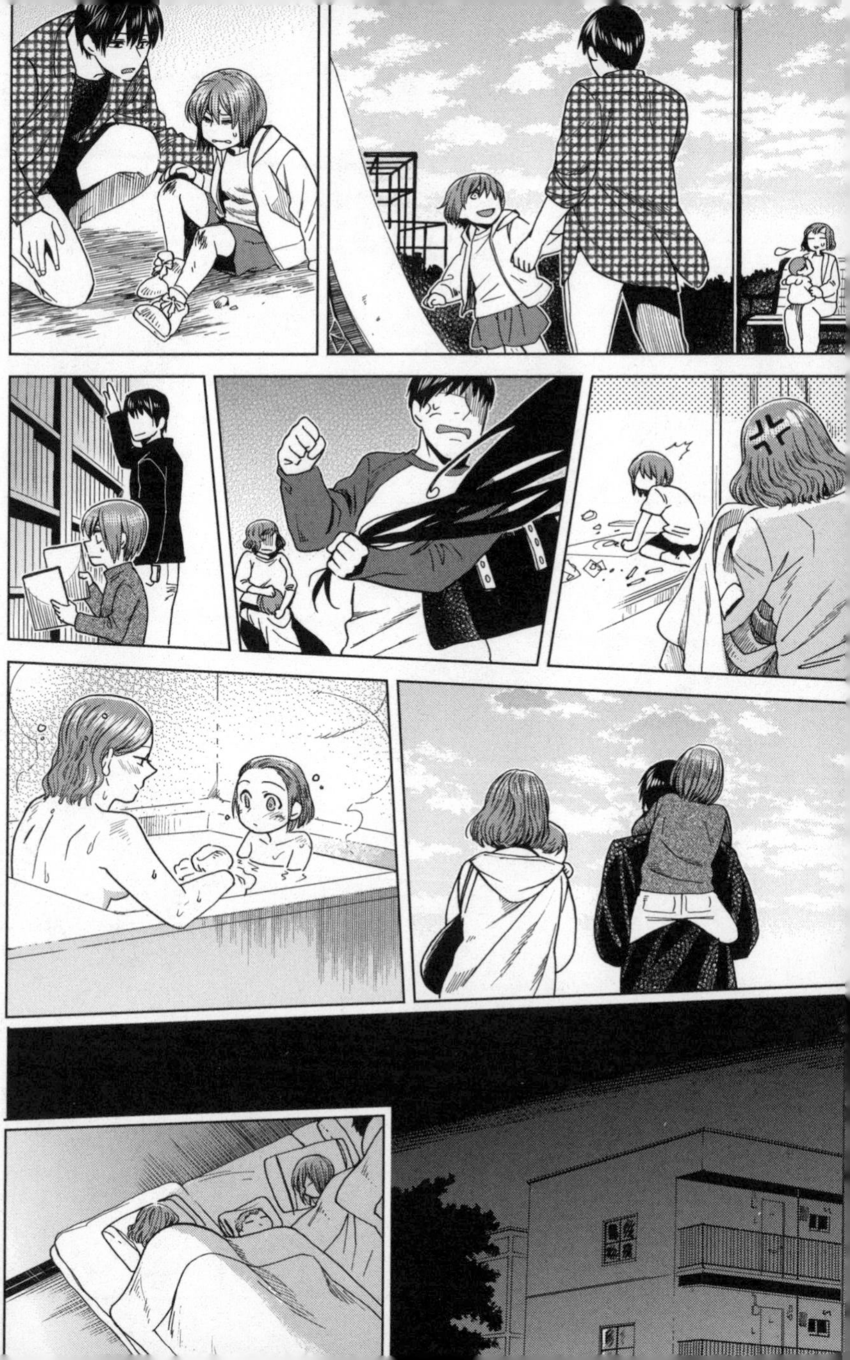

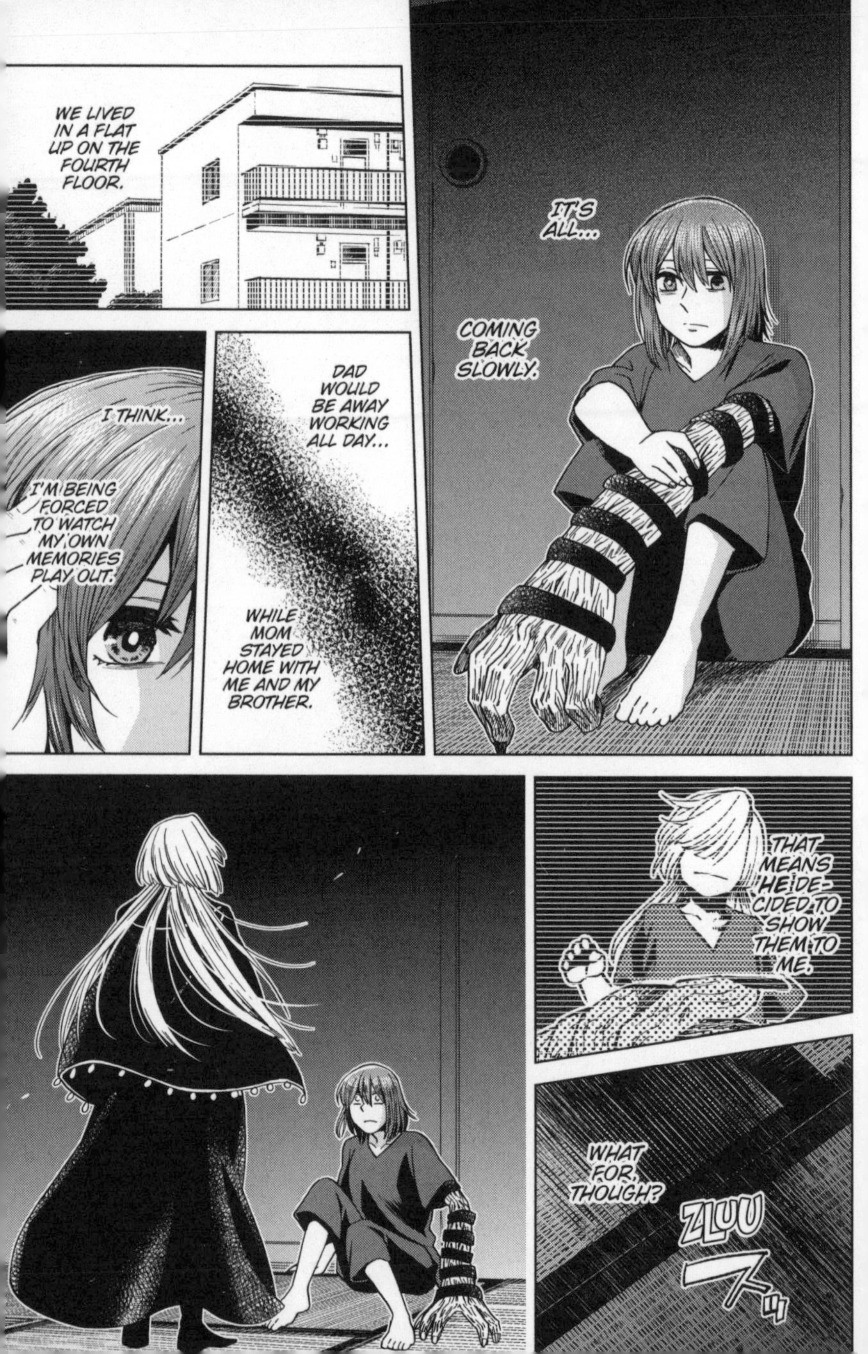
IT'S ALL...
COMING BACK SLOWLY.
WE LIVED IN A FLAT UP ON THE FOURTH FLOOR.
DAD WOULD BE AWAY WORKING ALL DAY...
WHILE MOM STAYED HOME WITH ME AND MY BROTHER.
I THINK...
I'M BEING FORCED TO WATCH MY OWN MEMORIES PLAY OUT.
THAT MEANS HE DE-CIDED TO SHOW THEM TO ME.
WHAT FOR, THOUGH?
ZLUU

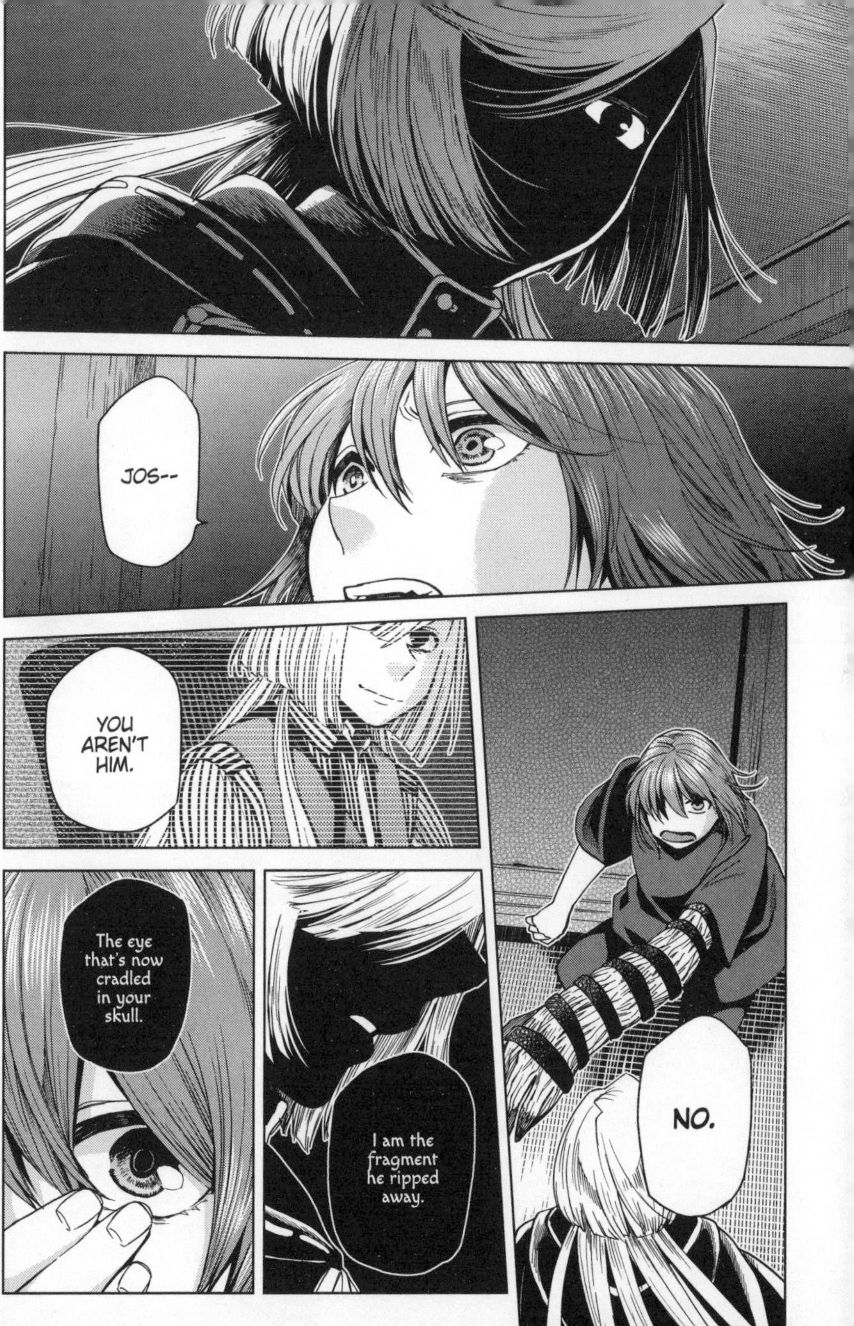
JOS--
NO.
YOU AREN'T HIM.
I am the fragment he ripped away.
The eye that's now cradled in your skull.

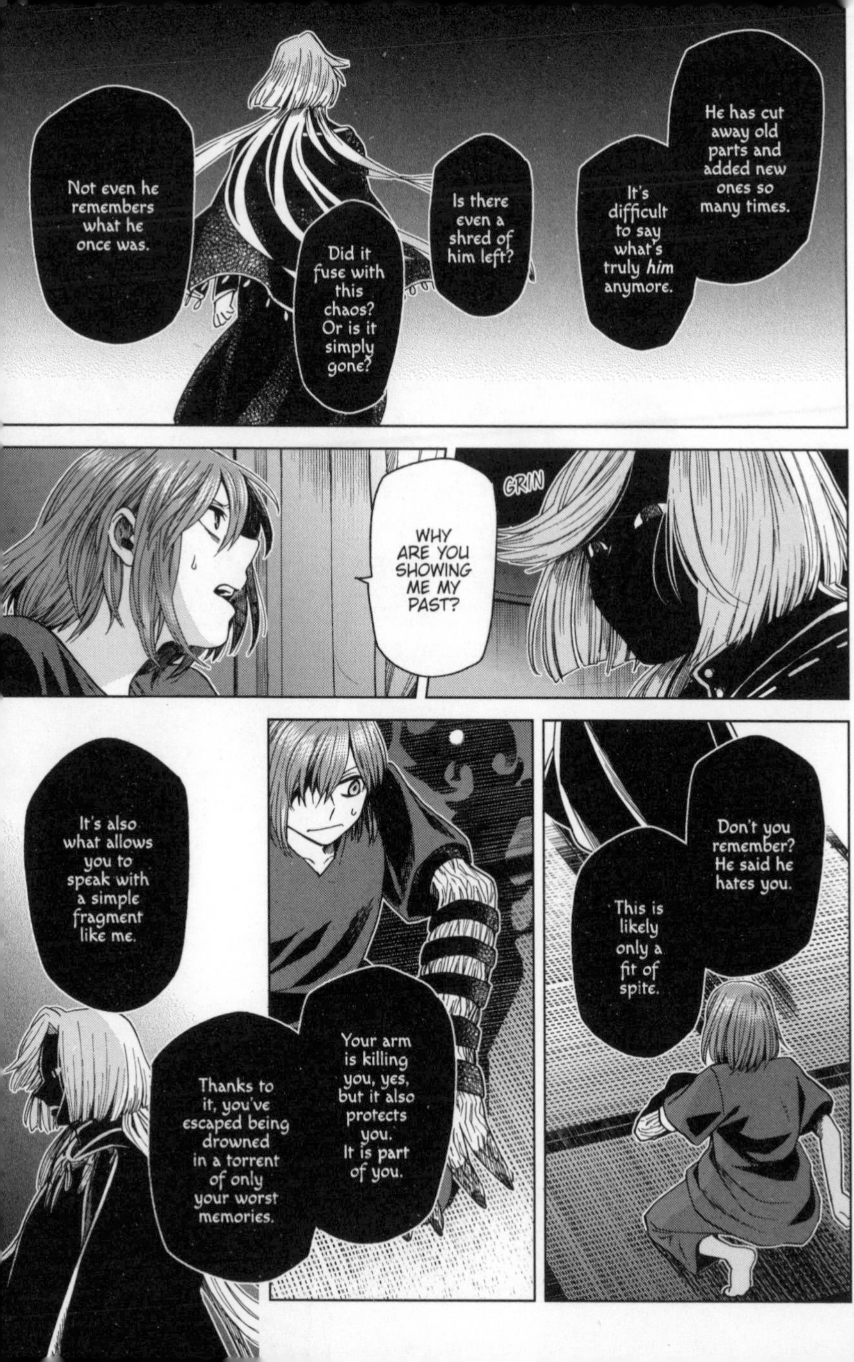
He has cut away old parts and added new ones so many times.
It's difficult to say what's truly *him* anymore.
Is there even a shred of him left?
Did it fuse with this chaos? Or is it simply gone?
Not even he remembers what he once was.
GRIN
WHY ARE YOU SHOWING ME MY PAST?
Don't you remember? He said he hates you.
This is likely only a fit of spite.
Your arm is killing you, yes, but it also protects you. It is part of you.
Thanks to it, you've escaped being drowned in a torrent of only your worst memories.
It's also what allows you to speak with a simple fragment like me.

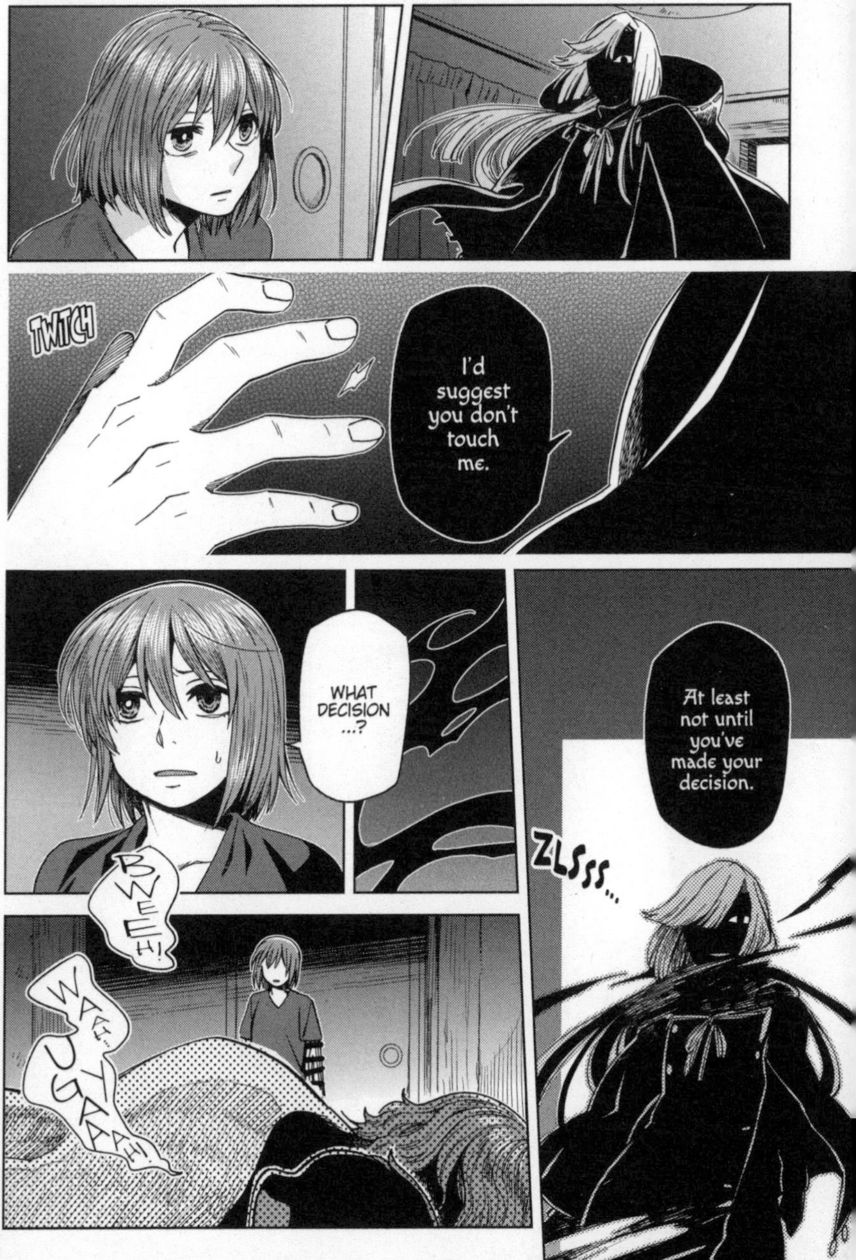
TWITCH
I'd suggest you don't touch me.
At least not until you've made your decision.
ZLSSS...
WHAT DECISION ...?
BWEEH!
WAAH...
UGYAAH!

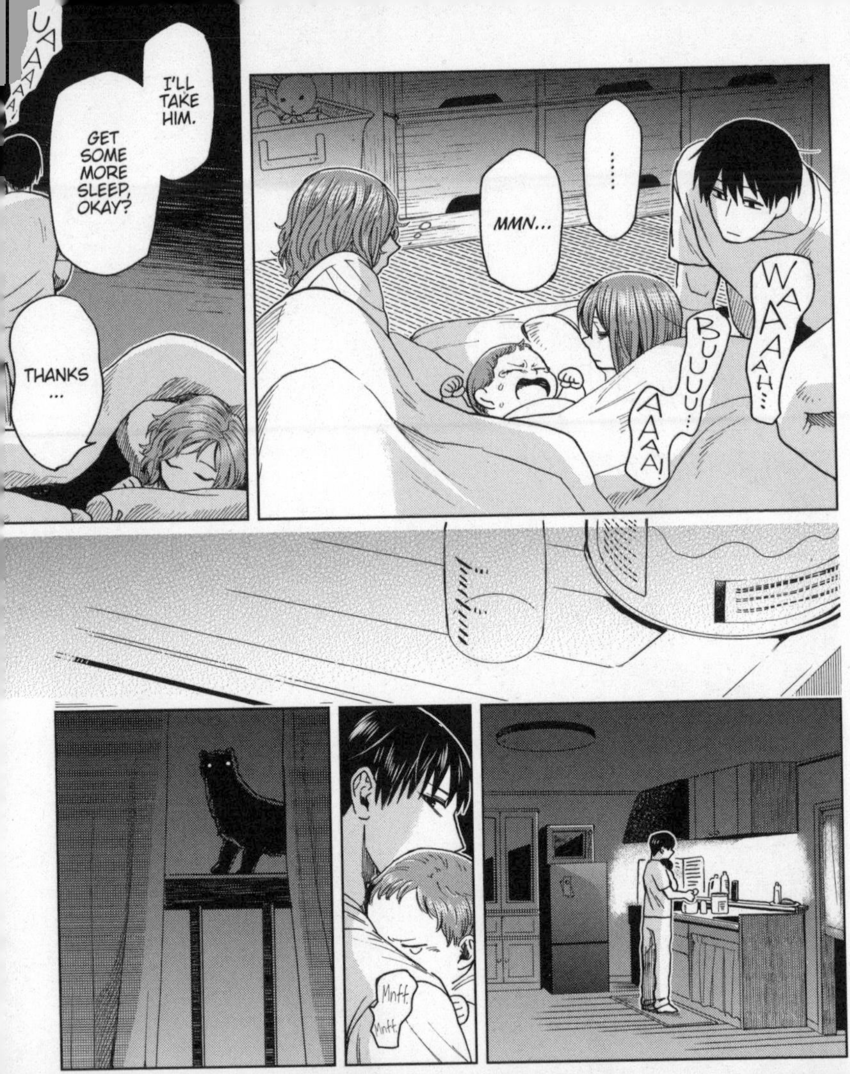
......
MMN...
WAAAAH...
BUUUU... AAAA!
UAAAA!
I'LL TAKE HIM.
GET SOME MORE SLEEP, OKAY?
THANKS ...
Mnff, Mnff.

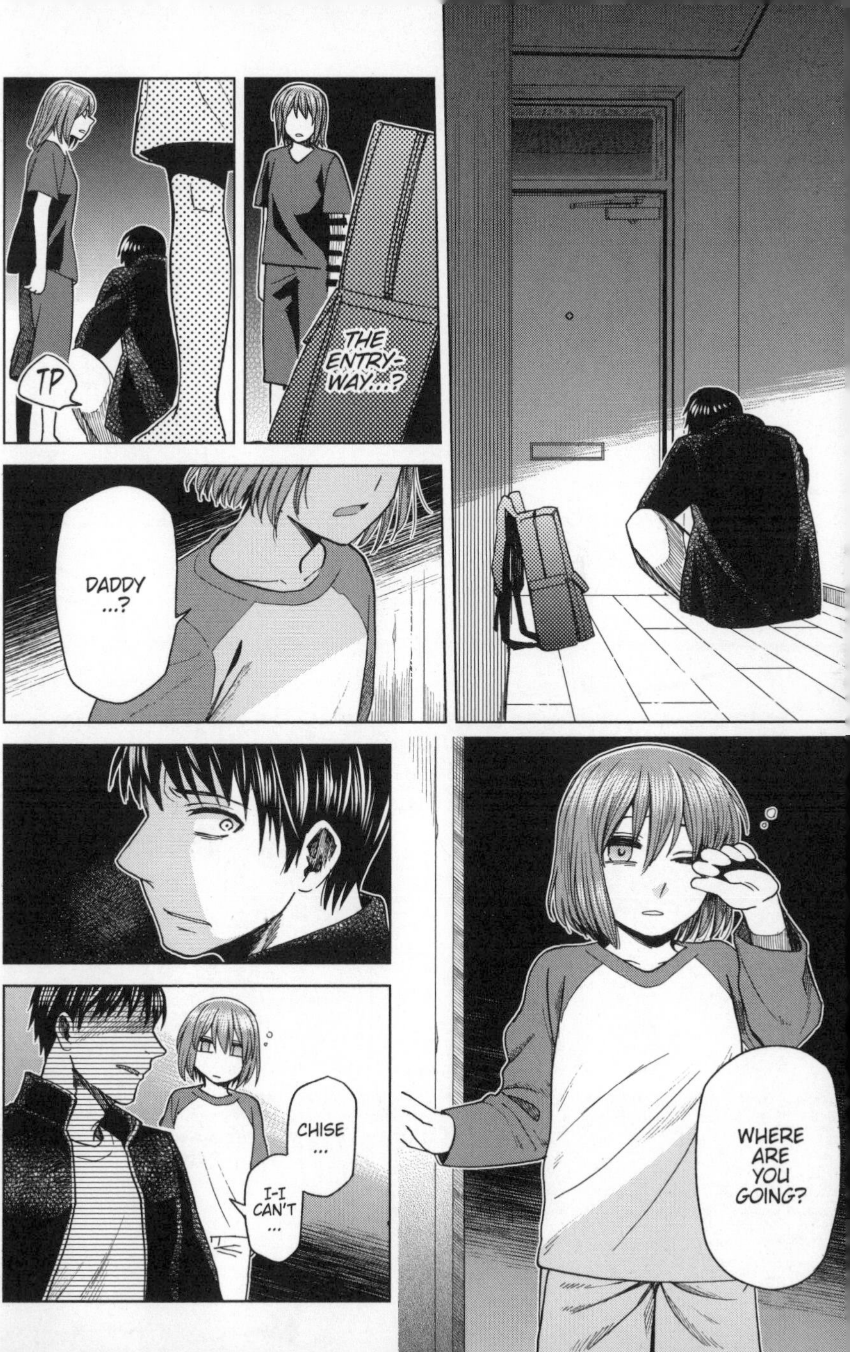
THE ENTRY-WAY...?
TP
DADDY ...?
WHERE ARE YOU GOING?
CHISE ...
I-I CAN'T ...

TOUSLE

I *PROMISE* I'LL BE BACK FOR YOU TWO.

JUST BE PATIENT, OKAY?

NO.

BACK TO BED, NOW. GOOD NIGHT.

OKAY...

?

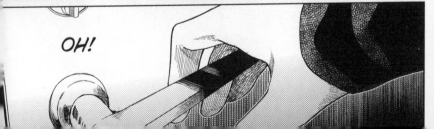

OH!

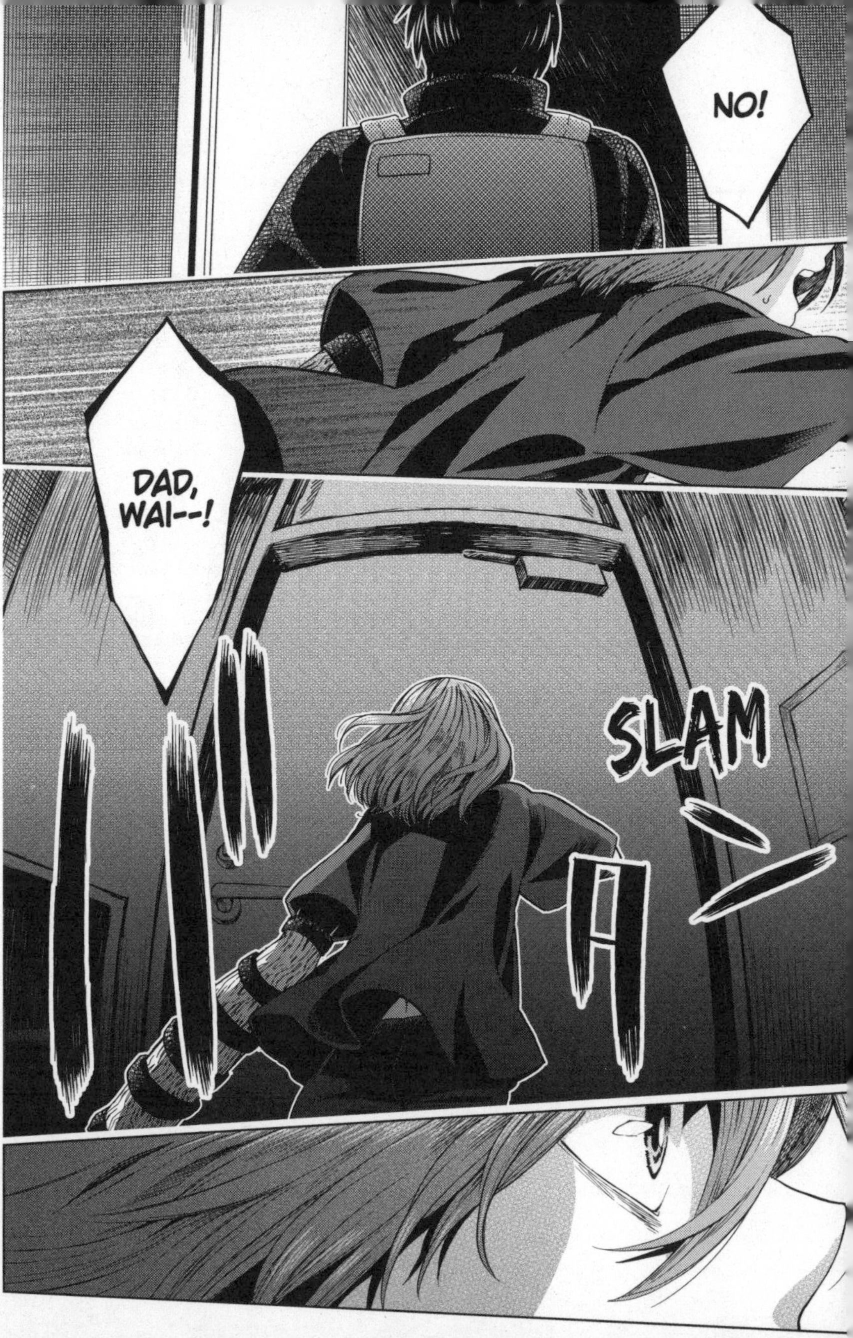
NO!
DAD, WAI--!
SLAM

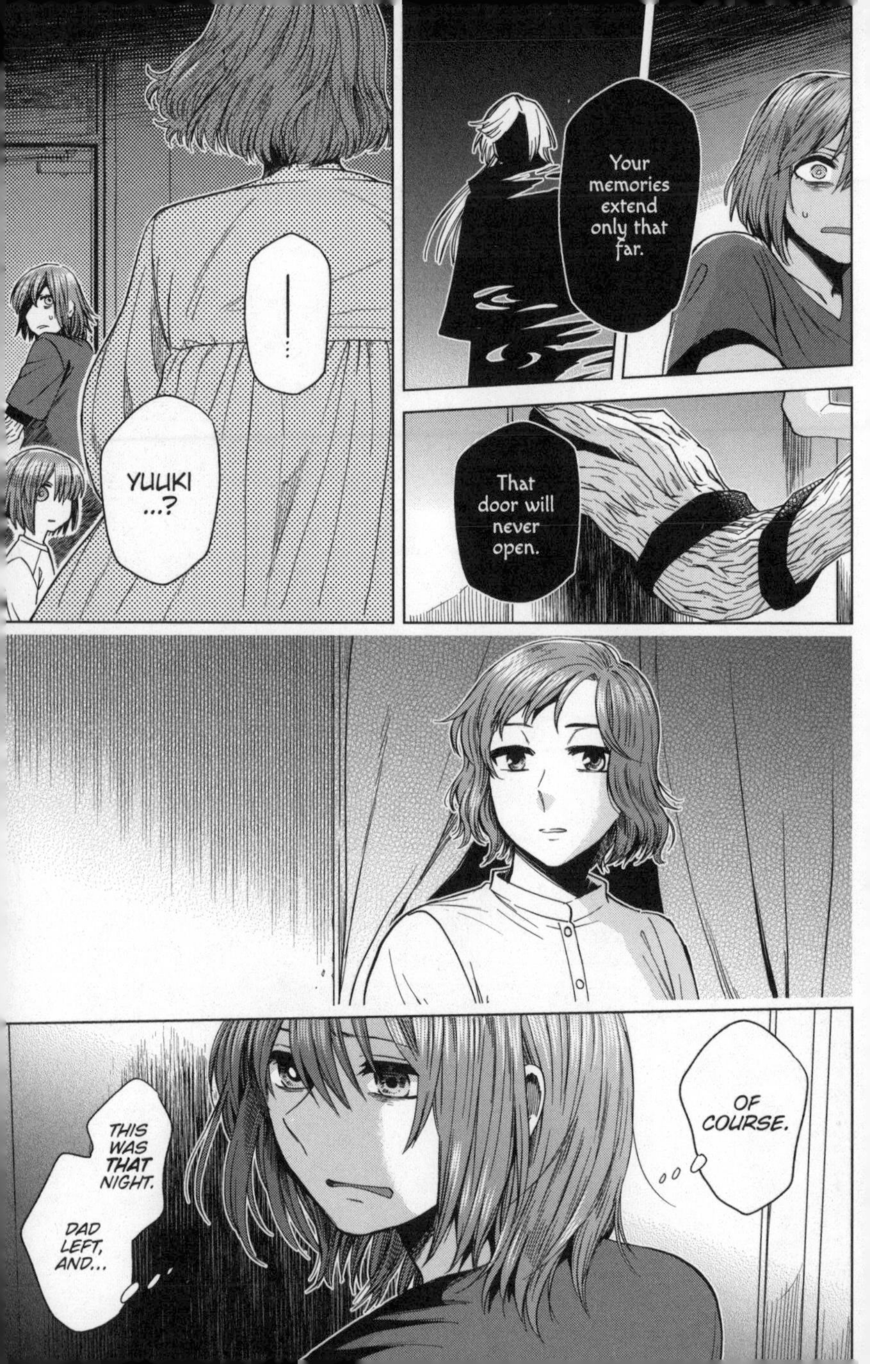

Your memories extend only that far.
That door will never open.
!
YUUKI ...?
OF COURSE.
THIS WAS THAT NIGHT.
DAD LEFT, AND...

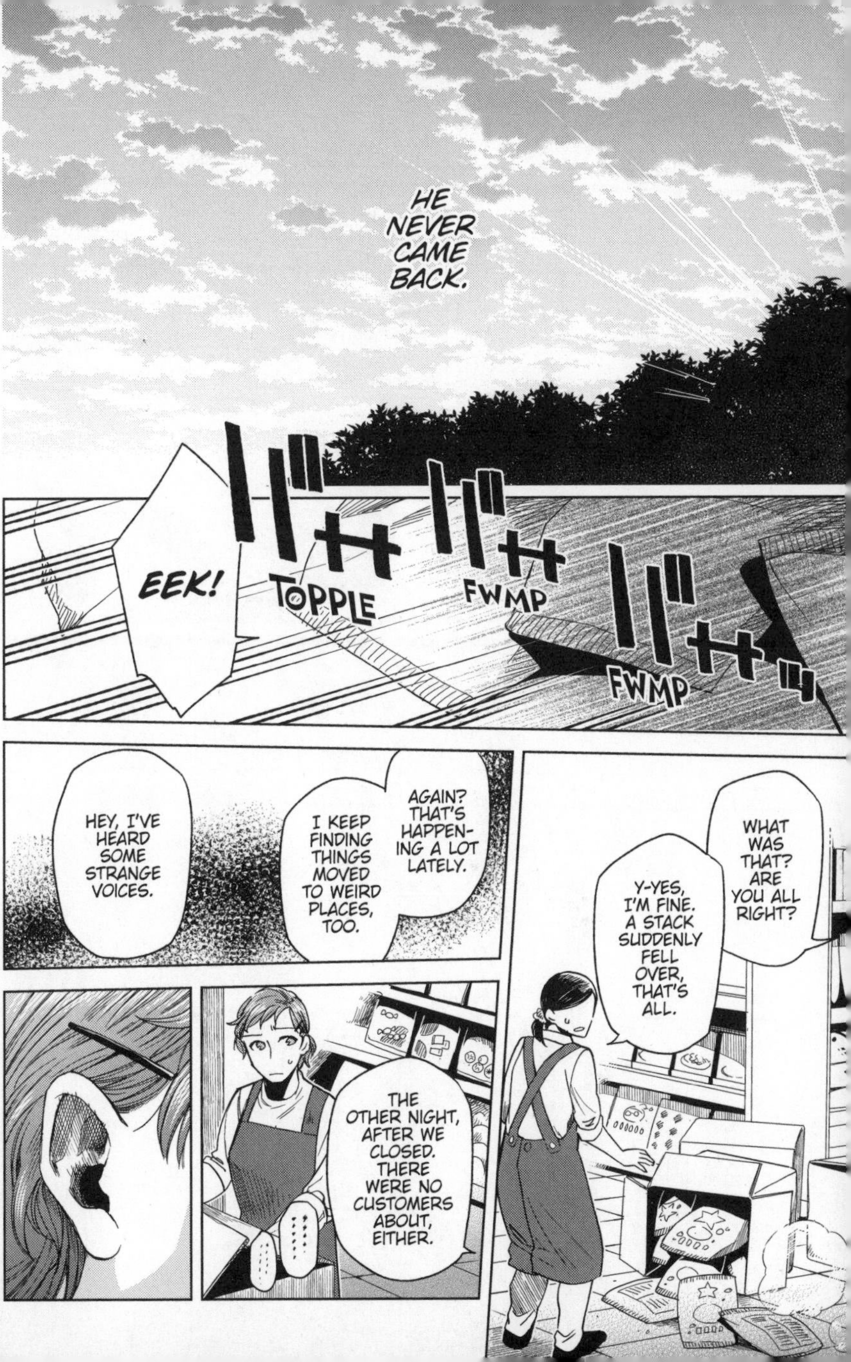
HE NEVER CAME BACK.
FWMP
FWMP
TOPPLE
EEK!
WHAT WAS THAT? ARE YOU ALL RIGHT?
Y-YES, I'M FINE. A STACK SUDDENLY FELL OVER, THAT'S ALL.
AGAIN? THAT'S HAPPEN-ING A LOT LATELY.
I KEEP FINDING THINGS MOVED TO WEIRD PLACES, TOO.
HEY, I'VE HEARD SOME STRANGE VOICES.
THE OTHER NIGHT, AFTER WE CLOSED. THERE WERE NO CUSTOMERS ABOUT, EITHER.

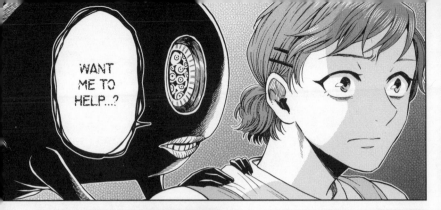

WANT ME TO HELP...?

HEE HEE HEE...

WHRL

GLOMP

WELCOME HOME...

DA...

MOMMY?

BTAM

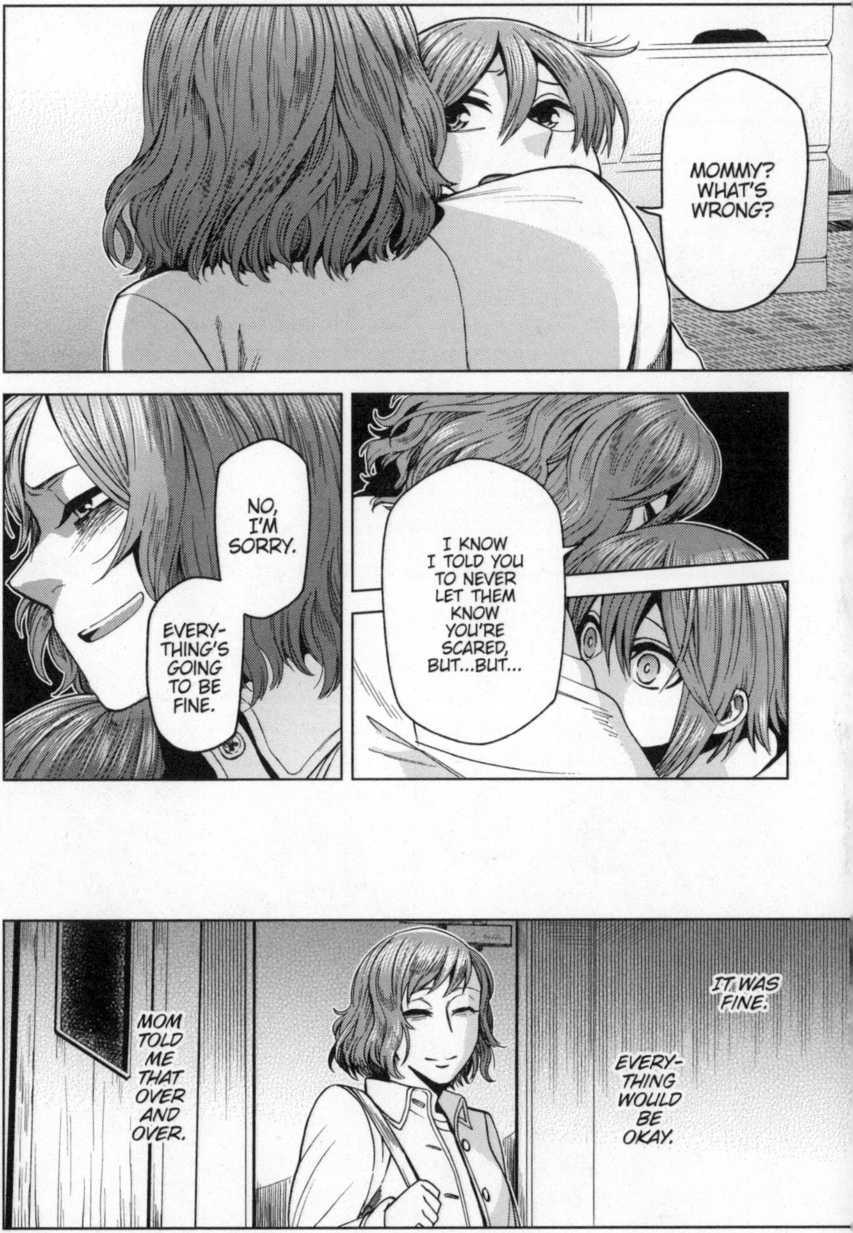
MOMMY? WHAT'S WRONG?
I KNOW I TOLD YOU TO NEVER LET THEM KNOW YOU'RE SCARED, BUT...BUT...
NO, I'M SORRY.
EVERY-THING'S GOING TO BE FINE.
IT WAS FINE.
EVERY-THING WOULD BE OKAY.
MOM TOLD ME THAT OVER AND OVER.

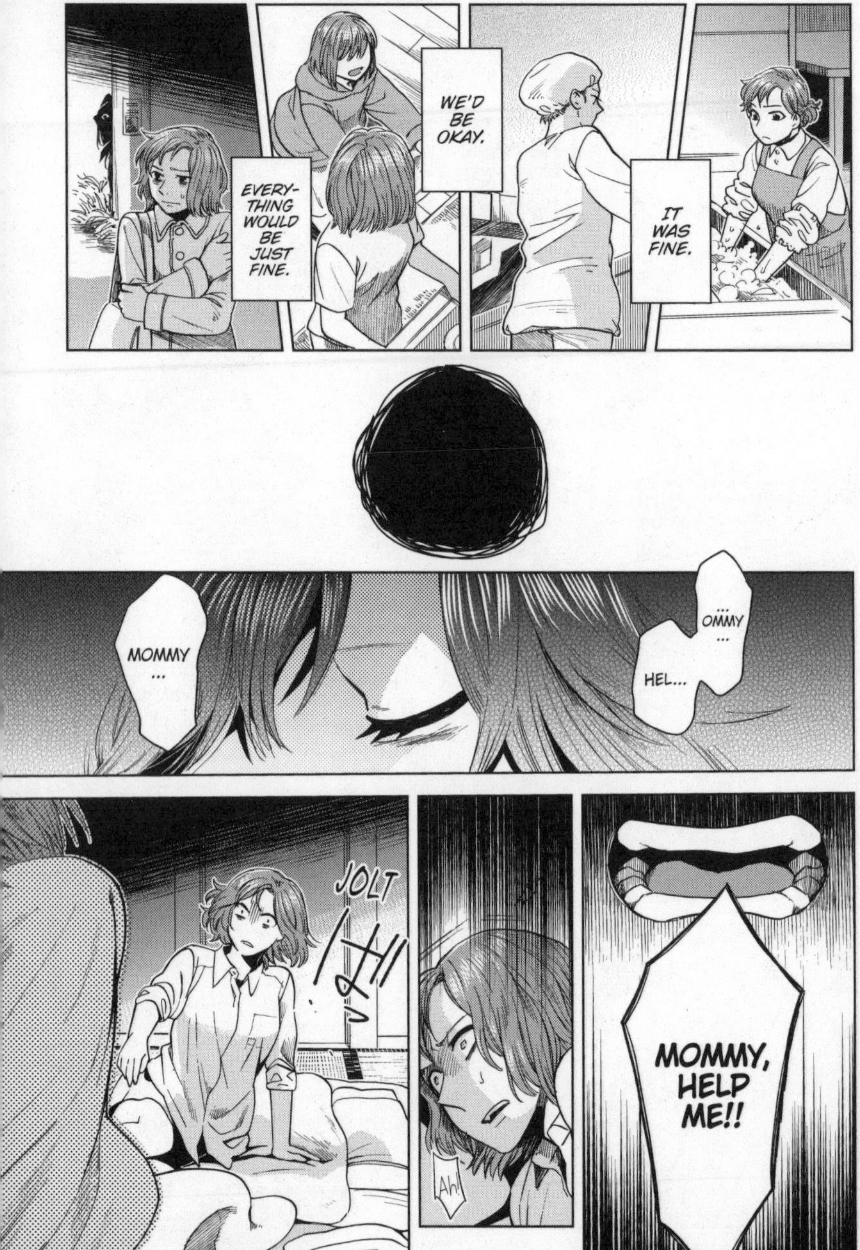
IT WAS FINE.
WE'D BE OKAY.
EVERYTHING WOULD BE JUST FINE.
...OMMY... HEL...
MOMMY...
MOMMY, HELP ME!!
Ah!
JOLT

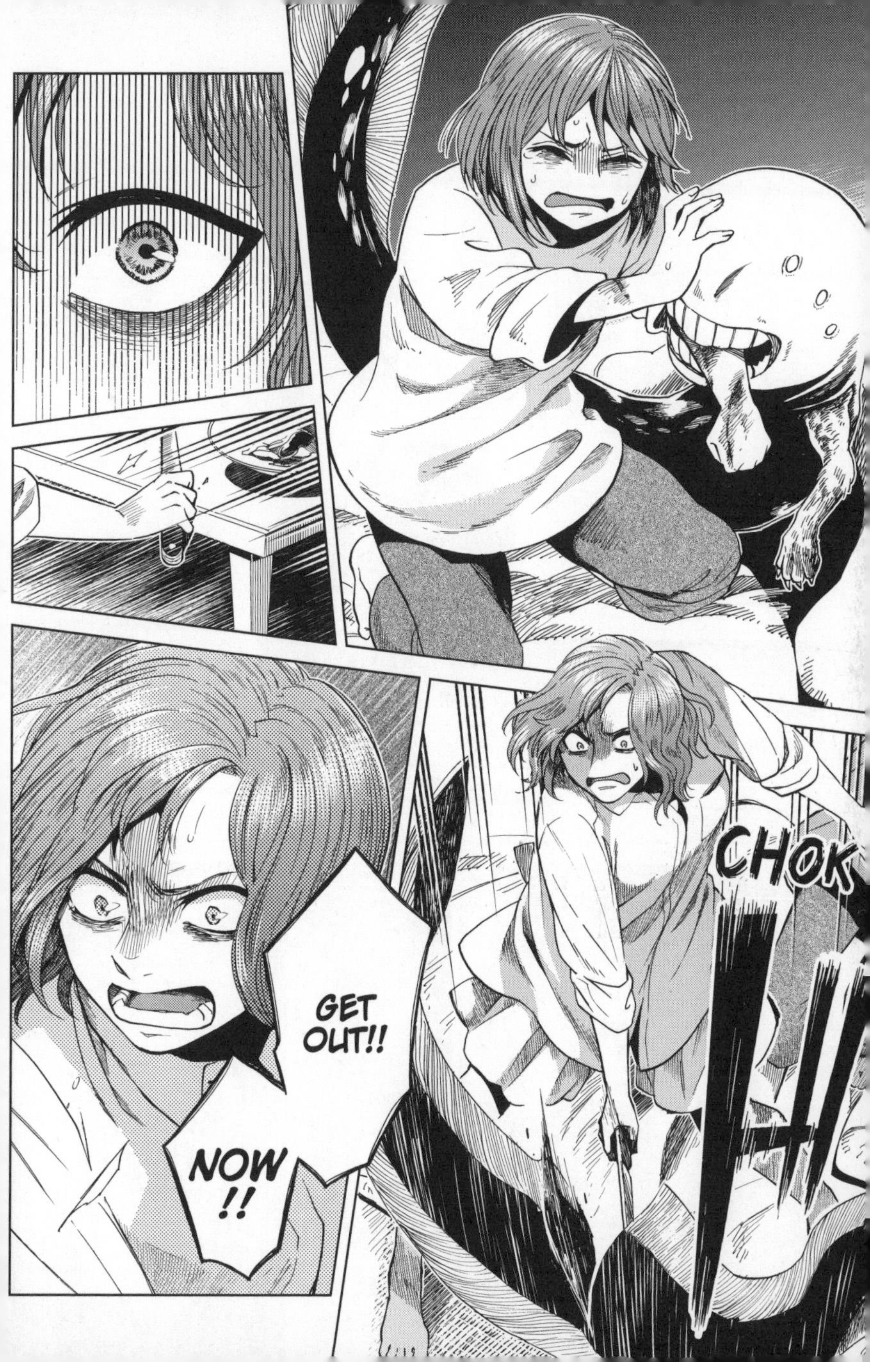
CHOK
GET OUT!!
NOW !!

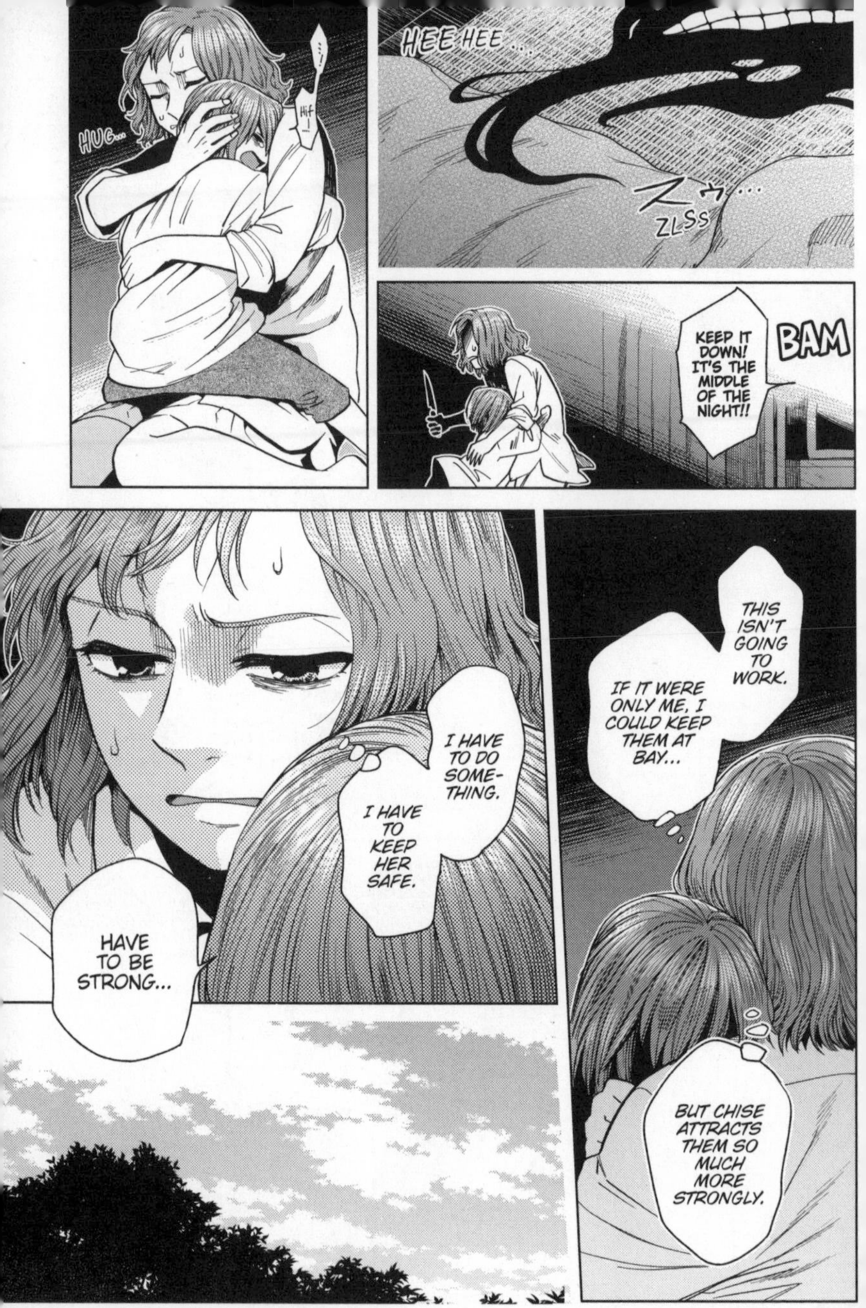
HEE HEE...
ZLSS
BAM
KEEP IT DOWN! IT'S THE MIDDLE OF THE NIGHT!!
Hif...!
HUG...
THIS ISN'T GOING TO WORK.
IF IT WERE ONLY ME, I COULD KEEP THEM AT BAY...
BUT CHISE ATTRACTS THEM SO MUCH MORE STRONGLY.
I HAVE TO DO SOMETHING.
I HAVE TO KEEP HER SAFE.
HAVE TO BE STRONG...

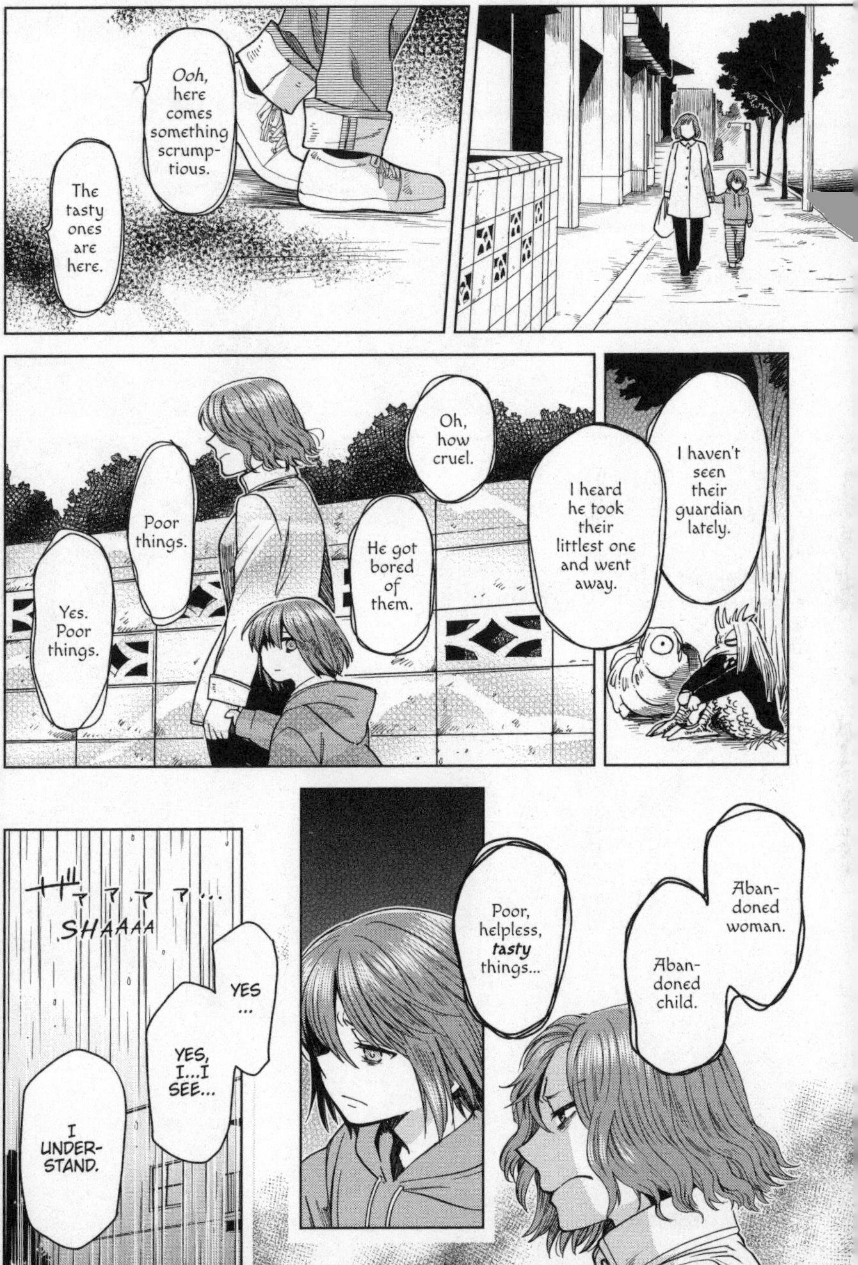
Ooh, here comes something scrump-tious.
The tasty ones are here.
I haven't seen their guardian lately.
I heard he took their littlest one and went away.
Oh, how cruel.
He got bored of them.
Poor things.
Yes. Poor things.
Aban-doned woman.
Aban-doned child.
Poor, helpless, *tasty* things...
ザァァァァ...
SHAAAA
YES...
YES, I...I SEE...
I UNDER-STAND.

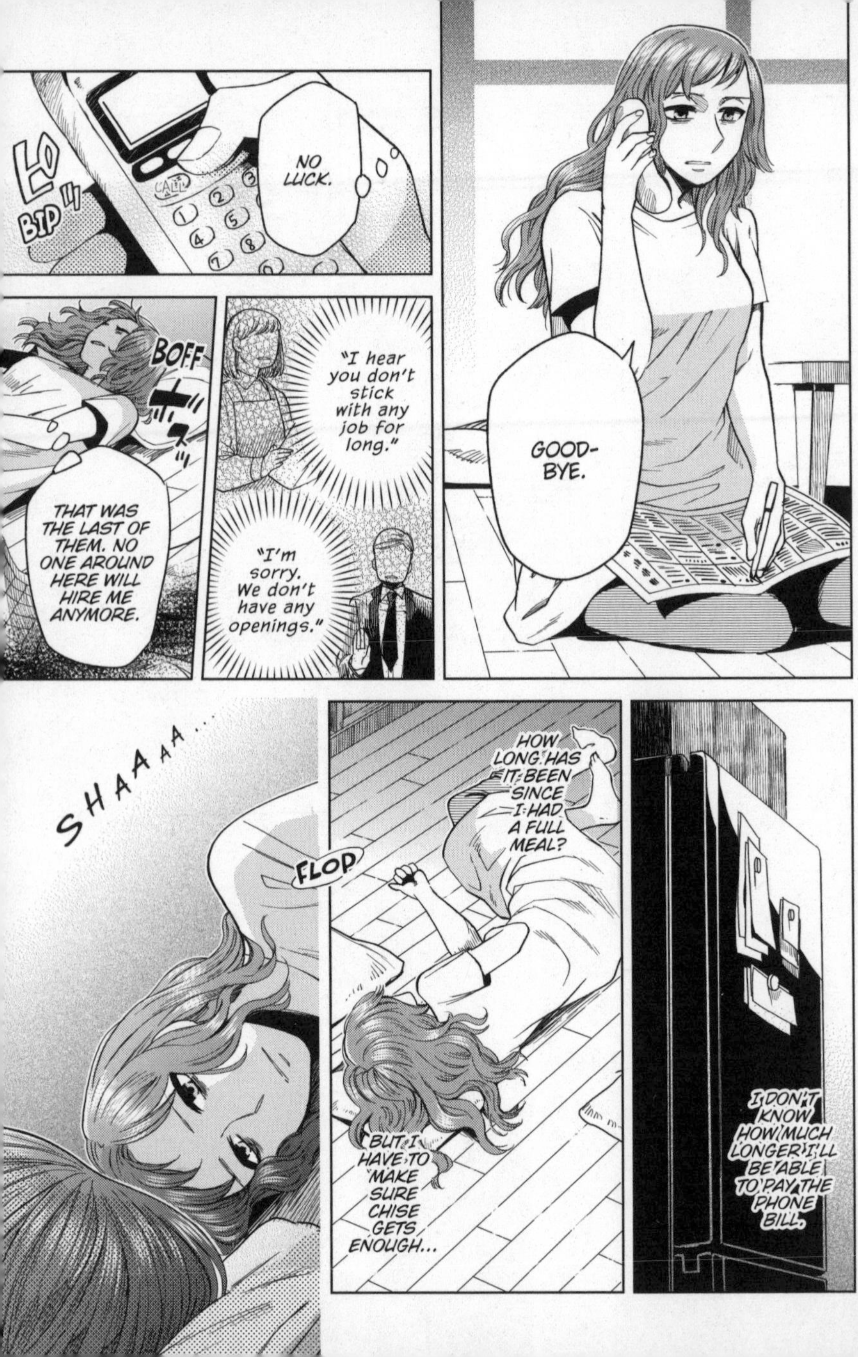
GOOD-BYE.
NO LUCK.
BIP
"I hear you don't stick with any job for long."
"I'm sorry. We don't have any openings."
BOFF
THAT WAS THE LAST OF THEM. NO ONE AROUND HERE WILL HIRE ME ANYMORE.
I DON'T KNOW HOW MUCH LONGER I'LL BE ABLE TO PAY THE PHONE BILL.
HOW LONG HAS IT BEEN SINCE I HAD A FULL MEAL?
FLOP
BUT I HAVE TO MAKE SURE CHISE GETS ENOUGH...
SHAAAA...

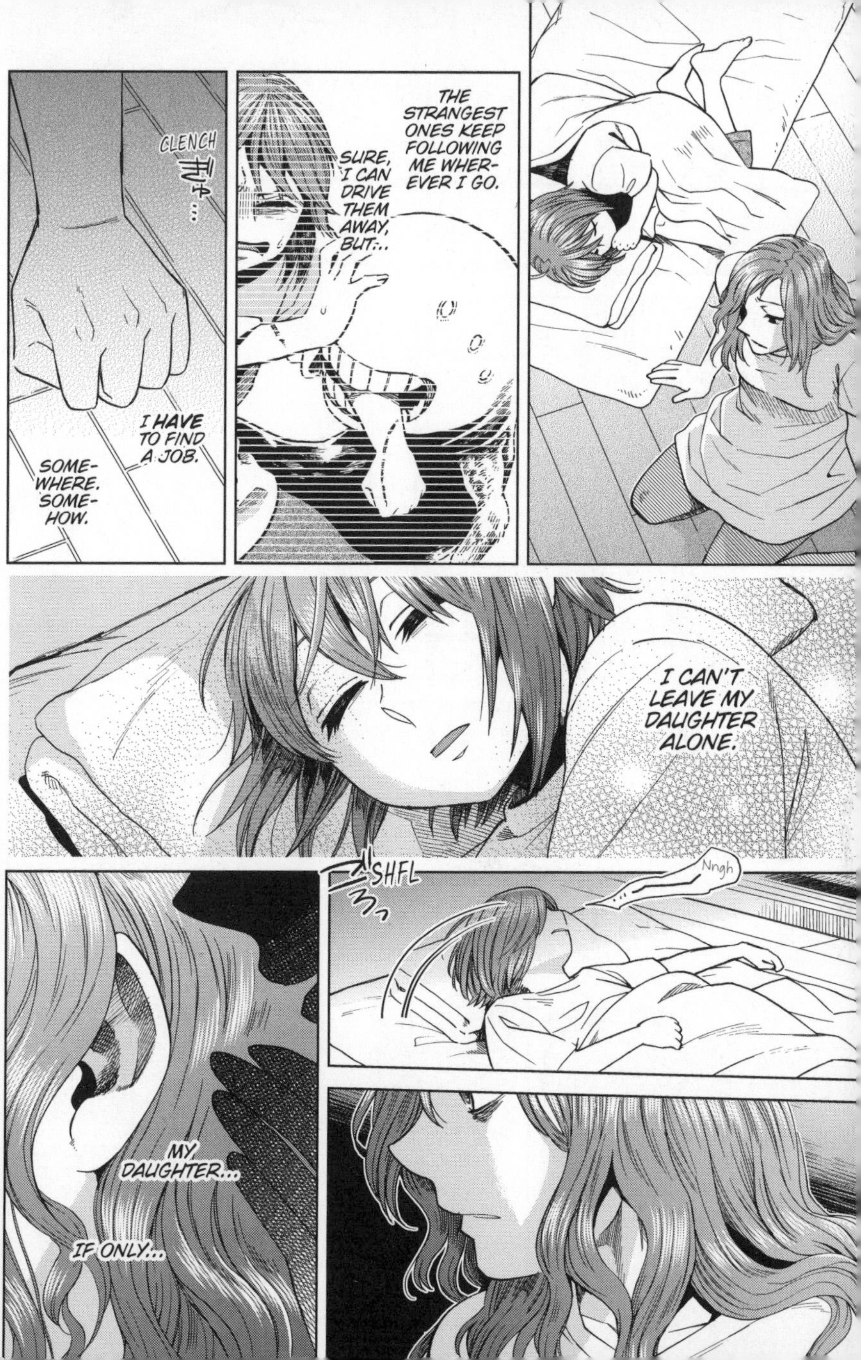

THE STRANGEST ONES KEEP FOLLOWING ME WHEREVER I GO.
SURE, I CAN DRIVE THEM AWAY, BUT...
CLENCH
ぎゅ…
I HAVE TO FIND A JOB.
SOMEWHERE. SOMEHOW.
I CAN'T LEAVE MY DAUGHTER ALONE.
SHFL
Nngh
MY DAUGHTER...
IF ONLY...

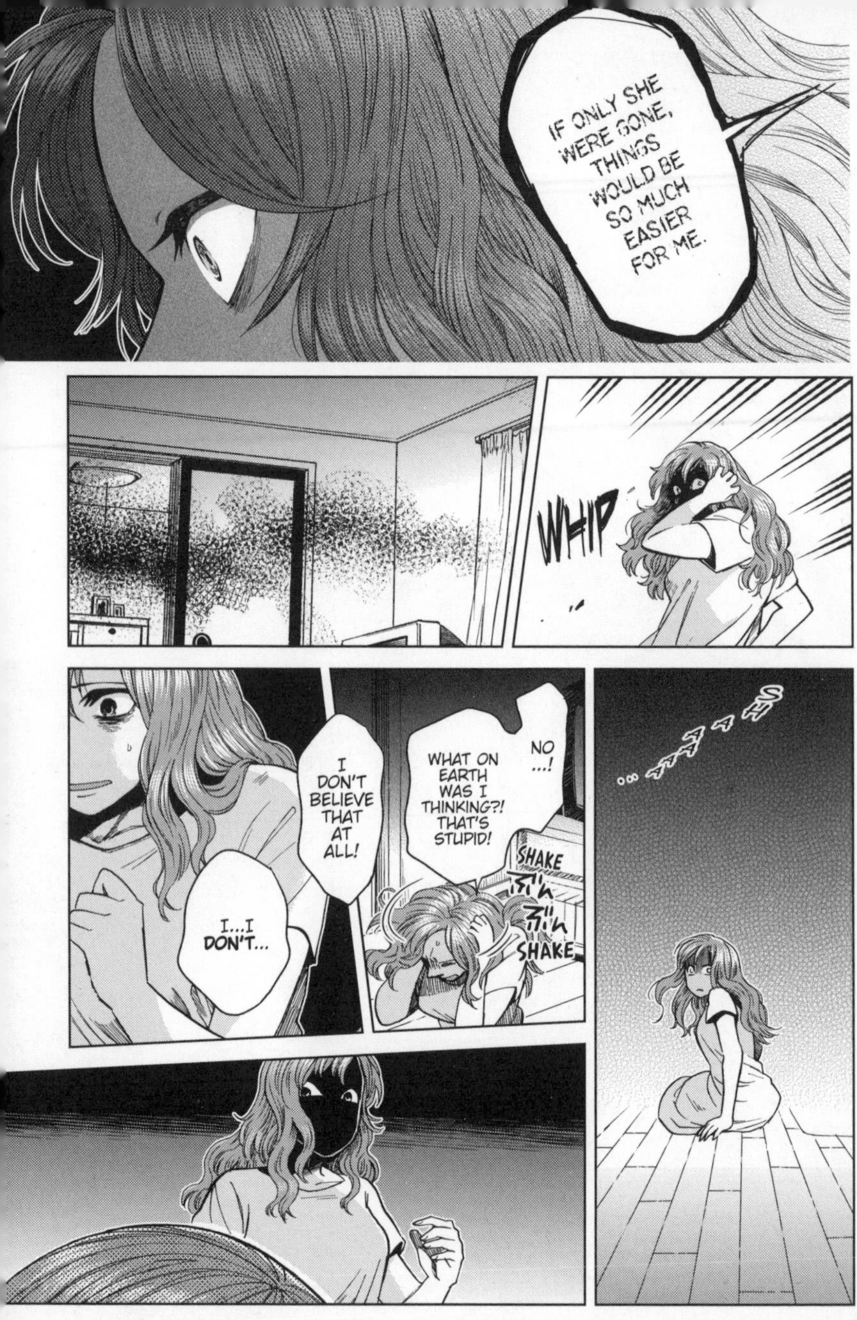
IF ONLY SHE WERE GONE, THINGS WOULD BE SO MUCH EASIER FOR ME.
WHIP
SHAAAAAA..
NO...!
WHAT ON EARTH WAS I THINKING?! THAT'S STUPID!
SHAKE
ぶん
ぶん
SHAKE
I DON'T BELIEVE THAT AT ALL!
I...I DON'T...

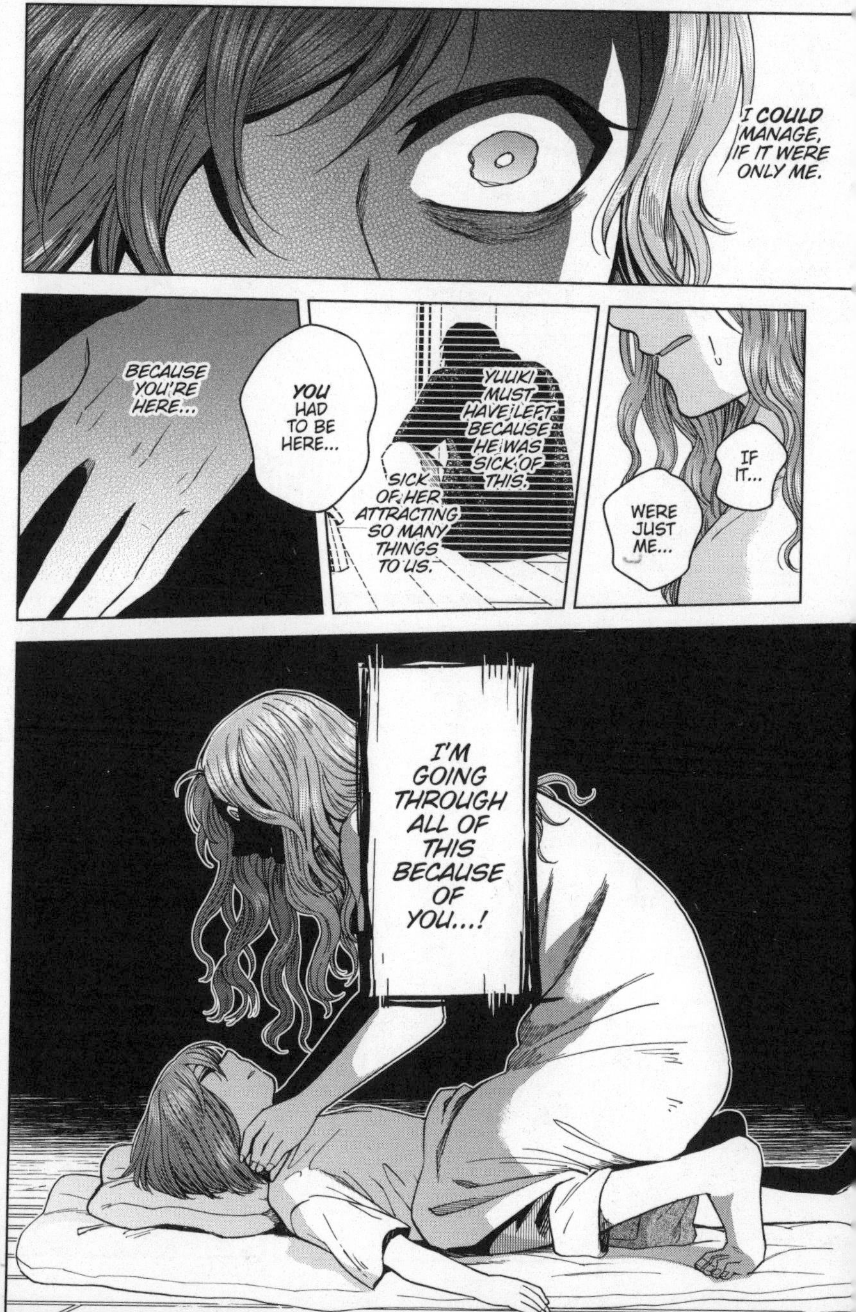
I COULD MANAGE, IF IT WERE ONLY ME.
IF IT...
WERE JUST ME...
YUUKI MUST HAVE LEFT BECAUSE HE WAS SICK OF THIS.
SICK OF HER ATTRACTING SO MANY THINGS TO US.
YOU HAD TO BE HERE...
BECAUSE YOU'RE HERE...
I'M GOING THROUGH ALL OF THIS BECAUSE OF YOU...!

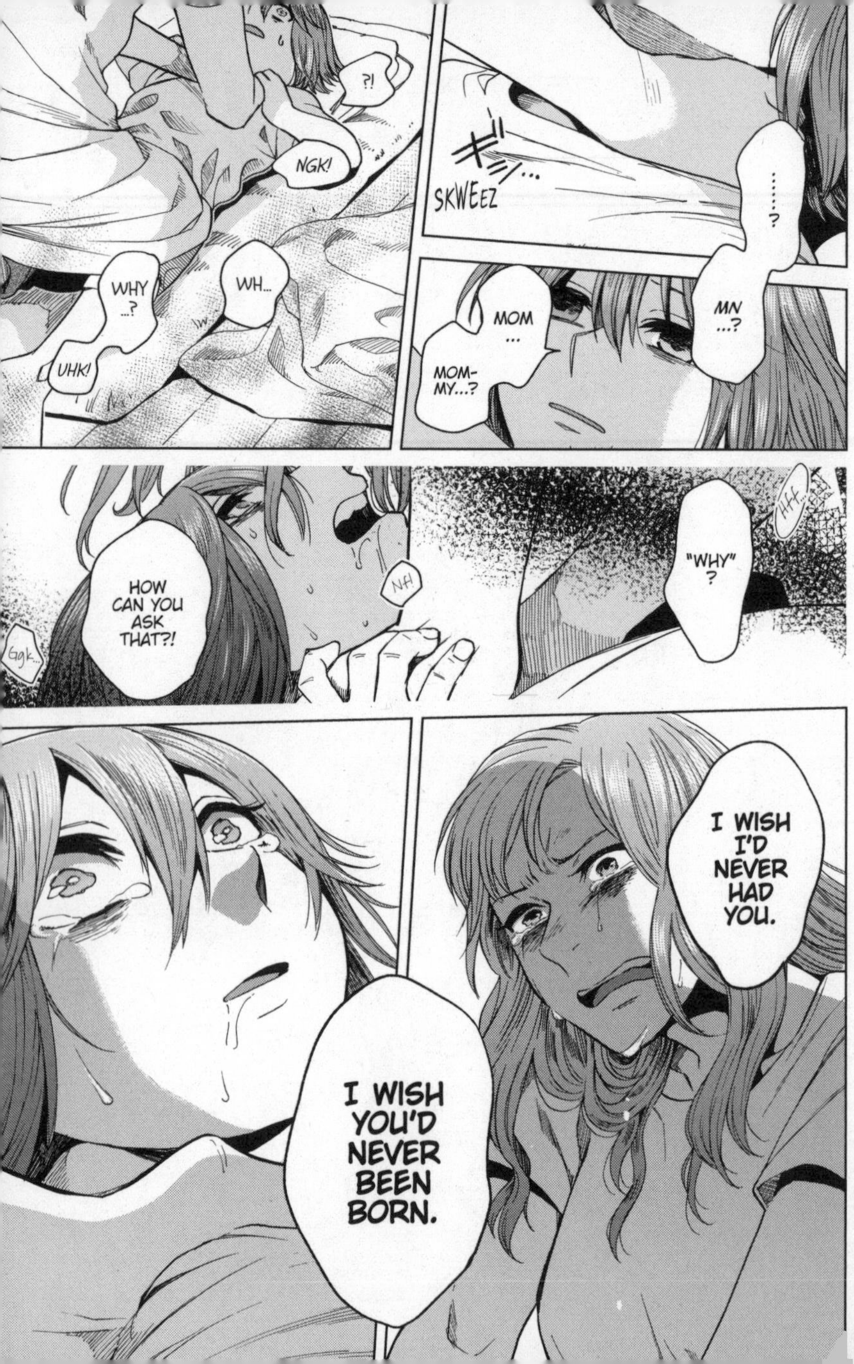
SKWEEZ
......?
MN ...?
MOM ...
MOM-MY...?
?!
NGK!
WH...
WHY ...?
UHK!
Hff...
"WHY" ?
Nf!
HOW CAN YOU ASK THAT?!
Ggk...
I WISH I'D NEVER HAD YOU.
I WISH YOU'D NEVER BEEN BORN.

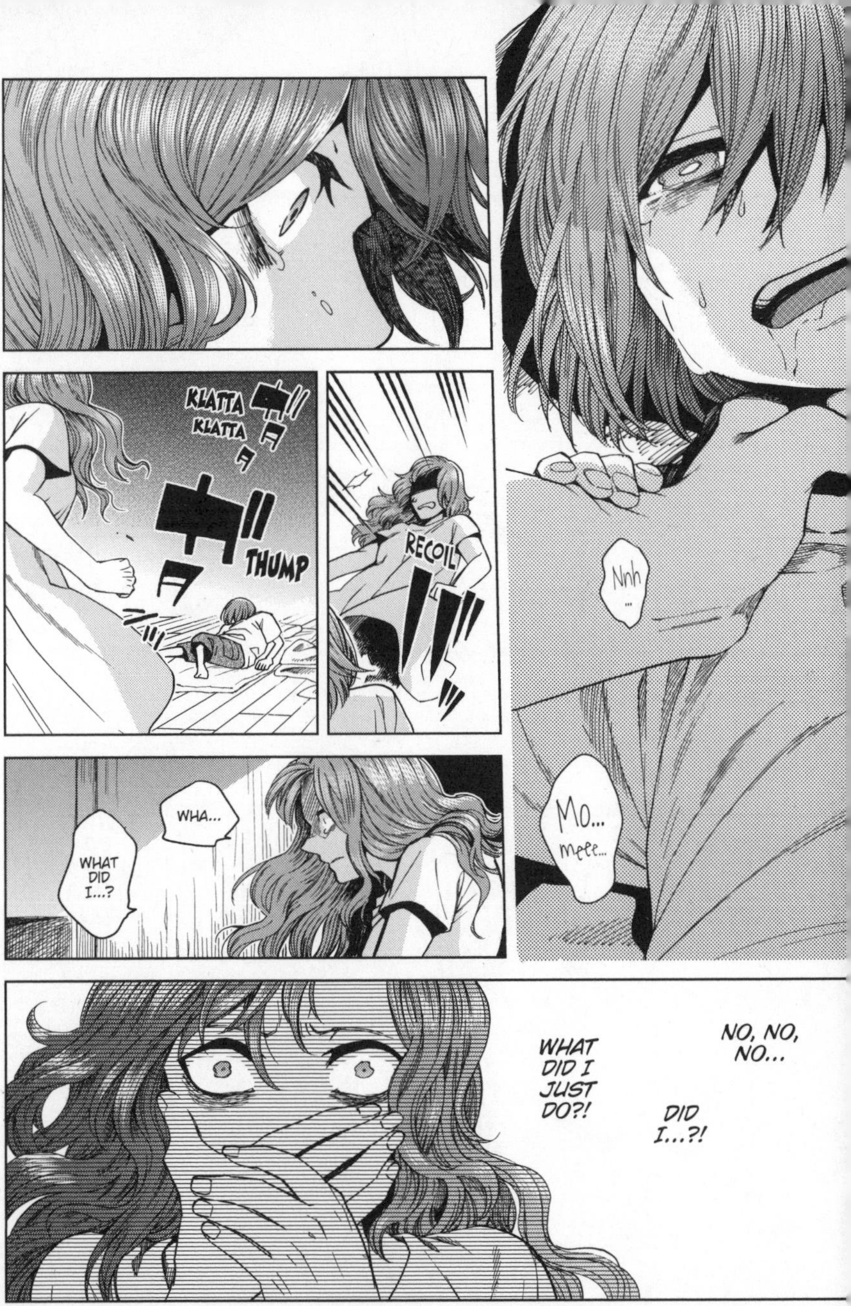
Nnh...
Mo... meee...
RECOIL
KLATTA KLATTA
THUMP
WHA...
WHAT DID I...?
NO, NO, NO...
DID I...?!
WHAT DID I JUST DO?!

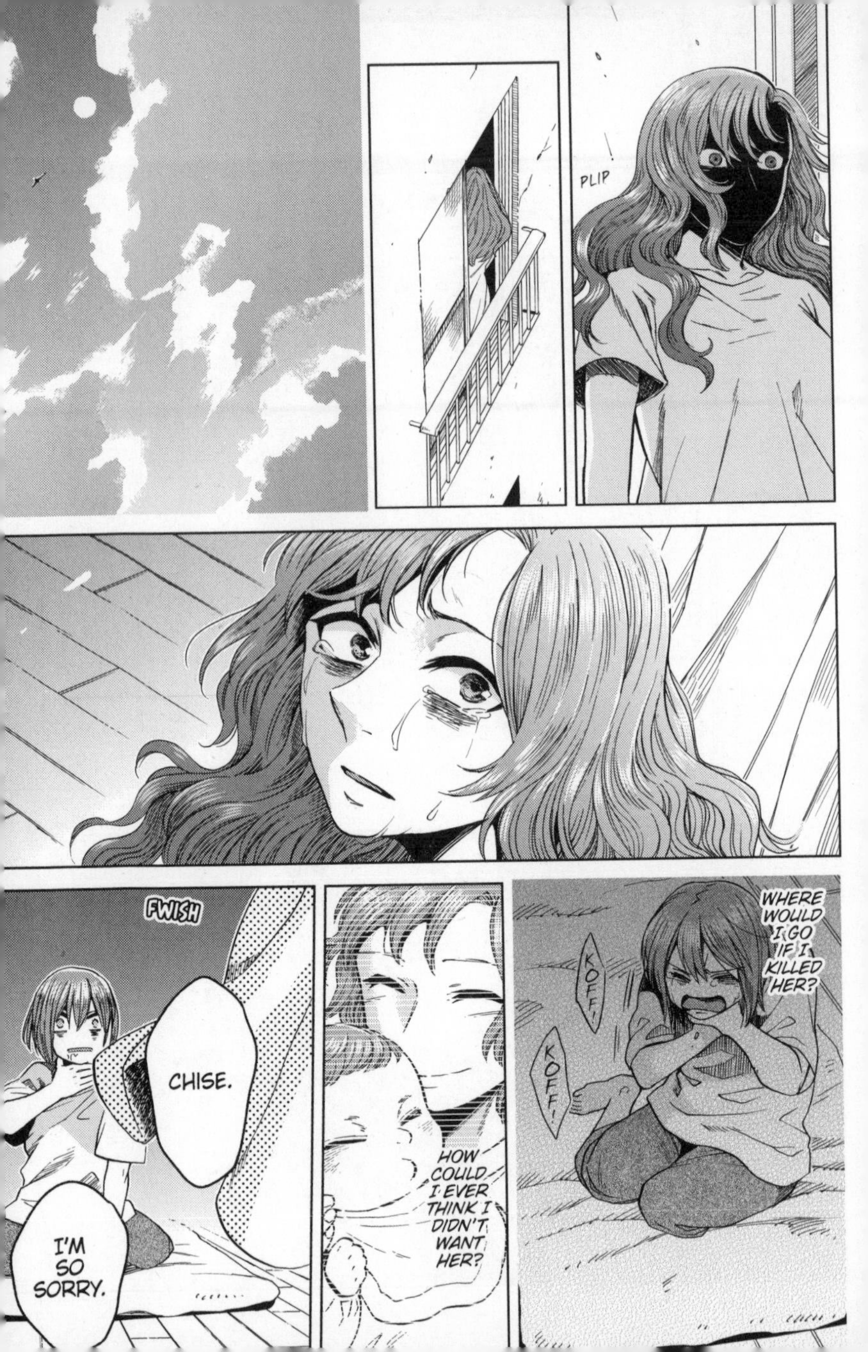
PLIP
WHERE WOULD I GO IF I KILLED HER?
KOFF!
KOFF!
HOW COULD I EVER THINK I DIDN'T WANT HER?
FWISH
CHISE.
I'M SO SORRY.

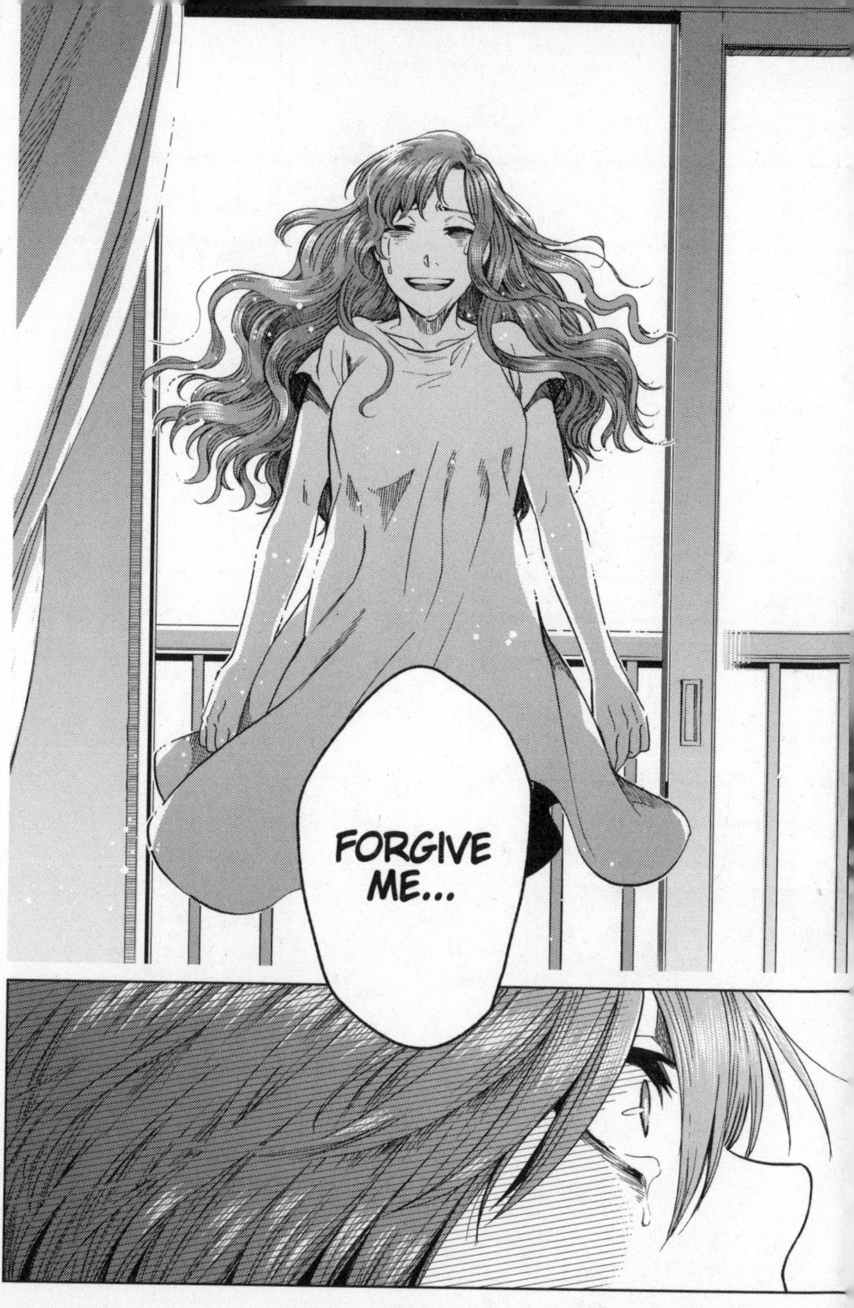
FORGIVE ME...

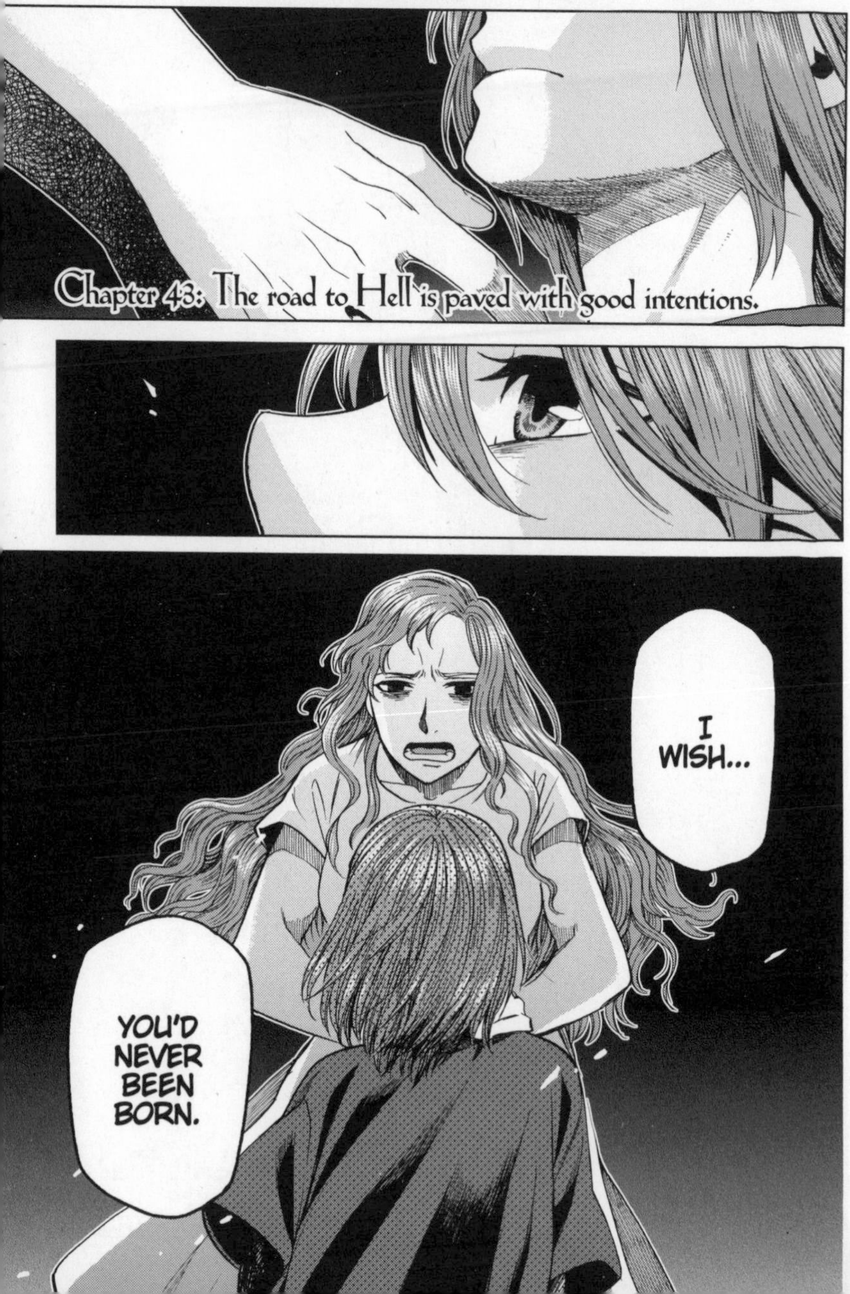
Chapter 43: The road to Hell is paved with good intentions.
I WISH...
YOU'D NEVER BEEN BORN.

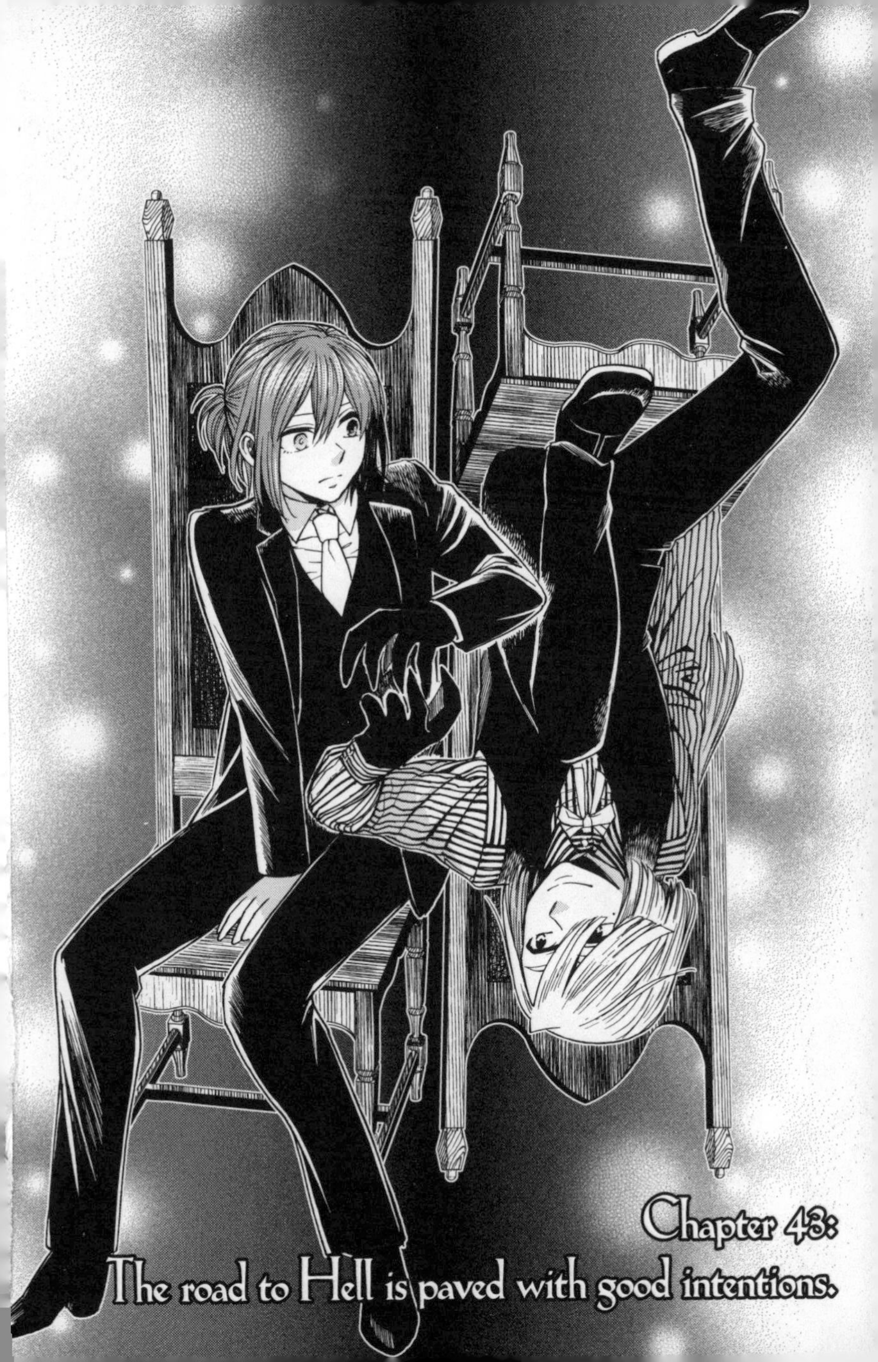

Chapter 43: The road to Hell is paved with good intentions.

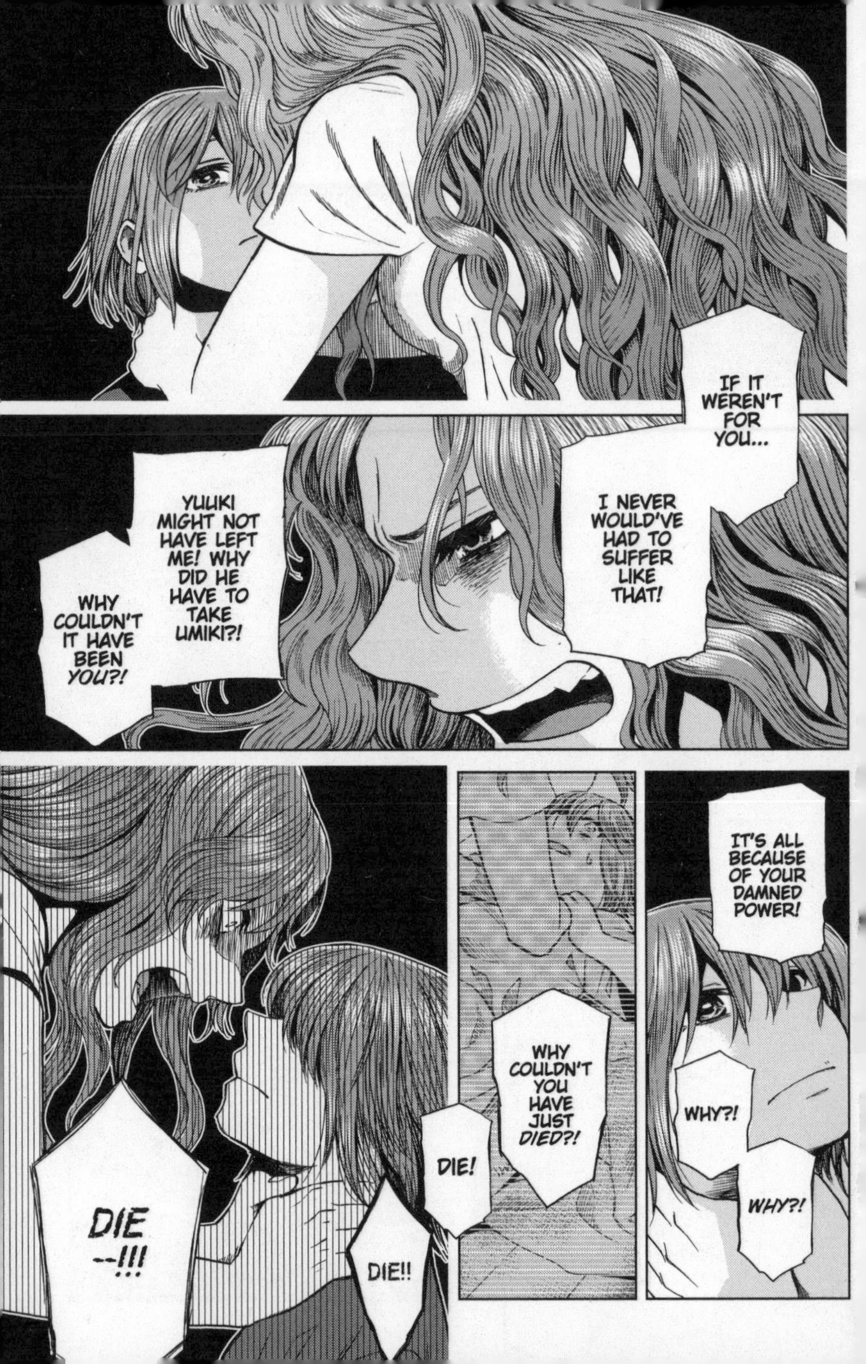
IF IT WEREN'T FOR YOU...
I NEVER WOULD'VE HAD TO SUFFER LIKE THAT!
YUUKI MIGHT NOT HAVE LEFT ME! WHY DID HE HAVE TO TAKE UMIKI?!
WHY COULDN'T IT HAVE BEEN *YOU*?!
IT'S ALL BECAUSE OF YOUR DAMNED POWER!
WHY?!
WHY?!
WHY COULDN'T YOU HAVE JUST *DIED*?!
DIE!
DIE!!
DIE --!!!

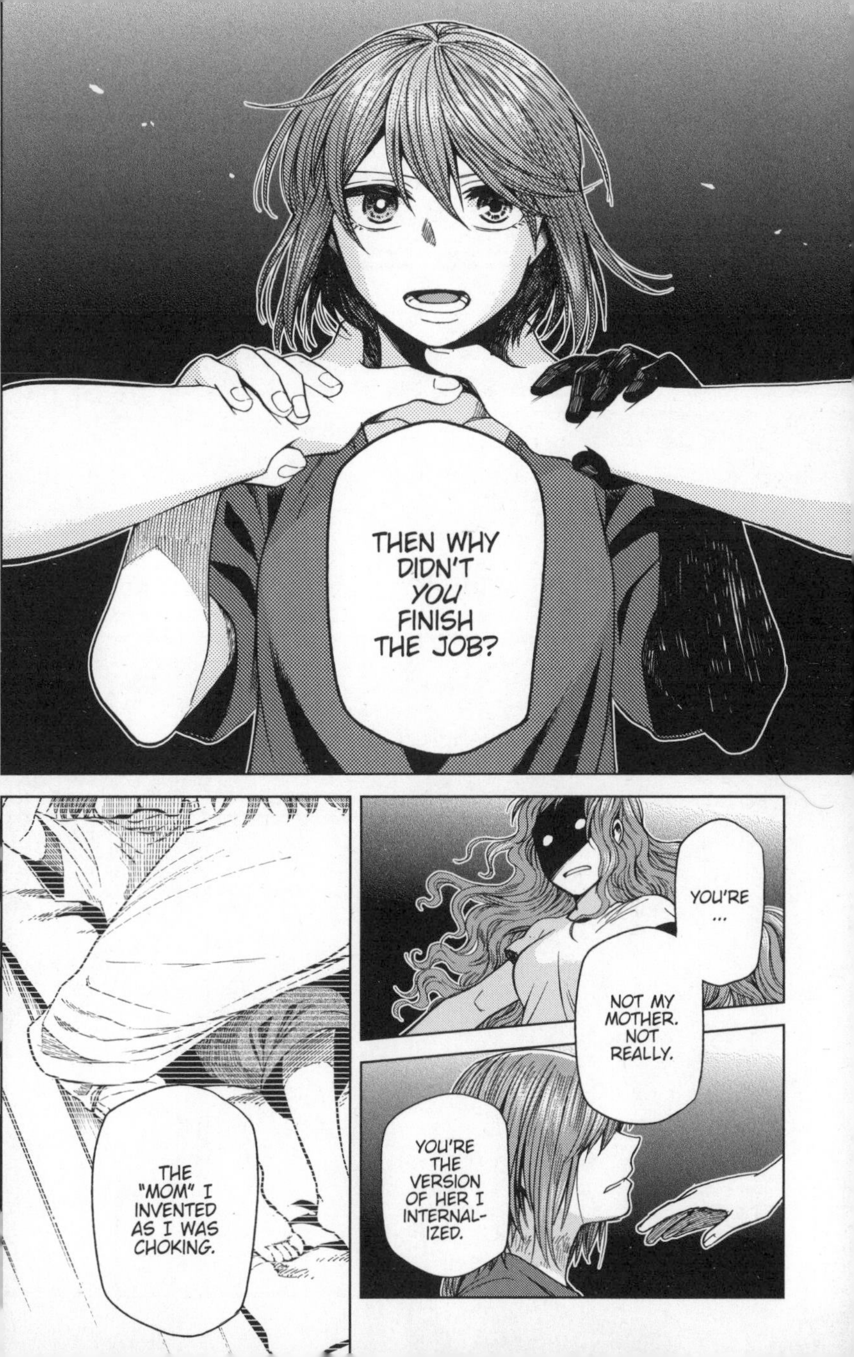
THEN WHY DIDN'T *YOU* FINISH THE JOB?
YOU'RE ...
NOT MY MOTHER. NOT REALLY.
YOU'RE THE VERSION OF HER I INTERNAL-IZED.
THE "MOM" I INVENTED AS I WAS CHOKING.

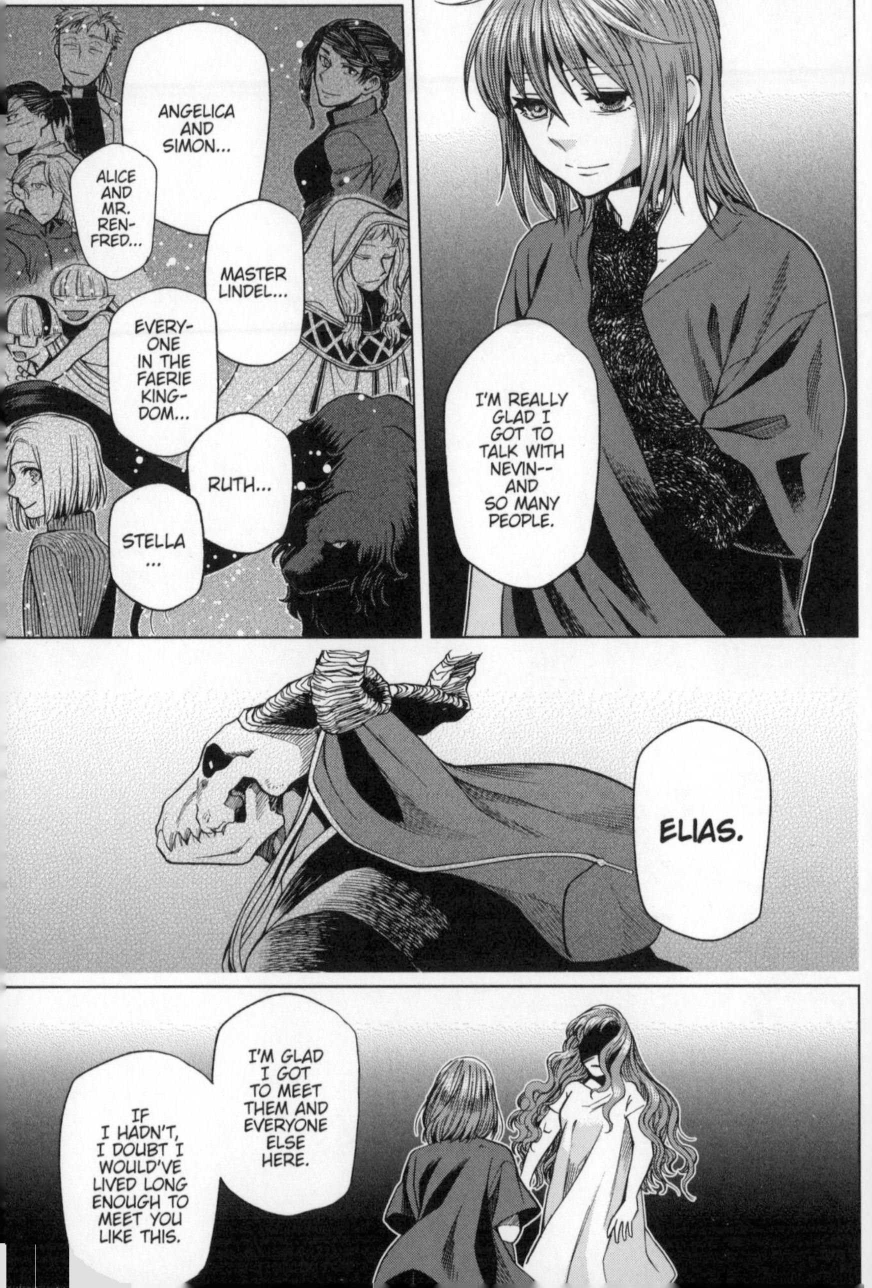
I'M REALLY GLAD I GOT TO TALK WITH NEVIN--AND SO MANY PEOPLE.
ANGELICA AND SIMON...
ALICE AND MR. REN-FRED...
MASTER LINDEL...
EVERY-ONE IN THE FAERIE KING-DOM...
RUTH...
STELLA ...
ELIAS.
I'M GLAD I GOT TO MEET THEM AND EVERYONE ELSE HERE.
IF I HADN'T, I DOUBT I WOULD'VE LIVED LONG ENOUGH TO MEET YOU LIKE THIS.

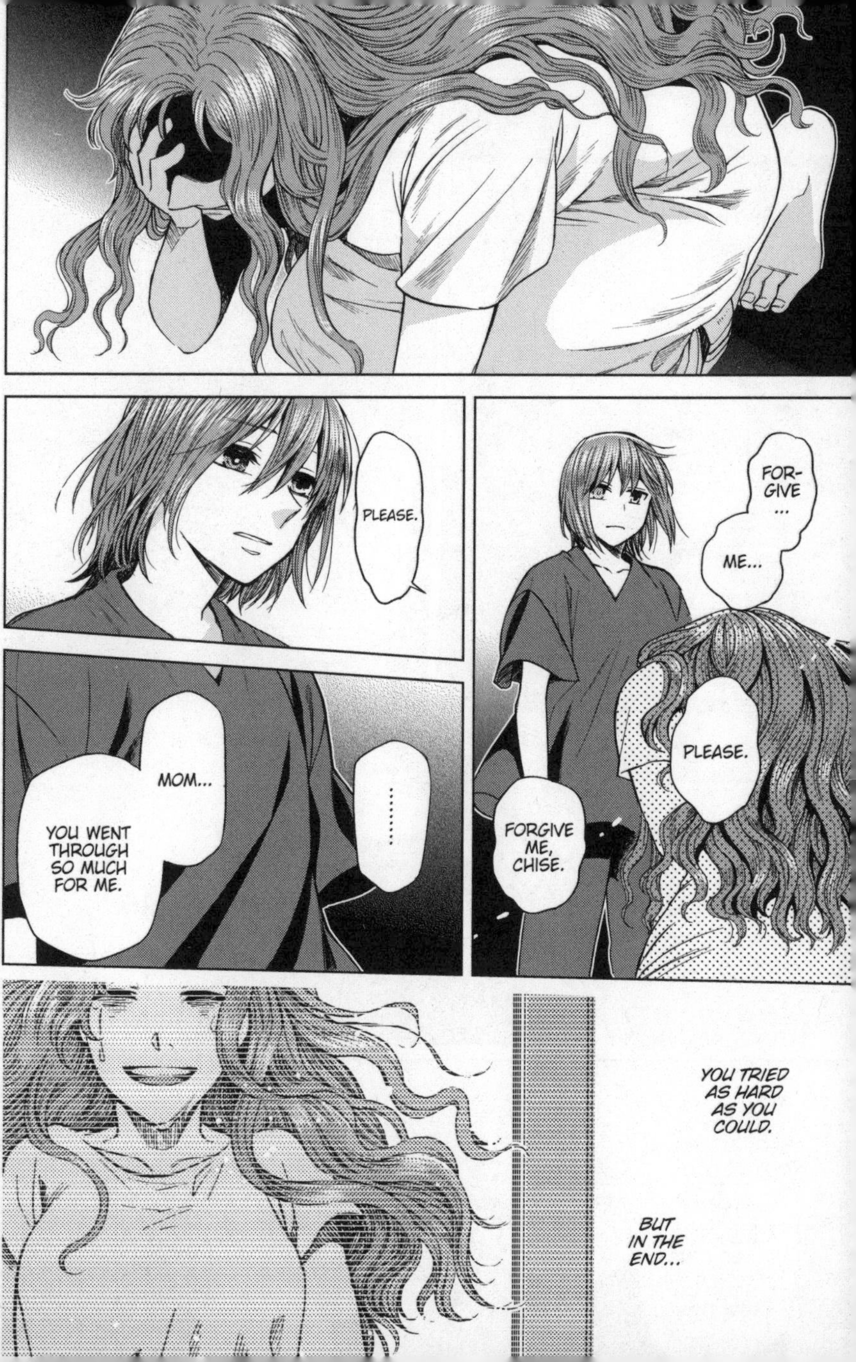
FOR-GIVE...
ME...
PLEASE.
FORGIVE ME, CHISE.
PLEASE.
......
MOM...
YOU WENT THROUGH SO MUCH FOR ME.
YOU TRIED AS HARD AS YOU COULD.
BUT IN THE END...

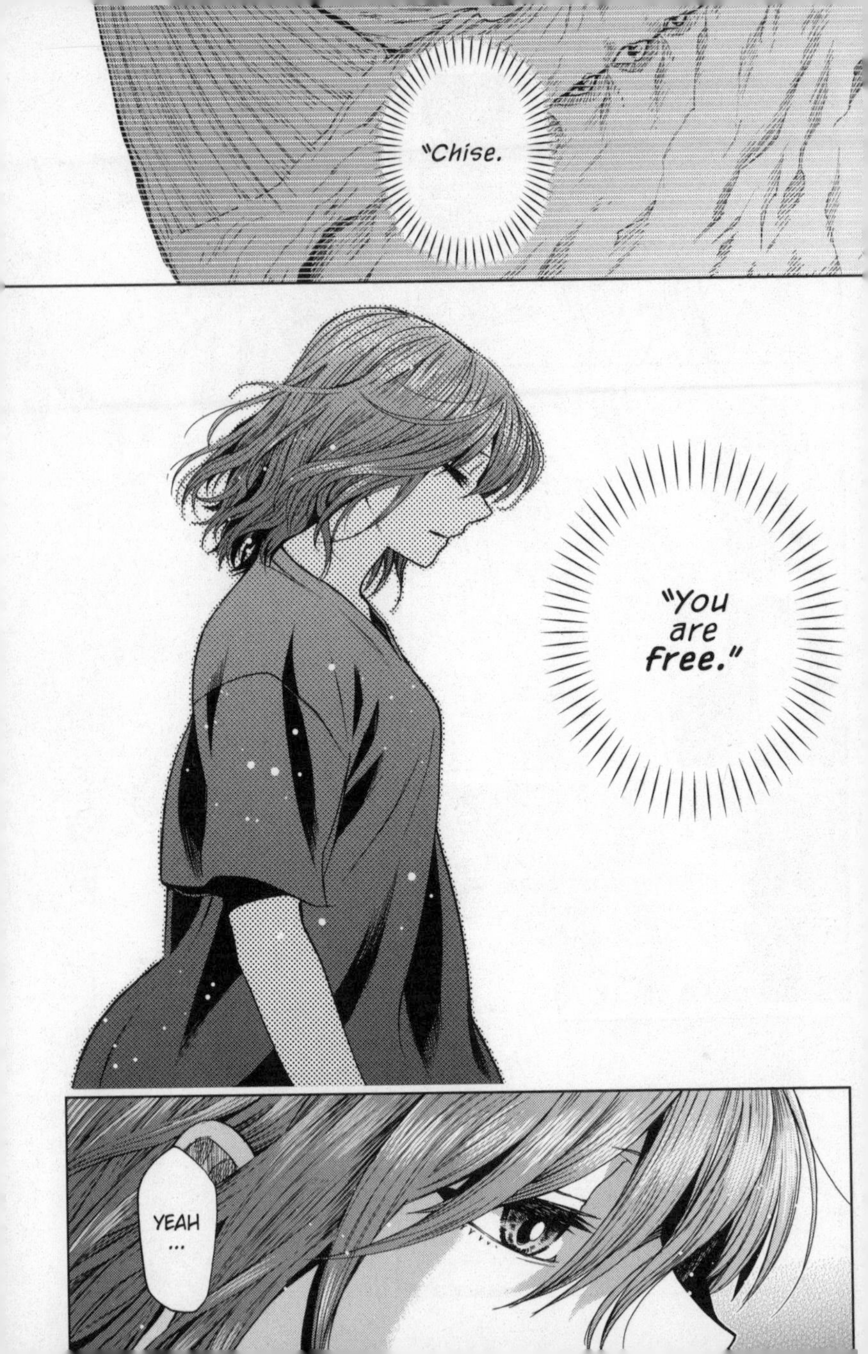
"Chise.
"You are free."
YEAH ...

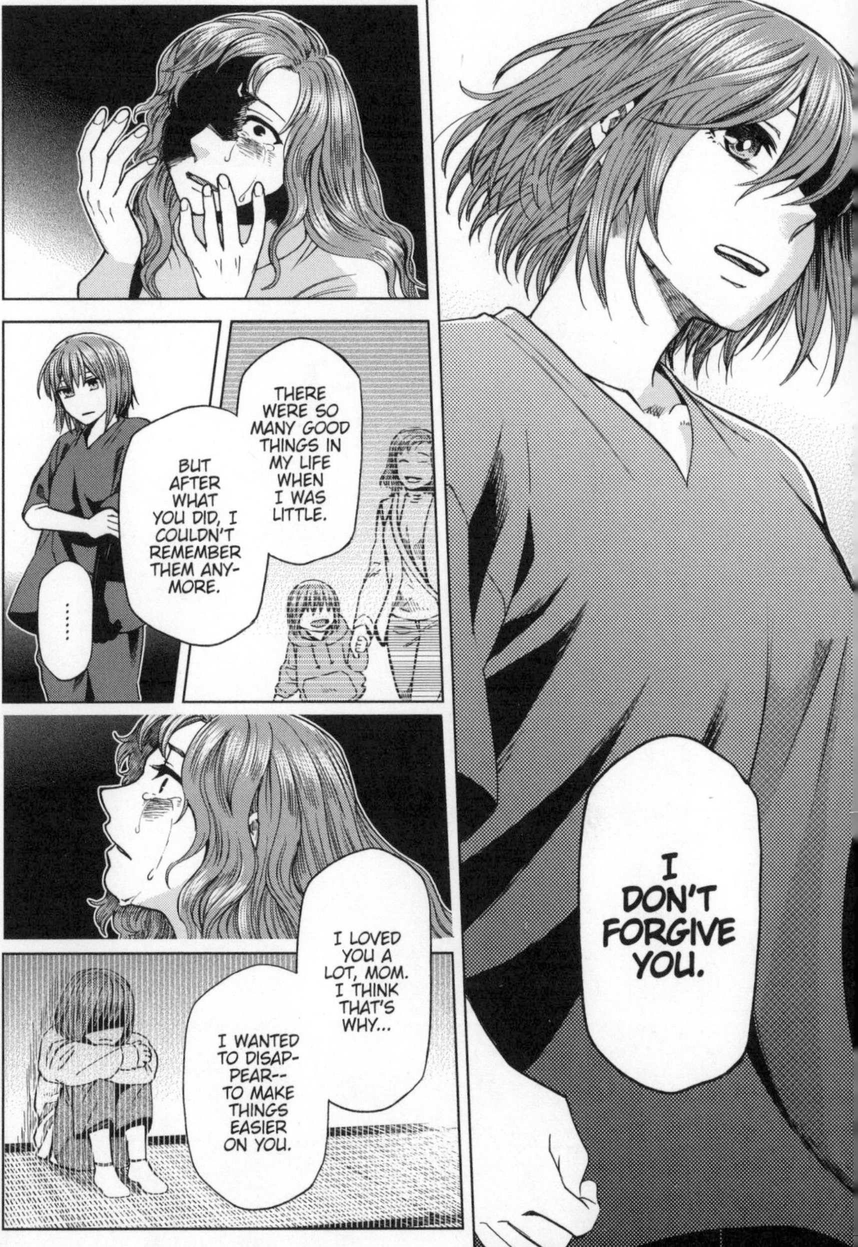
I DON'T FORGIVE YOU.
THERE WERE SO MANY GOOD THINGS IN MY LIFE WHEN I WAS LITTLE.
BUT AFTER WHAT YOU DID, I COULDN'T REMEMBER THEM ANY-MORE.
......
I LOVED YOU A LOT, MOM. I THINK THAT'S WHY...
I WANTED TO DISAP-PEAR-- TO MAKE THINGS EASIER ON YOU.

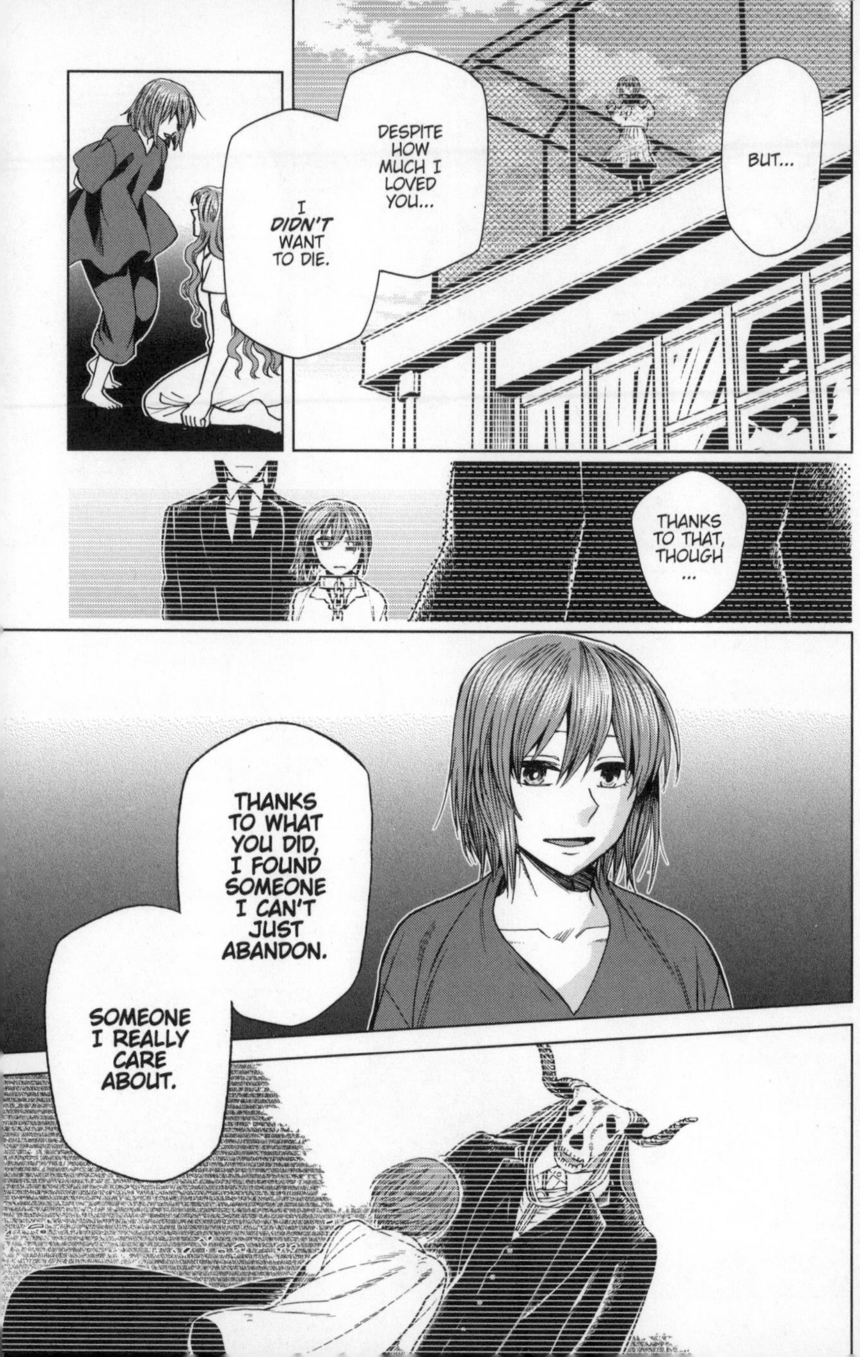
BUT...
DESPITE HOW MUCH I LOVED YOU...
I *DIDN'T* WANT TO DIE.
THANKS TO THAT, THOUGH ...
THANKS TO WHAT YOU DID, I FOUND SOMEONE I CAN'T JUST ABANDON.
SOMEONE I REALLY CARE ABOUT.

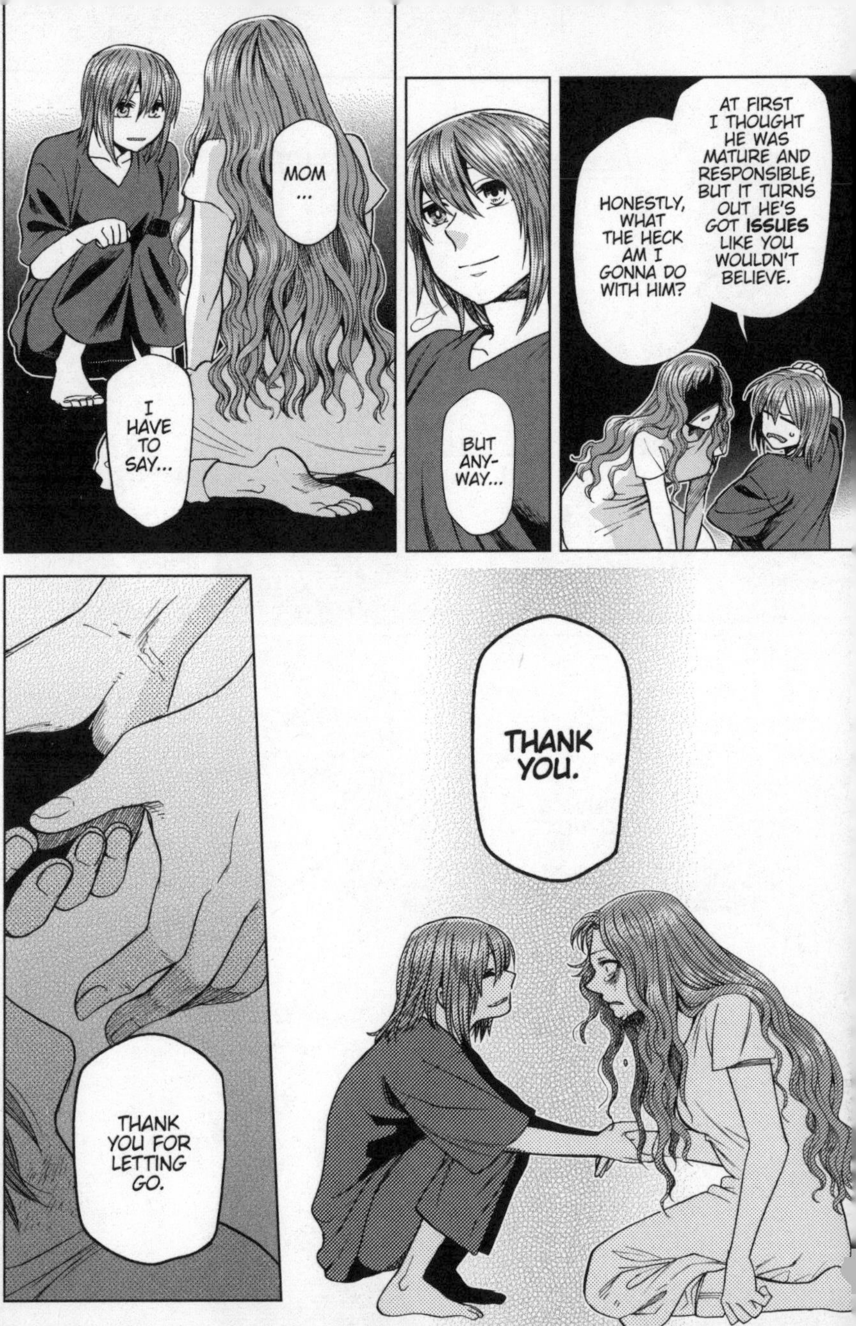
AT FIRST I THOUGHT HE WAS MATURE AND RESPONSIBLE, BUT IT TURNS OUT HE'S GOT **ISSUES** LIKE YOU WOULDN'T BELIEVE.
HONESTLY, WHAT THE HECK AM I GONNA DO WITH HIM?
BUT ANYWAY...
MOM ...
I HAVE TO SAY...
THANK YOU.
THANK YOU FOR LETTING GO.

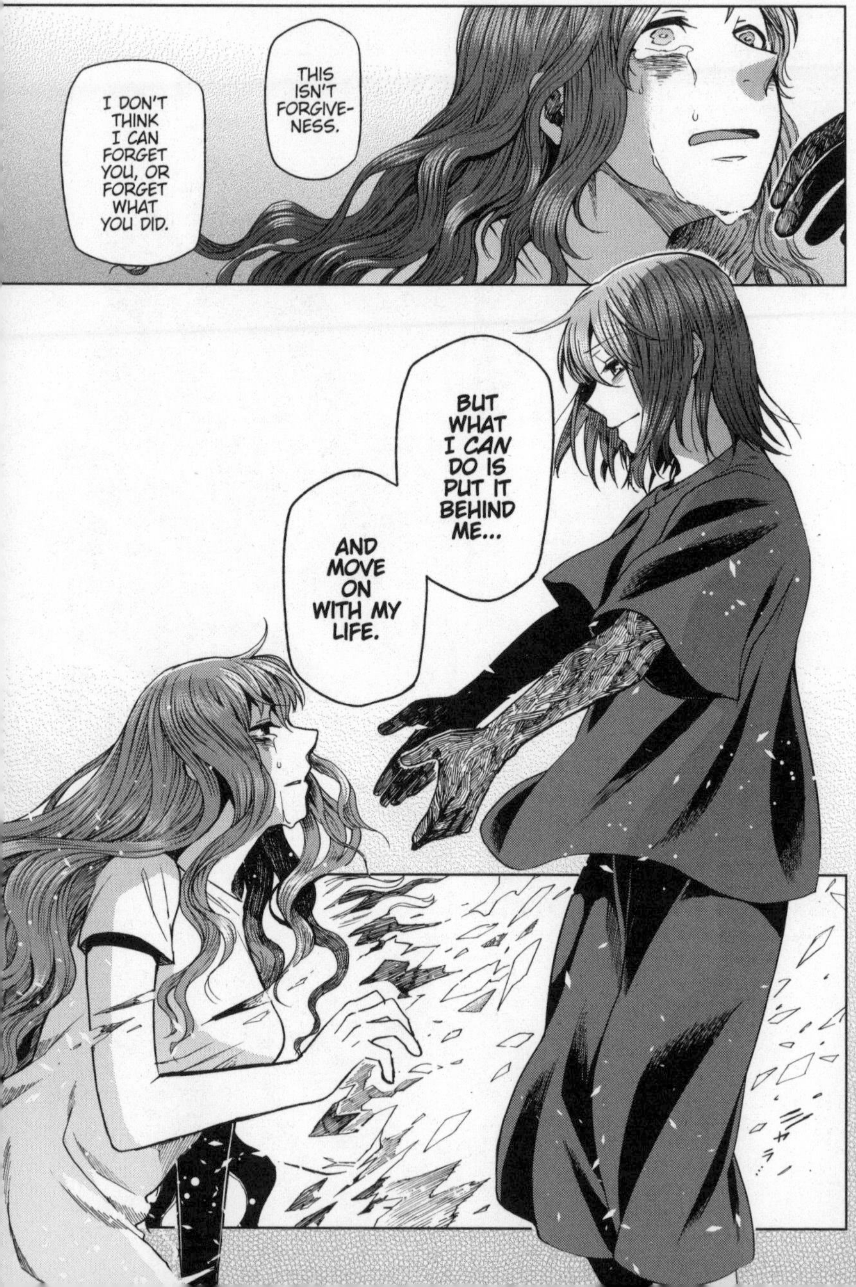
THIS ISN'T FORGIVE-NESS.
I DON'T THINK I CAN FORGET YOU, OR FORGET WHAT YOU DID.
BUT WHAT I CAN DO IS PUT IT BEHIND ME...
AND MOVE ON WITH MY LIFE.

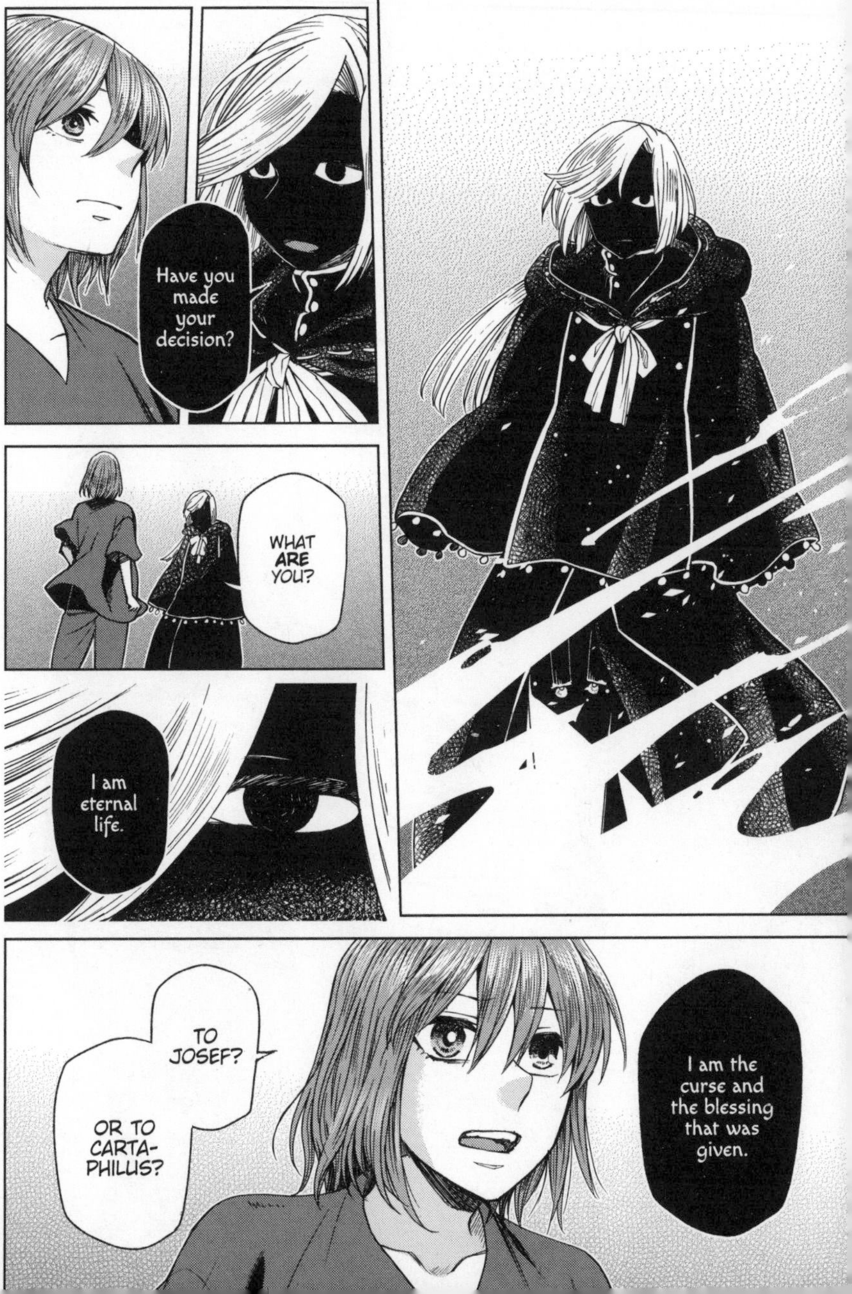
Have you made your decision?
WHAT ARE YOU?
I am eternal life.
I am the curse and the blessing that was given.
TO JOSEF?
OR TO CARTA-PHILUS?

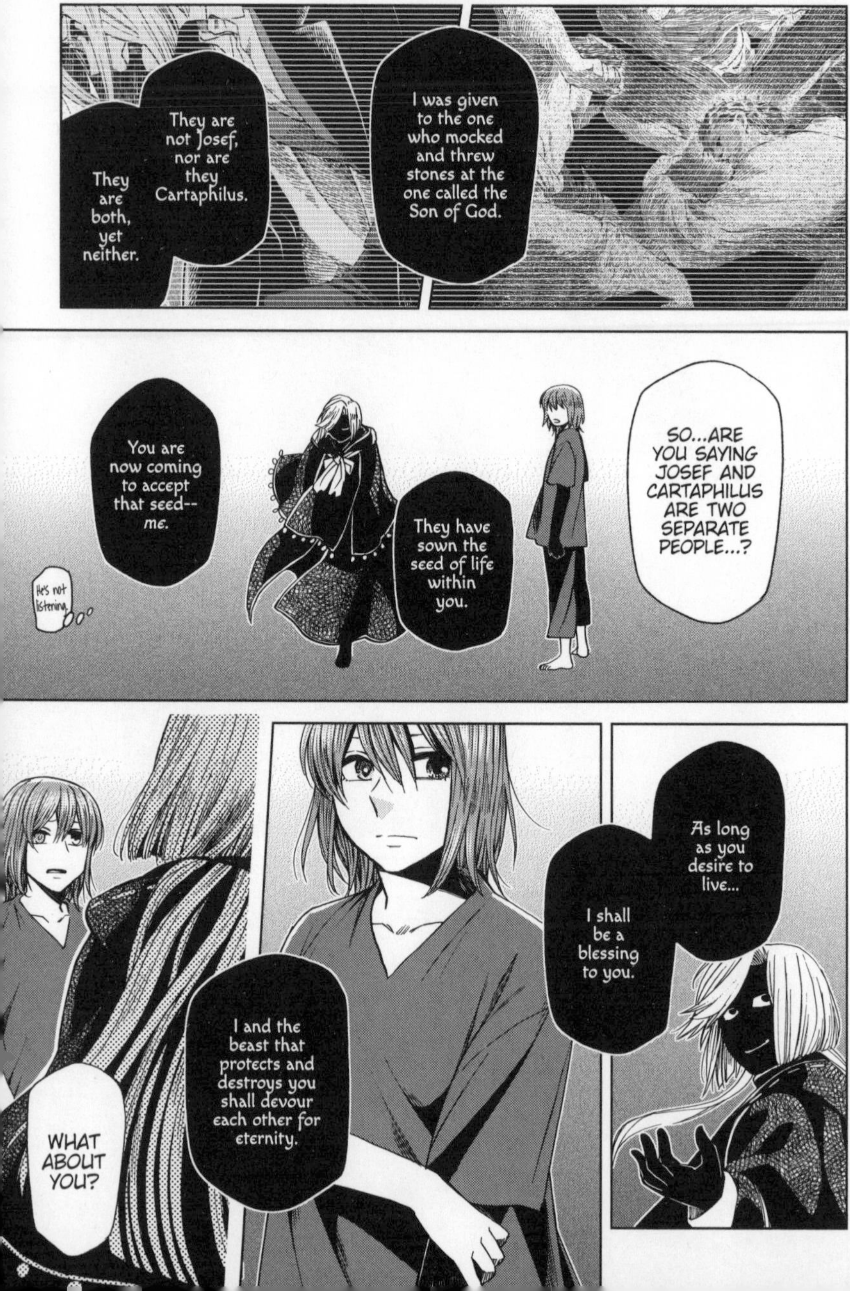
I was given to the one who mocked and threw stones at the one called the Son of God.
They are not Josef, nor are they Cartaphilus.
They are both, yet neither.
SO...ARE YOU SAYING JOSEF AND CARTAPHILUS ARE TWO SEPARATE PEOPLE...?
They have sown the seed of life within you.
You are now coming to accept that seed--me.
He's not listening.
As long as you desire to live...
I shall be a blessing to you.
I and the beast that protects and destroys you shall devour each other for eternity.
WHAT ABOUT YOU?

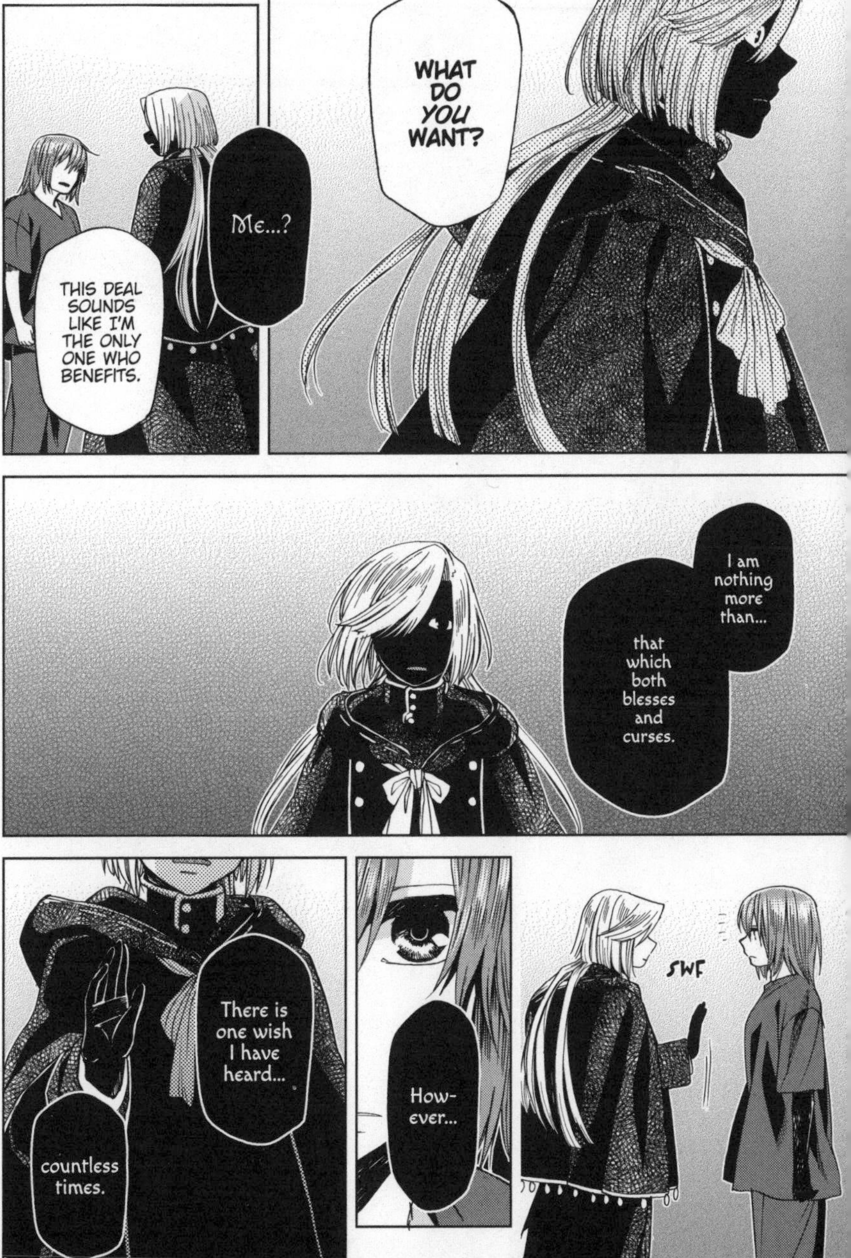
WHAT DO YOU WANT?
Me...?
THIS DEAL SOUNDS LIKE I'M THE ONLY ONE WHO BENEFITS.
I am nothing more than...
that which both blesses and curses.
SWF
How-ever...
There is one wish I have heard...
countless times.

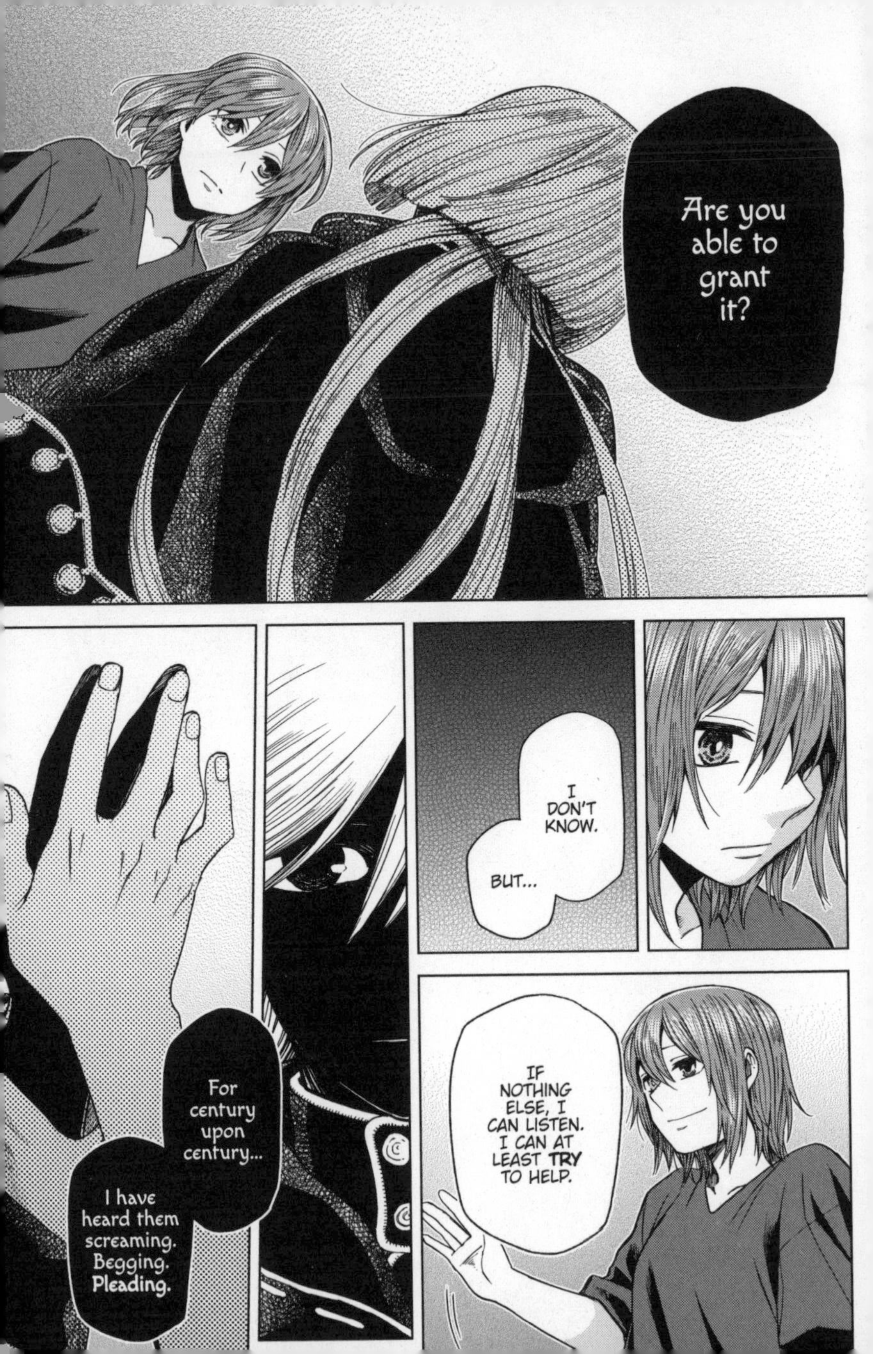
Are you able to grant it?
I DON'T KNOW.
BUT...
IF NOTHING ELSE, I CAN LISTEN. I CAN AT LEAST **TRY** TO HELP.
For century upon century...
I have heard them screaming. Begging. **Pleading.**

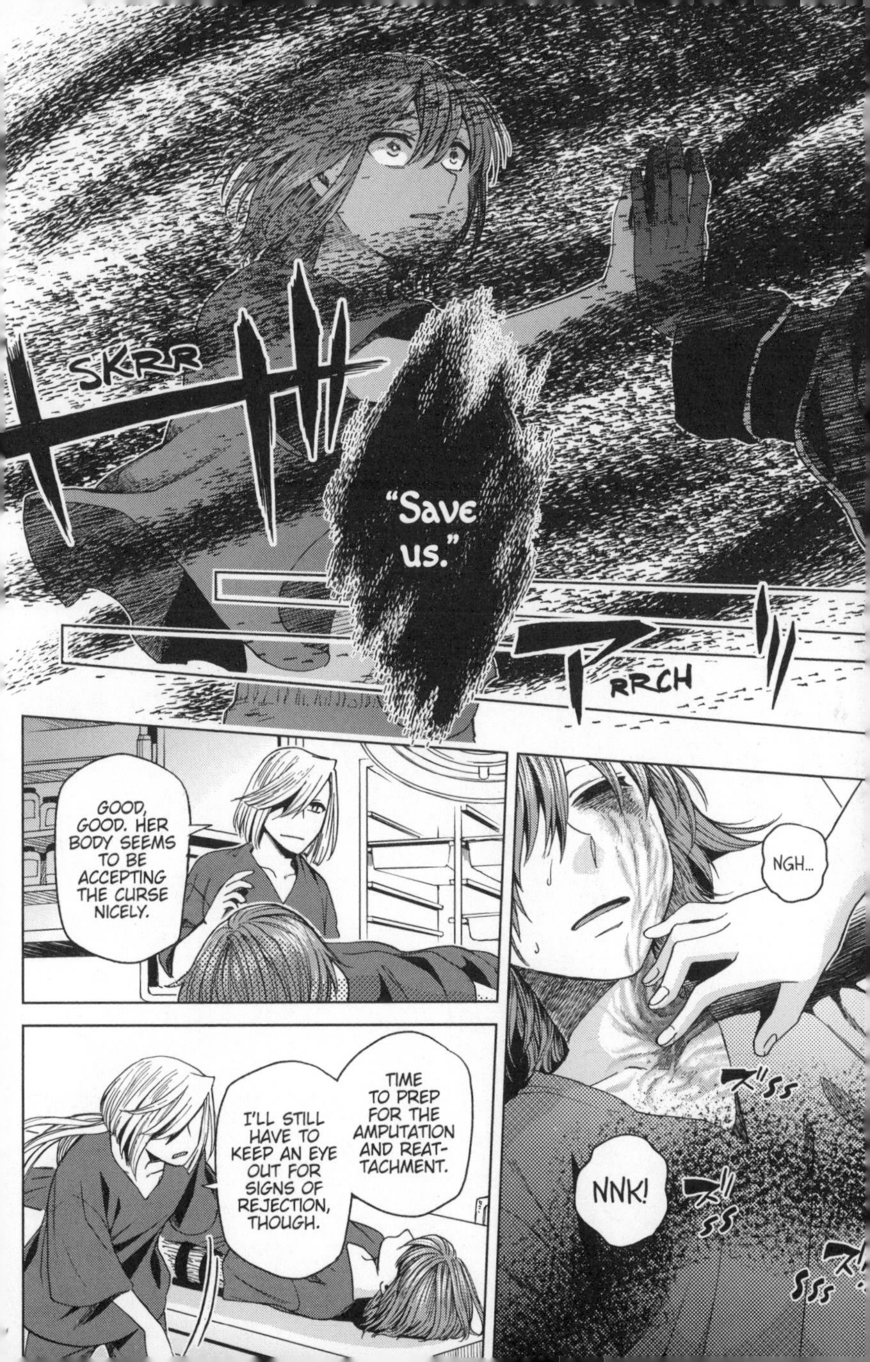
SKRR
"Save us."
RRCH
NGH...
ズss
NNK!
ズss
ズsss
GOOD, GOOD. HER BODY SEEMS TO BE ACCEPTING THE CURSE NICELY.
TIME TO PREP FOR THE AMPUTATION AND REAT-TACHMENT.
I'LL STILL HAVE TO KEEP AN EYE OUT FOR SIGNS OF REJECTION, THOUGH.

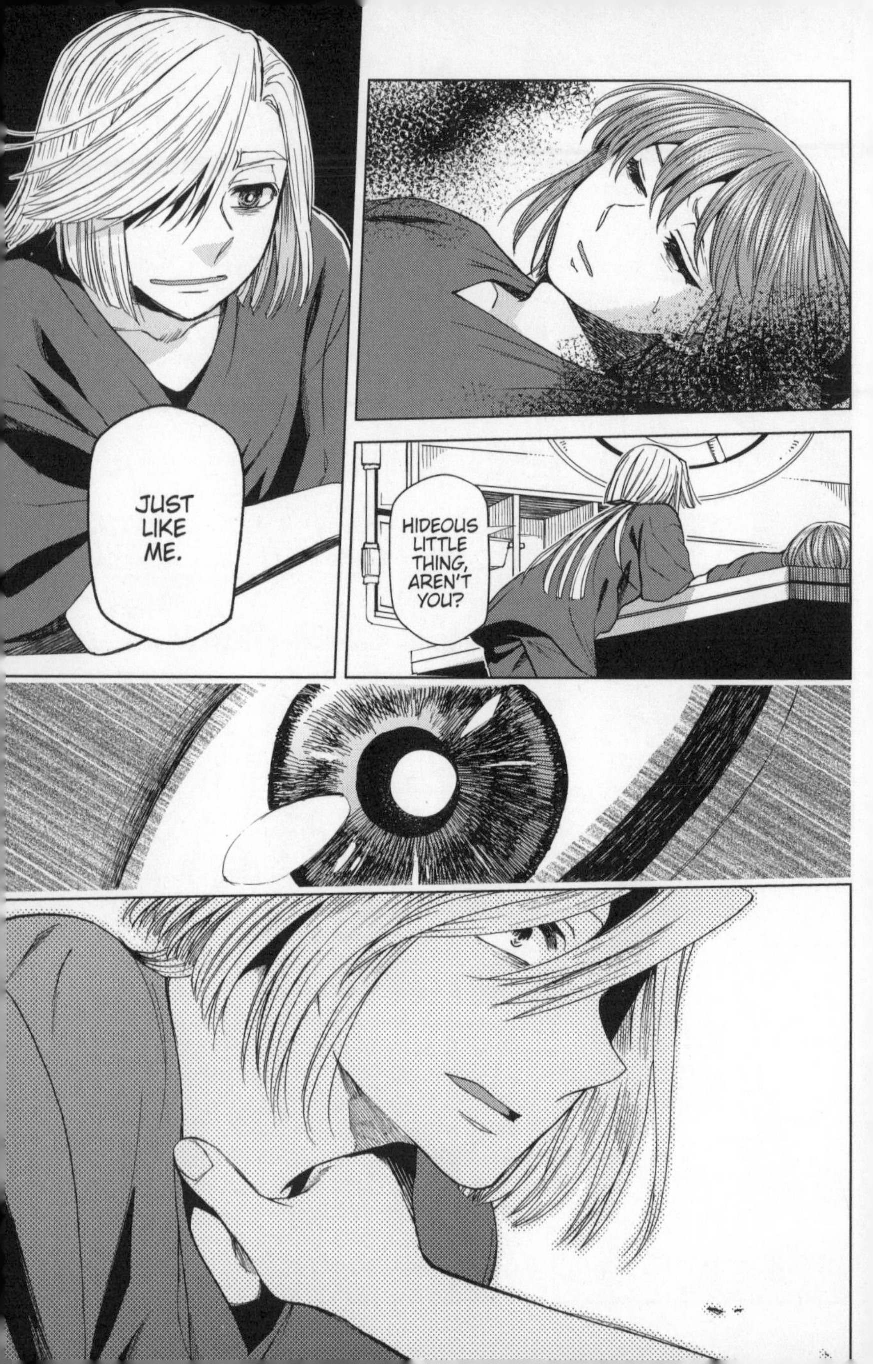
HIDEOUS LITTLE THING, AREN'T YOU?
JUST LIKE ME.

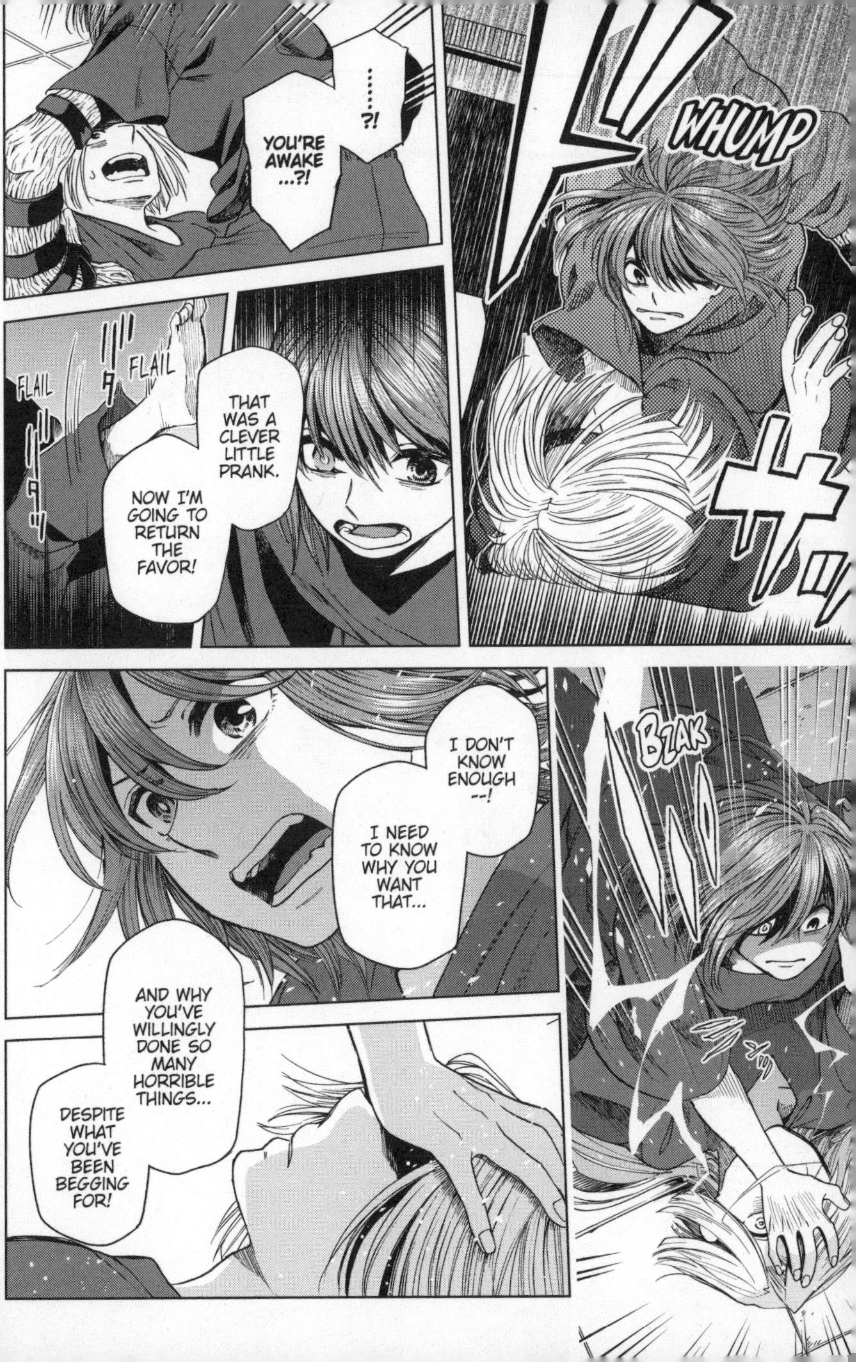
WHUMP
......?!
YOU'RE AWAKE ...?!
THAT WAS A CLEVER LITTLE PRANK.
NOW I'M GOING TO RETURN THE FAVOR!
FLAIL
FLAIL
BZAK
I DON'T KNOW ENOUGH --!
I NEED TO KNOW WHY YOU WANT THAT...
AND WHY YOU'VE WILLINGLY DONE SO MANY HORRIBLE THINGS...
DESPITE WHAT YOU'VE BEEN BEGGING FOR!

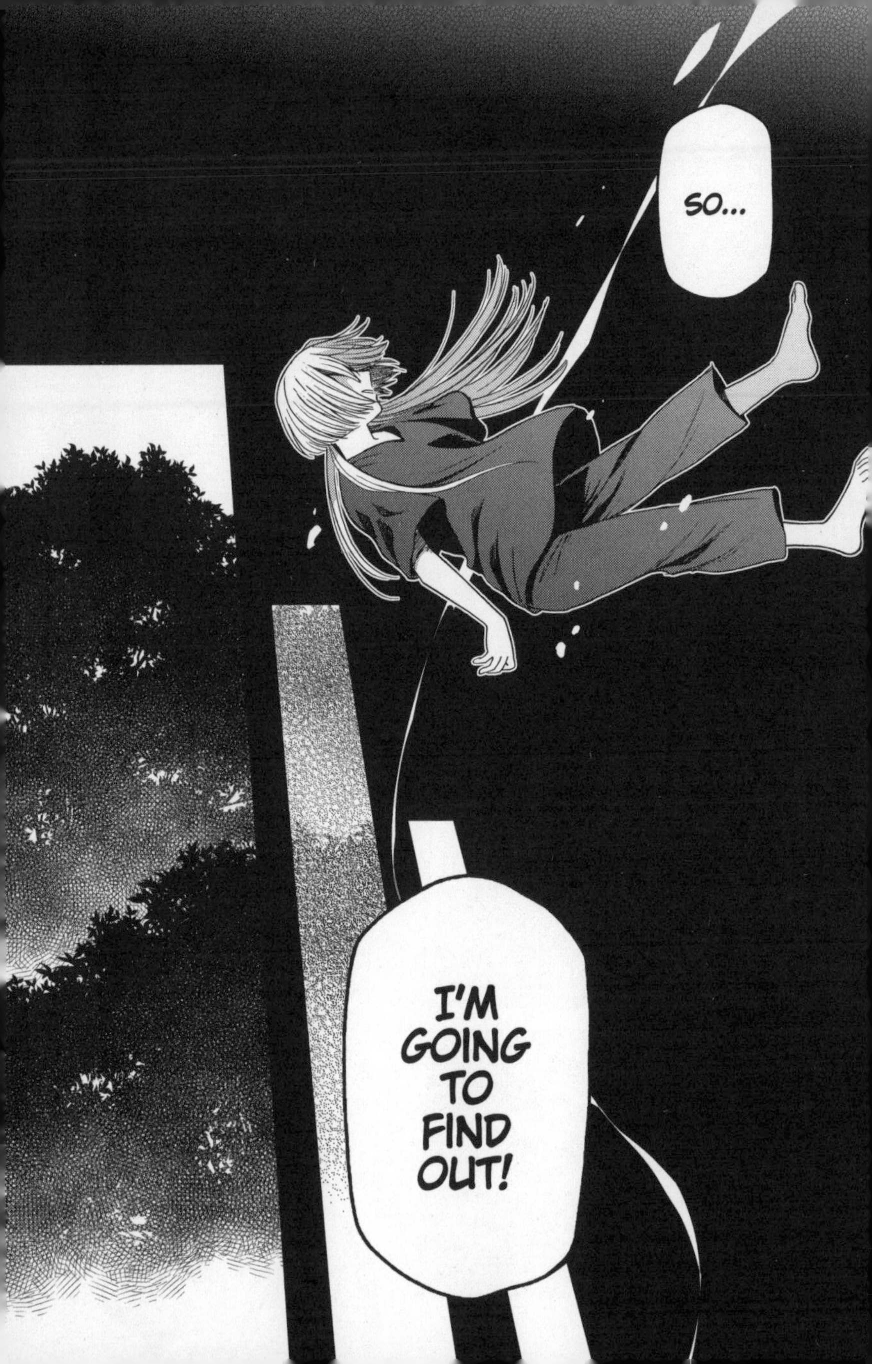
SO...
I'M GOING TO FIND OUT!

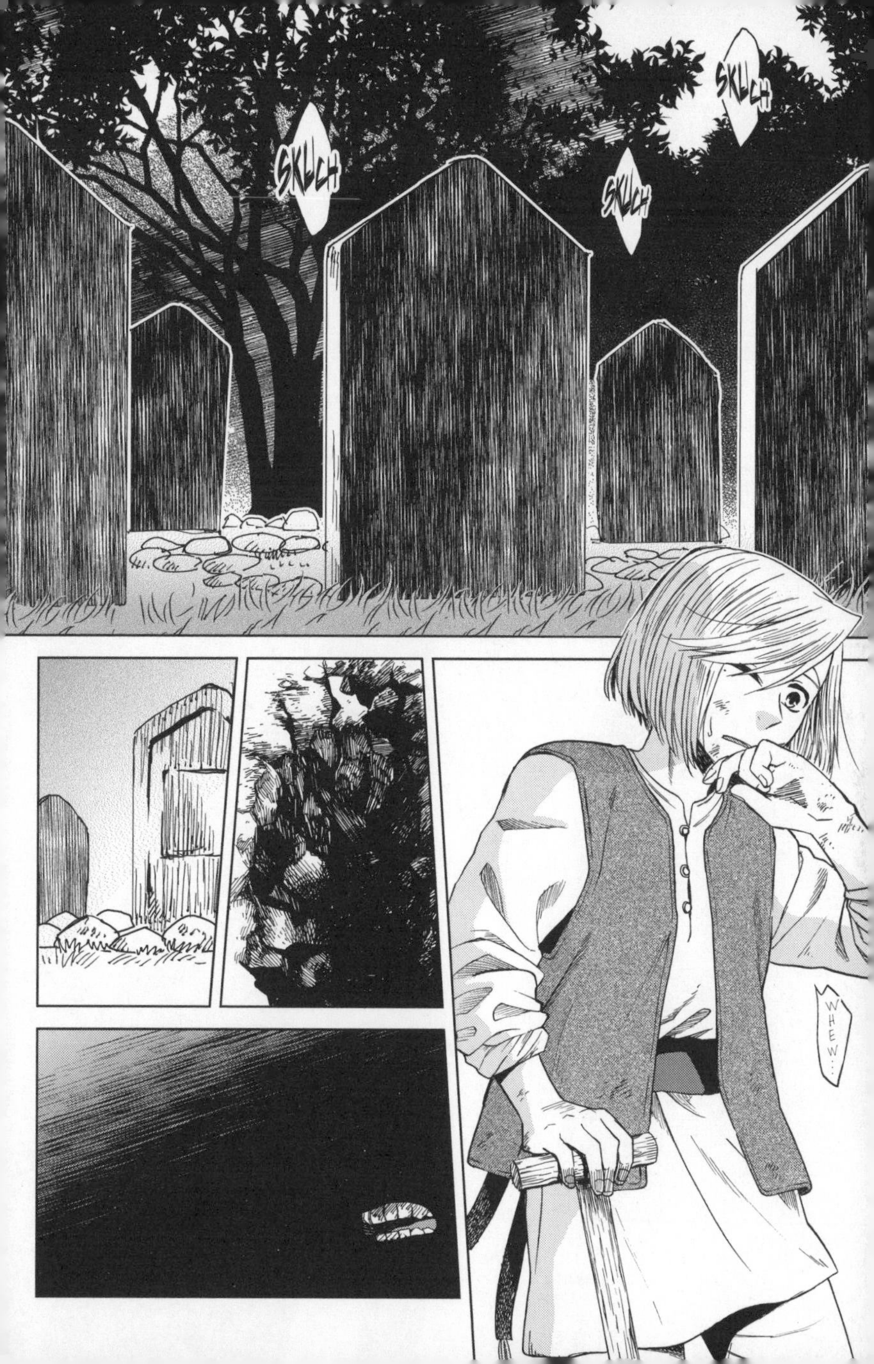
SKLCH
SKLCH
SKLCH
WHEW...

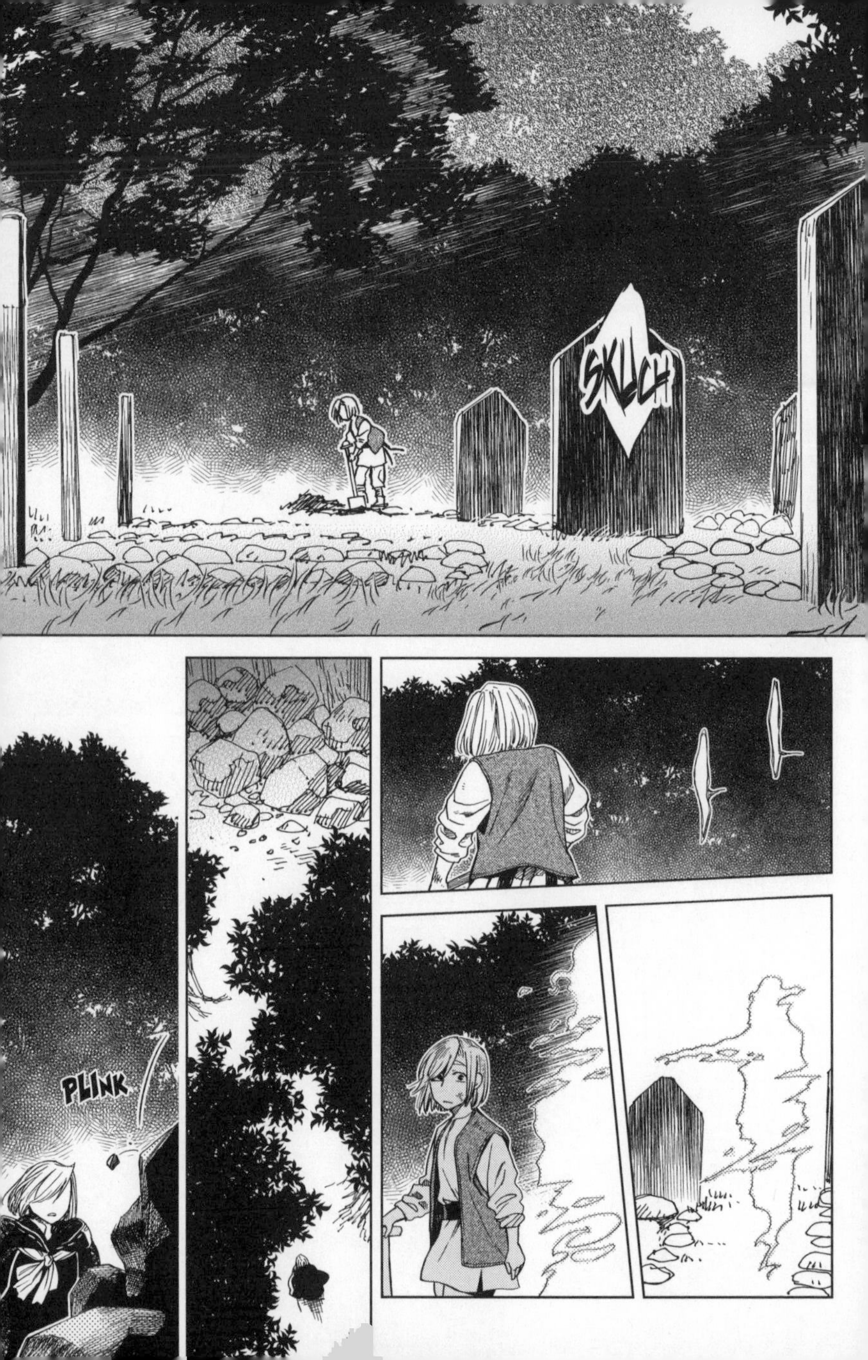
SKLLCH
PLINK

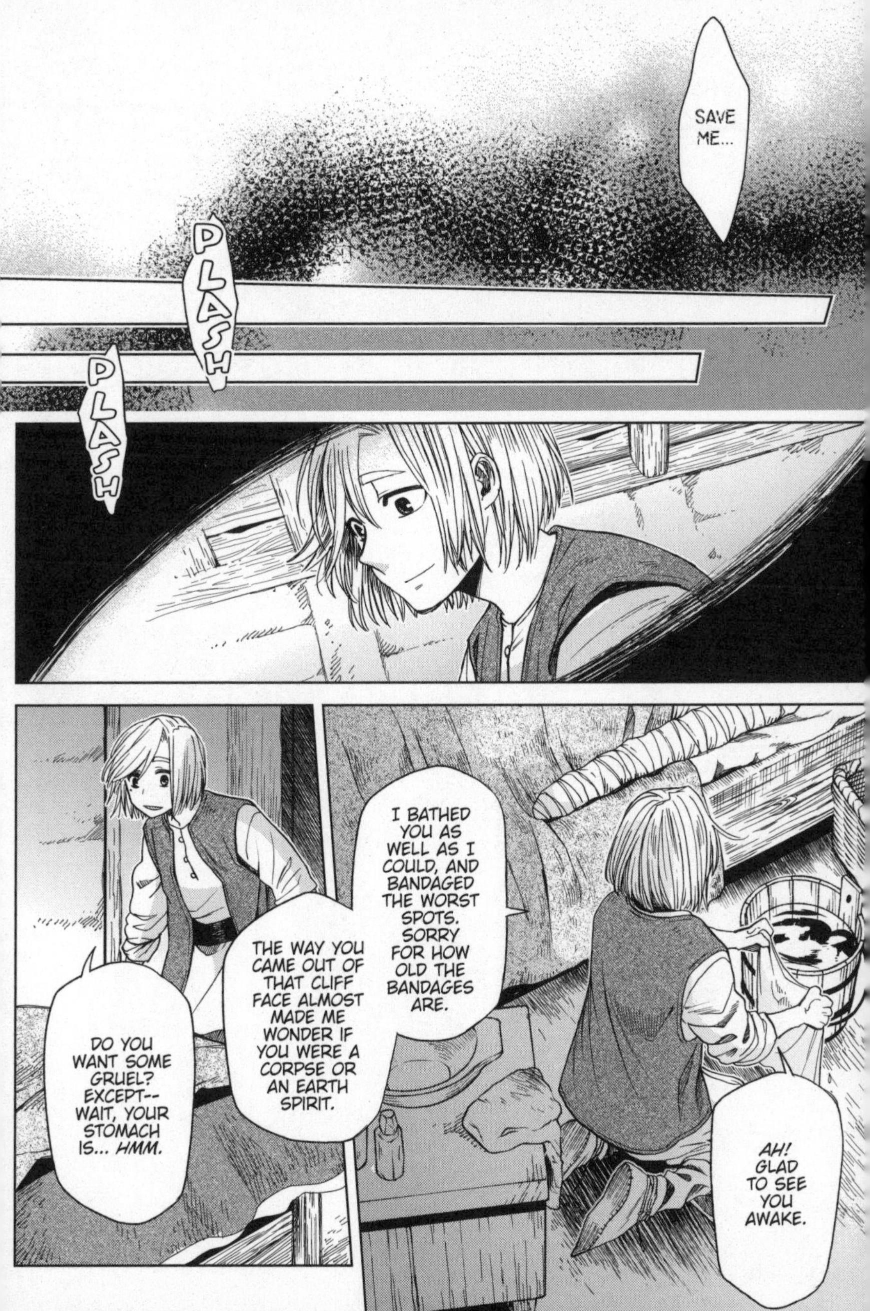
SAVE ME...
PLASH
PLASH
AH! GLAD TO SEE YOU AWAKE.
I BATHED YOU AS WELL AS I COULD, AND BANDAGED THE WORST SPOTS. SORRY FOR HOW OLD THE BANDAGES ARE.
THE WAY YOU CAME OUT OF THAT CLIFF FACE ALMOST MADE ME WONDER IF YOU WERE A CORPSE OR AN EARTH SPIRIT.
DO YOU WANT SOME GRUEL? EXCEPT-- WAIT, YOUR STOMACH IS... *HMM.*

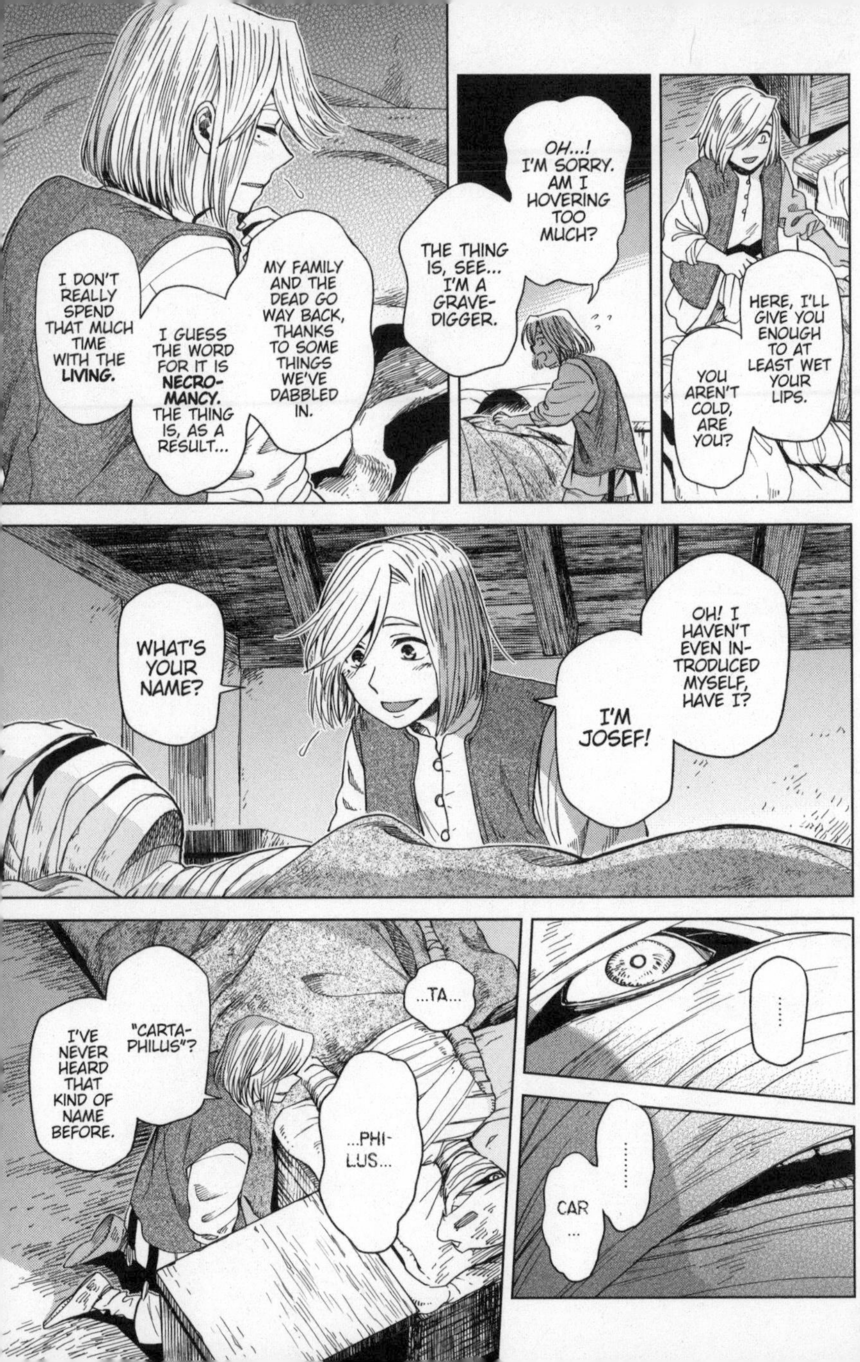
HERE, I'LL GIVE YOU ENOUGH TO AT LEAST WET YOUR LIPS.
YOU AREN'T COLD, ARE YOU?
OH...! I'M SORRY. AM I HOVERING TOO MUCH?
THE THING IS, SEE... I'M A GRAVE-DIGGER.
MY FAMILY AND THE DEAD GO WAY BACK, THANKS TO SOME THINGS WE'VE DABBLED IN.
I GUESS THE WORD FOR IT IS **NECRO-MANCY.** THE THING IS, AS A RESULT...
I DON'T REALLY SPEND THAT MUCH TIME WITH THE **LIVING.**
OH! I HAVEN'T EVEN IN-TRODUCED MYSELF, HAVE I?
I'M JOSEF!
WHAT'S YOUR NAME?
......
......
CAR...
...TA...
...PHI-LUS...
"CARTA-PHILUS"?
I'VE NEVER HEARD THAT KIND OF NAME BEFORE.

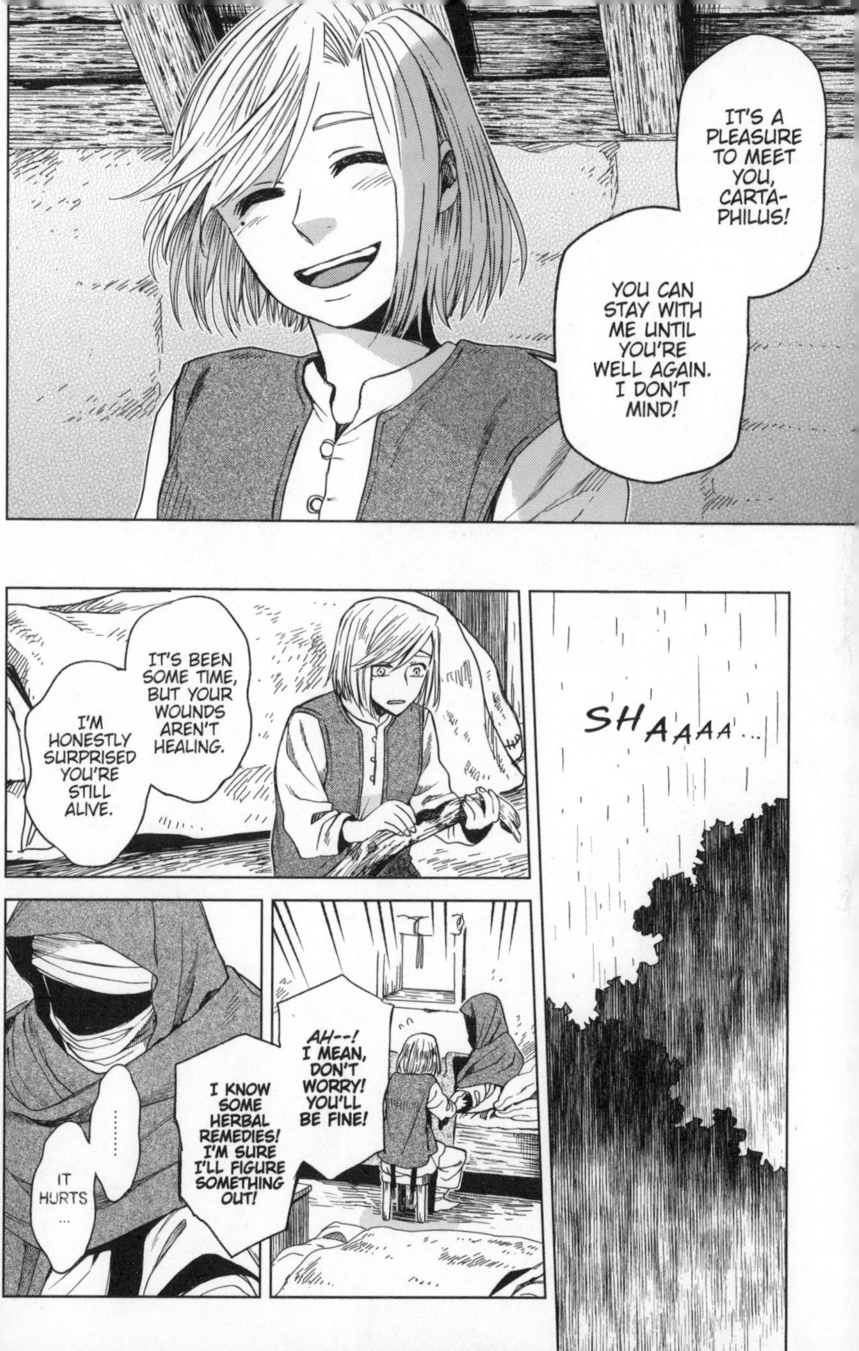
IT'S A PLEASURE TO MEET YOU, CARTA-PHILUS!
YOU CAN STAY WITH ME UNTIL YOU'RE WELL AGAIN. I DON'T MIND!
SHAAAA...
IT'S BEEN SOME TIME, BUT YOUR WOUNDS AREN'T HEALING.
I'M HONESTLY SURPRISED YOU'RE STILL ALIVE.
AH--! I MEAN, DON'T WORRY! YOU'LL BE FINE!
I KNOW SOME HERBAL REMEDIES! I'M SURE I'LL FIGURE SOMETHING OUT!
......
IT HURTS ...

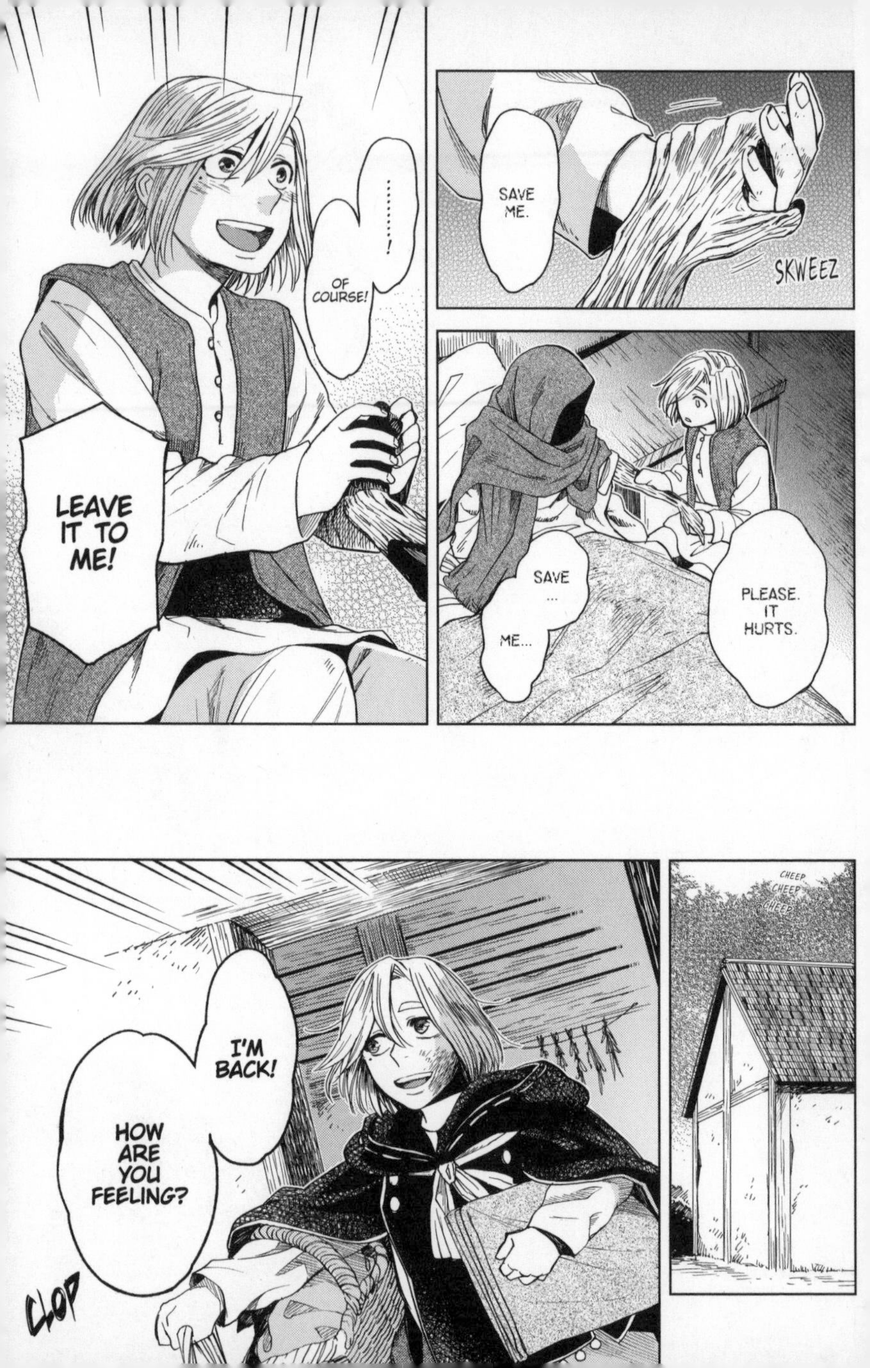
SAVE ME.
SKWEEZ
PLEASE. IT HURTS.
SAVE... ME...
......!
OF COURSE!
LEAVE IT TO ME!
CHEEP CHEEP CHEEP
I'M BACK!
HOW ARE YOU FEELING?
CLOP

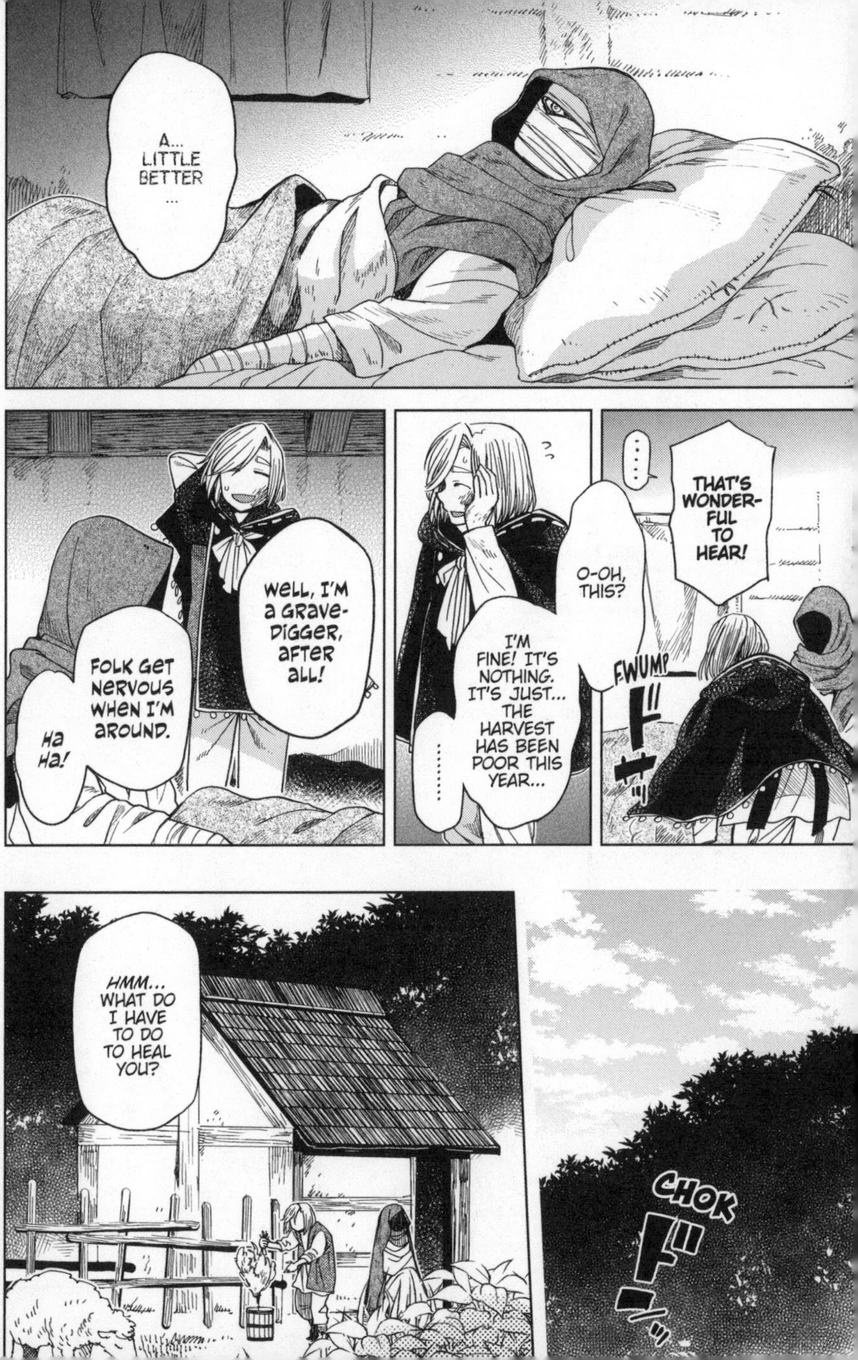
A... LITTLE BETTER ...
......
THAT'S WONDERFUL TO HEAR!
FWUMP
ドッ
O-OH, THIS?
I'M FINE! IT'S NOTHING. IT'S JUST... THE HARVEST HAS BEEN POOR THIS YEAR...
......
WELL, I'M A GRAVE-DIGGER, AFTER ALL!
FOLK GET NERVOUS WHEN I'M AROUND.
Ha Ha!
CHOK
ドッ
HMM... WHAT DO I HAVE TO DO TO HEAL YOU?

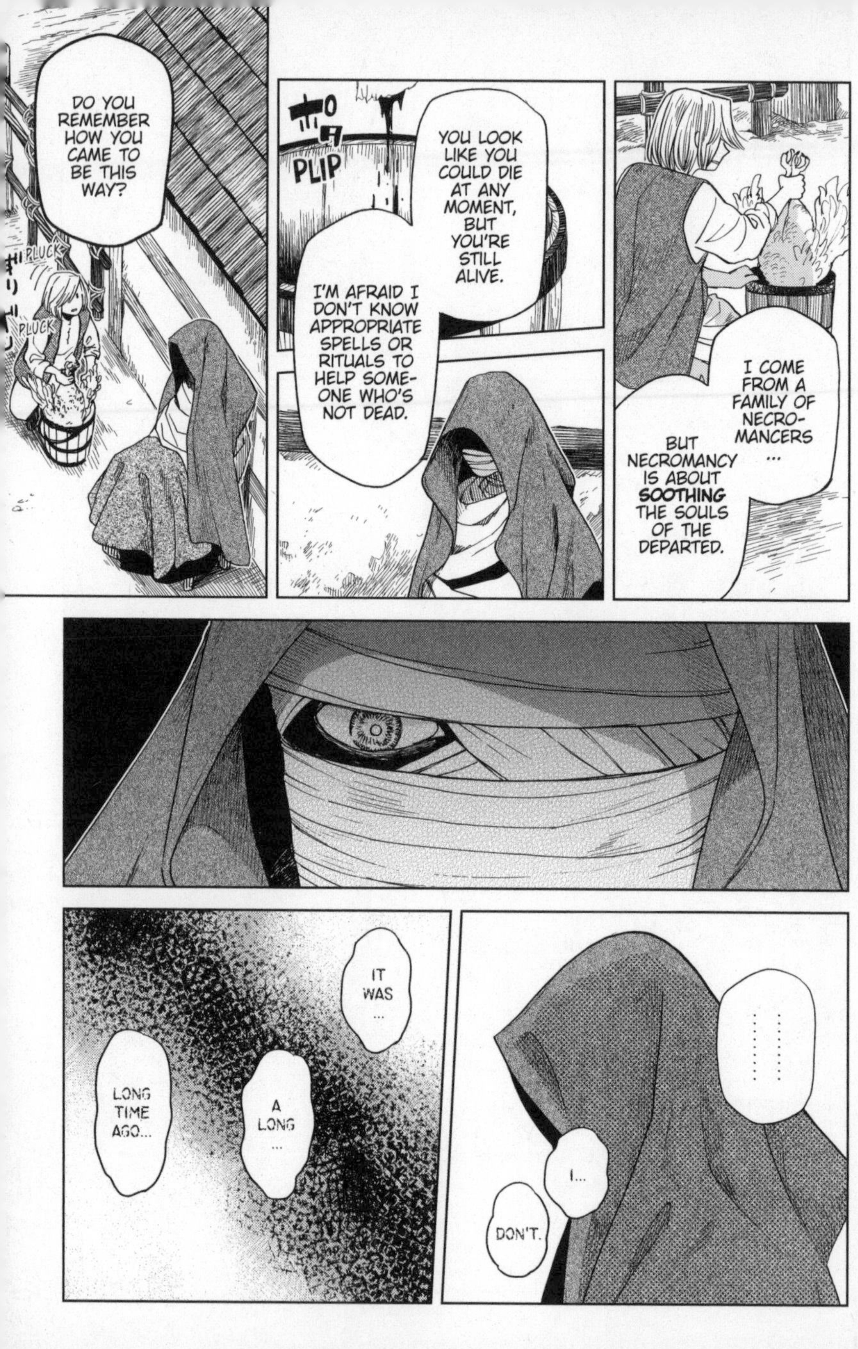

I COME FROM A FAMILY OF NECRO-MANCERS...
BUT NECROMANCY IS ABOUT **SOOTHING** THE SOULS OF THE DEPARTED.
PLIP
YOU LOOK LIKE YOU COULD DIE AT ANY MOMENT, BUT YOU'RE STILL ALIVE.
I'M AFRAID I DON'T KNOW APPROPRIATE SPELLS OR RITUALS TO HELP SOME-ONE WHO'S NOT DEAD.
DO YOU REMEMBER HOW YOU CAME TO BE THIS WAY?
PLUCK
PLUCK
......
I...
DON'T.
IT WAS...
A LONG...
LONG TIME AGO...

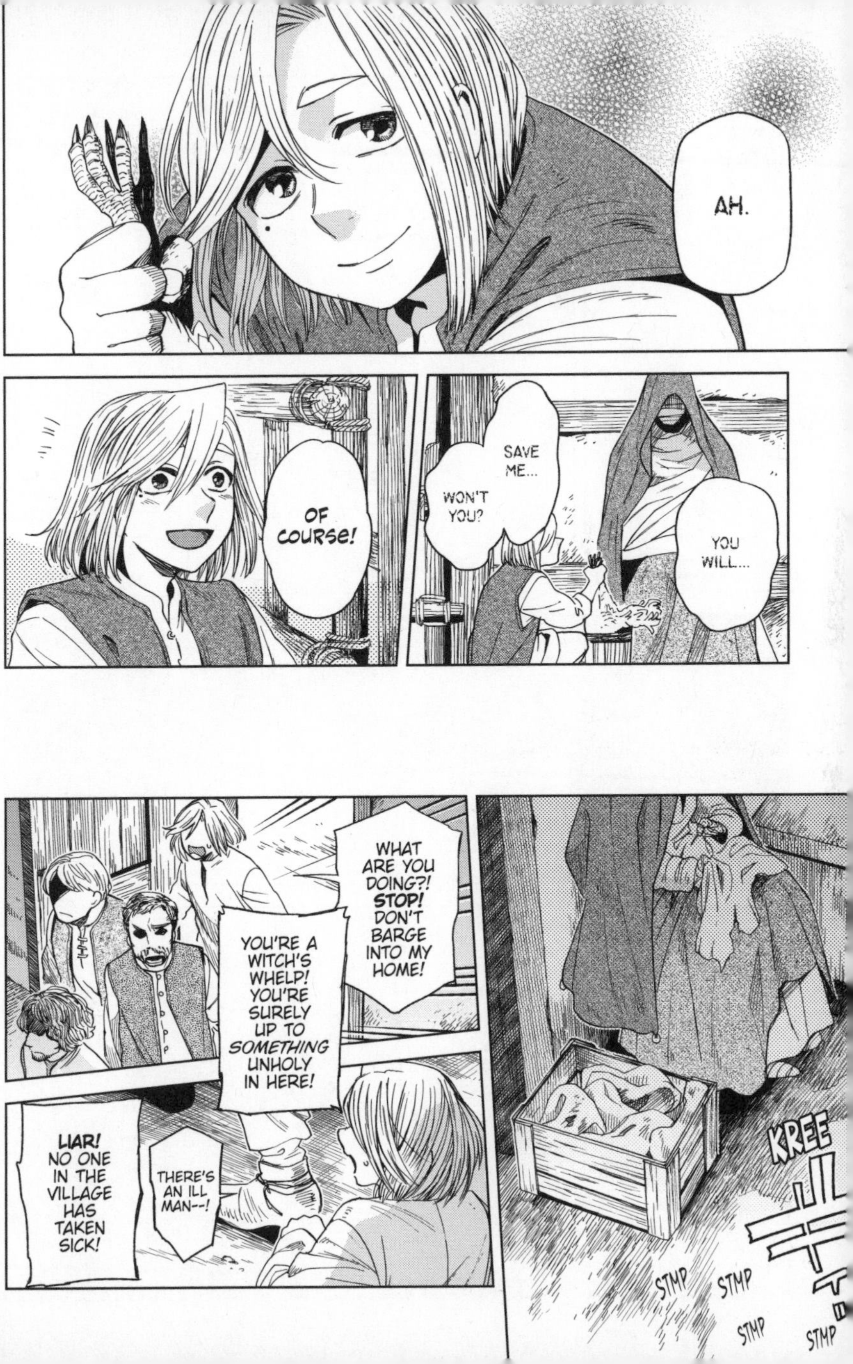
AH.
SAVE ME... WON'T YOU?
YOU WILL...
OF COURSE!
KREE
STMP STMP STMP STMP
WHAT ARE YOU DOING?! **STOP!** DON'T BARGE INTO MY HOME!
YOU'RE A WITCH'S WHELP! YOU'RE SURELY UP TO *SOMETHING* UNHOLY IN HERE!
THERE'S AN ILL MAN--!
LIAR! NO ONE IN THE VILLAGE HAS TAKEN SICK!

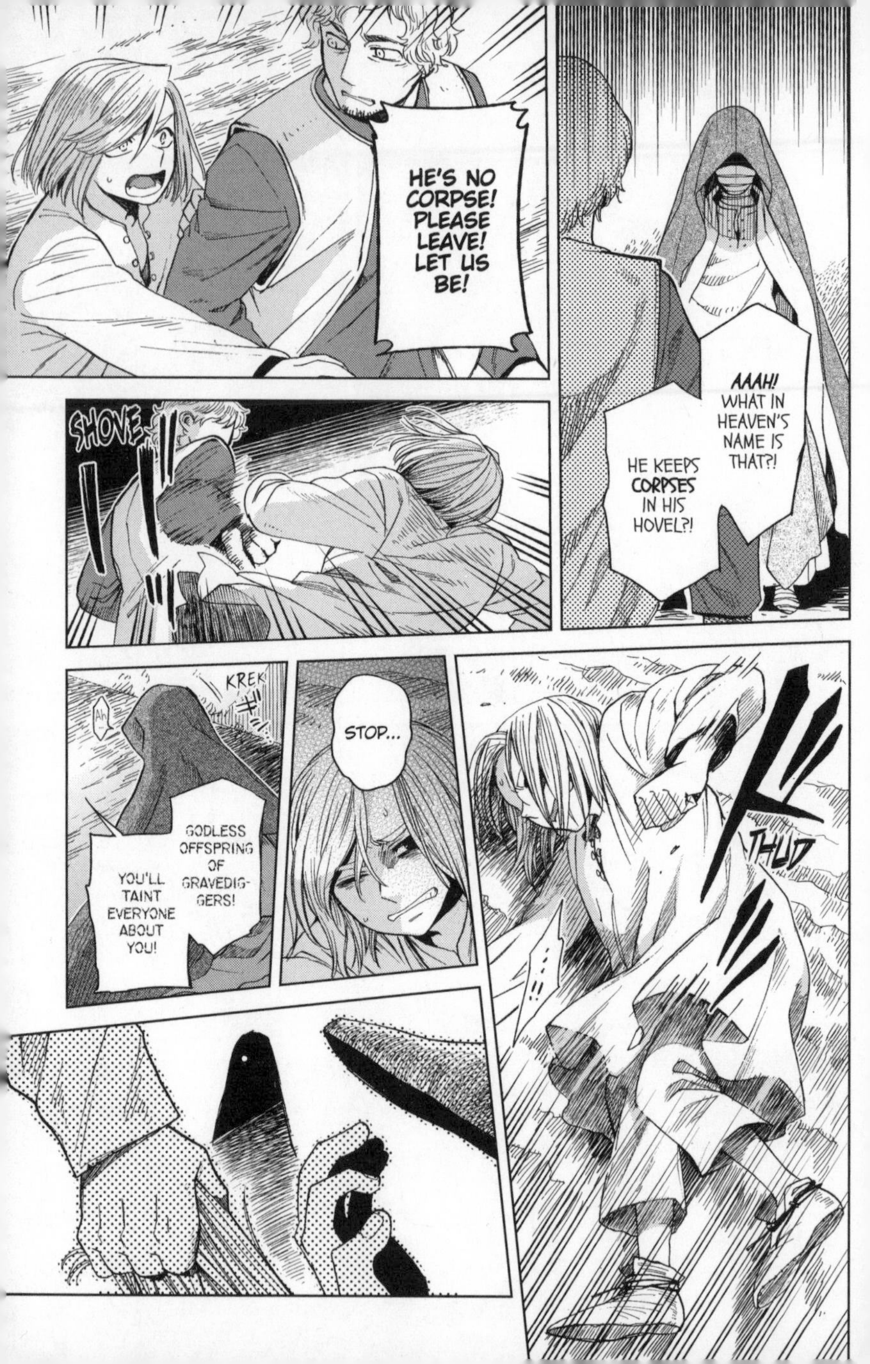

AAAH! WHAT IN HEAVEN'S NAME IS THAT?!
HE KEEPS CORPSES IN HIS HOVEL?!
HE'S NO CORPSE! PLEASE LEAVE! LET US BE!
SHOVE
THUD
...!
STOP...
KREK
Ah...
GODLESS OFFSPRING OF GRAVEDIGGERS!
YOU'LL TAINT EVERYONE ABOUT YOU!

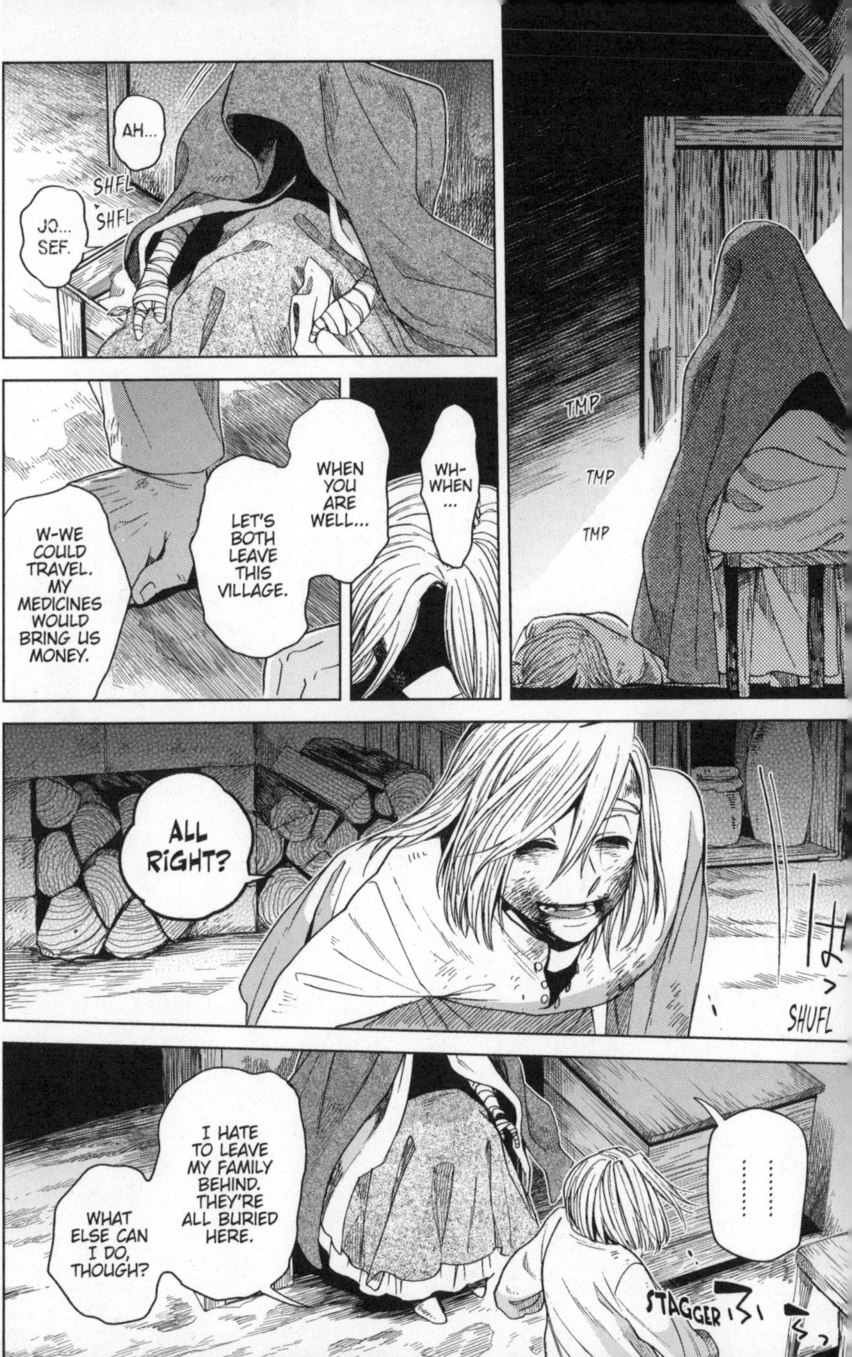
TMP
TMP
TMP
AH...
SHFL
SHFL
JO... SEF.
WH-WHEN ...
WHEN YOU ARE WELL... LET'S BOTH LEAVE THIS VILLAGE.
W-WE COULD TRAVEL. MY MEDICINES WOULD BRING US MONEY.
SHUFL
ALL RIGHT?
......
I HATE TO LEAVE MY FAMILY BEHIND. THEY'RE ALL BURIED HERE.
WHAT ELSE CAN I DO, THOUGH?
STAGGER

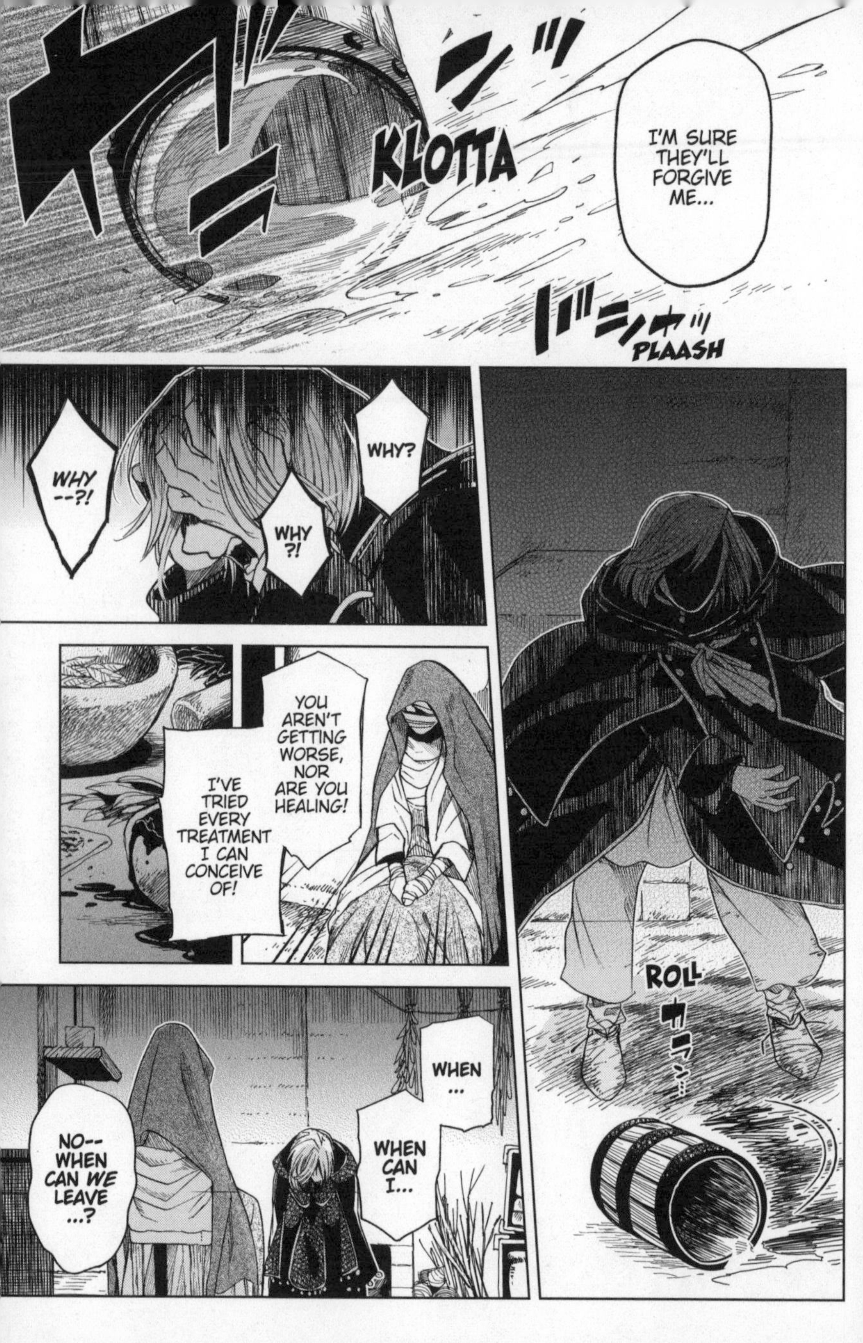
I'M SURE THEY'LL FORGIVE ME...
KLOTTA
PLAASH
ROLL
WHY?
WHY ?!
WHY --?!
YOU AREN'T GETTING WORSE, NOR ARE YOU HEALING!
I'VE TRIED EVERY TREATMENT I CAN CONCEIVE OF!
WHEN ...
WHEN CAN I...
NO-- WHEN CAN WE LEAVE ...?

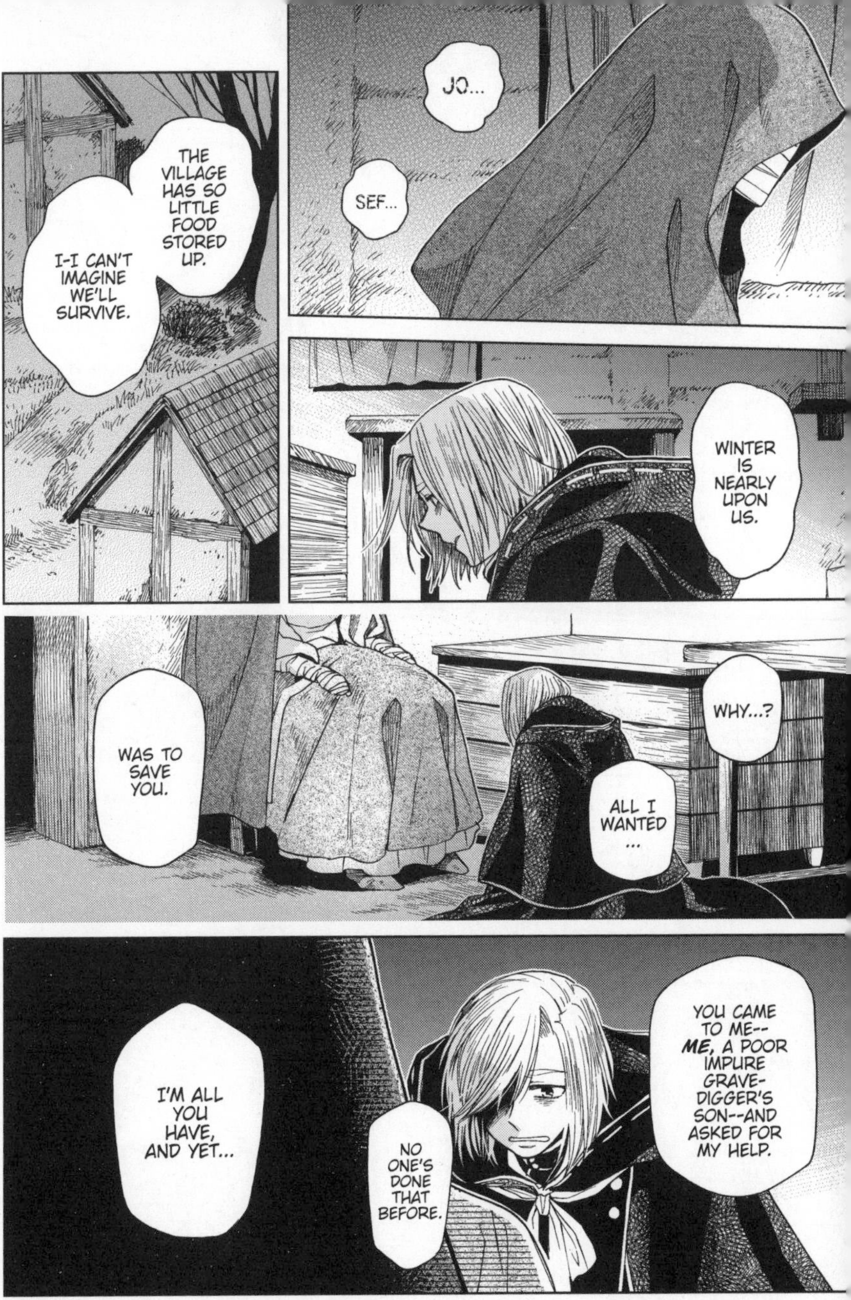
JO...
SEF...
WINTER IS NEARLY UPON US.
THE VILLAGE HAS SO LITTLE FOOD STORED UP.
I-I CAN'T IMAGINE WE'LL SURVIVE.
WHY...?
ALL I WANTED...
WAS TO SAVE YOU.
YOU CAME TO ME-- *ME,* A POOR IMPURE GRAVE-DIGGER'S SON--AND ASKED FOR MY HELP.
NO ONE'S DONE THAT BEFORE.
I'M ALL YOU HAVE, AND YET...

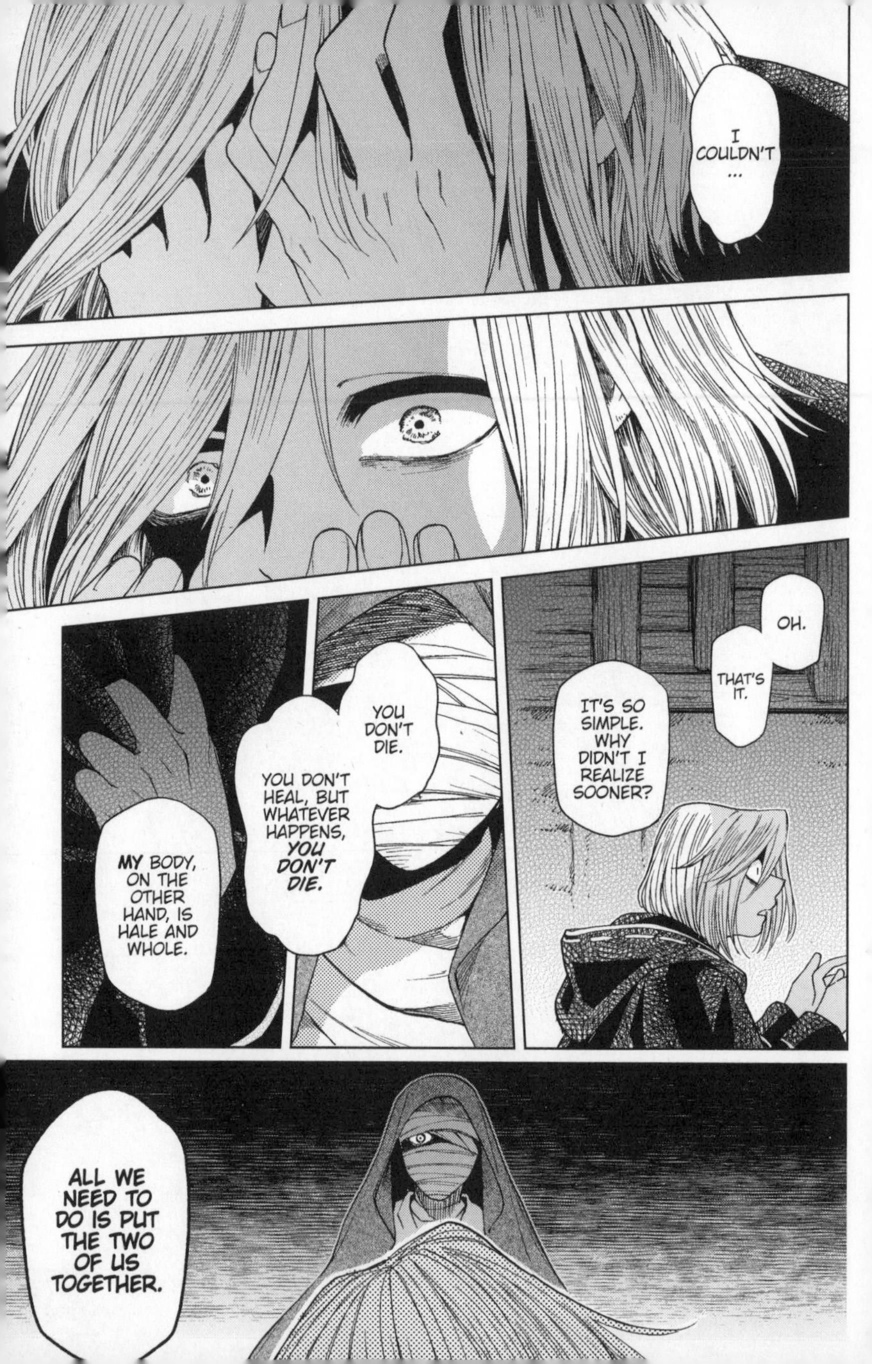
I COULDN'T ...
OH.
THAT'S IT.
IT'S SO SIMPLE. WHY DIDN'T I REALIZE SOONER?
YOU DON'T DIE.
YOU DON'T HEAL, BUT WHATEVER HAPPENS, ***YOU DON'T DIE.***
MY BODY, ON THE OTHER HAND, IS HALE AND WHOLE.
ALL WE NEED TO DO IS PUT THE TWO OF US TOGETHER.

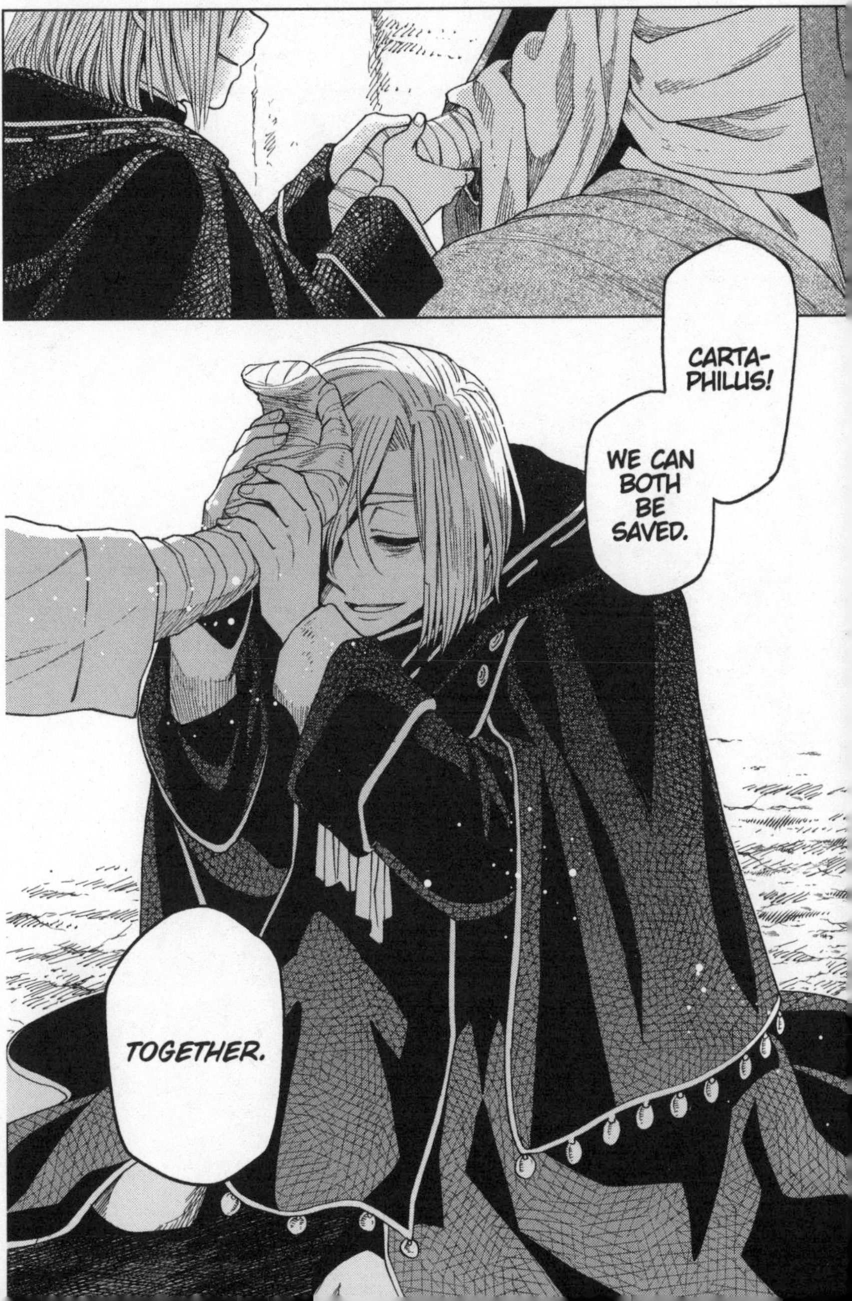
CARTA-
PHILUS!
WE CAN BOTH BE SAVED.
TOGETHER.

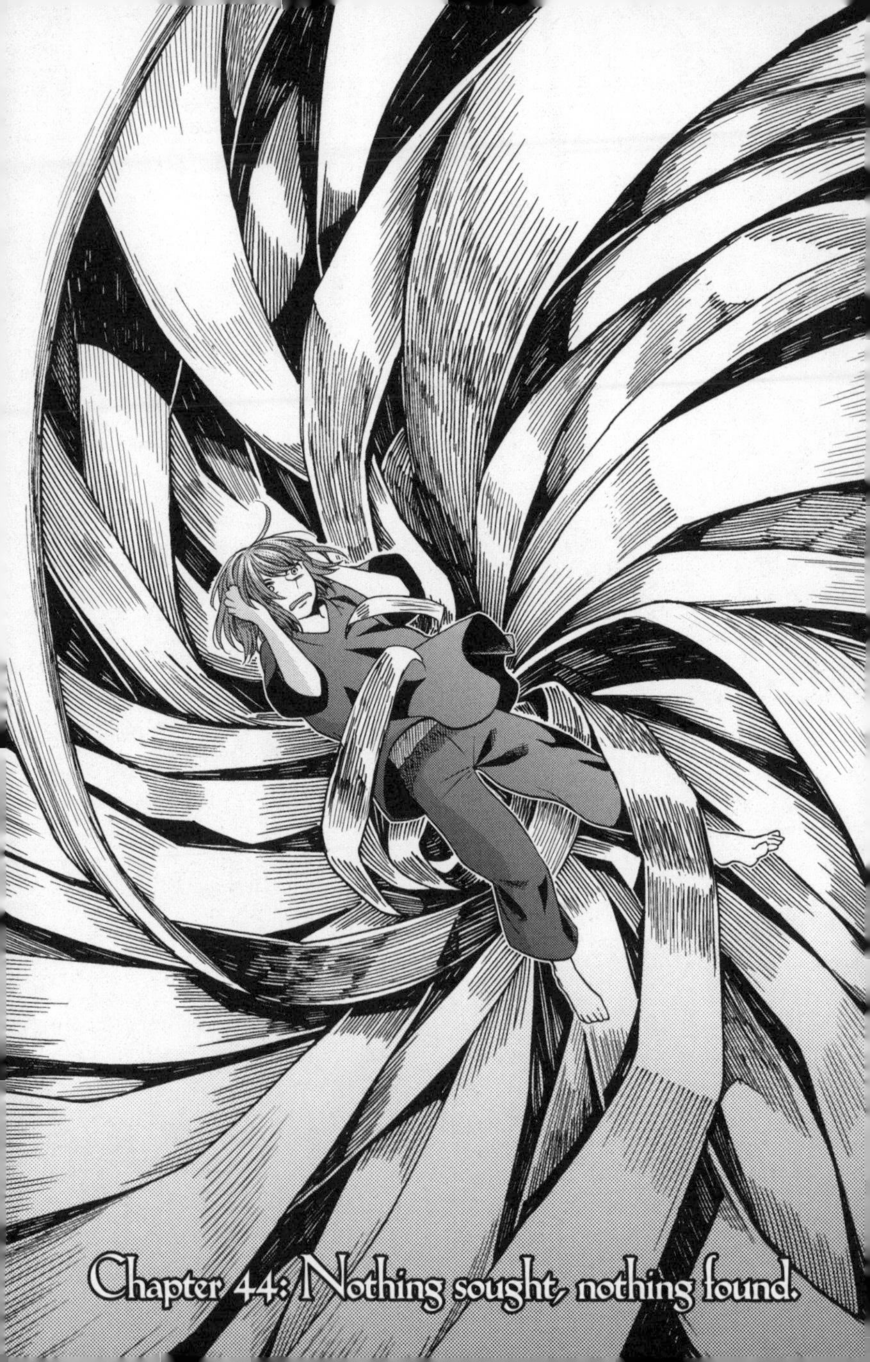

Chapter 44: Nothing sought, nothing found.

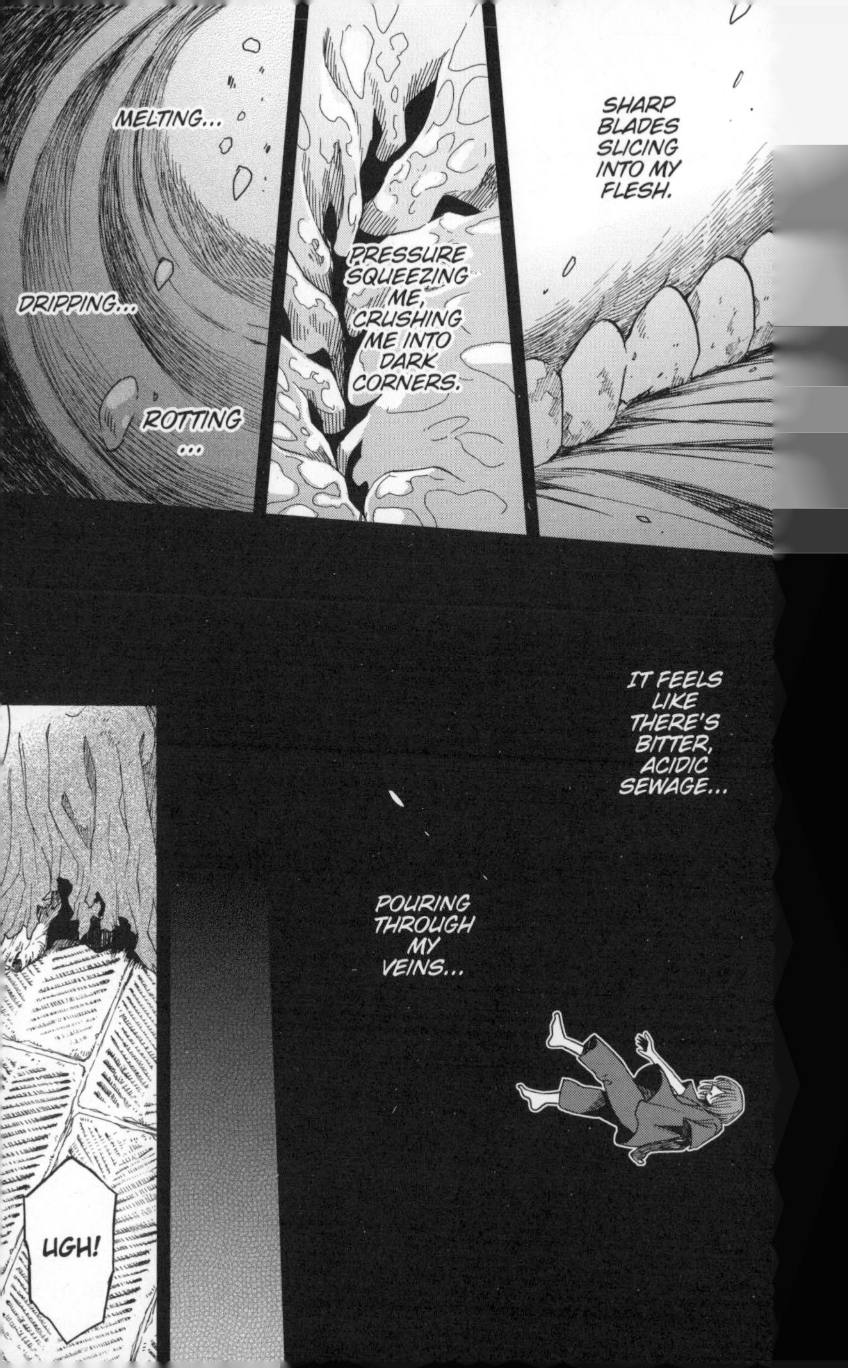
SHARP BLADES SLICING INTO MY FLESH.
PRESSURE SQUEEZING ME, CRUSHING ME INTO DARK CORNERS.
MELTING...
DRIPPING...
ROTTING...
IT FEELS LIKE THERE'S BITTER, ACIDIC SEWAGE...
POURING THROUGH MY VEINS...
UGH!

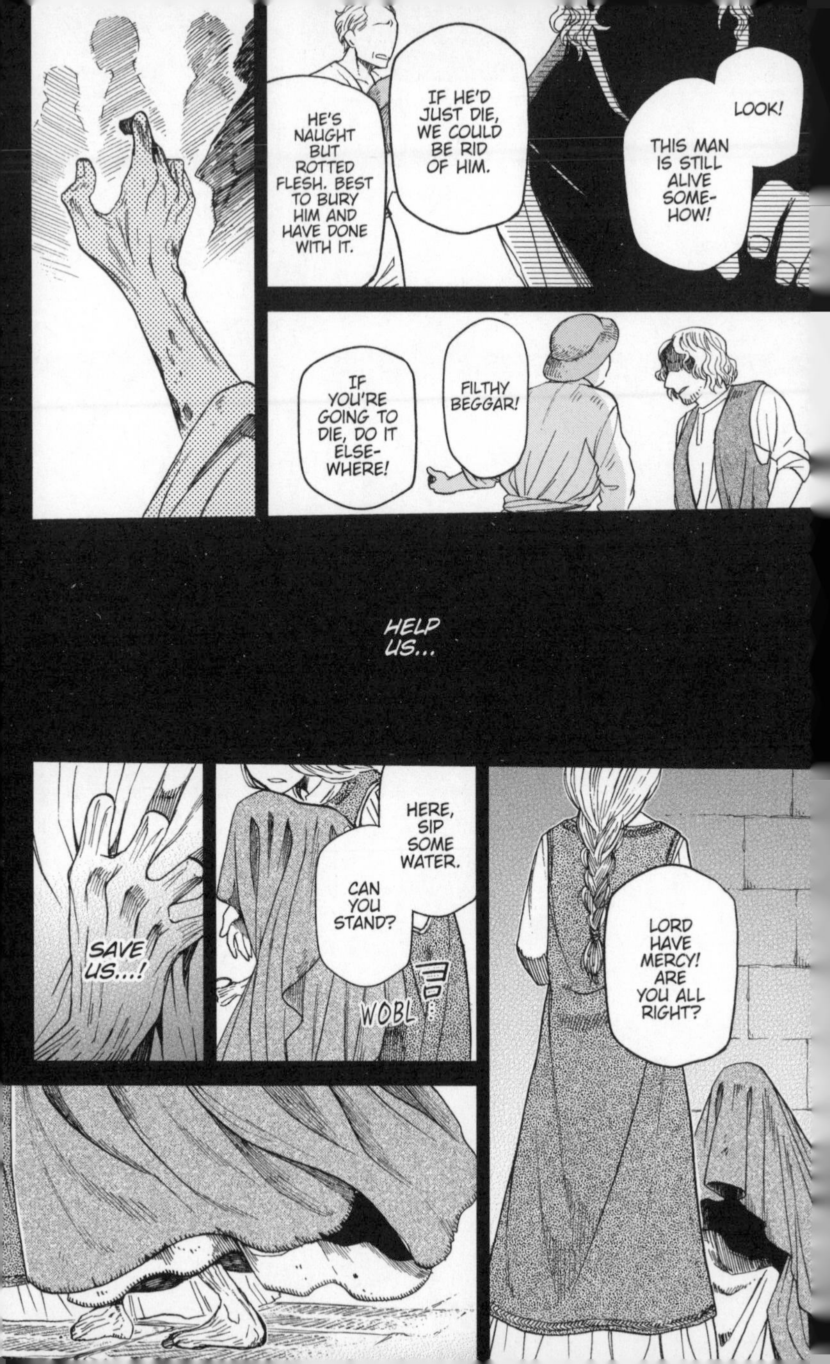
LOOK!
THIS MAN IS STILL ALIVE SOME-HOW!
IF HE'D JUST DIE, WE COULD BE RID OF HIM.
HE'S NAUGHT BUT ROTTED FLESH. BEST TO BURY HIM AND HAVE DONE WITH IT.
FILTHY BEGGAR!
IF YOU'RE GOING TO DIE, DO IT ELSE-WHERE!
HELP US...
LORD HAVE MERCY! ARE YOU ALL RIGHT?
HERE, SIP SOME WATER.
CAN YOU STAND?
WOBL...
SAVE US...!

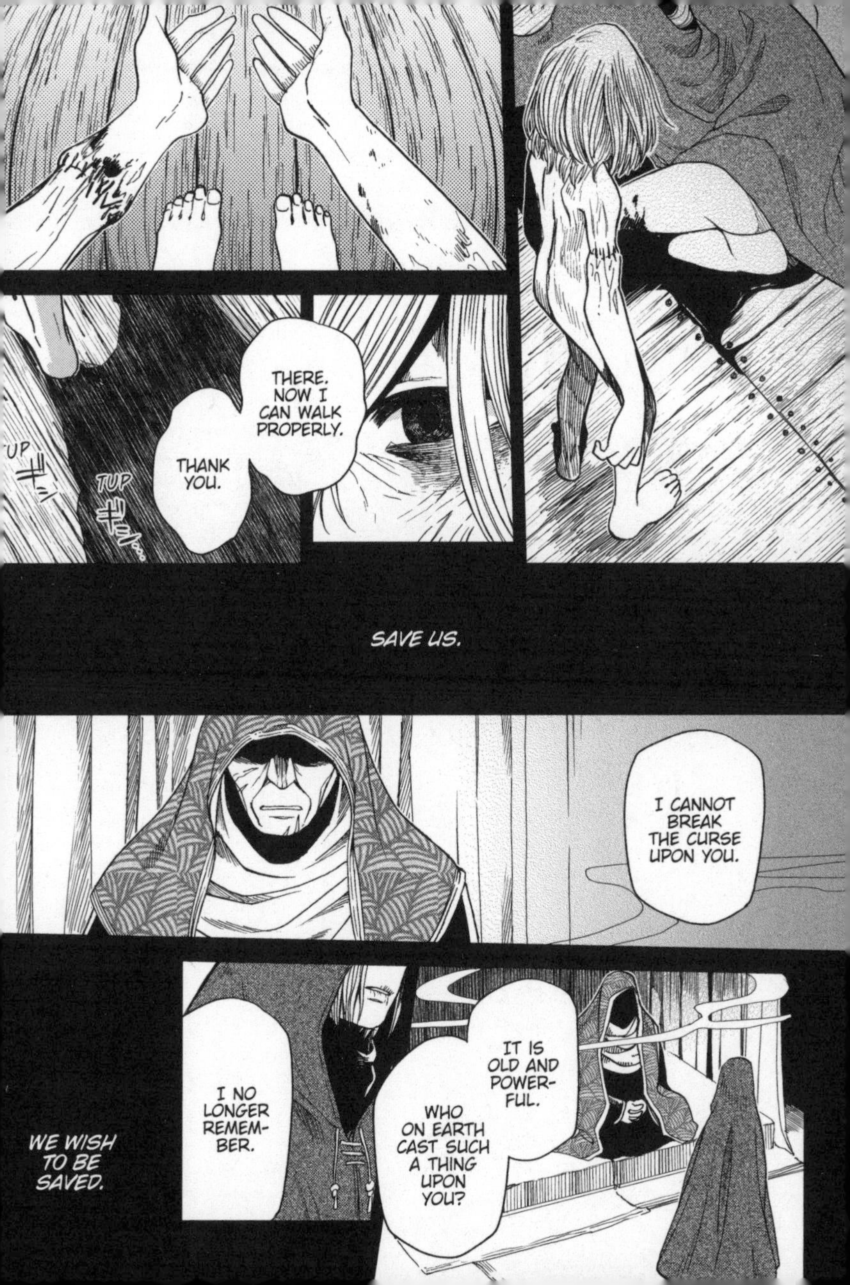
THERE. NOW I CAN WALK PROPERLY.
THANK YOU.
TUP
TUP
SAVE US.
I CANNOT BREAK THE CURSE UPON YOU.
IT IS OLD AND POWER-FUL.
WHO ON EARTH CAST SUCH A THING UPON YOU?
I NO LONGER REMEM-BER.
WE WISH TO BE SAVED.

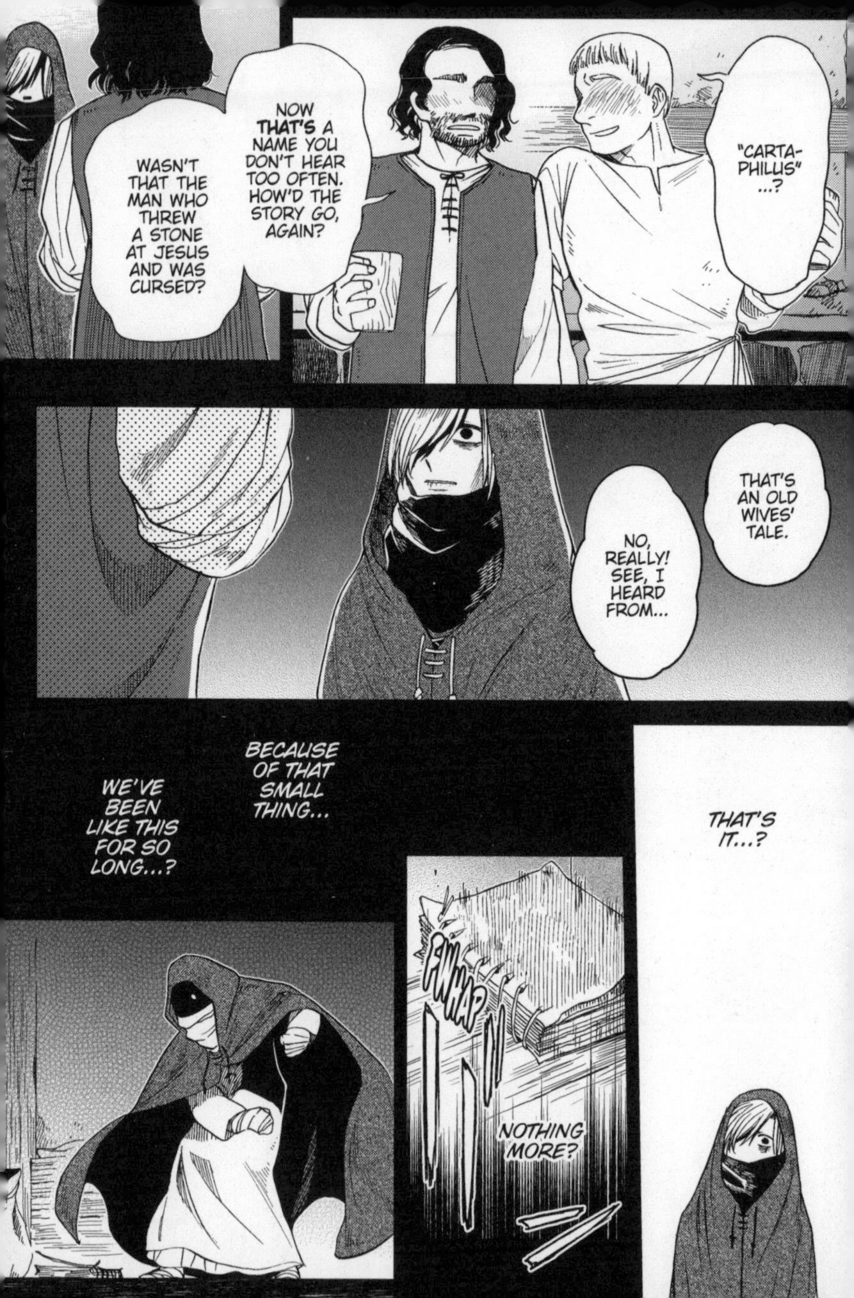
"CARTA-PHILUS"...?
NOW THAT'S A NAME YOU DON'T HEAR TOO OFTEN. HOW'D THE STORY GO, AGAIN?
WASN'T THAT THE MAN WHO THREW A STONE AT JESUS AND WAS CURSED?
THAT'S AN OLD WIVES' TALE.
NO, REALLY! SEE, I HEARD FROM...
THAT'S IT...?
BECAUSE OF THAT SMALL THING...
WE'VE BEEN LIKE THIS FOR SO LONG...?
FWHAP
NOTHING MORE?

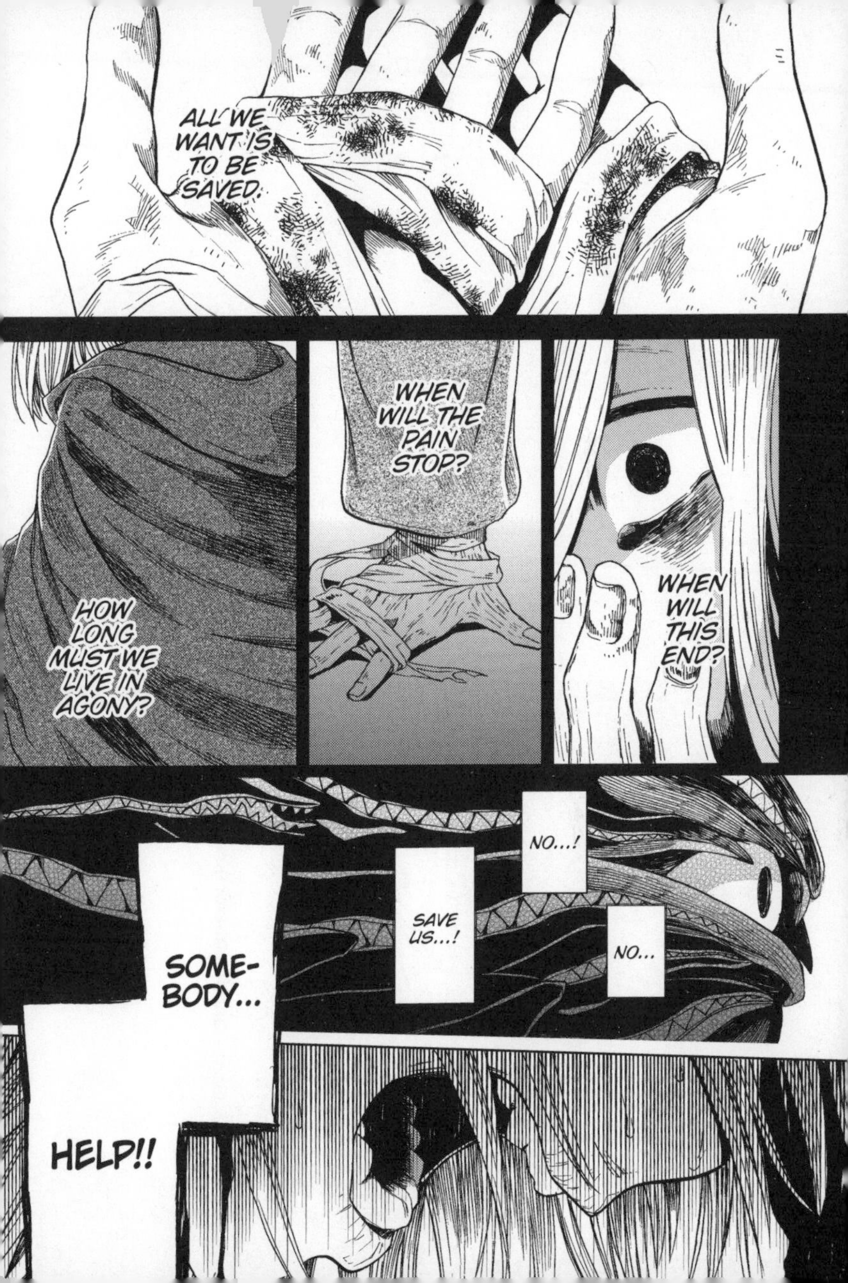
ALL WE WANT IS TO BE SAVED.
WHEN WILL THIS END?
WHEN WILL THE PAIN STOP?
HOW LONG MUST WE LIVE IN AGONY?
NO...
NO...!
SAVE US...!
SOME-BODY...
HELP!!

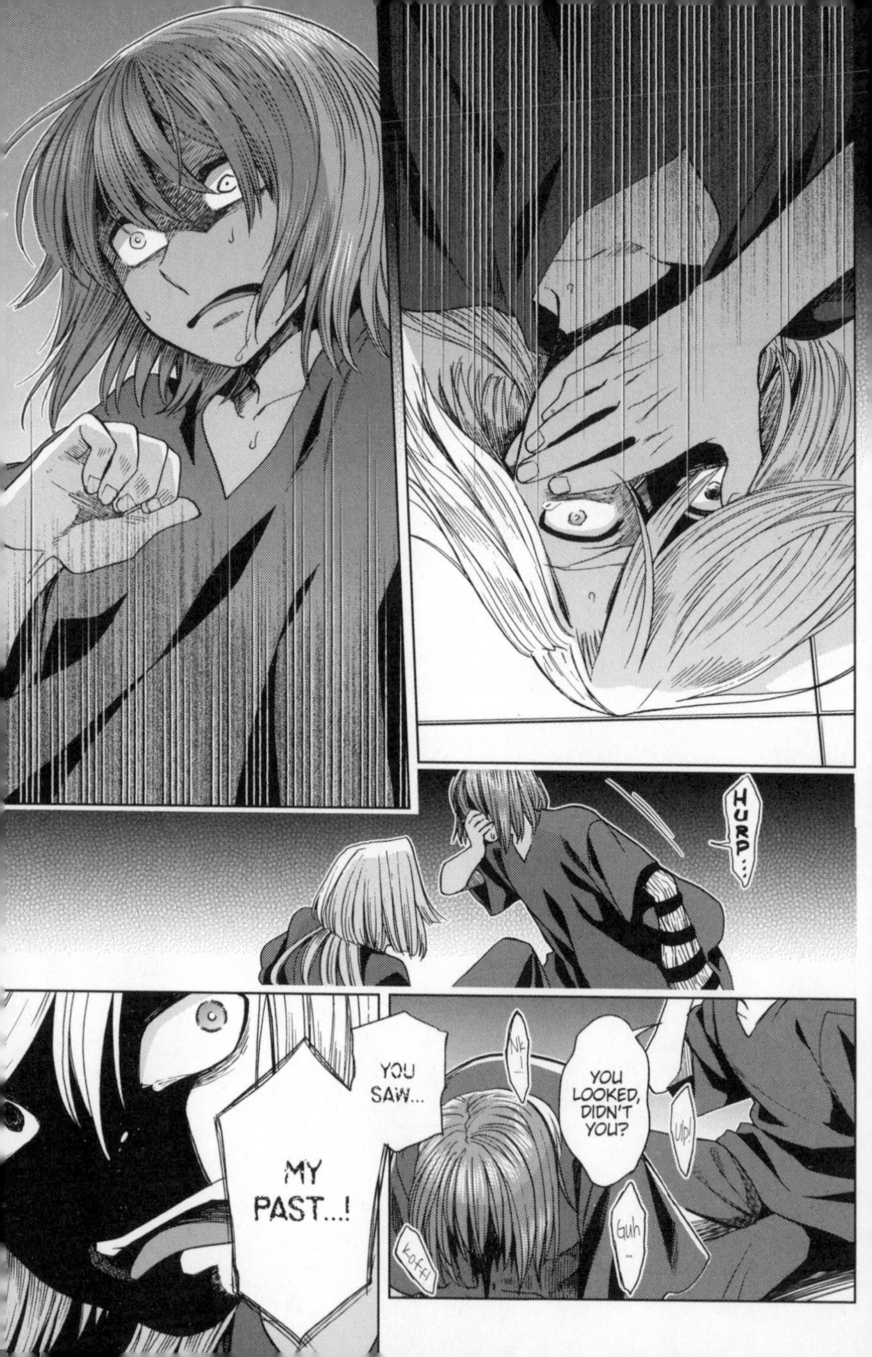
HURP...
YOU LOOKED, DIDN'T YOU?
Nk!...
Ulp!
Guh...
koff!
YOU SAW...
MY PAST...!

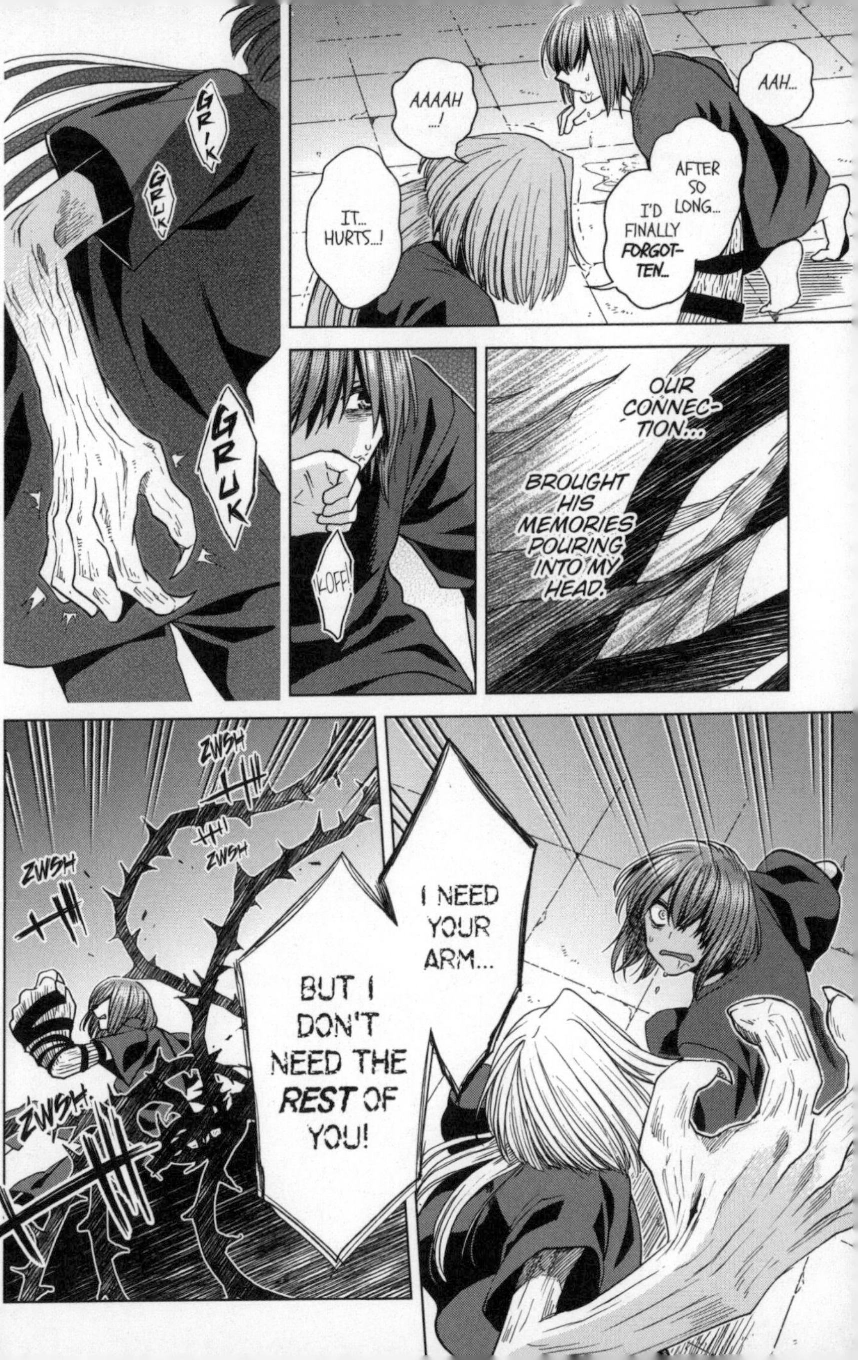
AAH...
AFTER SO LONG... I'D FINALLY FORGOT-TEN...
AAAAH...!
IT... HURTS...!
OUR CONNEC-TION...
BROUGHT HIS MEMORIES POURING INTO MY HEAD.
KOFF!
GRIK
GRUK
GRUK
I NEED YOUR ARM...
BUT I DON'T NEED THE REST OF YOU!
ZWSH
ZWSH
ZWSH
ZWSH

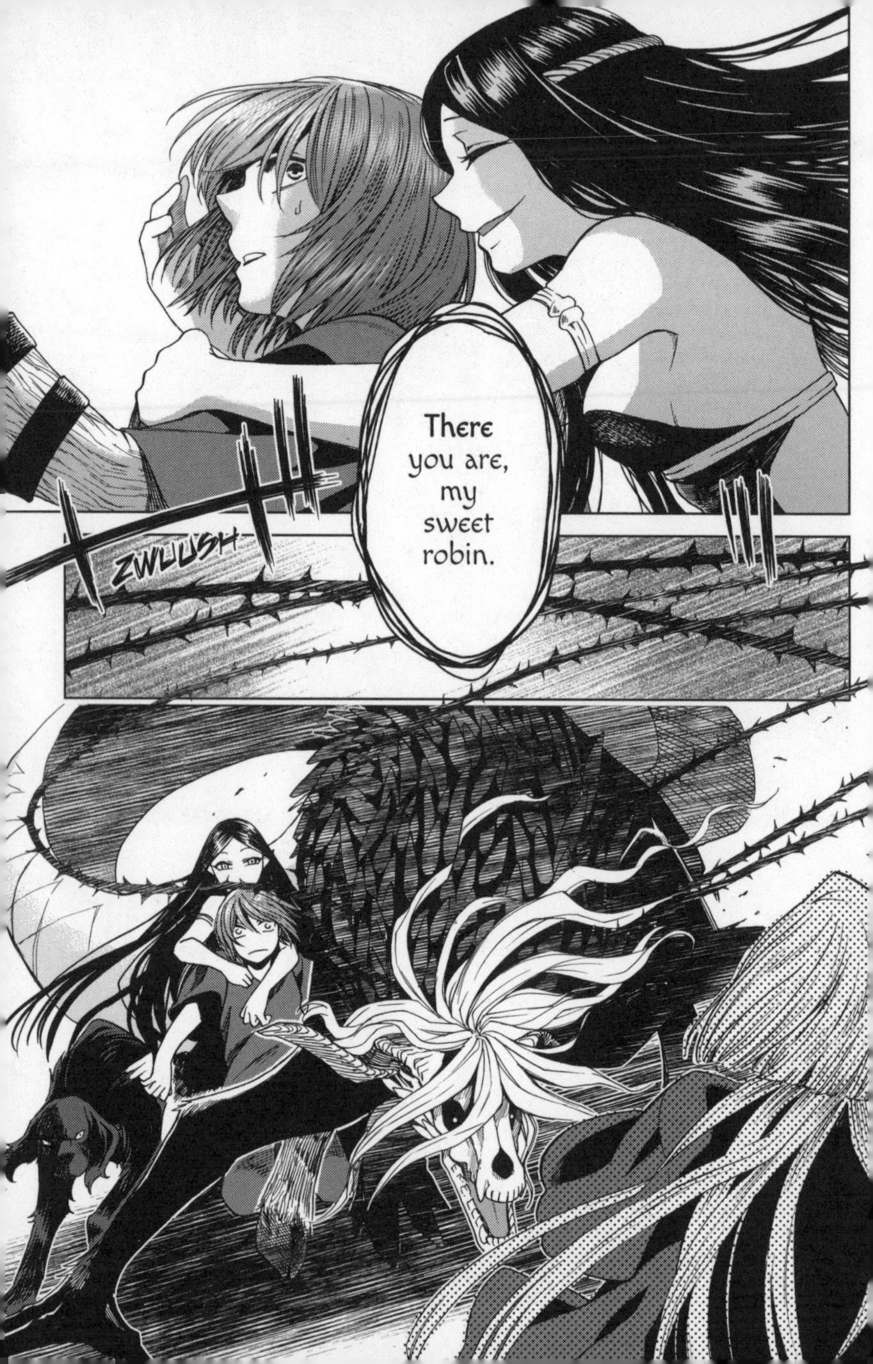
There you are, my sweet robin.
ZWUUSH

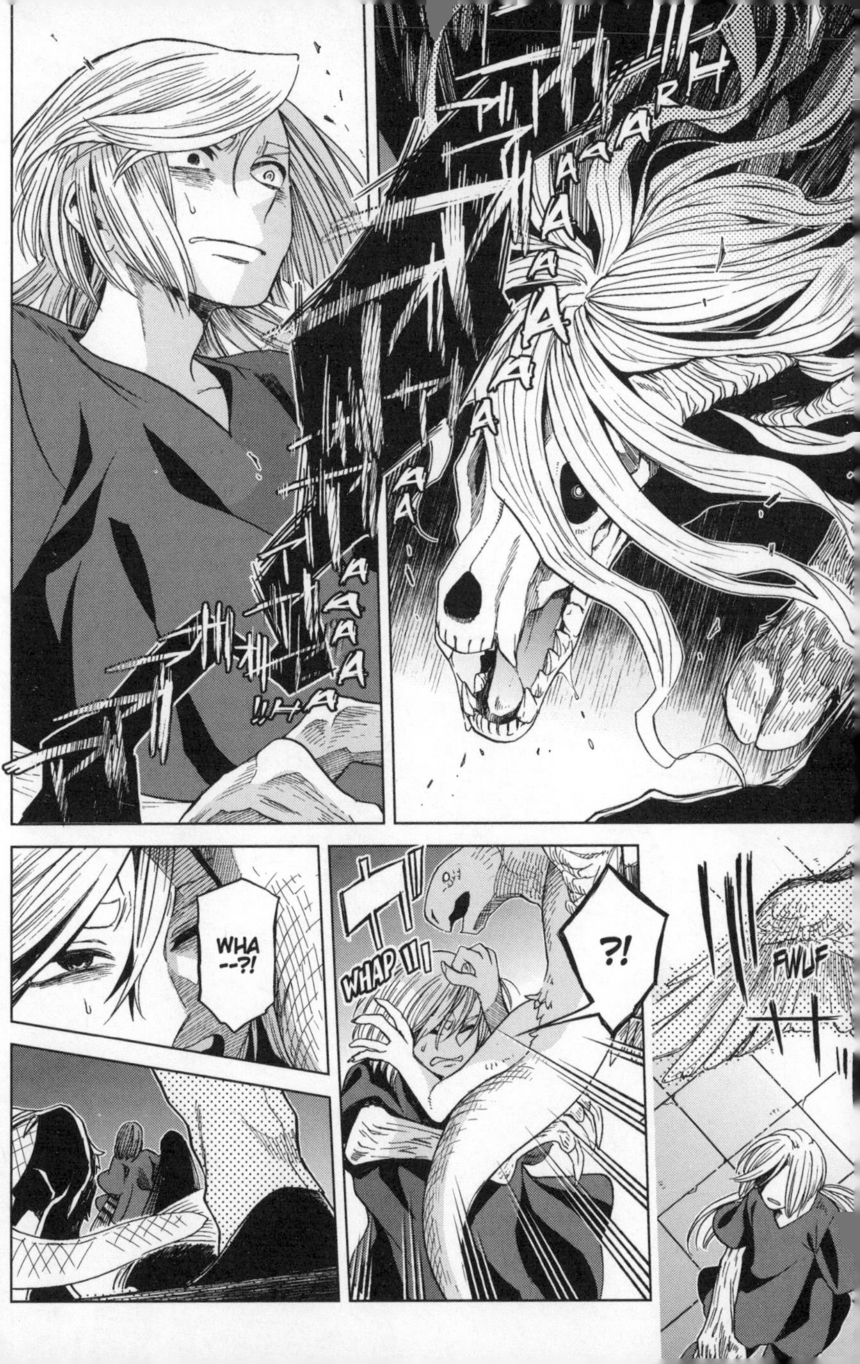
FWUF
?!
WHAP!!!
WHA --?!

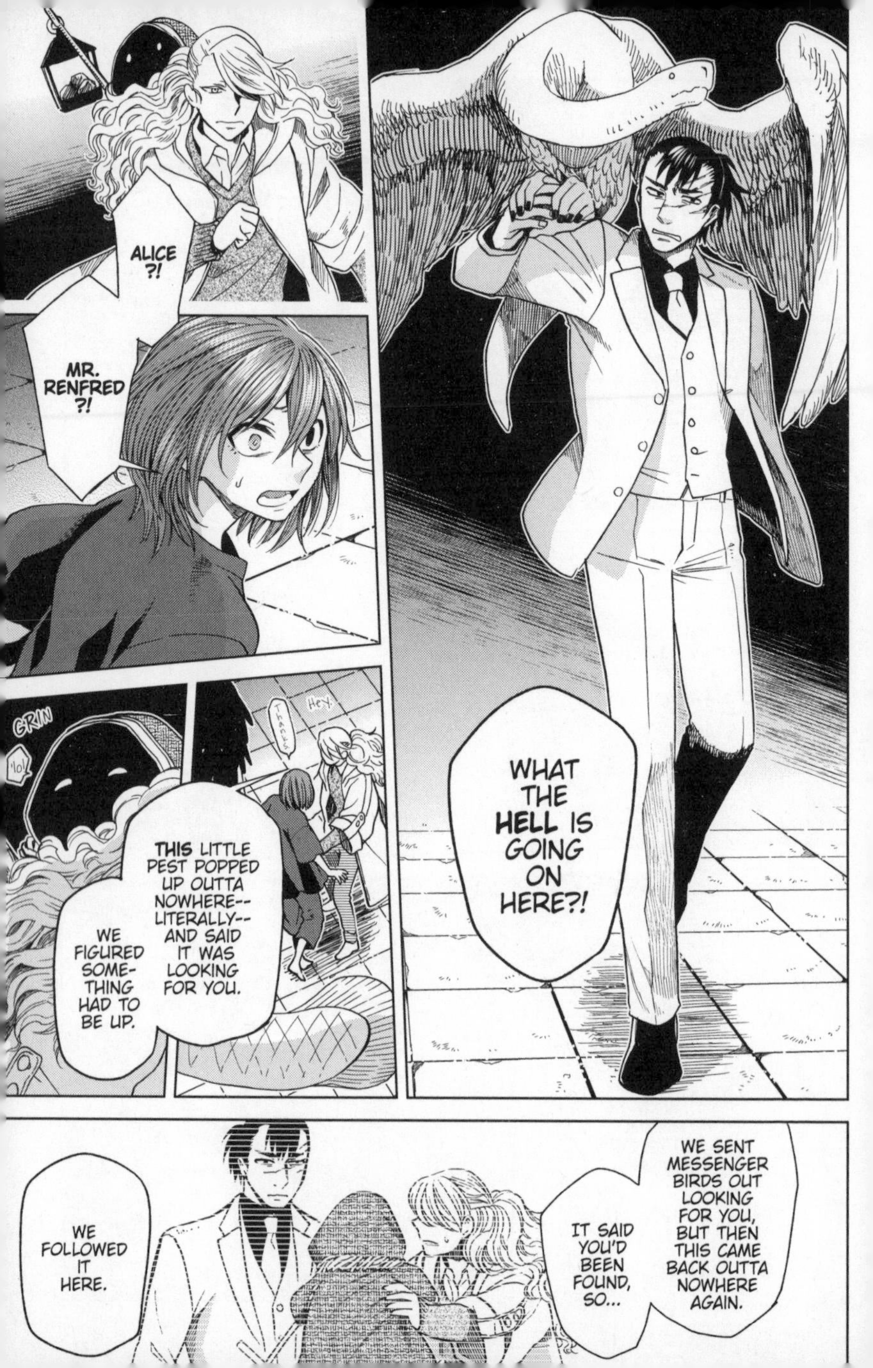
WHAT THE HELL IS GOING ON HERE?!
ALICE ?!
MR. RENFRED ?!
Hey.
Thanks.
GRIN
'lo!
THIS LITTLE PEST POPPED UP OUTTA NOWHERE--LITERALLY--AND SAID IT WAS LOOKING FOR YOU.
WE FIGURED SOME-THING HAD TO BE UP.
WE SENT MESSENGER BIRDS OUT LOOKING FOR YOU, BUT THEN THIS CAME BACK OUTTA NOWHERE AGAIN.
IT SAID YOU'D BEEN FOUND, SO...
WE FOLLOWED IT HERE.

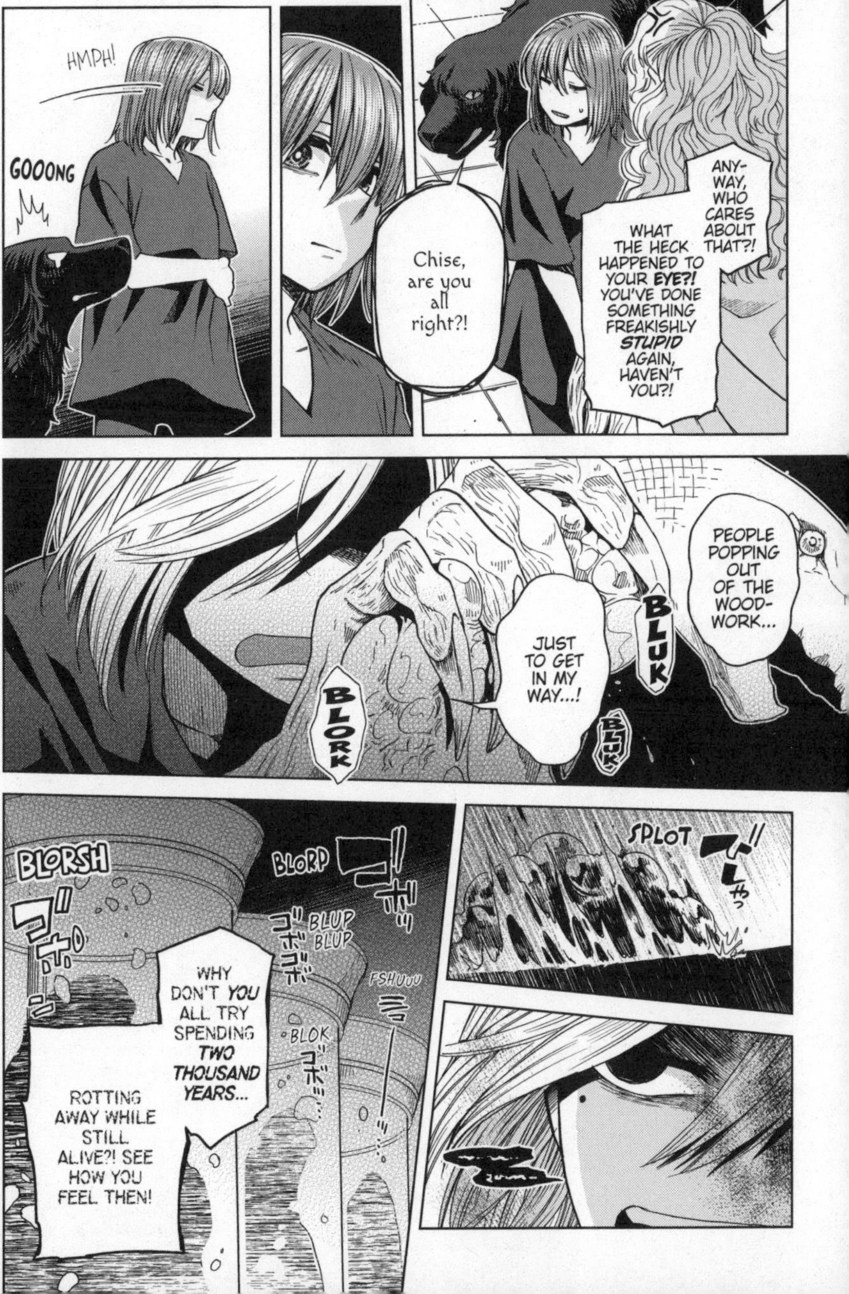
ANY-WAY, WHO CARES ABOUT THAT?!
WHAT THE HECK HAPPENED TO YOUR EYE?! YOU'VE DONE SOMETHING FREAKISHLY STUPID AGAIN, HAVEN'T YOU?!
Chise, are you all right?!
HMPH!
GOOONG
PEOPLE POPPING OUT OF THE WOOD-WORK...
BLUK
JUST TO GET IN MY WAY...!
BLORK
BLUK
SPLOT
BLORP
BLORSH
BLUP BLUP
WHY DON'T YOU ALL TRY SPENDING TWO THOUSAND YEARS...
ROTTING AWAY WHILE STILL ALIVE?! SEE HOW YOU FEEL THEN!
FSHUUU
BLOK

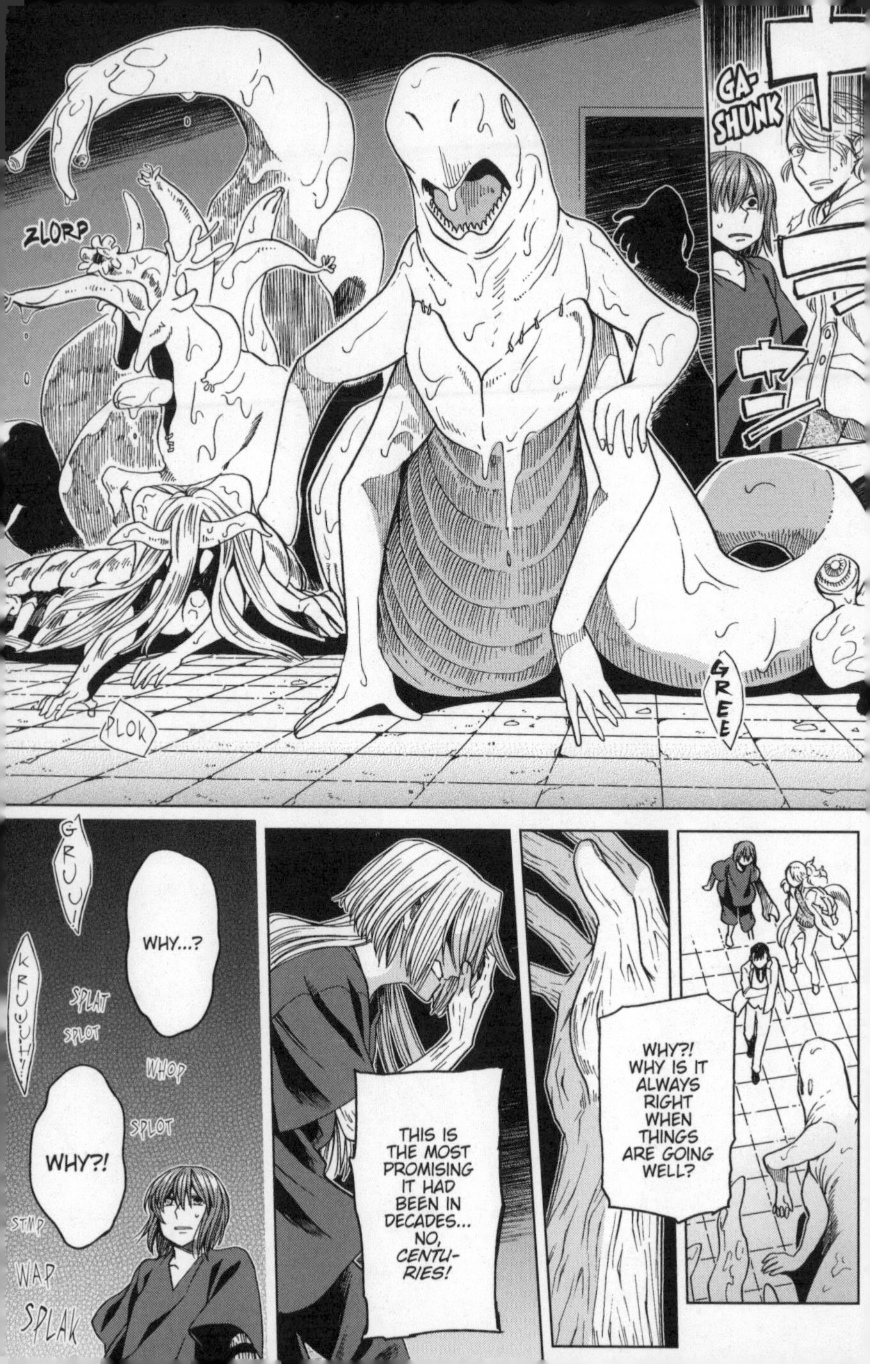
GA-SHUNK
ZLORP
GREE
PLOK
WHY?! WHY IS IT ALWAYS RIGHT WHEN THINGS ARE GOING WELL?
THIS IS THE MOST PROMISING IT HAD BEEN IN DECADES... NO, CENTURIES!
GRUU!
WHY...?
KRUUUH!!
SPLAT
SPLOT
WHOP
SPLOT
WHY?!
STMP
WAP
SPLAK

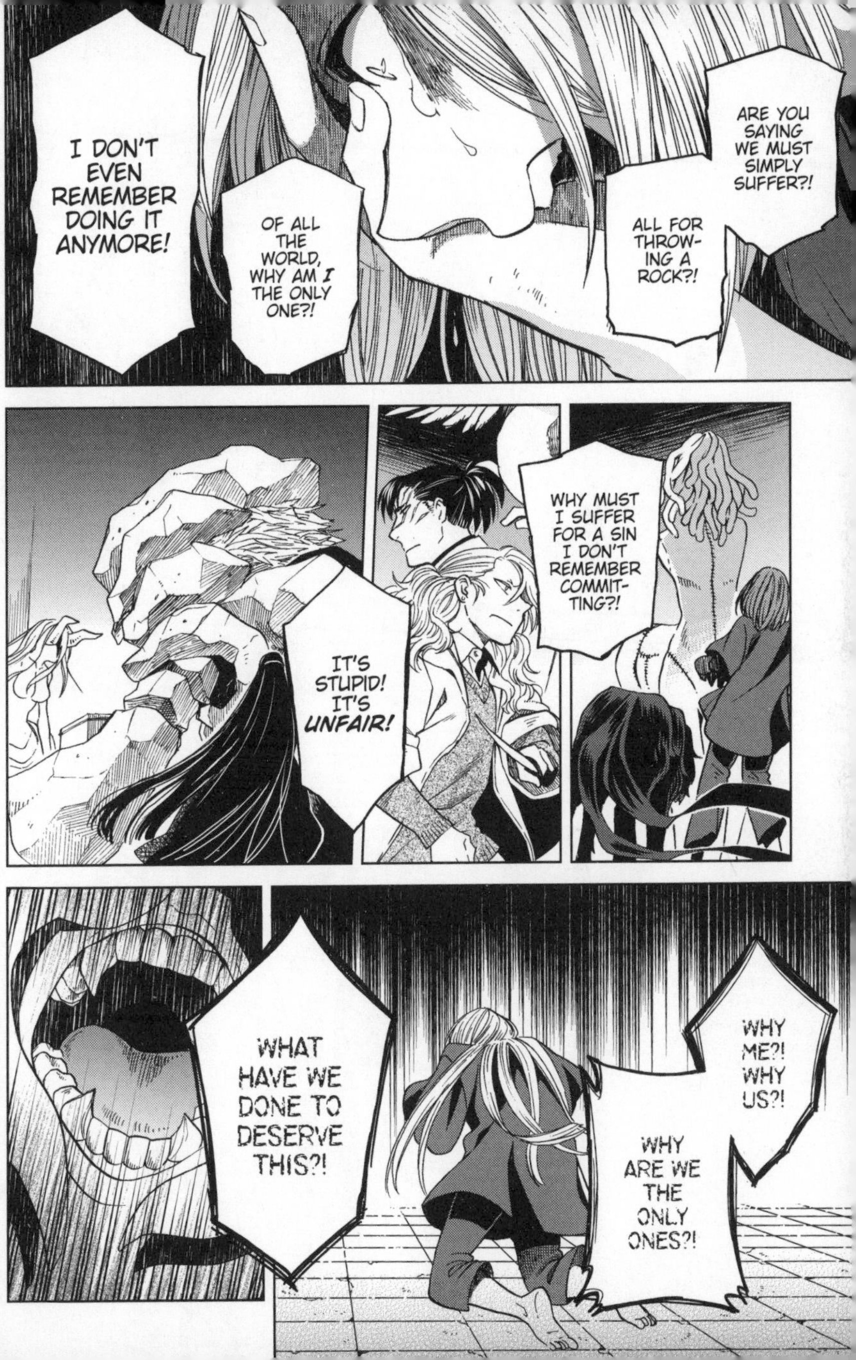
ARE YOU SAYING WE MUST SIMPLY SUFFER?!
ALL FOR THROWING A ROCK?!
OF ALL THE WORLD, WHY AM I THE ONLY ONE?!
I DON'T EVEN REMEMBER DOING IT ANYMORE!
WHY MUST I SUFFER FOR A SIN I DON'T REMEMBER COMMITTING?!
IT'S STUPID! IT'S UNFAIR!
WHY ME?! WHY US?!
WHY ARE WE THE ONLY ONES?!
WHAT HAVE WE DONE TO DESERVE THIS?!

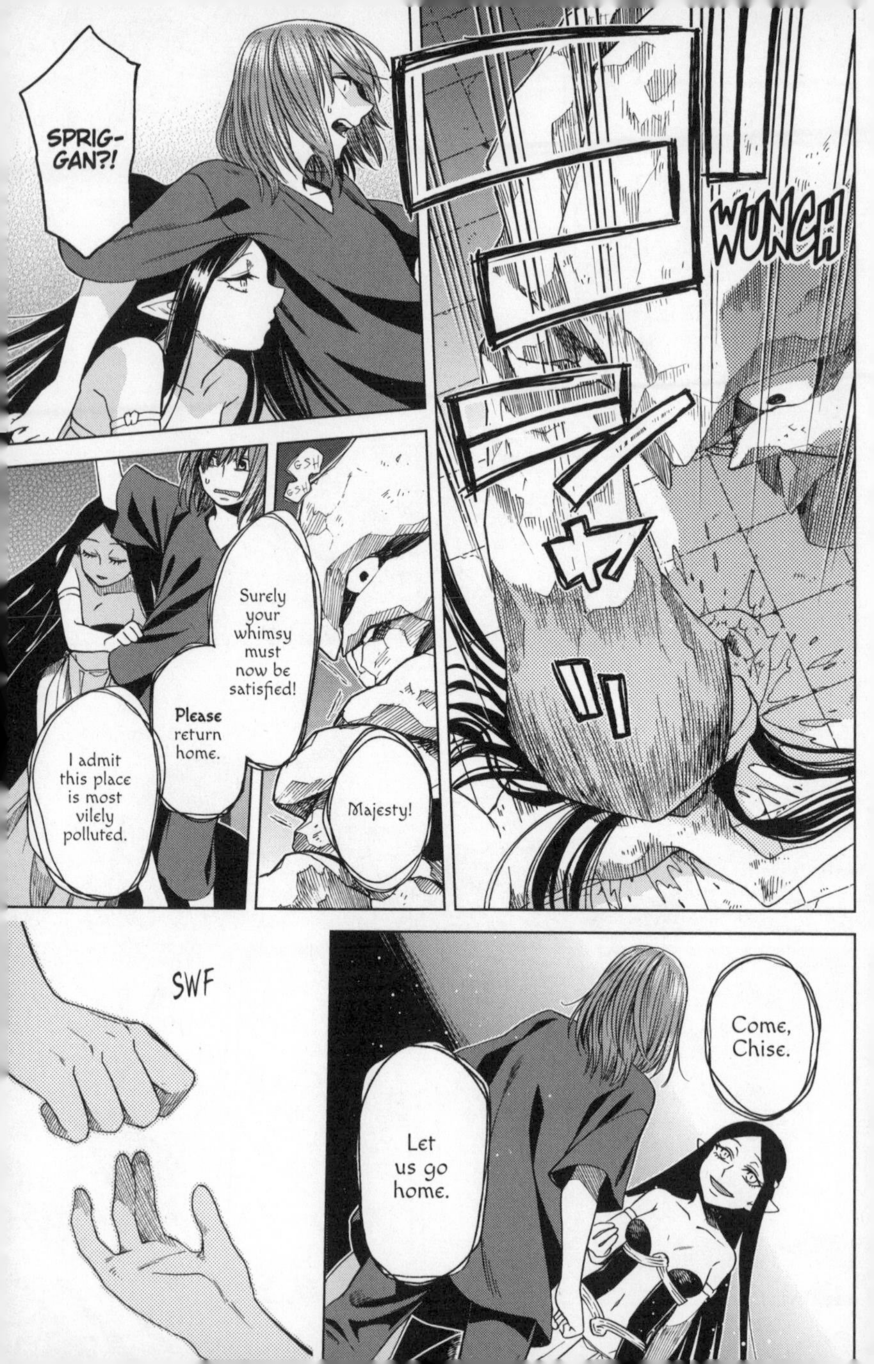
WUNCH
SPRIG-GAN?!
GSH GSH
Majesty!
Surely your whimsy must now be satisfied!
Please return home.
I admit this place is most vilely polluted.
Come, Chise.
Let us go home.
SWF

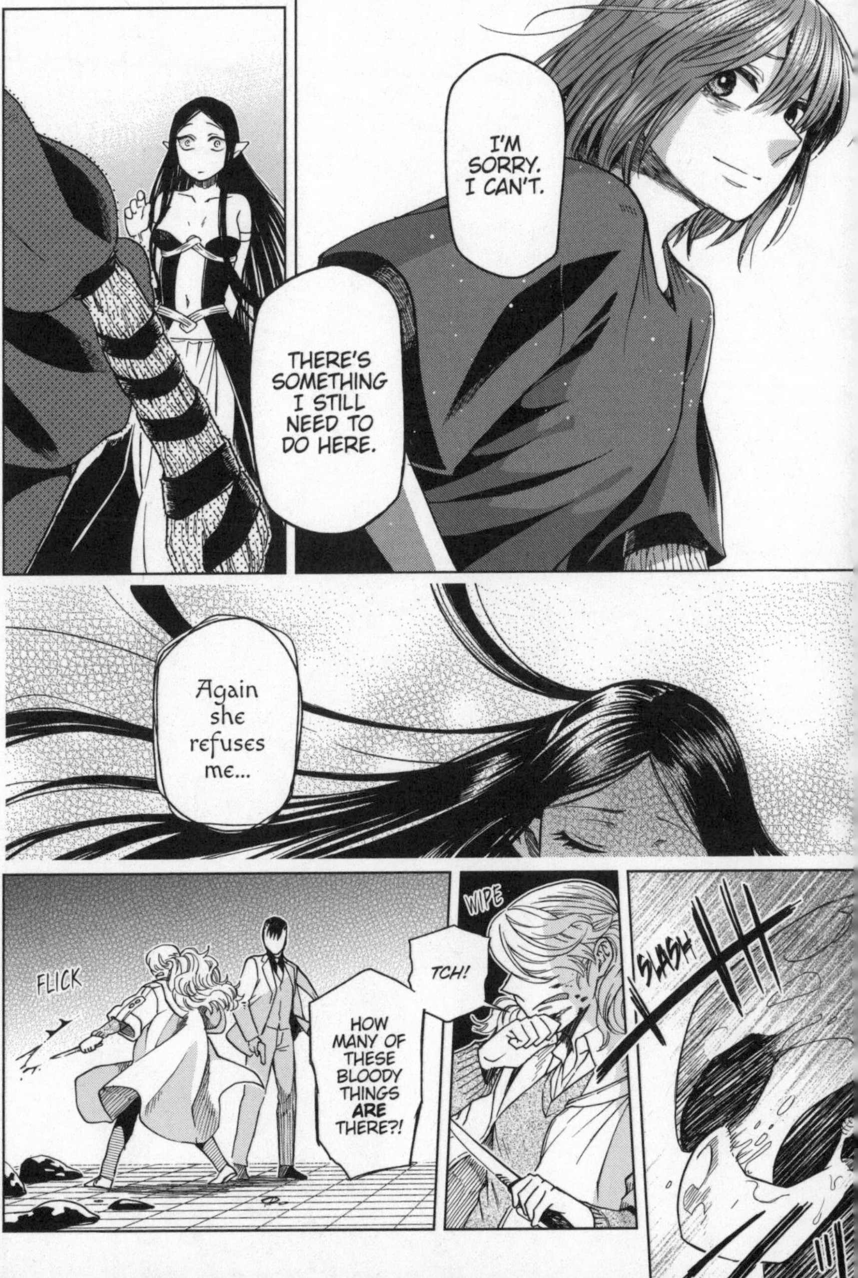
I'M SORRY. I CAN'T.
THERE'S SOMETHING I STILL NEED TO DO HERE.
Again she refuses me...
SLASH
WIPE
TCH!
HOW MANY OF THESE BLOODY THINGS **ARE** THERE?!
FLICK

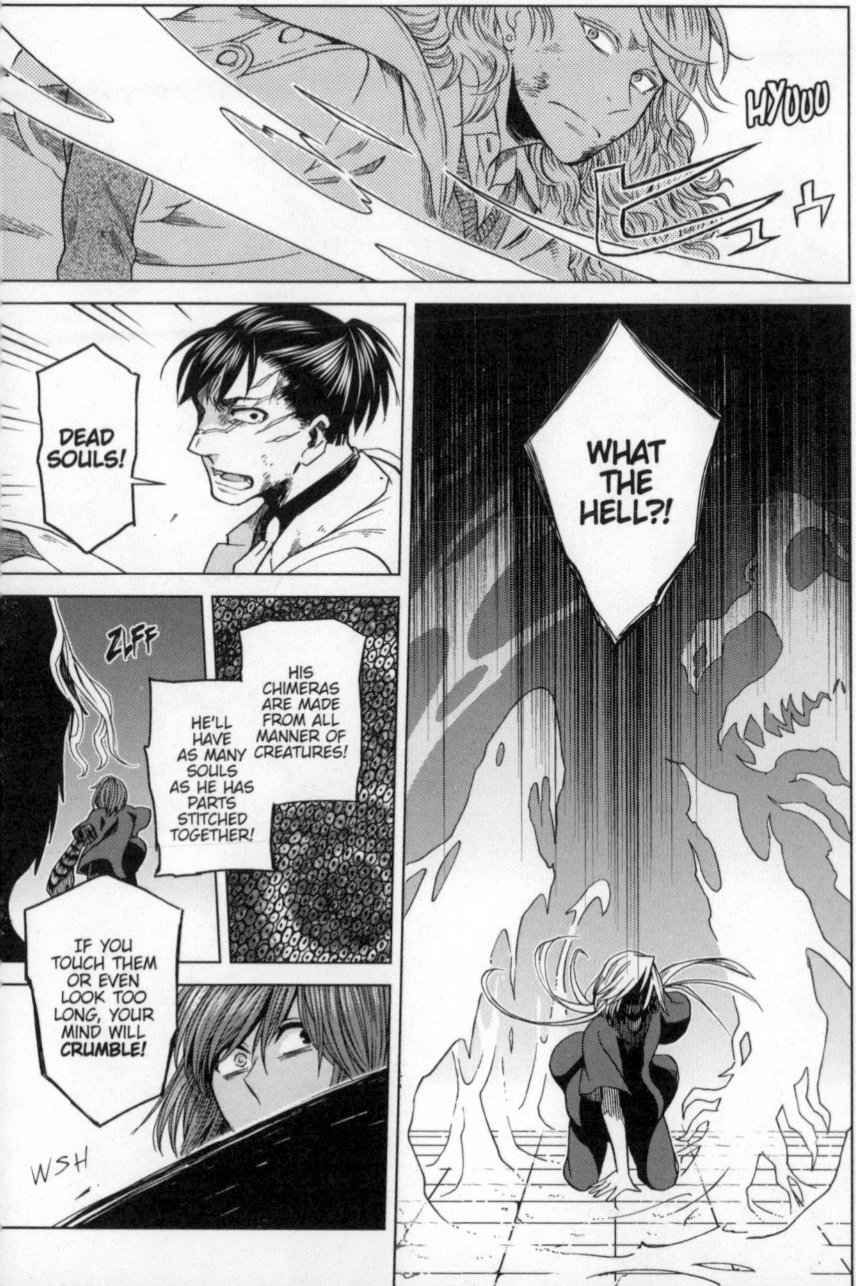
HYUUU
WHAT THE HELL?!
DEAD SOULS!
ZLFF
HIS CHIMERAS ARE MADE FROM ALL MANNER OF CREATURES!
HE'LL HAVE AS MANY SOULS AS HE HAS PARTS STITCHED TOGETHER!
IF YOU TOUCH THEM OR EVEN LOOK TOO LONG, YOUR MIND WILL **CRUMBLE!**
WSH

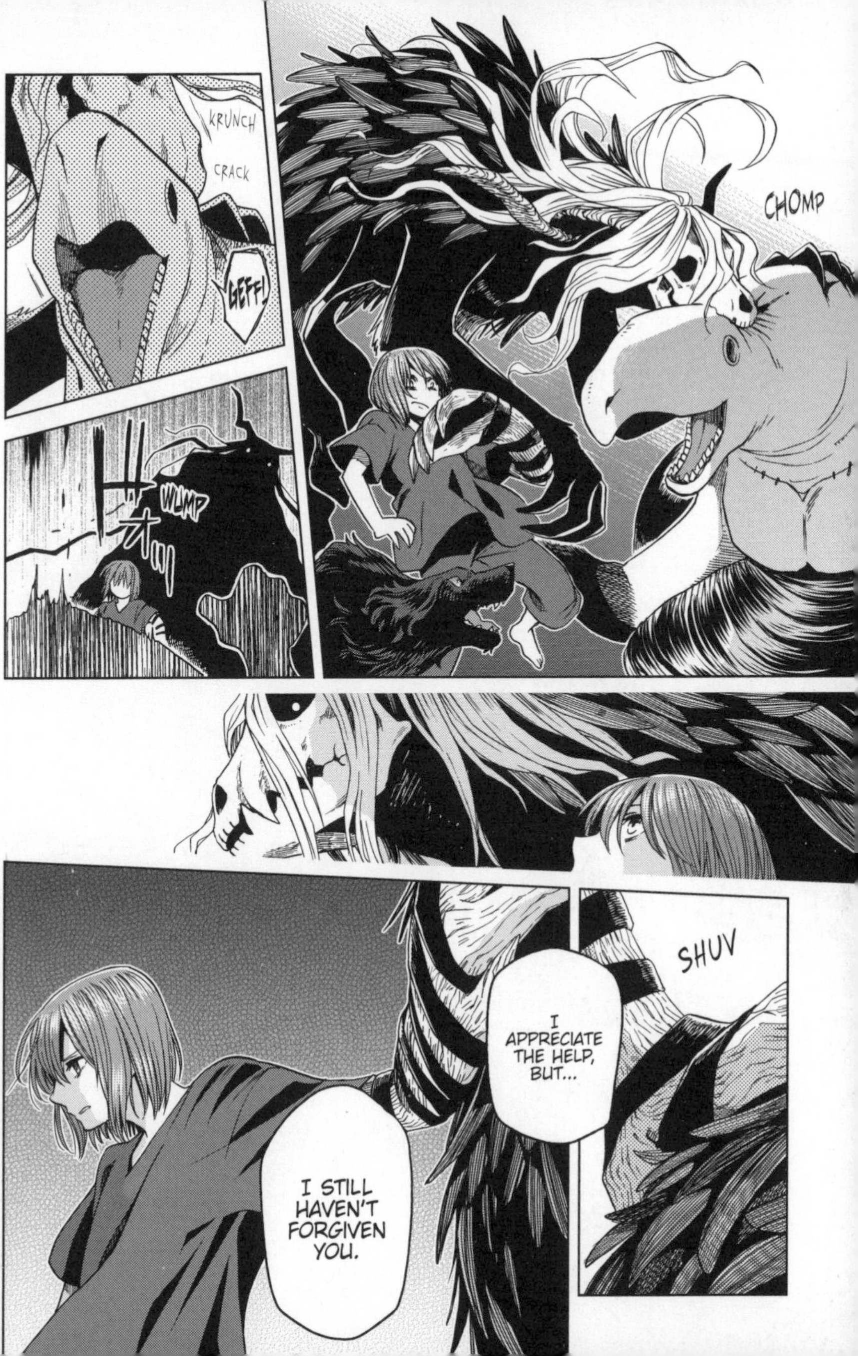
CHOMP
KRUNCH
CRACK
GEFF!
WUMP
SHUV
I APPRECIATE THE HELP, BUT...
I STILL HAVEN'T FORGIVEN YOU.

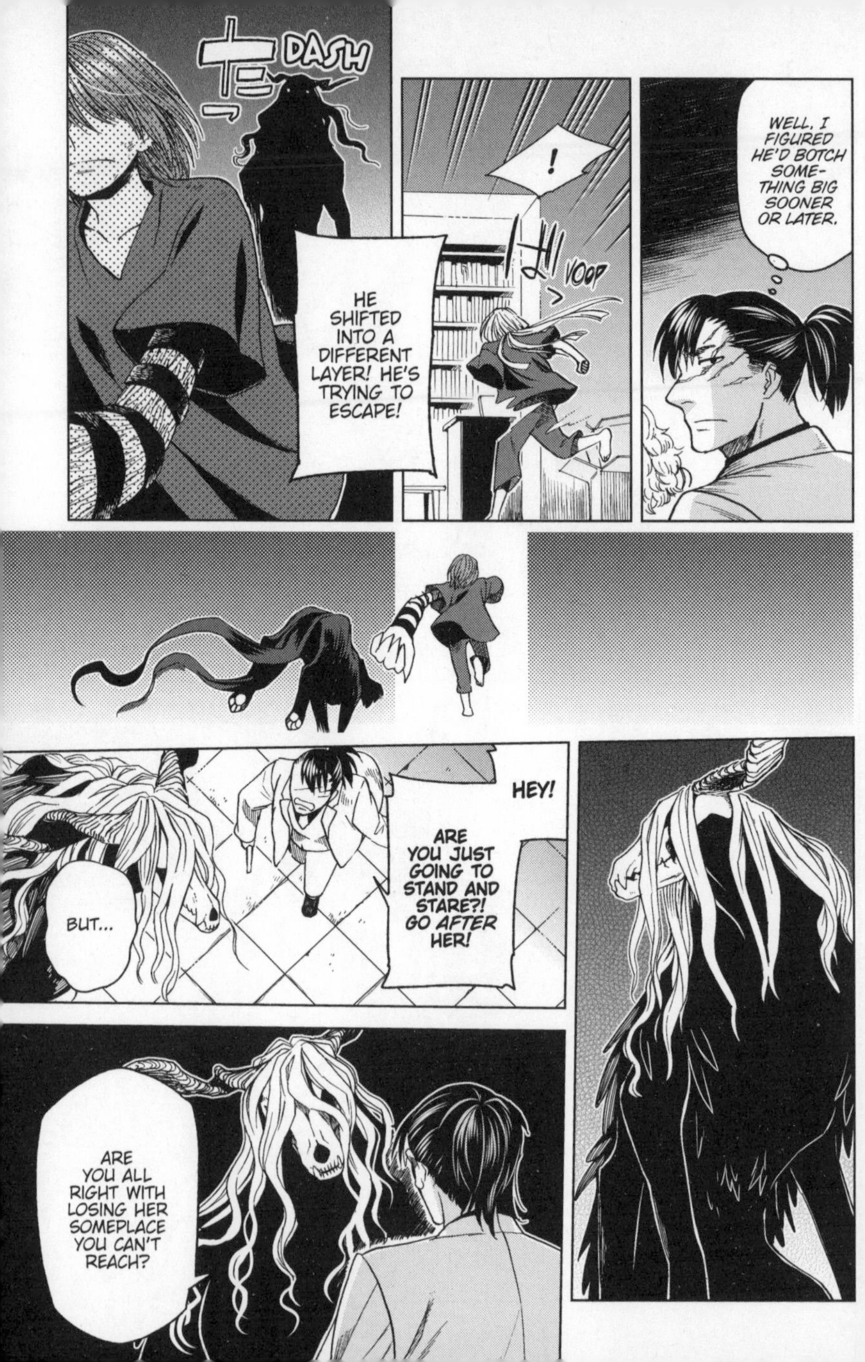
WELL, I FIGURED HE'D BOTCH SOME-THING BIG SOONER OR LATER.
!
VOOP
DASH
HE SHIFTED INTO A DIFFERENT LAYER! HE'S TRYING TO ESCAPE!
HEY!
ARE YOU JUST GOING TO STAND AND STARE?! GO AFTER HER!
BUT...
ARE YOU ALL RIGHT WITH LOSING HER SOMEPLACE YOU CAN'T REACH?

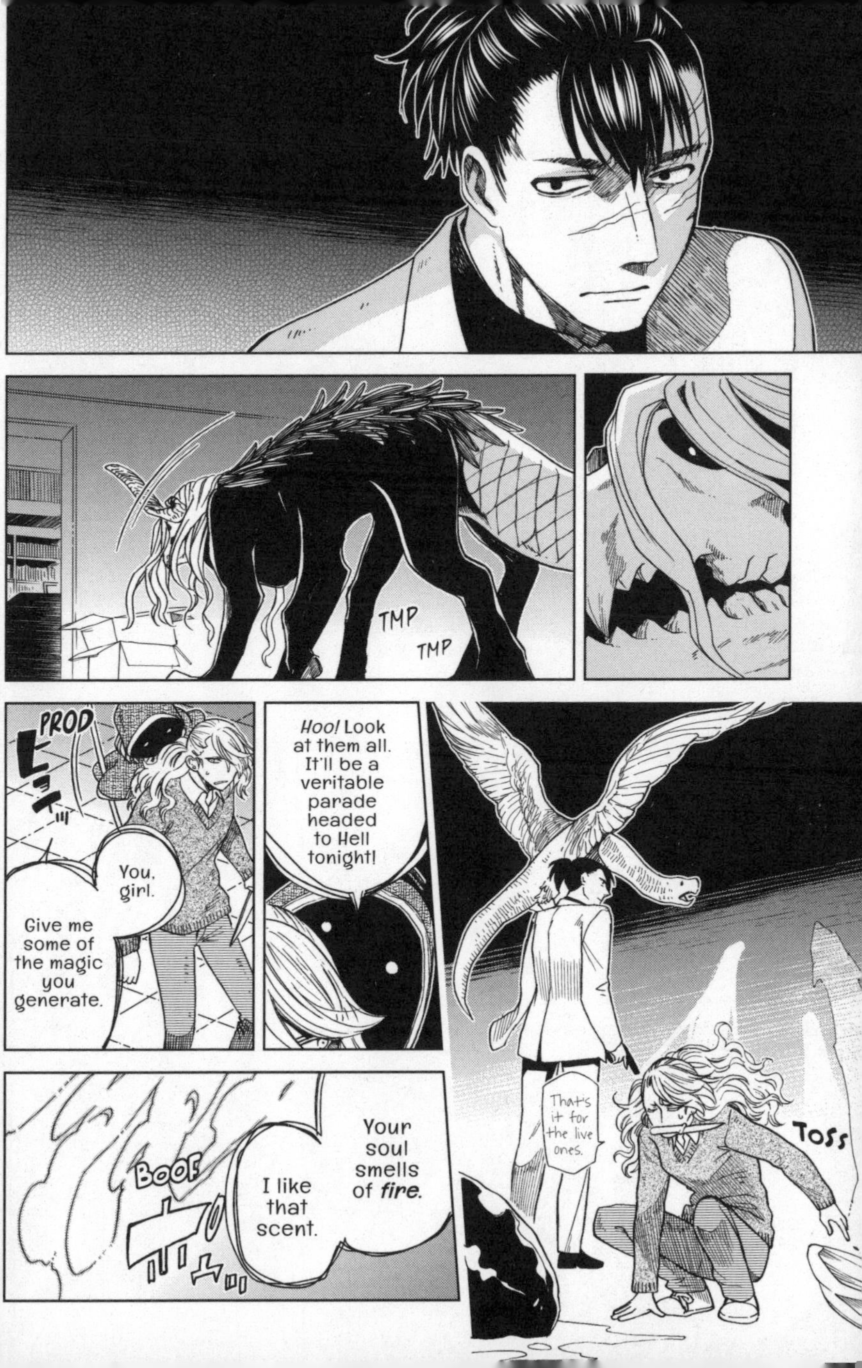
TMP
TMP
That's it for the live ones.
TOSS
Hoo! Look at them all. It'll be a veritable parade headed to Hell tonight!
PROD
You, girl.
Give me some of the magic you generate.
Your soul smells of *fire*.
I like that scent.
BOOF

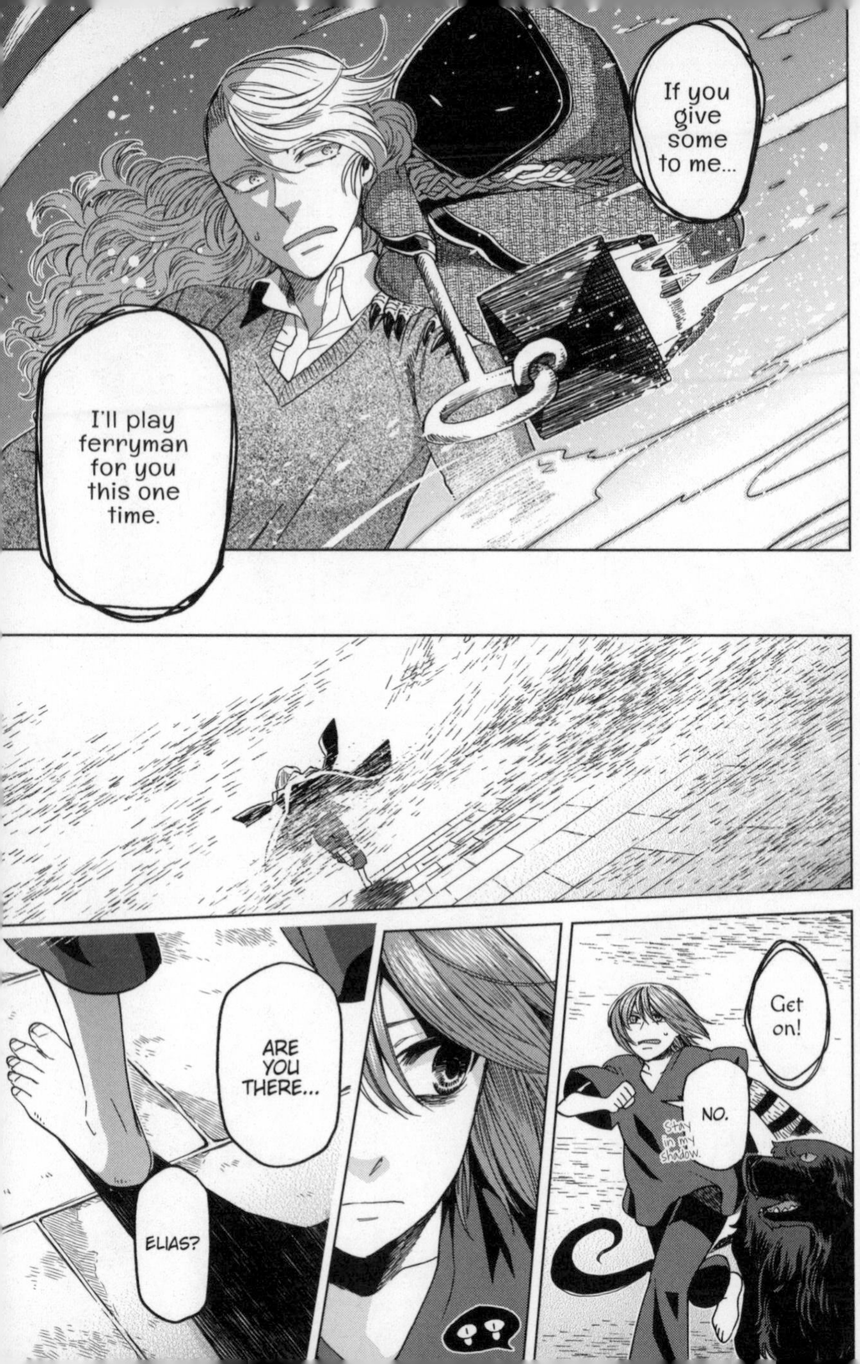
If you give some to me...
I'll play ferryman for you this one time.
Get on!
NO.
Stay in my shadow.
ARE YOU THERE...
ELIAS?

I'M SORRY.

I'M STILL ANGRY WITH YOU.

VERY ANGRY.

| | | | |

I AM.

DON'T BOTHER APOLOGIZING IF YOU DON'T MEAN IT.

| | | | |

"MAKE IT UP" ...?

IF YOU WANT BACK IN MY GOOD GRACES ...

YOU'LL HAVE TO MAKE IT UP TO ME.

SO...

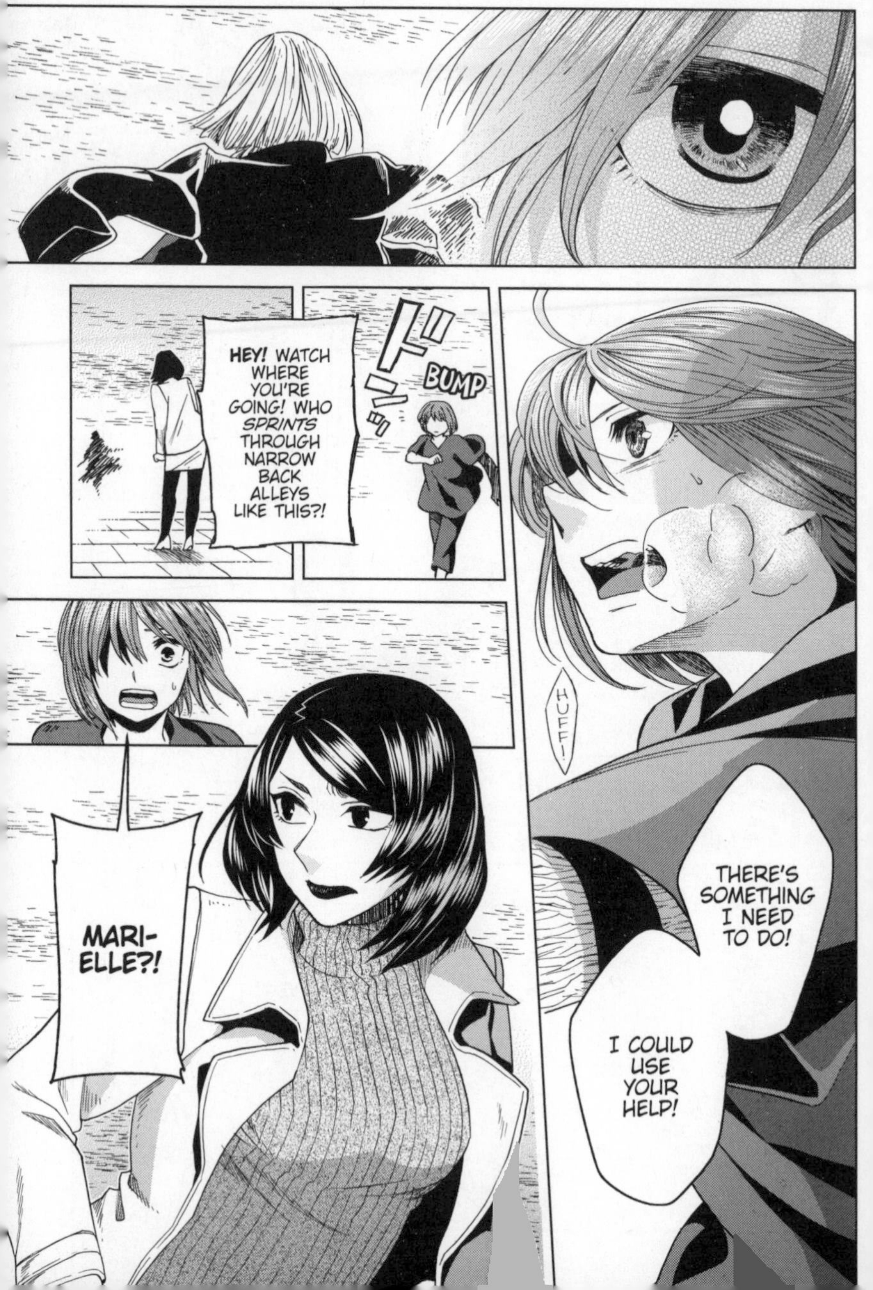
HUFF!
THERE'S SOMETHING I NEED TO DO!
I COULD USE YOUR HELP!
BUMP
HEY! WATCH WHERE YOU'RE GOING! WHO *SPRINTS* THROUGH NARROW BACK ALLEYS LIKE THIS?!
MARI-ELLE?!

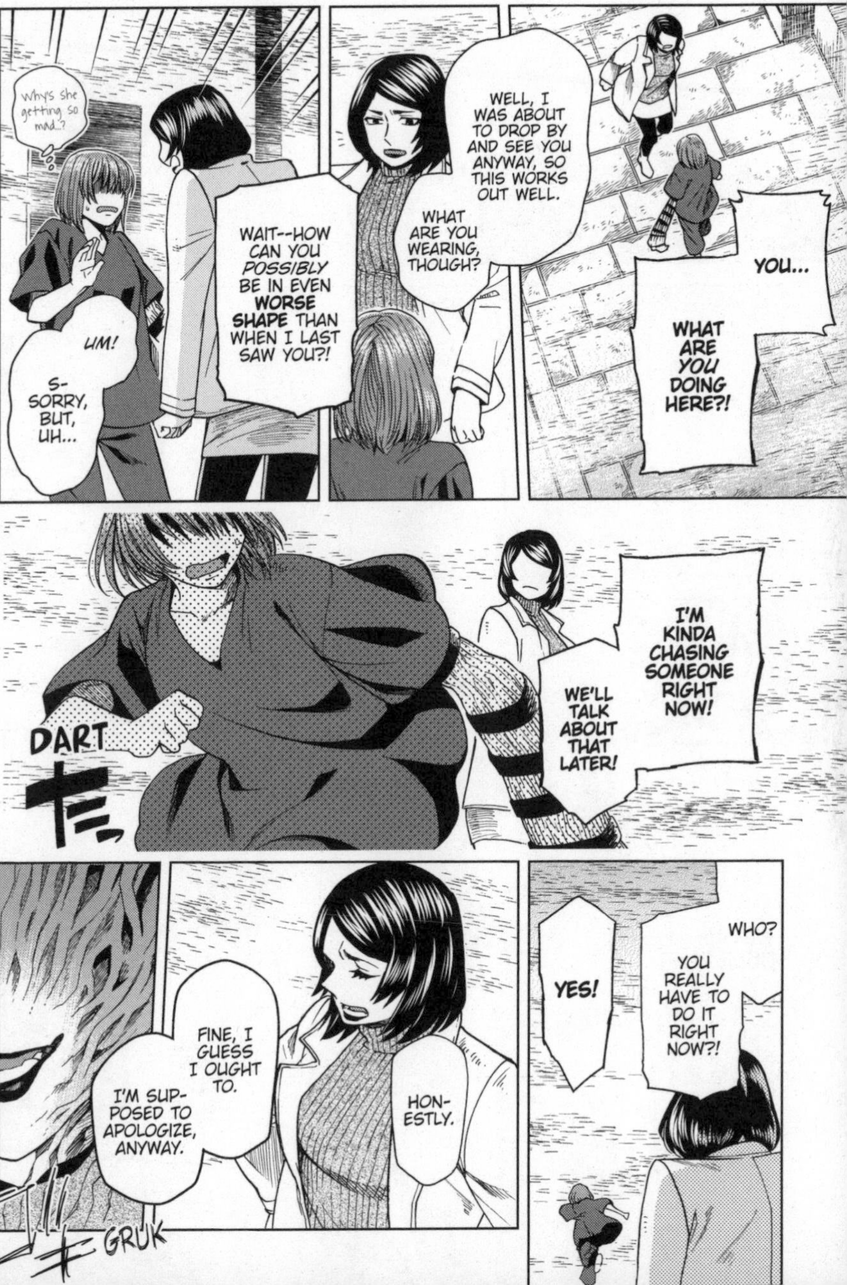
YOU...
WHAT ARE YOU DOING HERE?!
WELL, I WAS ABOUT TO DROP BY AND SEE YOU ANYWAY, SO THIS WORKS OUT WELL.
WHAT ARE YOU WEARING, THOUGH?
WAIT--HOW CAN YOU POSSIBLY BE IN EVEN WORSE SHAPE THAN WHEN I LAST SAW YOU?!
Why's she getting so mad..?
UM!
S-SORRY, BUT, UH...
I'M KINDA CHASING SOMEONE RIGHT NOW!
WE'LL TALK ABOUT THAT LATER!
DART
WHO?
YOU REALLY HAVE TO DO IT RIGHT NOW?!
YES!
HON-ESTLY.
FINE, I GUESS I OUGHT TO.
I'M SUP-POSED TO APOLOGIZE, ANYWAY.
GRUK

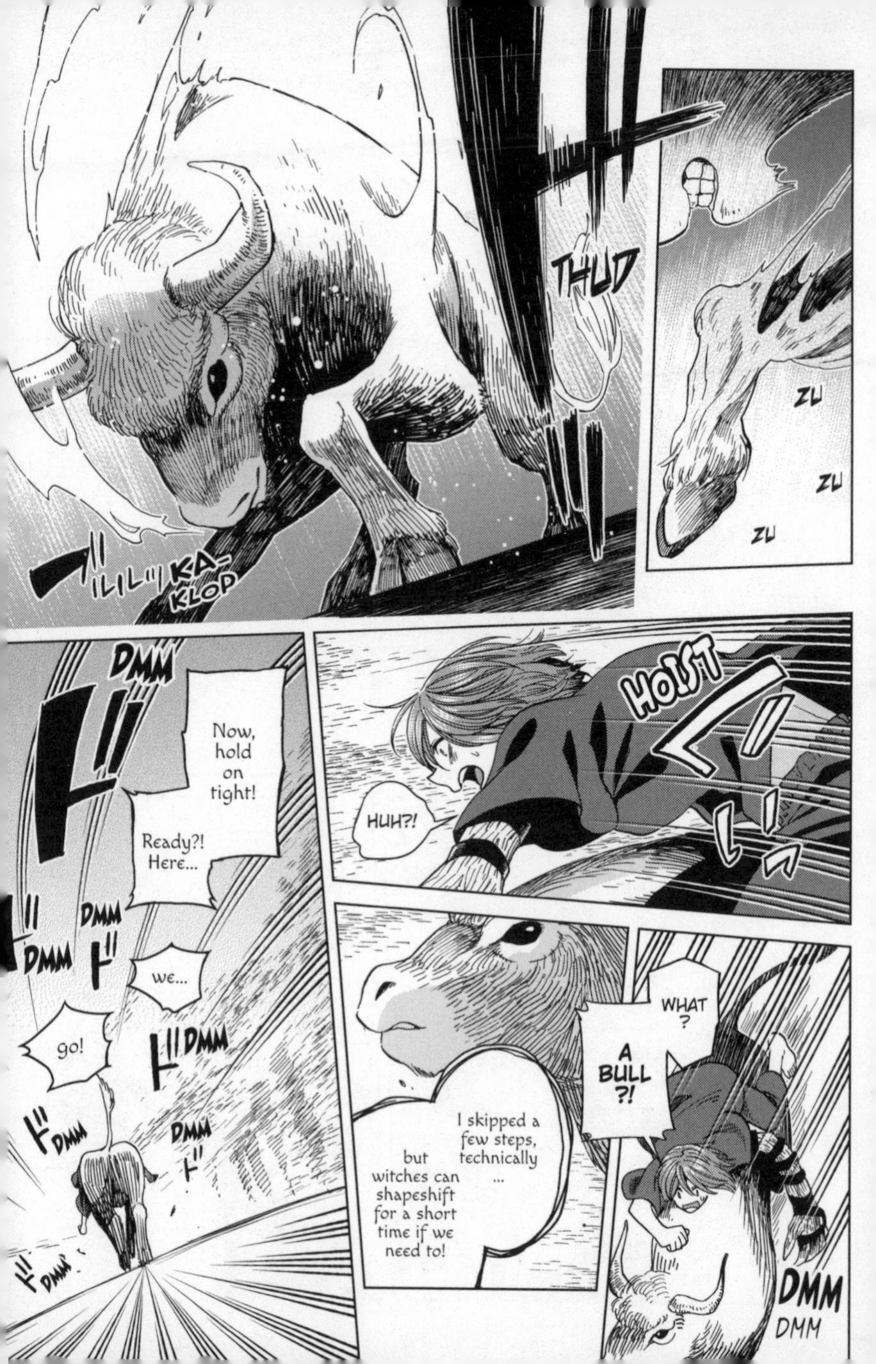
ZU
ZU
ZU
THUD
KA-
KLOP
HOIST
HUH?!
WHAT?
A BULL?!
DMM
DMM
I skipped a few steps, technically...
but witches can shapeshift for a short time if we need to!
DMM
Now, hold on tight!
Ready?! Here...
DMM
DMM
we...
go!
DMM
DMM
DMM
DMM

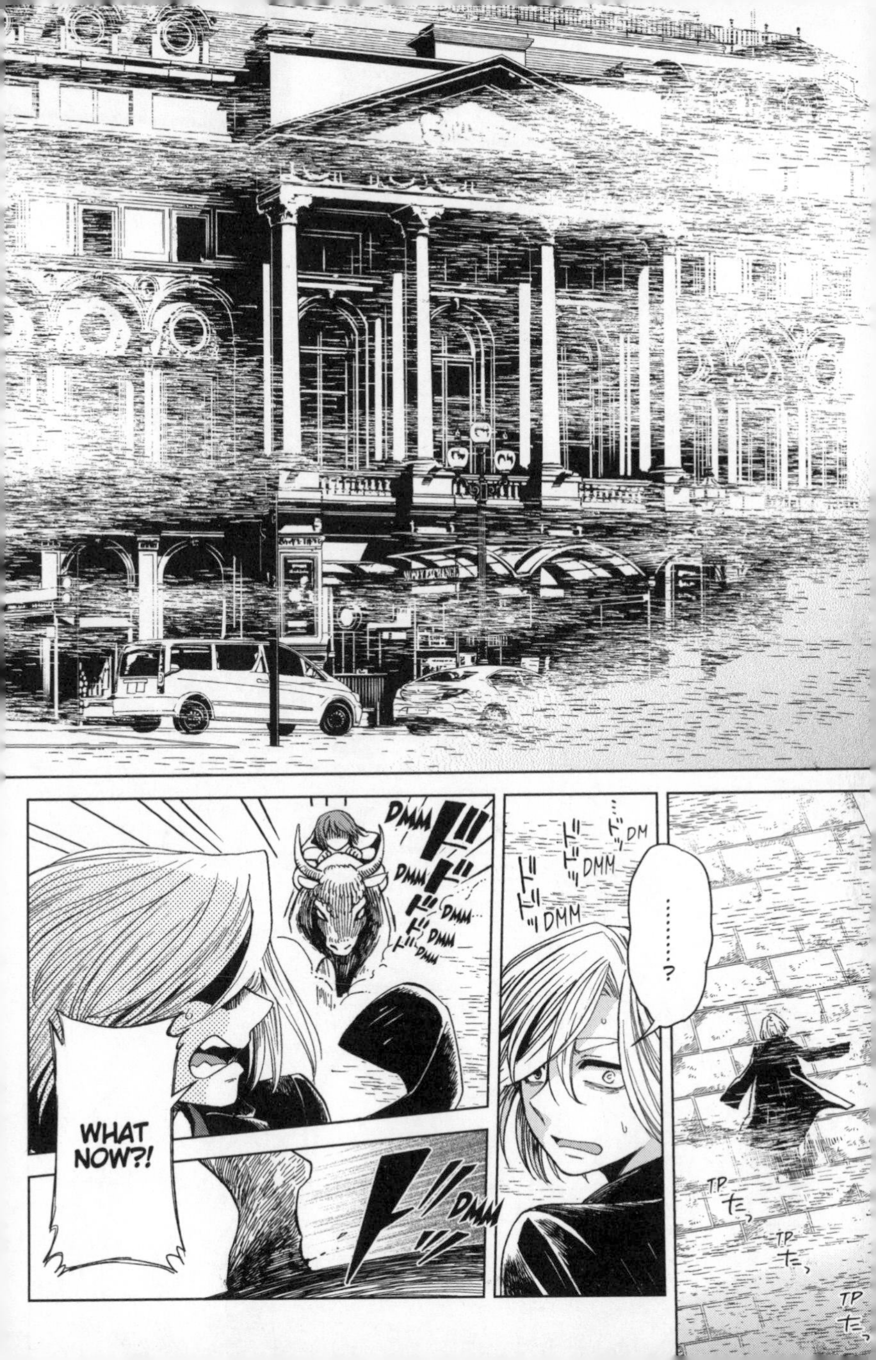
MONEY EXCHANGE
TP たっ
TP たっ
TP たっ
ドッ DM
ドッドッ DMM
ドッドッ DMM
......?
DMM ド!!
DMM ド
ドッ DMM
ド DMM
ドッ DMM
WHAT NOW?!
DMM

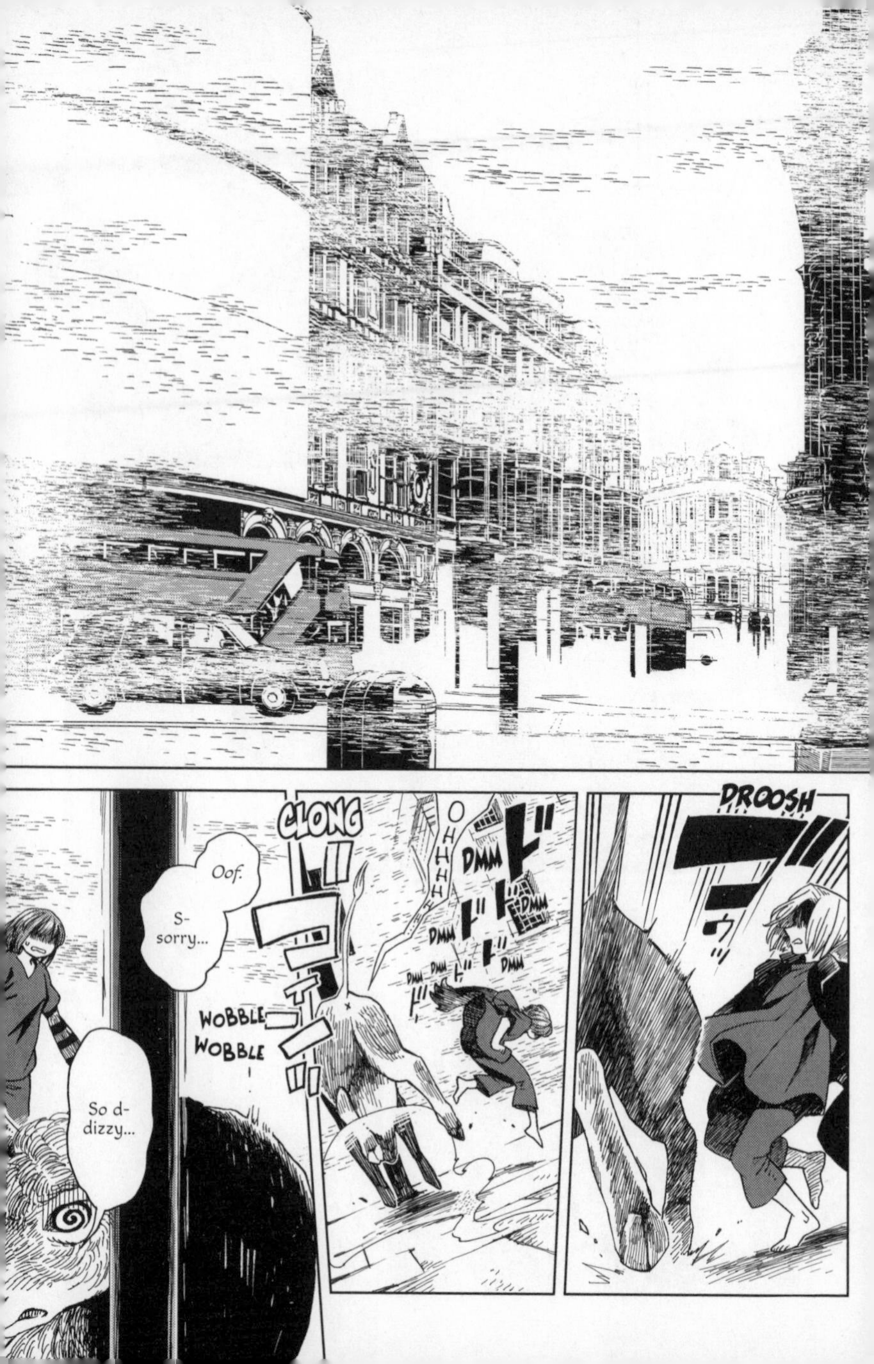
DROOSH
CLONG
OHHHHH
DMM
DMM
DMM
DMM
DMM
DMM
WOBBLE WOBBLE
Oof.
S-sorry...
So d-dizzy...

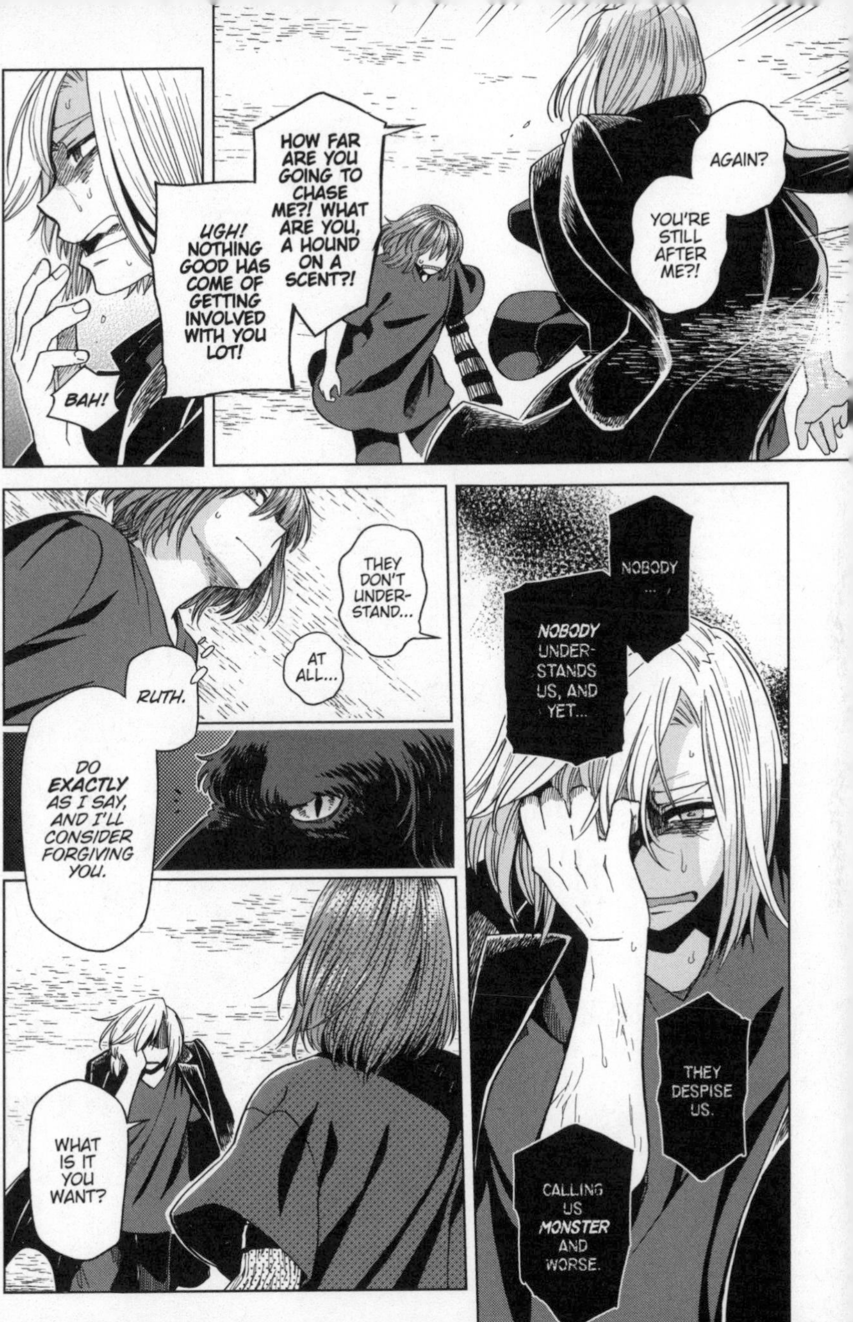
AGAIN?
YOU'RE STILL AFTER ME?!
HOW FAR ARE YOU GOING TO CHASE ME?! WHAT ARE YOU, A HOUND ON A SCENT?!
UGH! NOTHING GOOD HAS COME OF GETTING INVOLVED WITH YOU LOT!
BAH!
NOBODY...
NOBODY UNDERSTANDS US, AND YET...
THEY DESPISE US.
CALLING US MONSTER AND WORSE.
THEY DON'T UNDERSTAND...
AT ALL...
RUTH.
DO EXACTLY AS I SAY, AND I'LL CONSIDER FORGIVING YOU.
WHAT IS IT YOU WANT?

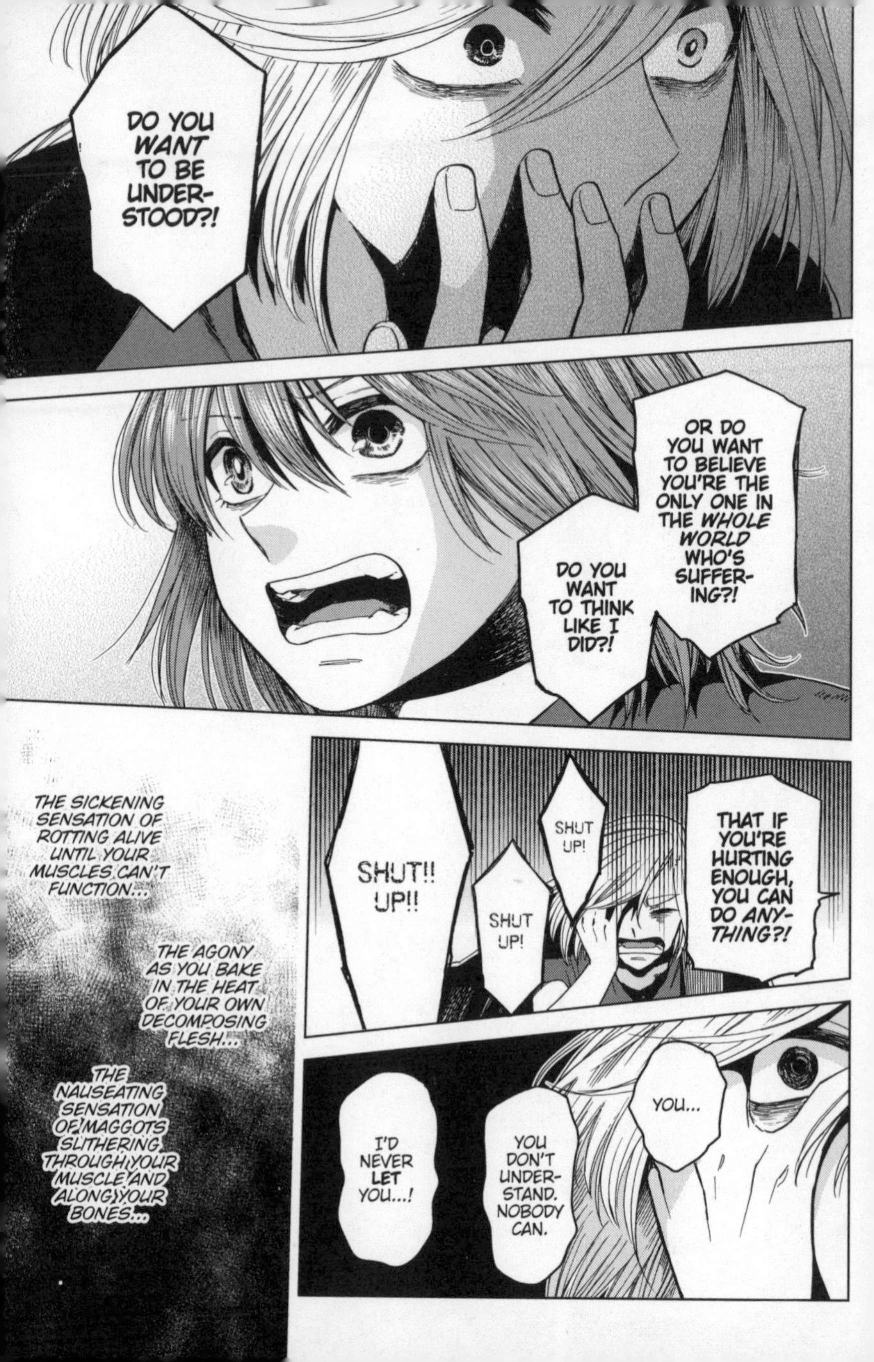
DO YOU WANT TO BE UNDERSTOOD?!
OR DO YOU WANT TO BELIEVE YOU'RE THE ONLY ONE IN THE WHOLE WORLD WHO'S SUFFERING?!
DO YOU WANT TO THINK LIKE I DID?!
THAT IF YOU'RE HURTING ENOUGH, YOU CAN DO ANYTHING?!
SHUT UP!
SHUT UP!
SHUT!! UP!!
YOU...
YOU DON'T UNDERSTAND. NOBODY CAN.
I'D NEVER LET YOU...!
THE SICKENING SENSATION OF ROTTING ALIVE UNTIL YOUR MUSCLES CAN'T FUNCTION...
THE AGONY AS YOU BAKE IN THE HEAT OF YOUR OWN DECOMPOSING FLESH...
THE NAUSEATING SENSATION OF MAGGOTS SLITHERING THROUGH YOUR MUSCLE AND ALONG YOUR BONES...

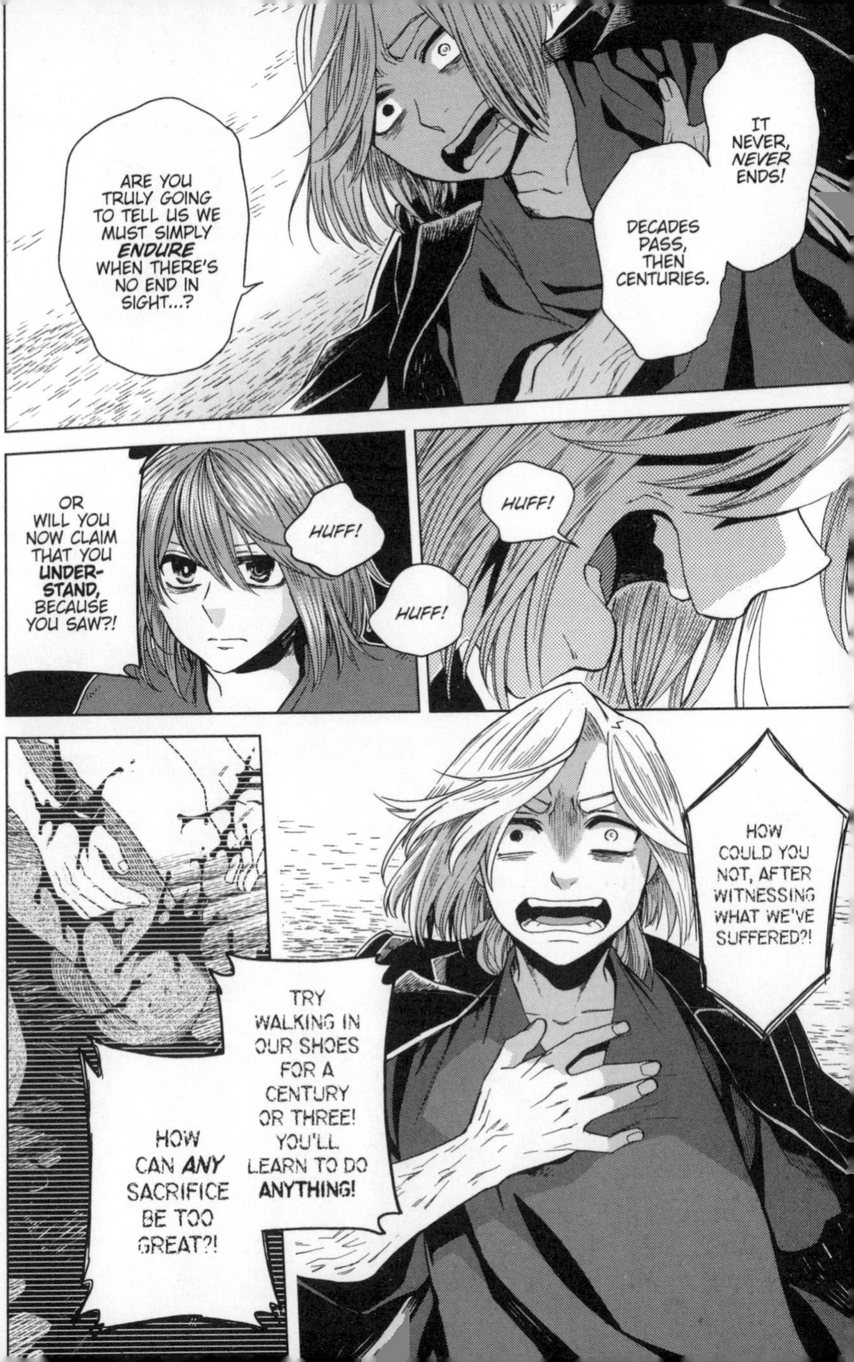
IT NEVER, NEVER ENDS!
DECADES PASS, THEN CENTURIES.
ARE YOU TRULY GOING TO TELL US WE MUST SIMPLY ENDURE WHEN THERE'S NO END IN SIGHT...?
HUFF!
HUFF!
HUFF!
OR WILL YOU NOW CLAIM THAT YOU UNDER-STAND, BECAUSE YOU SAW?!
HOW COULD YOU NOT, AFTER WITNESSING WHAT WE'VE SUFFERED?!
TRY WALKING IN OUR SHOES FOR A CENTURY OR THREE! YOU'LL LEARN TO DO ANYTHING!
HOW CAN ANY SACRIFICE BE TOO GREAT?!

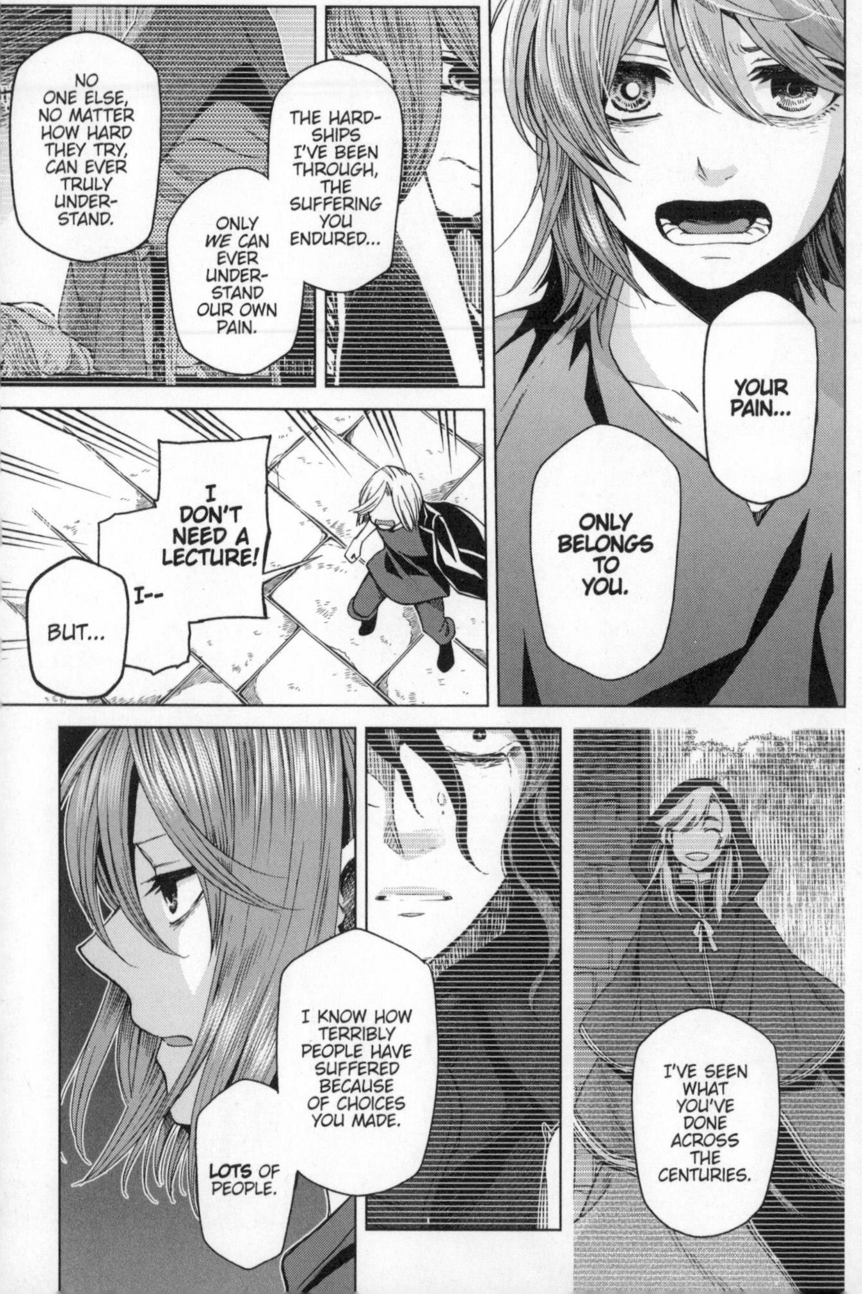
YOUR PAIN...
ONLY BELONGS TO YOU.
THE HARDSHIPS I'VE BEEN THROUGH, THE SUFFERING YOU ENDURED...
ONLY *WE* CAN EVER UNDERSTAND OUR OWN PAIN.
NO ONE ELSE, NO MATTER HOW HARD THEY TRY, CAN EVER TRULY UNDERSTAND.
I DON'T NEED A LECTURE!
I--
BUT...
I'VE SEEN WHAT YOU'VE DONE ACROSS THE CENTURIES.
I KNOW HOW TERRIBLY PEOPLE HAVE SUFFERED BECAUSE OF CHOICES YOU MADE.
LOTS OF PEOPLE.

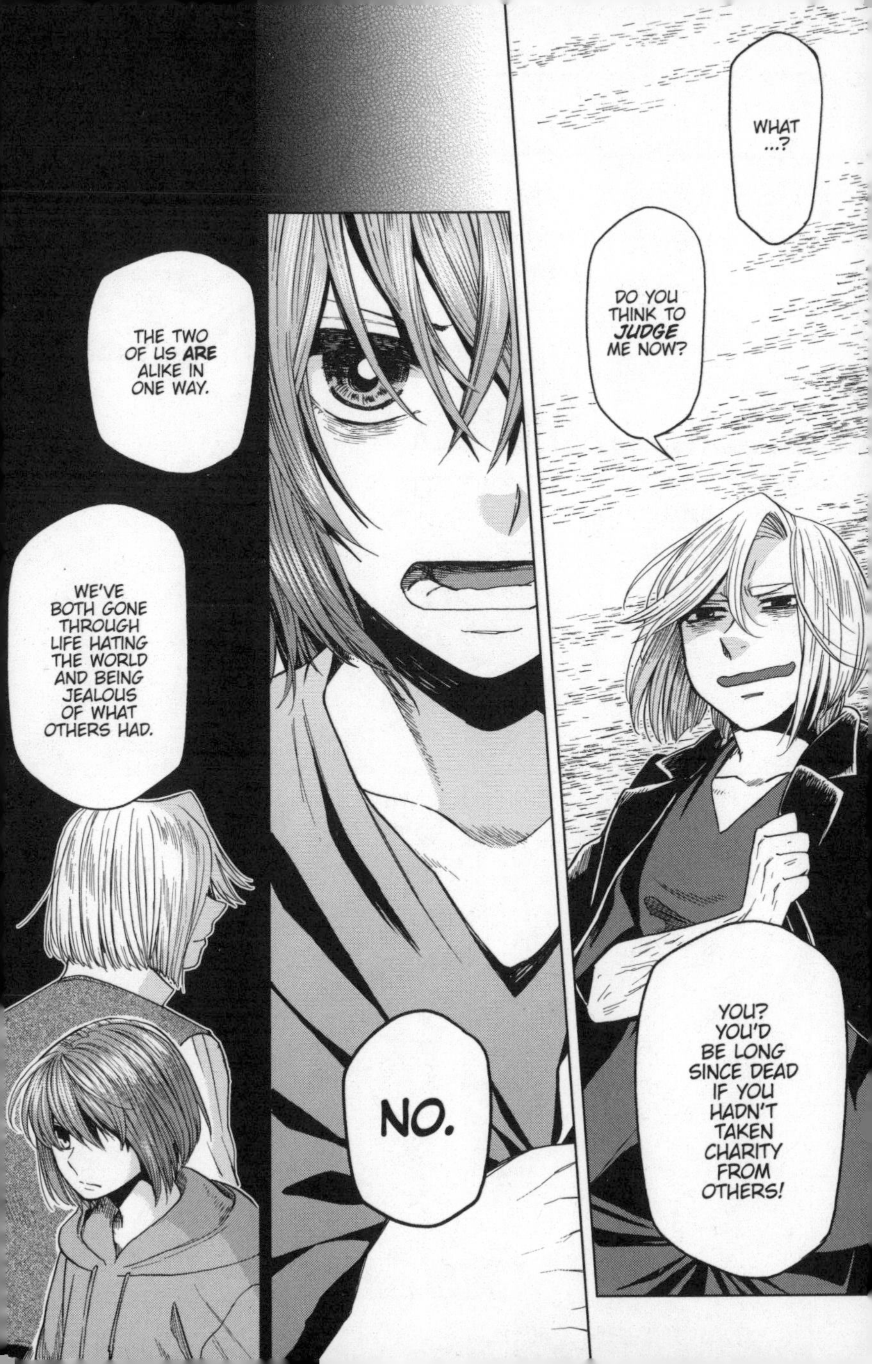
WHAT ...?
DO YOU THINK TO JUDGE ME NOW?
YOU? YOU'D BE LONG SINCE DEAD IF YOU HADN'T TAKEN CHARITY FROM OTHERS!
NO.
THE TWO OF US ARE ALIKE IN ONE WAY.
WE'VE BOTH GONE THROUGH LIFE HATING THE WORLD AND BEING JEALOUS OF WHAT OTHERS HAD.

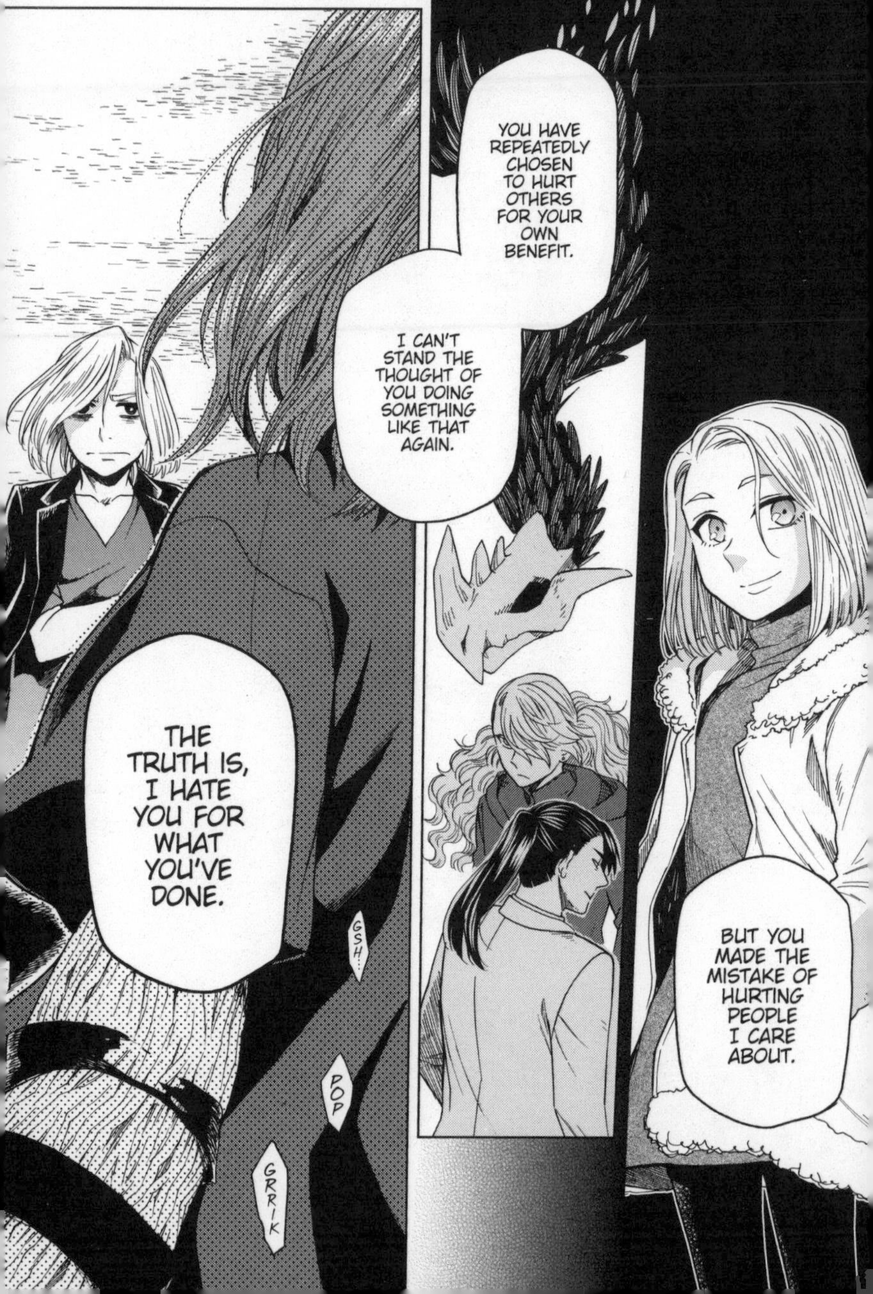
YOU HAVE REPEATEDLY CHOSEN TO HURT OTHERS FOR YOUR OWN BENEFIT.
I CAN'T STAND THE THOUGHT OF YOU DOING SOMETHING LIKE THAT AGAIN.
BUT YOU MADE THE MISTAKE OF HURTING PEOPLE I CARE ABOUT.
THE TRUTH IS, I HATE YOU FOR WHAT YOU'VE DONE.
GSH...
POP
GRRIK

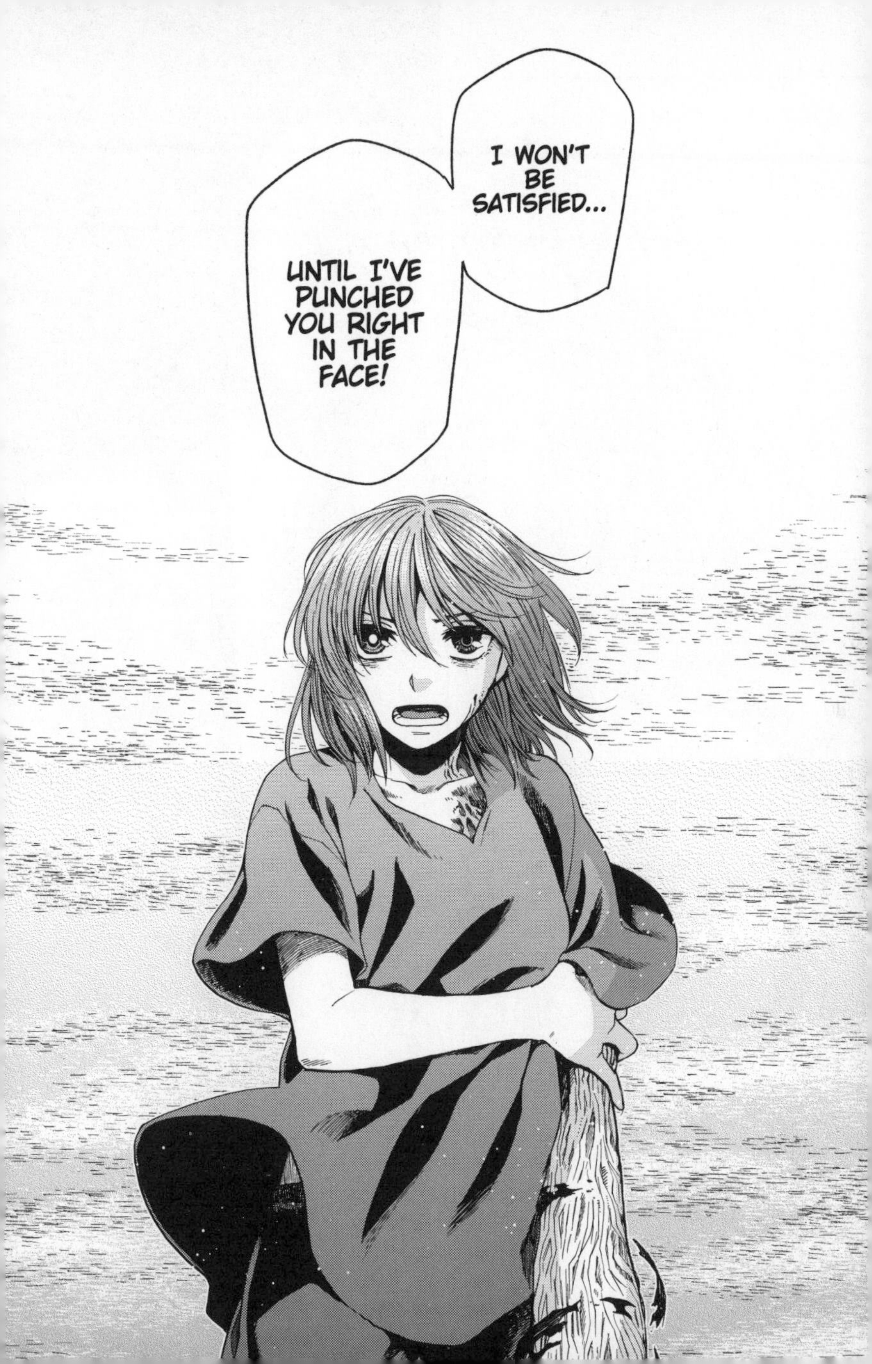
I WON'T BE SATISFIED...
UNTIL I'VE PUNCHED YOU RIGHT IN THE FACE!

Chapter 45: Live and let live.

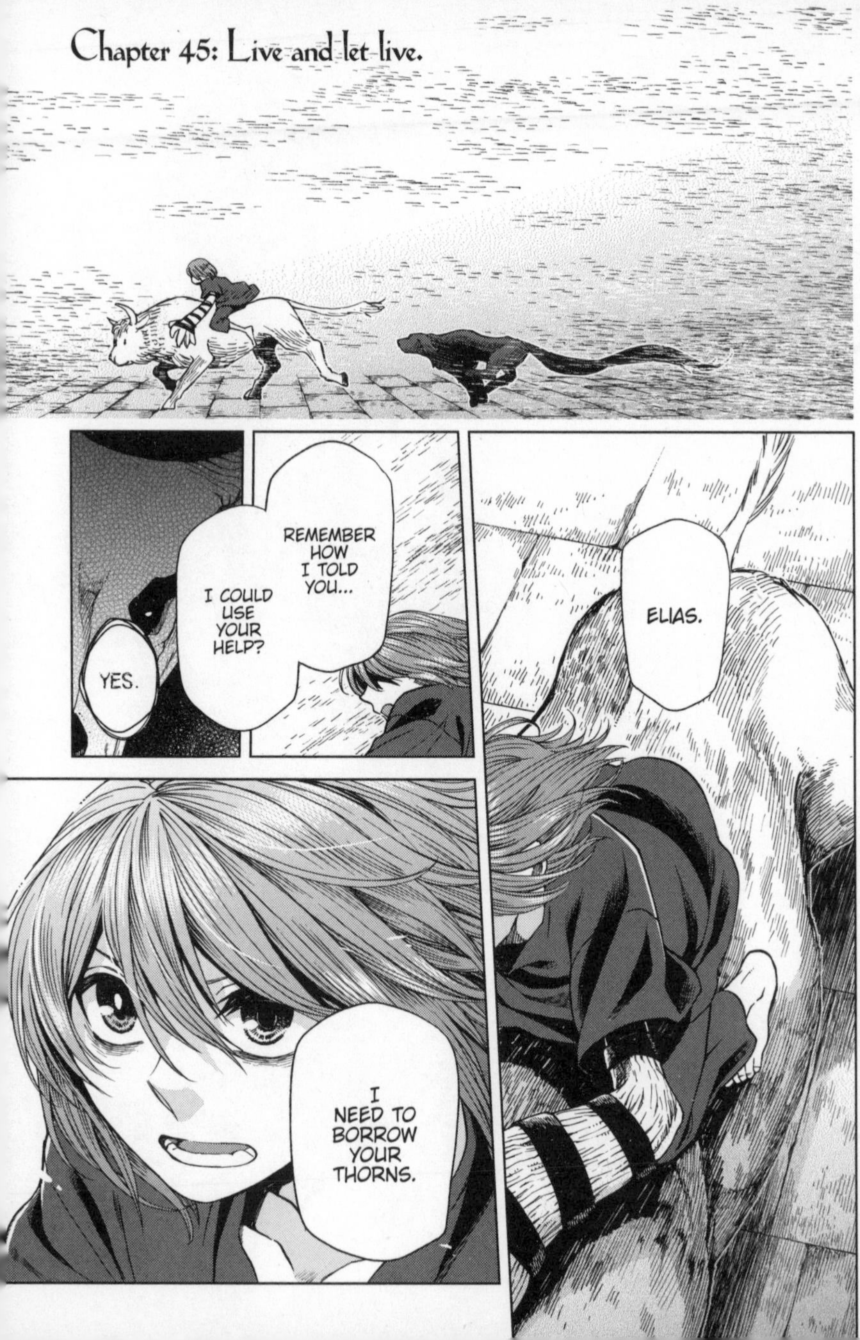
ELIAS.
REMEMBER HOW I TOLD YOU...
I COULD USE YOUR HELP?
YES.
I NEED TO BORROW YOUR THORNS.

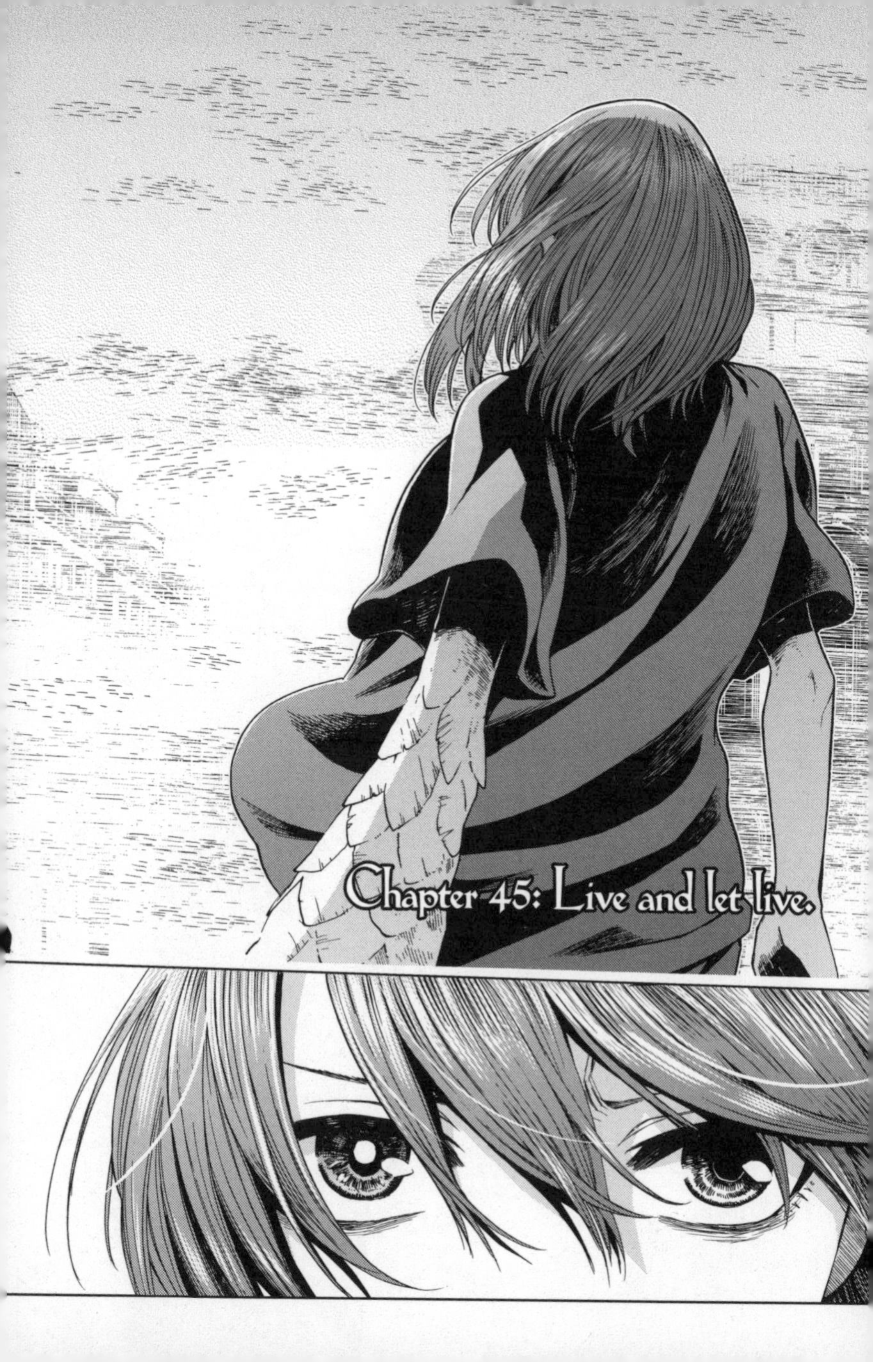
Chapter 45: Live and let live.

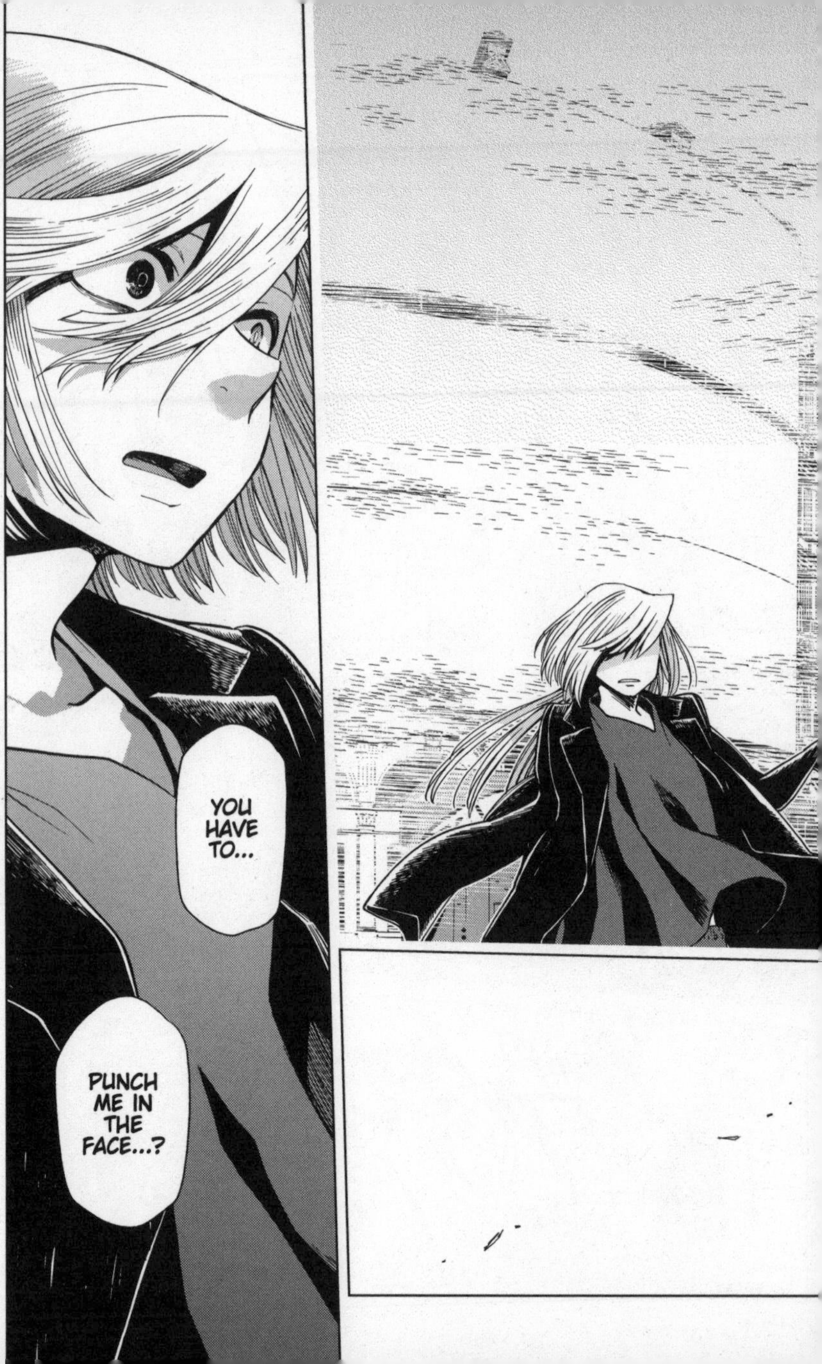
YOU HAVE TO...
PUNCH ME IN THE FACE...?

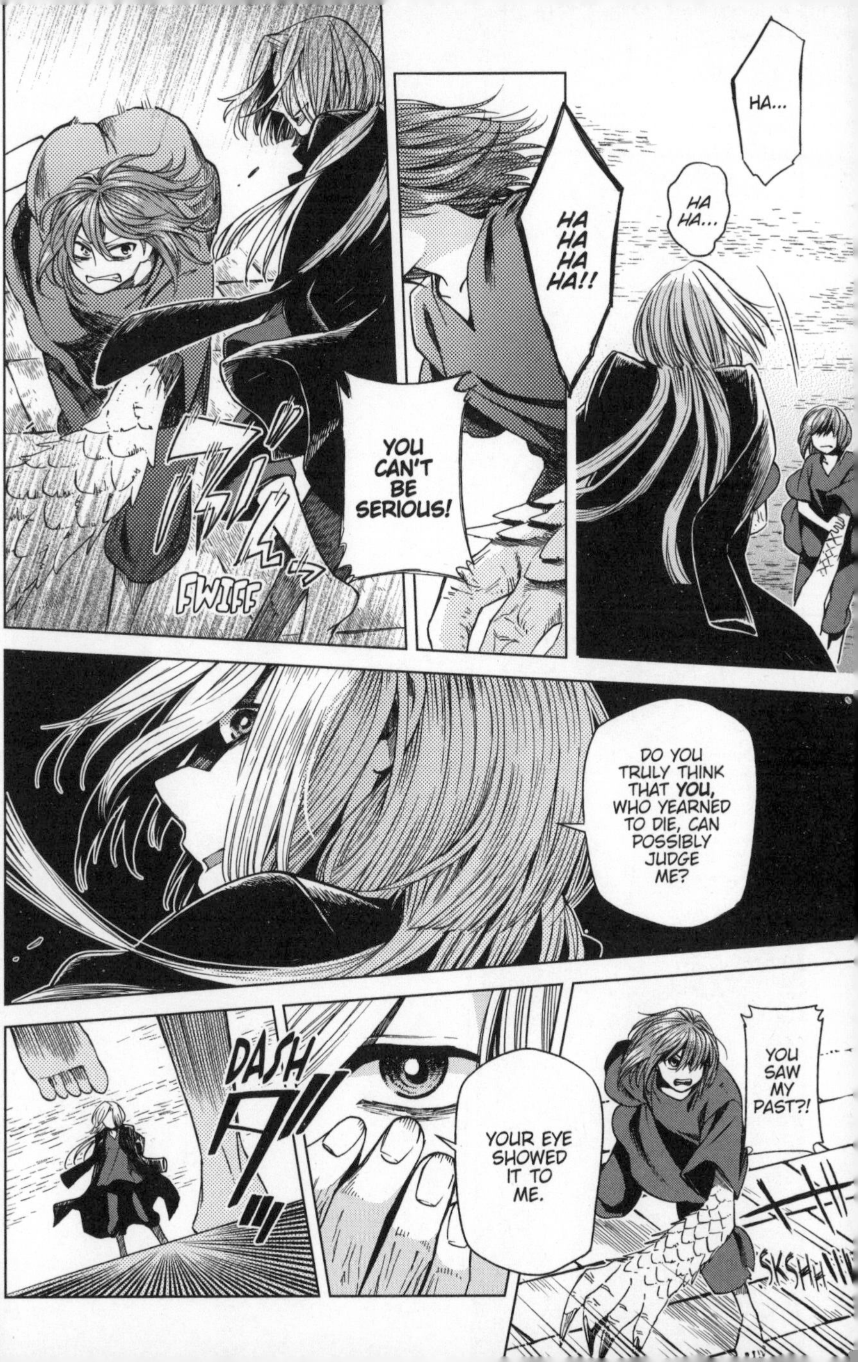
HA...
HA HA...
HA HA HA HA!!
YOU CAN'T BE SERIOUS!
FWIFF
DO YOU TRULY THINK THAT **YOU**, WHO YEARNED TO DIE, CAN POSSIBLY JUDGE ME?
YOU SAW MY PAST?!
SKSHH
YOUR EYE SHOWED IT TO ME.
DASH

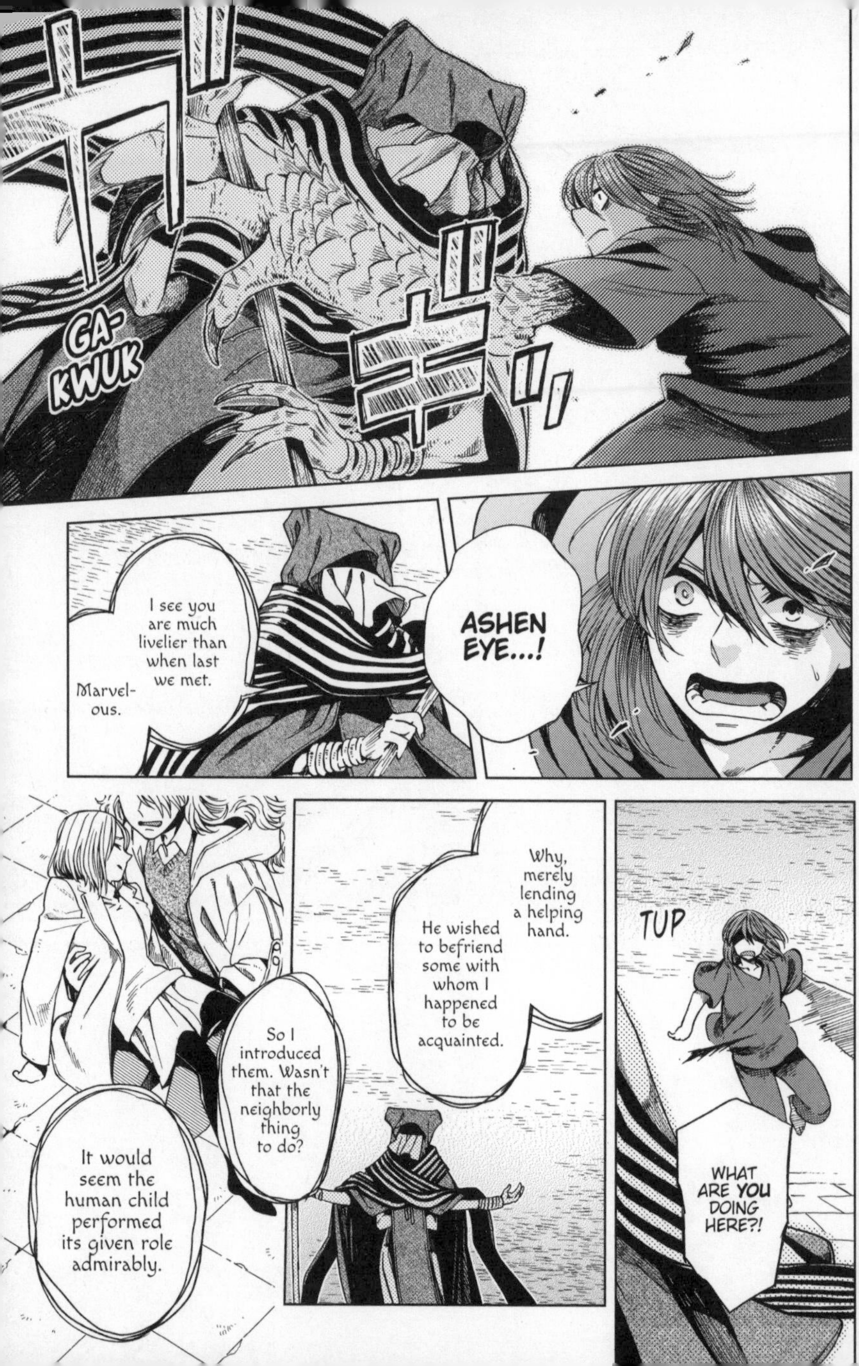
GA-KWUK
ASHEN EYE...!
I see you are much livelier than when last we met.
Marvelous.
TUP
WHAT ARE YOU DOING HERE?!
Why, merely lending a helping hand.
He wished to befriend some with whom I happened to be acquainted.
So I introduced them. Wasn't that the neighborly thing to do?
It would seem the human child performed its given role admirably.

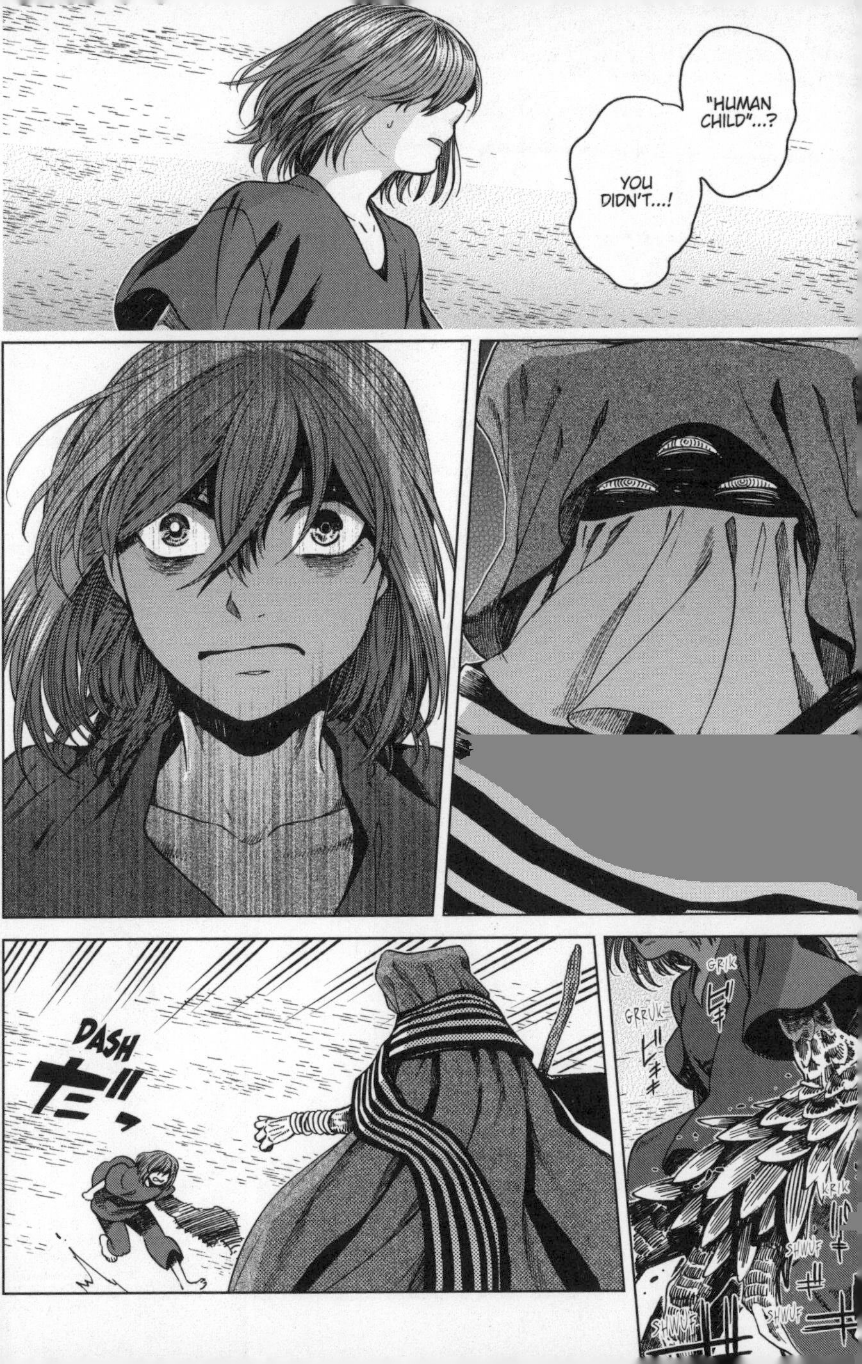
"HUMAN CHILD"...?
YOU DIDN'T...!
GRIK
GRRUK
KRIK
SHWUF
SHWUF
SHWUF
DASH

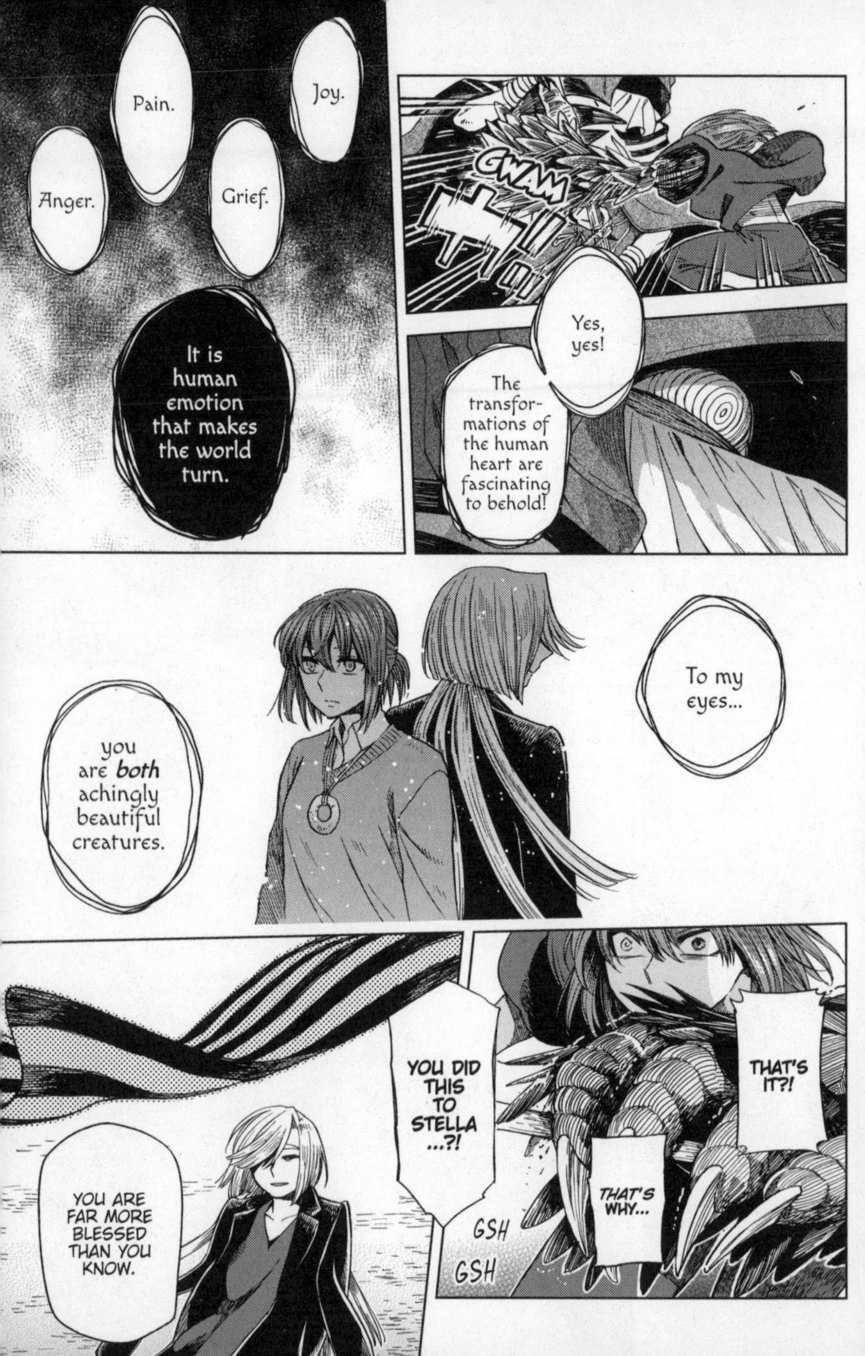
GWAM
Yes, yes!
The transformations of the human heart are fascinating to behold!
Joy.
Pain.
Grief.
Anger.
It is human emotion that makes the world turn.
To my eyes...
you are *both* achingly beautiful creatures.
THAT'S IT?!
THAT'S WHY...
YOU DID THIS TO STELLA ...?!
GSH
GSH
YOU ARE FAR MORE BLESSED THAN YOU KNOW.

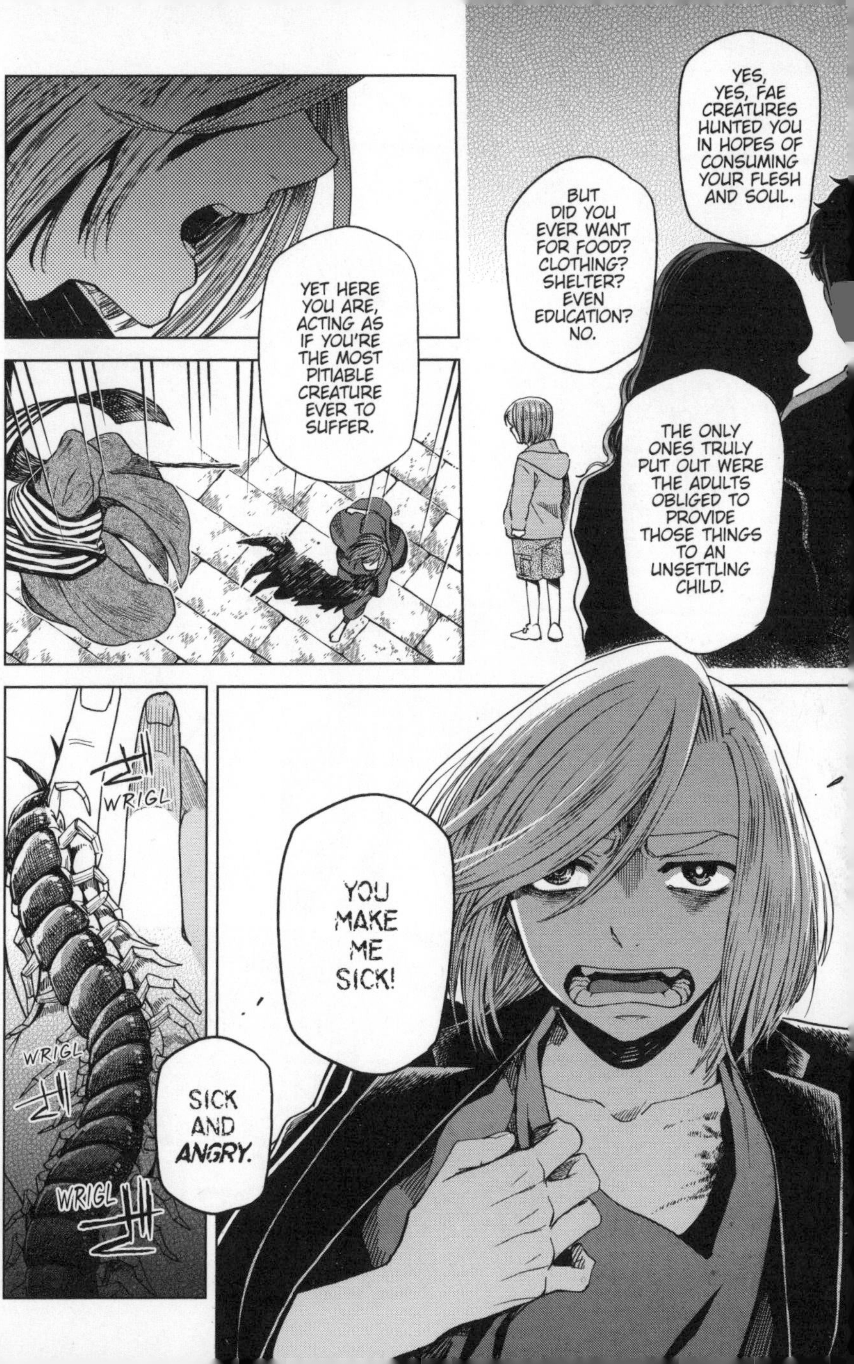
YES, YES, FAE CREATURES HUNTED YOU IN HOPES OF CONSUMING YOUR FLESH AND SOUL.
BUT DID YOU EVER WANT FOR FOOD? CLOTHING? SHELTER? EVEN EDUCATION? NO.
THE ONLY ONES TRULY PUT OUT WERE THE ADULTS OBLIGED TO PROVIDE THOSE THINGS TO AN UNSETTLING CHILD.
YET HERE YOU ARE, ACTING AS IF YOU'RE THE MOST PITIABLE CREATURE EVER TO SUFFER.
YOU MAKE ME SICK!
SICK AND ANGRY.
WRIGL
WRIGL
WRIGL

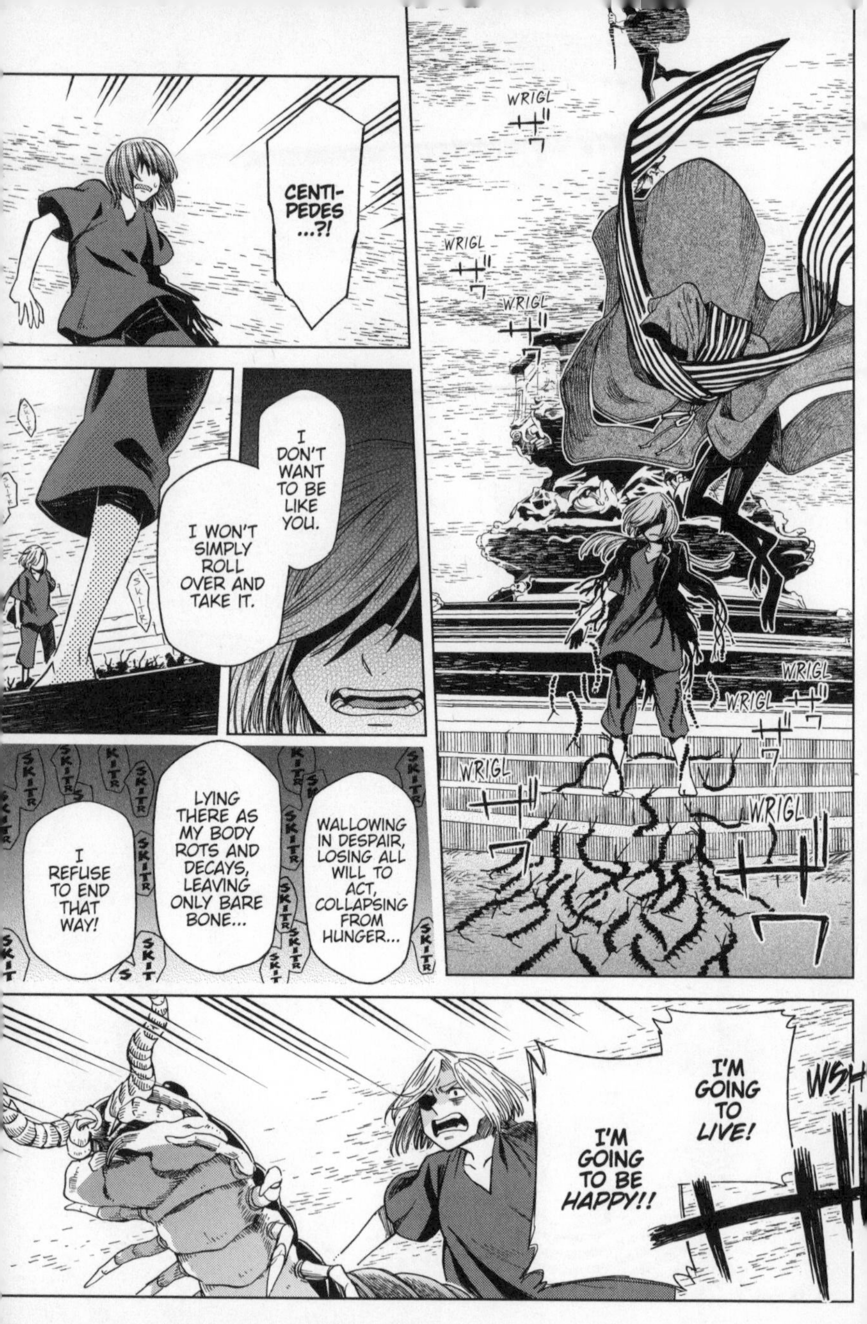
WRIGL
WRIGL
WRIGL
WRIGL
WRIGL
WRIGL
WRIGL
CENTIPEDES...?!
I DON'T WANT TO BE LIKE YOU.
I WON'T SIMPLY ROLL OVER AND TAKE IT.
SKITR
SKITR
SKITR
WALLOWING IN DESPAIR, LOSING ALL WILL TO ACT, COLLAPSING FROM HUNGER...
LYING THERE AS MY BODY ROTS AND DECAYS, LEAVING ONLY BARE BONE...
I REFUSE TO END THAT WAY!
SKITR
WSH
I'M GOING TO LIVE!
I'M GOING TO BE HAPPY!!

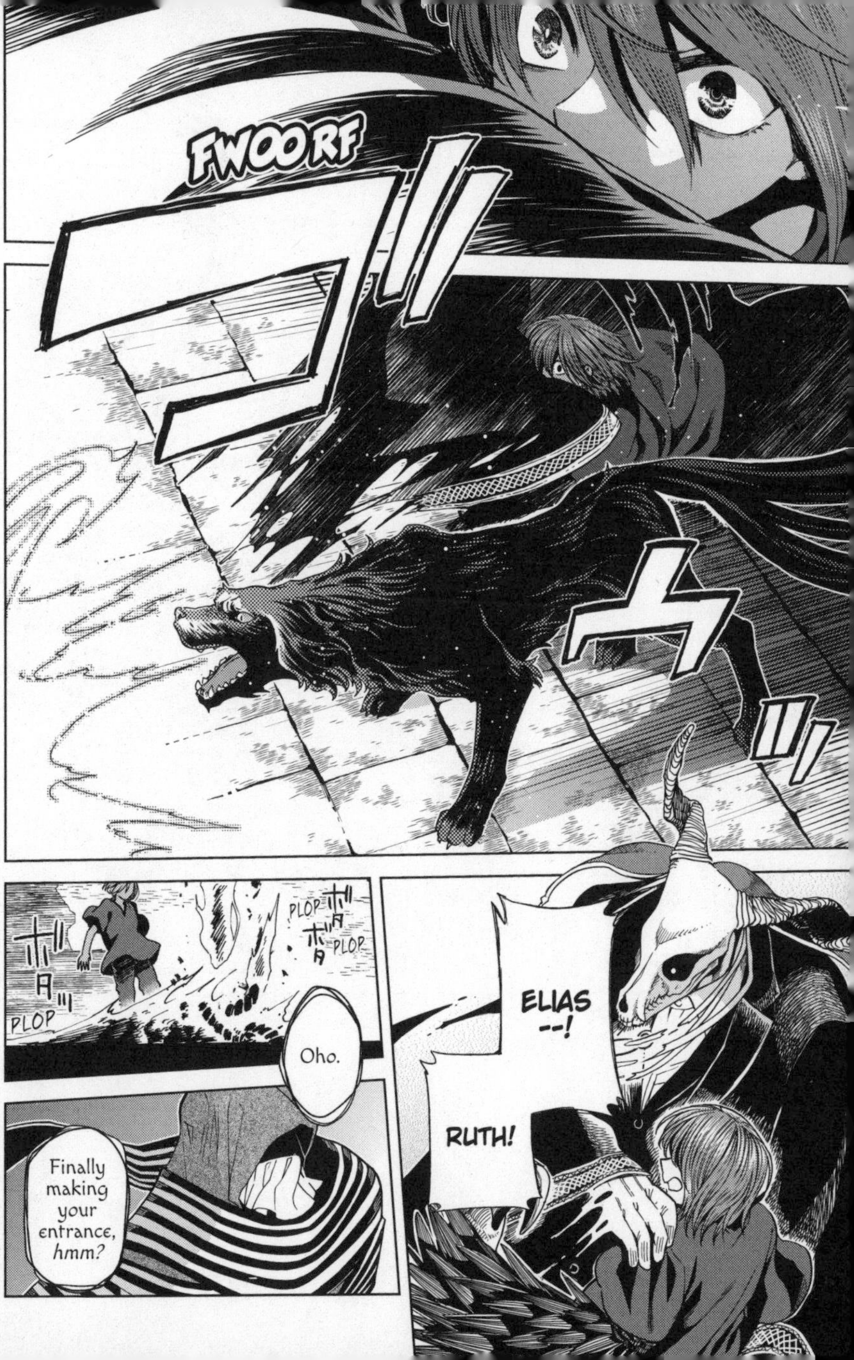
FWOORF
ELIAS --!
RUTH!
PLOP
PLOP
PLOP
Oho.
Finally making your entrance, hmm?

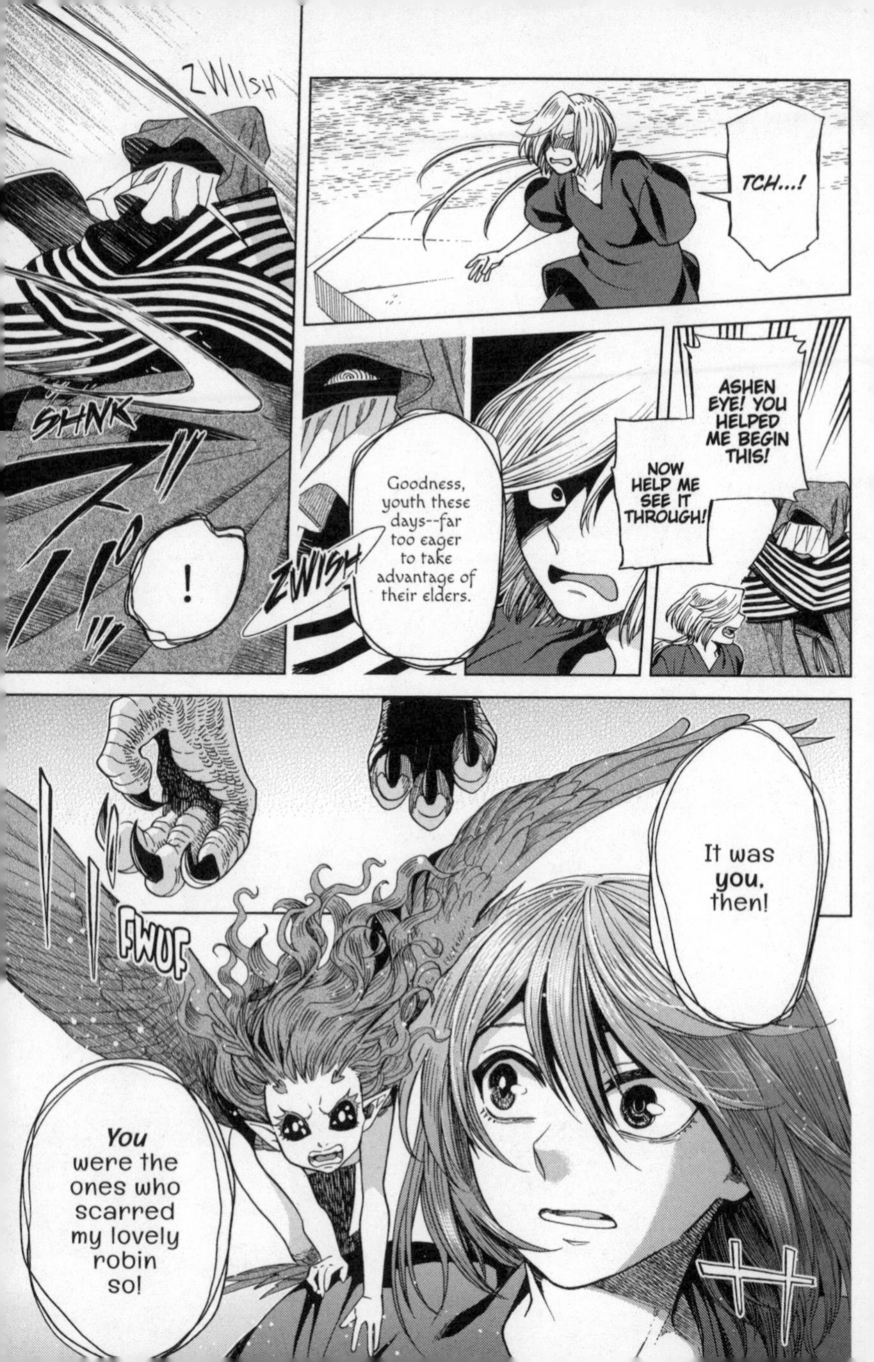
TCH...!
ASHEN EYE! YOU HELPED ME BEGIN THIS!
NOW HELP ME SEE IT THROUGH!
Goodness, youth these days--far too eager to take advantage of their elders.
ZWISH
ZWIISH
SHNK
!
It was you, then!
FWUF
You were the ones who scarred my lovely robin so!

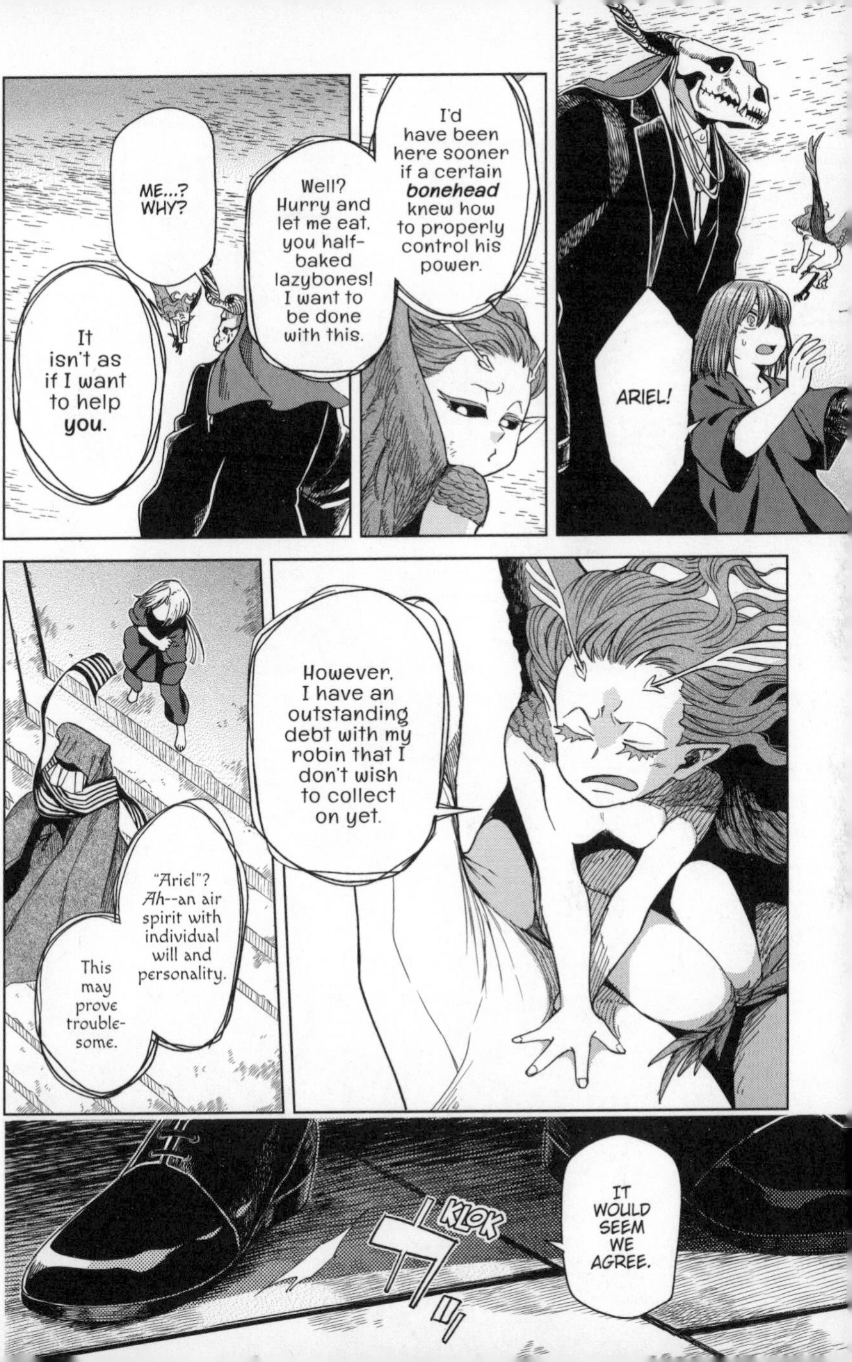
ARIEL!
I'd have been here sooner if a certain *bonehead* knew how to properly control his power.
Well? Hurry and let me eat, you half-baked lazybones! I want to be done with this.
ME...? WHY?
It isn't as if I want to help **you**.
However, I have an outstanding debt with my robin that I don't wish to collect on yet.
"Ariel"? *Ah*--an air spirit with individual will and personality.
This may prove trouble-some.
KLOK
IT WOULD SEEM WE AGREE.

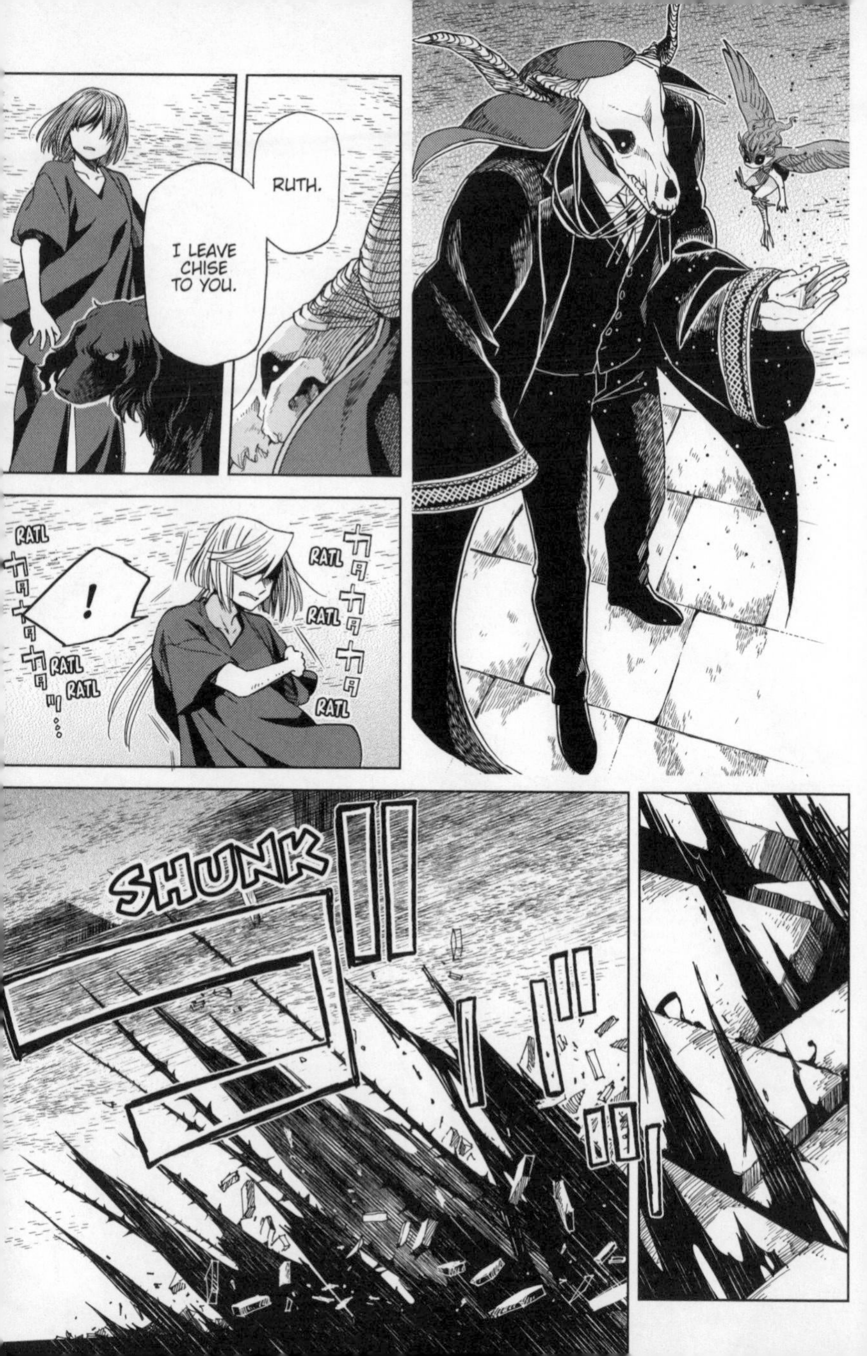
RUTH.
I LEAVE CHISE TO YOU.
RATL
RATL
RATL
!
RATL
RATL
RATL
...
SHUNK

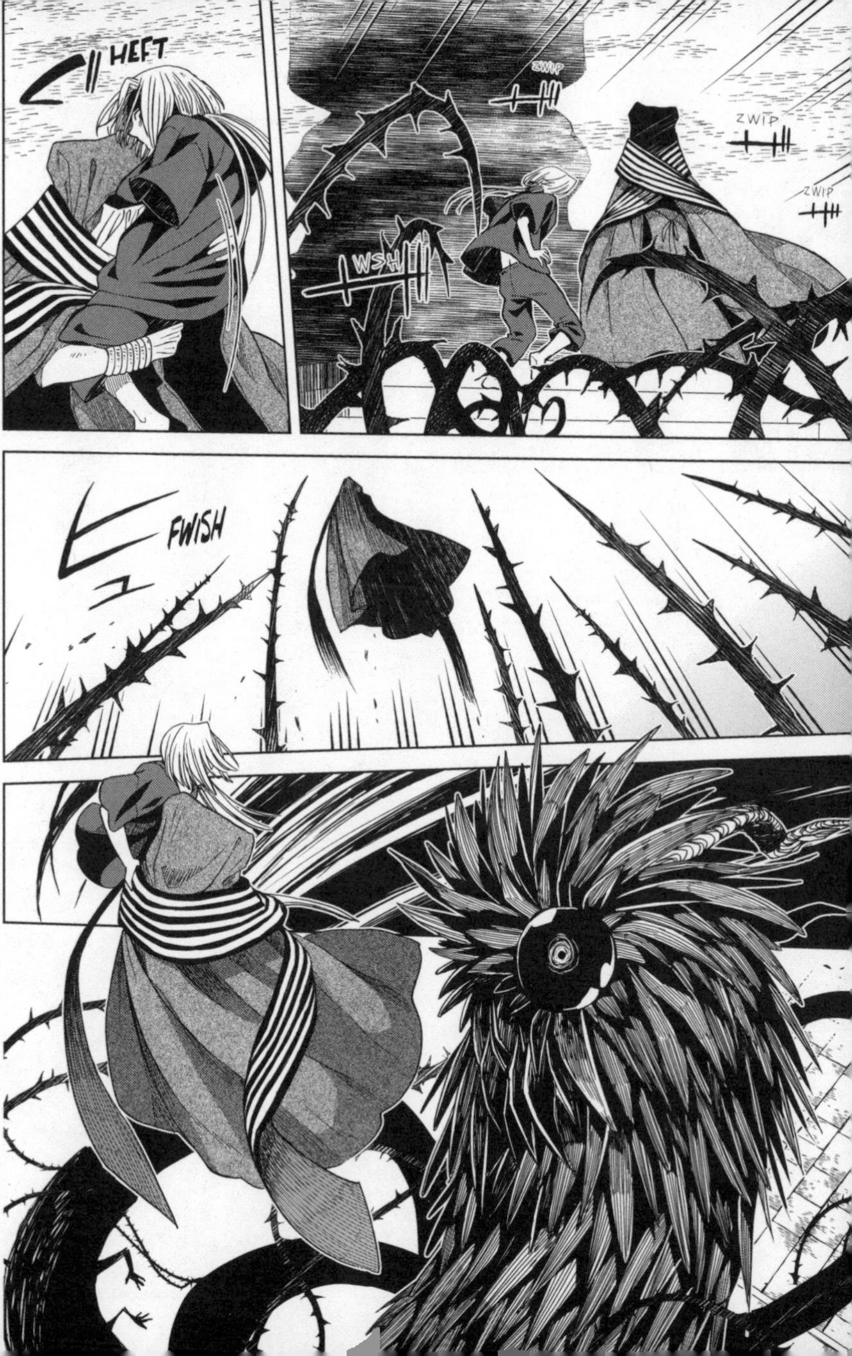
ZWIP
ZWIP
ZWIP
WSH
HEFT
FWISH

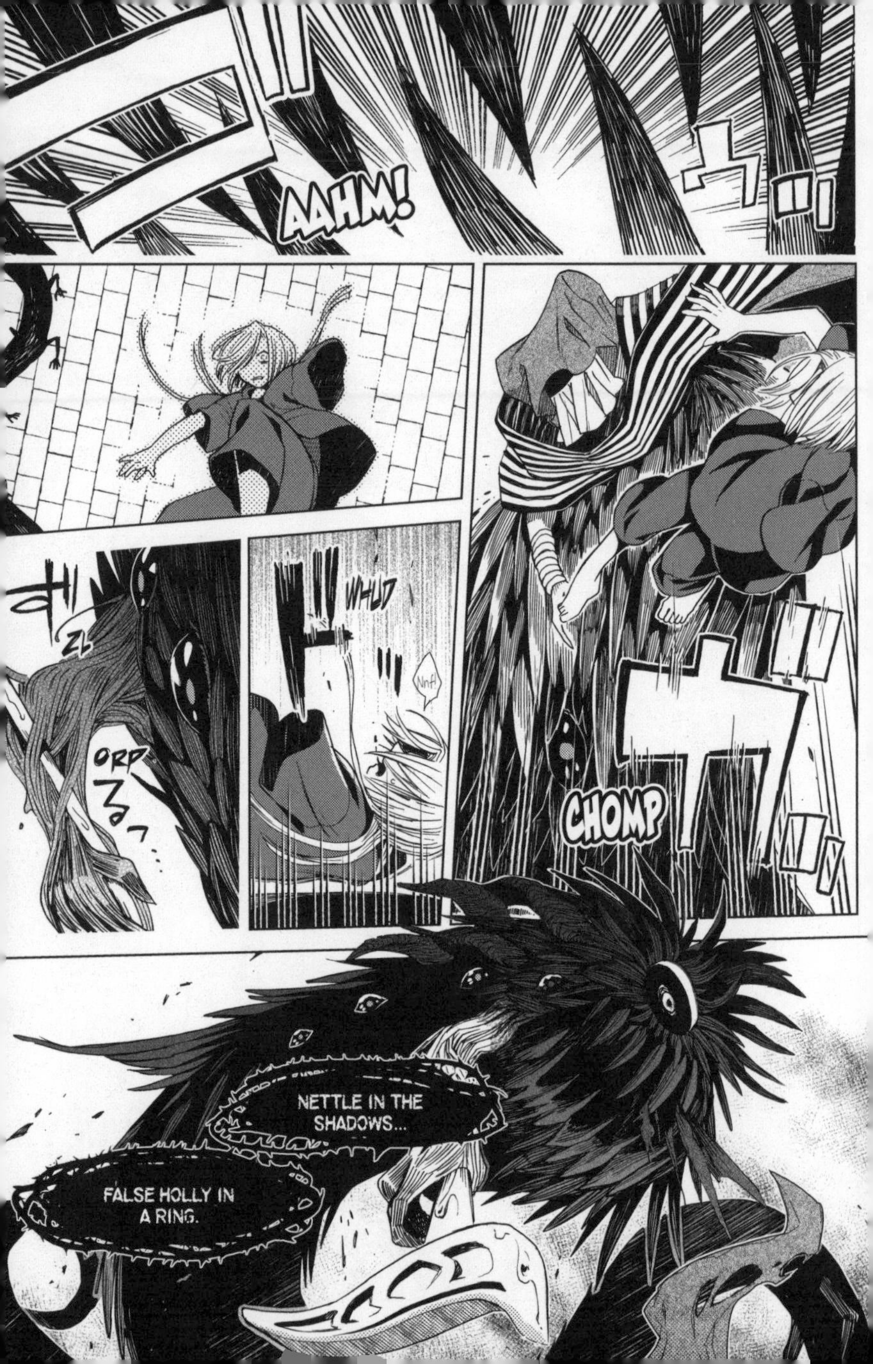
AAHM!
CHOMP
WHUD
Nnf!
ZL
ORP
NETTLE IN THE SHADOWS...
FALSE HOLLY IN A RING.

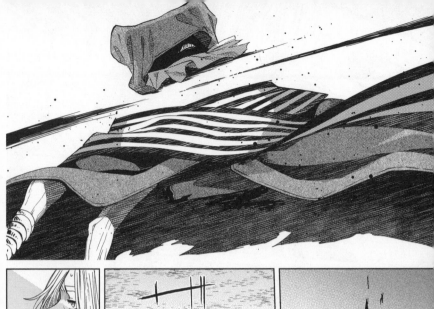

HUFF
HUFF

-SHIIIISHT

YANK

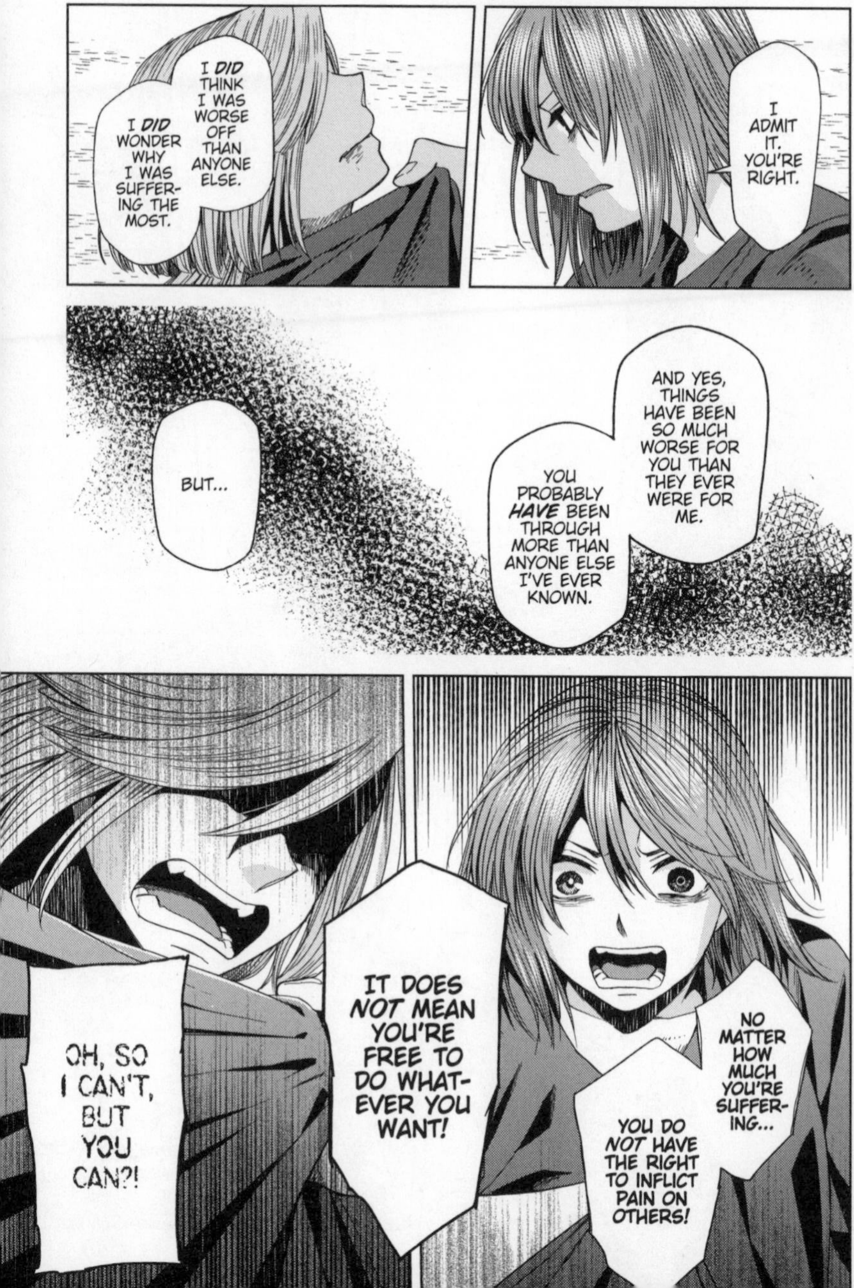
I ADMIT IT. YOU'RE RIGHT.
I *DID* THINK I WAS WORSE OFF THAN ANYONE ELSE.
I *DID* WONDER WHY I WAS SUFFERING THE MOST.
AND YES, THINGS HAVE BEEN SO MUCH WORSE FOR YOU THAN THEY EVER WERE FOR ME.
YOU PROBABLY ***HAVE*** BEEN THROUGH MORE THAN ANYONE ELSE I'VE EVER KNOWN.
BUT...
NO MATTER HOW MUCH YOU'RE SUFFERING...
IT DOES *NOT* MEAN YOU'RE FREE TO DO WHATEVER YOU WANT!
YOU DO *NOT* HAVE THE RIGHT TO INFLICT PAIN ON OTHERS!
OH, SO I CAN'T, BUT YOU CAN?!

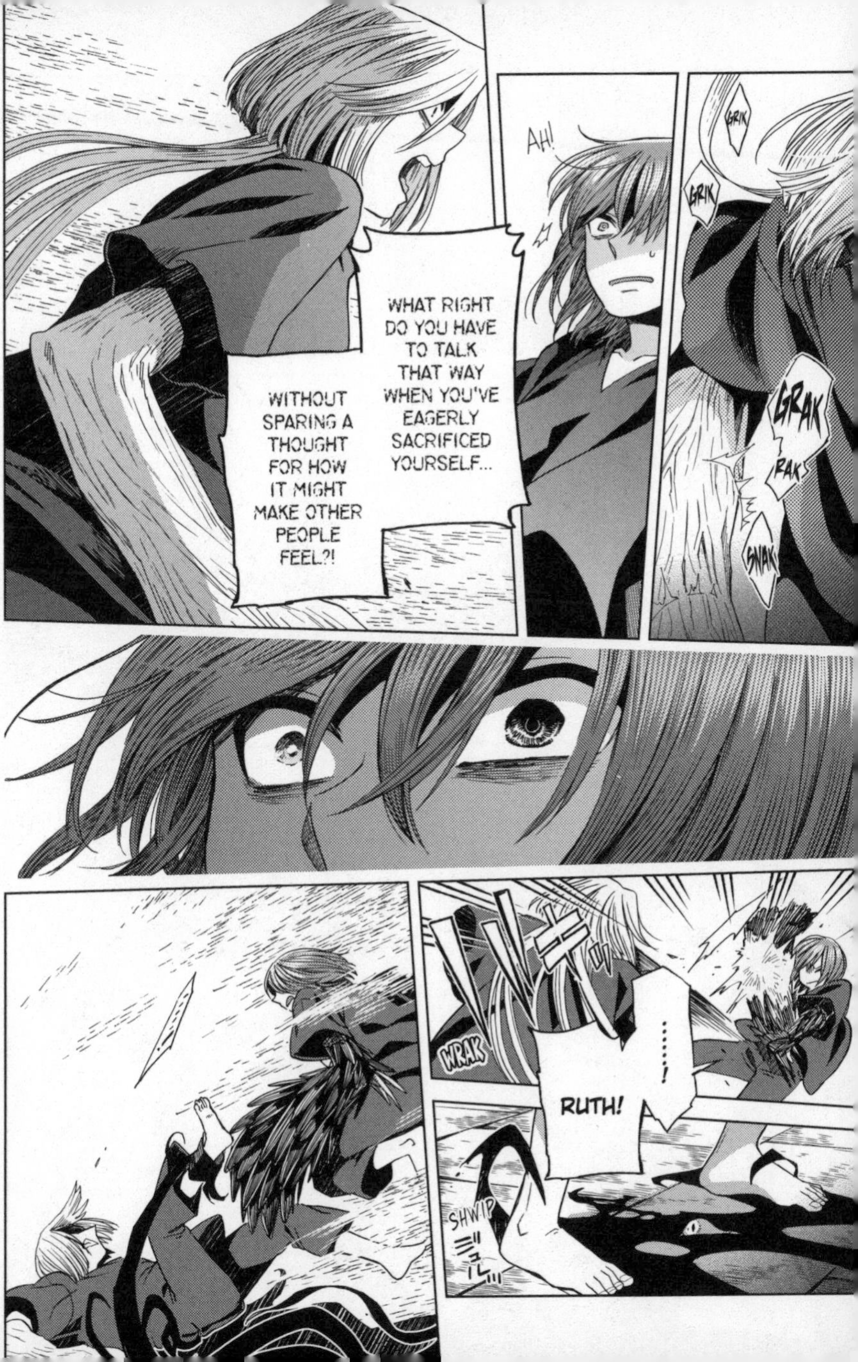
GRIK
GRIK
GRAK
RAK
SNAK
AH!
WHAT RIGHT DO YOU HAVE TO TALK THAT WAY WHEN YOU'VE EAGERLY SACRIFICED YOURSELF...
WITHOUT SPARING A THOUGHT FOR HOW IT MIGHT MAKE OTHER PEOPLE FEEL?!
......!
WRAK
RUTH!
SHWIP

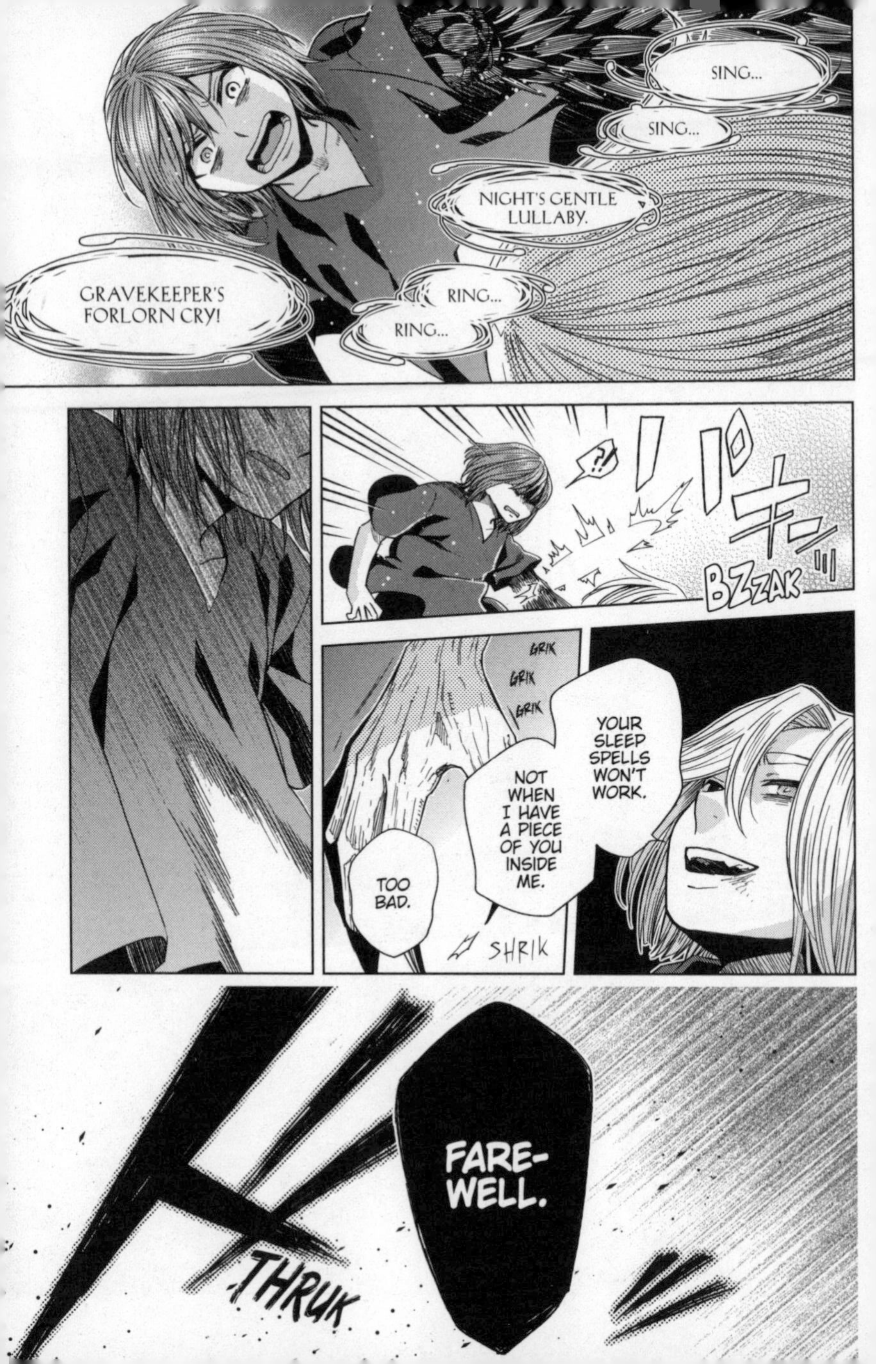
SING...
SING...
NIGHT'S GENTLE LULLABY.
RING...
RING...
GRAVEKEEPER'S FORLORN CRY!
?!
BZZAK
YOUR SLEEP SPELLS WON'T WORK.
NOT WHEN I HAVE A PIECE OF YOU INSIDE ME.
GRIK
GRIK
GRIK
TOO BAD.
SHRIK
FARE-WELL.
THRUK

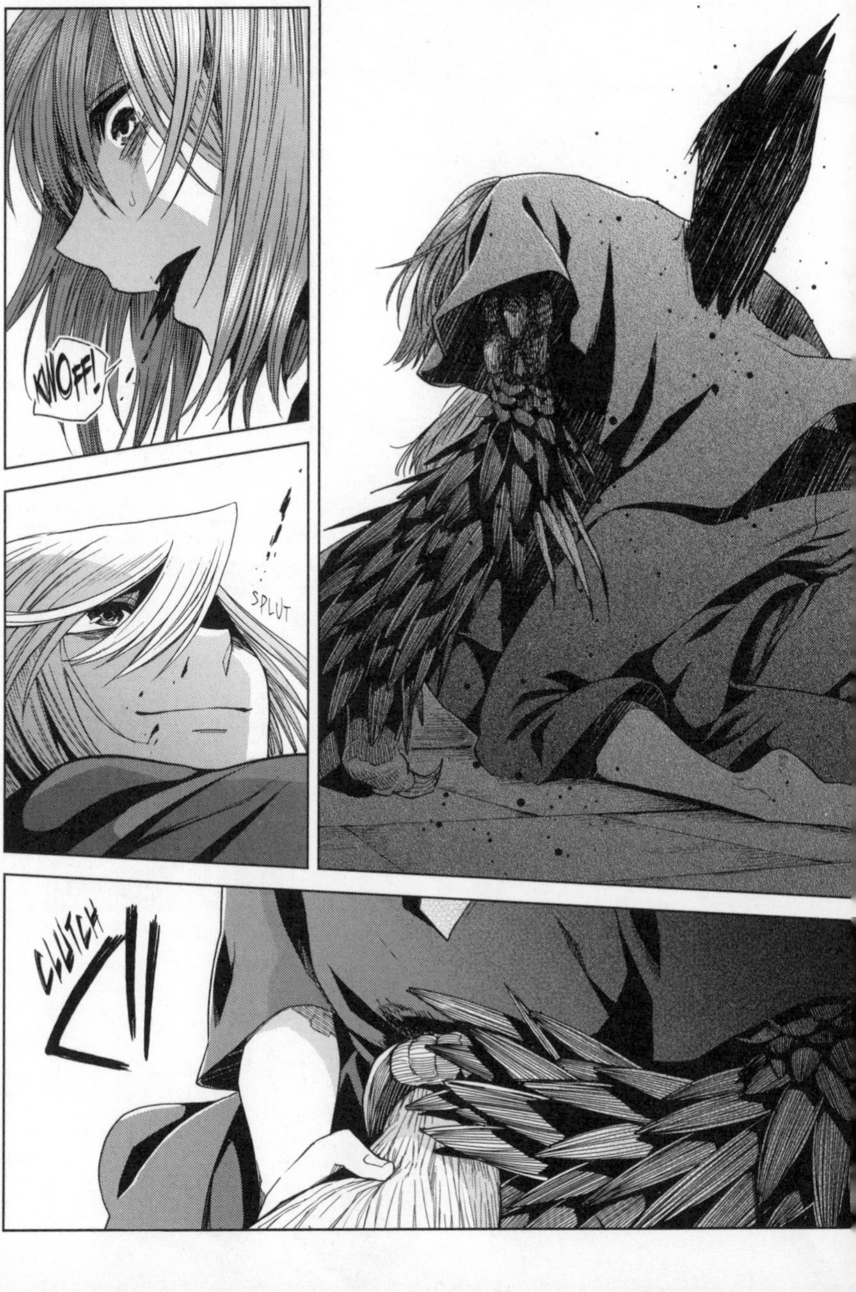
KWOFF!
SPLUT
CLUTCH

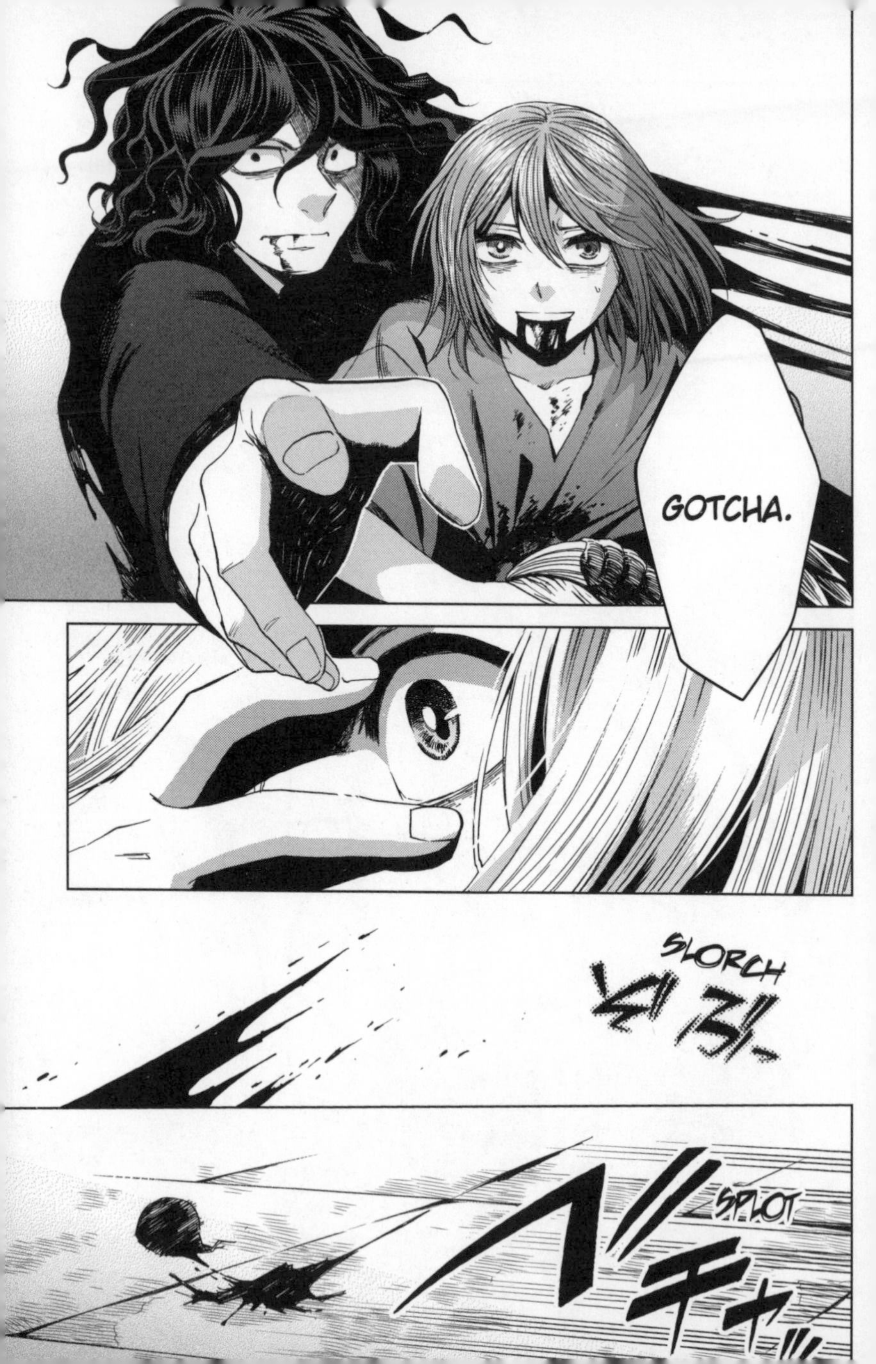
GOTCHA.
SLORCH
SPLOT

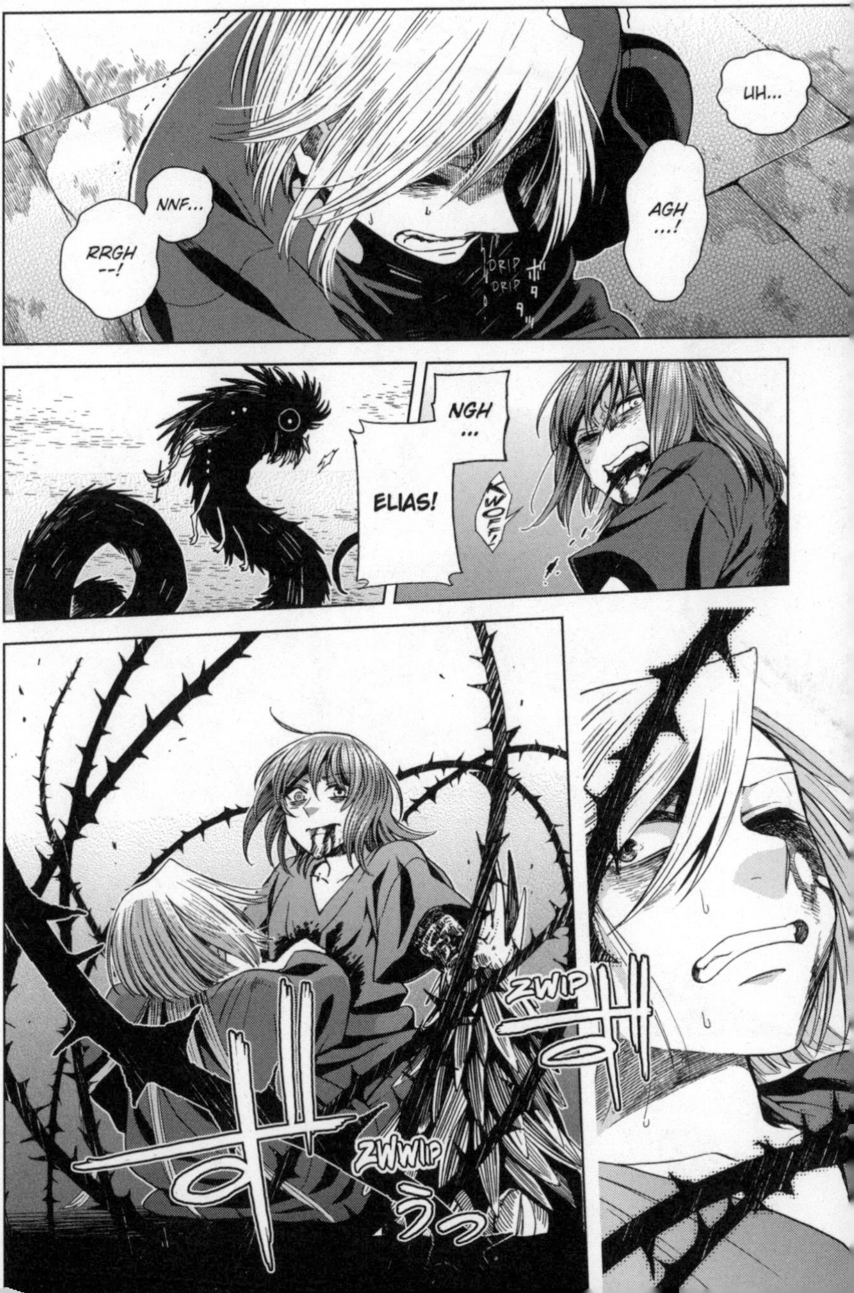
UH...
AGH ...!
DRIP DRIP
NNF...
RRGH --!
NGH ...
KWOFF!
ELIAS!
ZWIP
ZWWIP

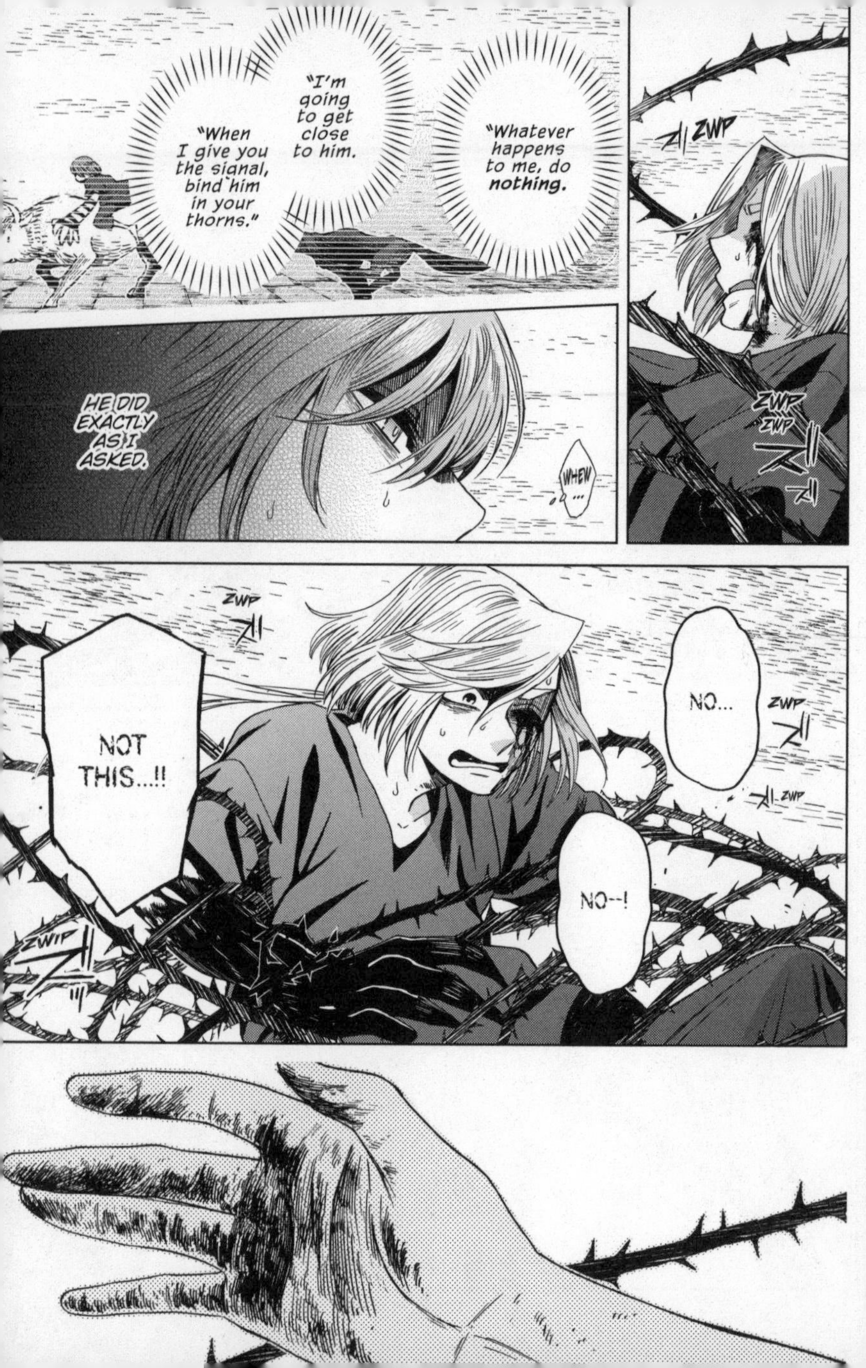
ZWP
ZWP ZWP
"Whatever happens to me, do **nothing.**
"I'm going to get close to him.
"When I give you the signal, bind him in your thorns."
WHEW...
HE DID EXACTLY AS I ASKED.
NO...
ZWP
ZWP
NO--!
ZWP
NOT THIS...!!
ZWIP

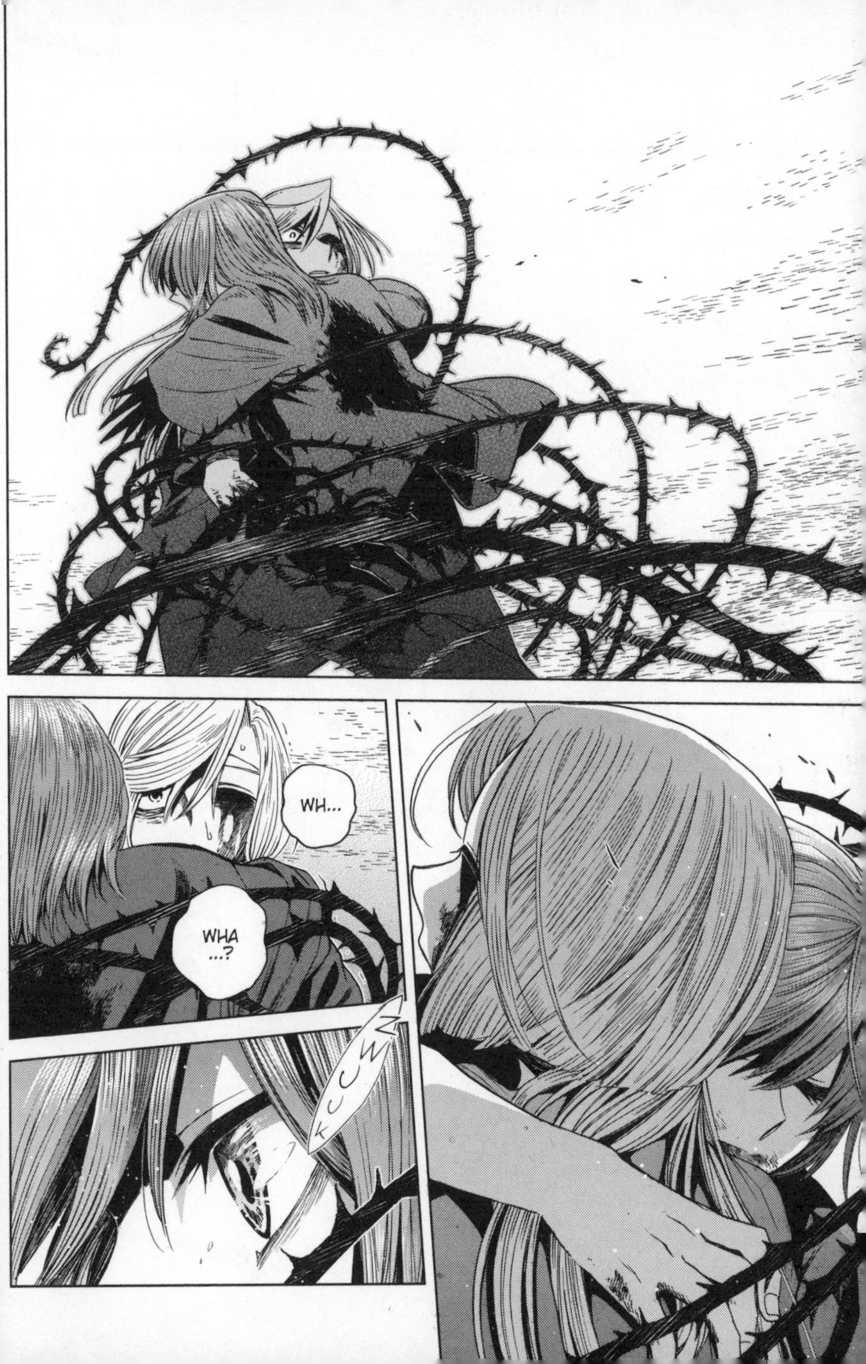
WH...
WHA ...?
KCCWN

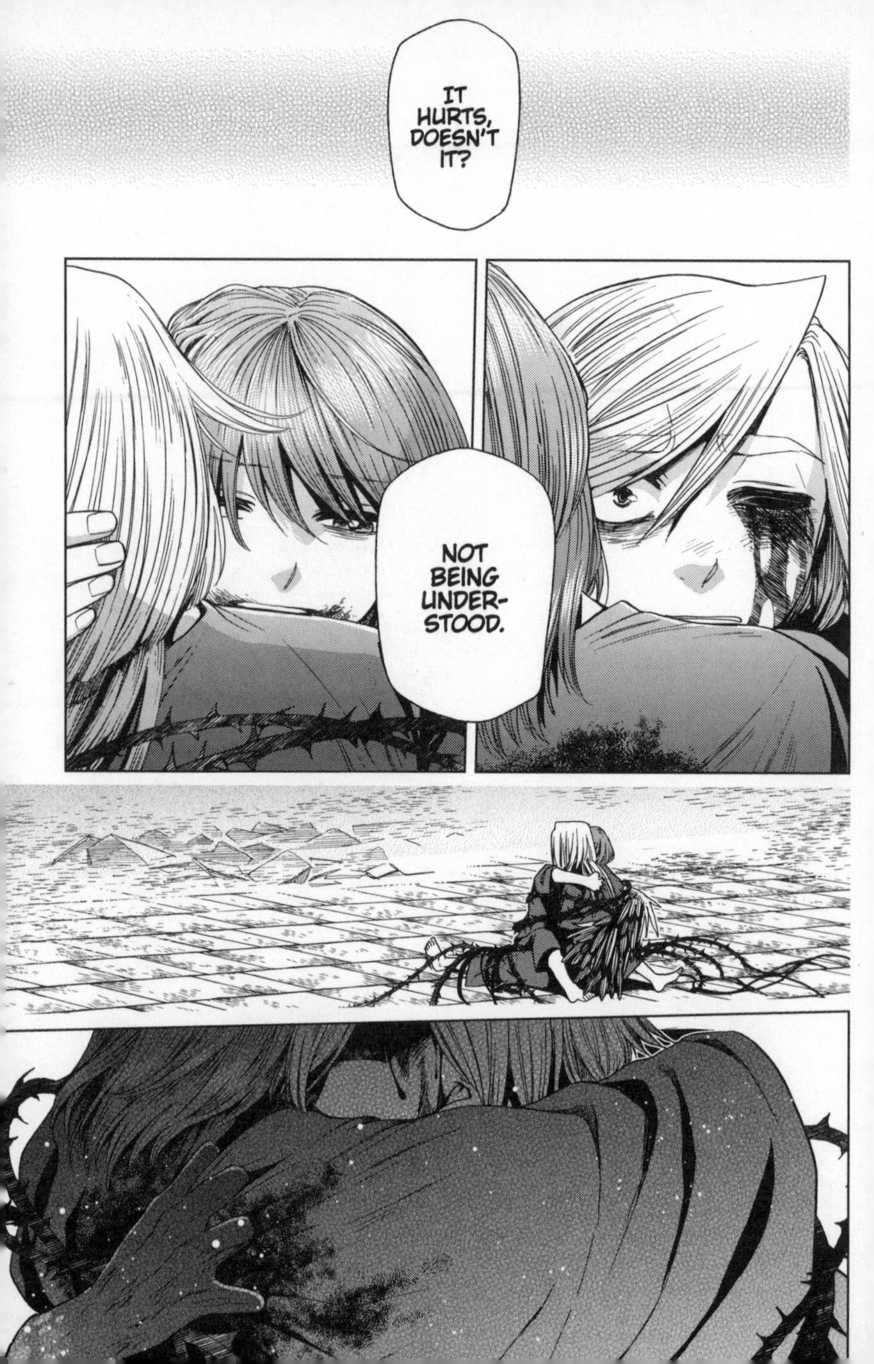
IT HURTS, DOESN'T IT?
NOT BEING UNDER-STOOD.

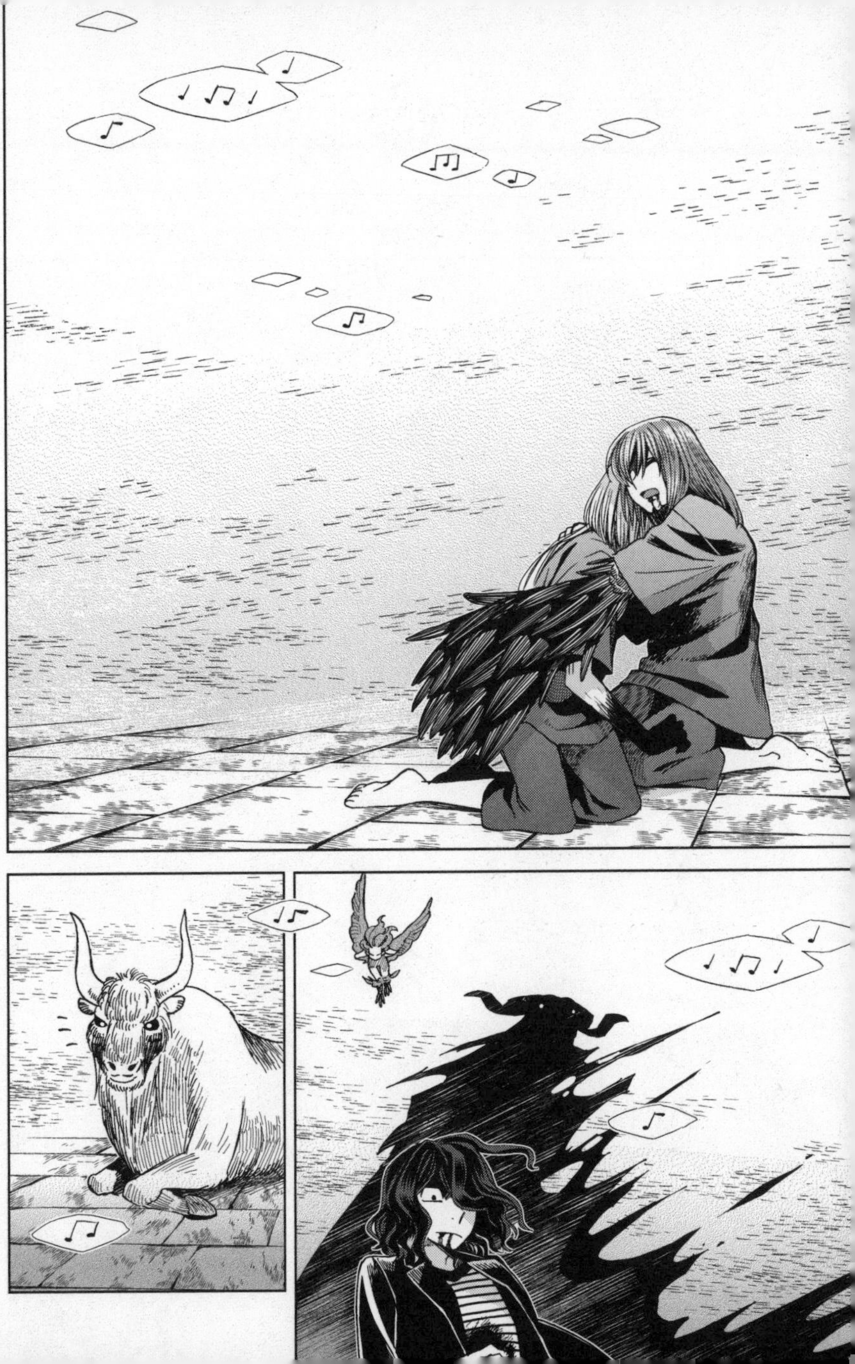

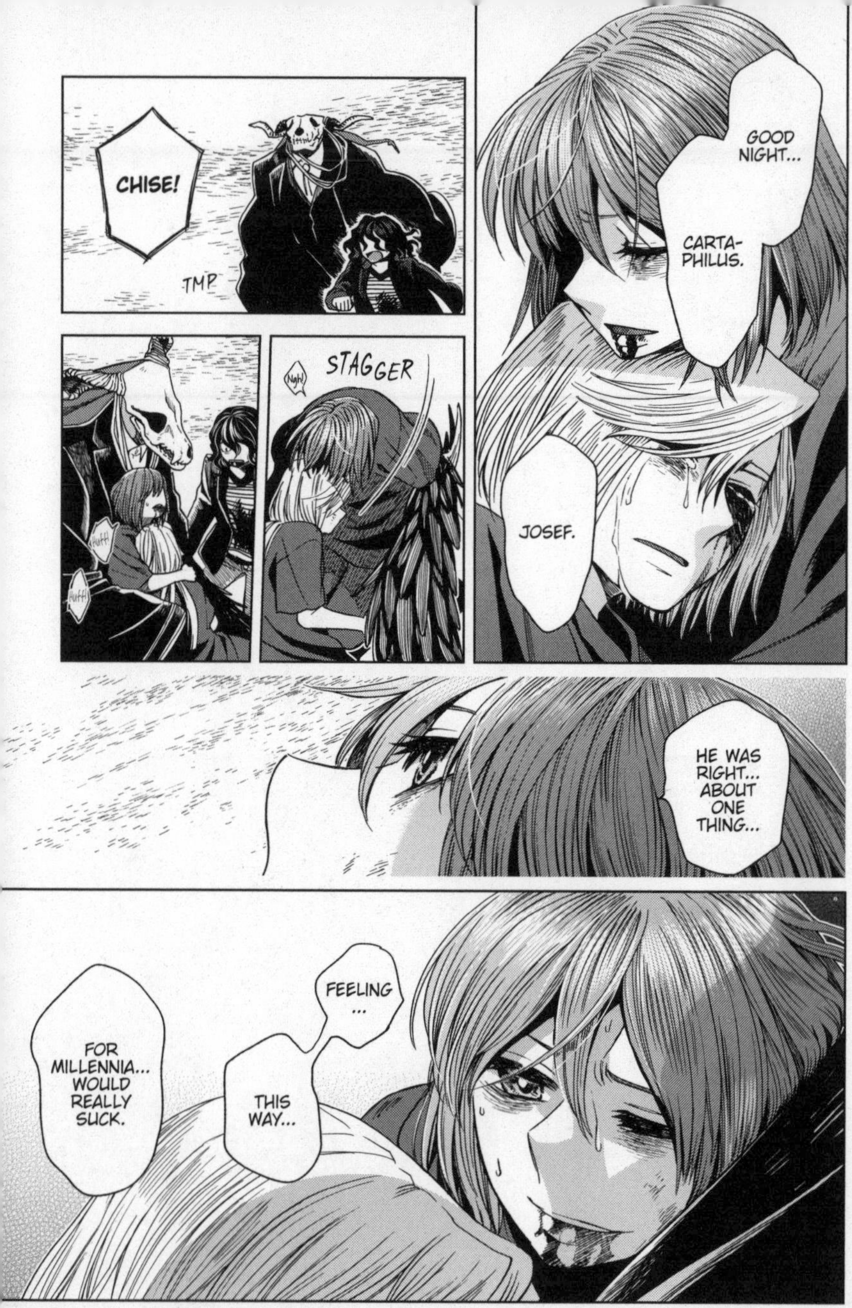
GOOD NIGHT...
CARTA-PHILUS.
JOSEF.
CHISE!
TMP
STAGGER
Ngh!
Huff!
Huff!
HE WAS RIGHT... ABOUT ONE THING...
FEELING ...
THIS WAY...
FOR MILLENNIA... WOULD REALLY SUCK.

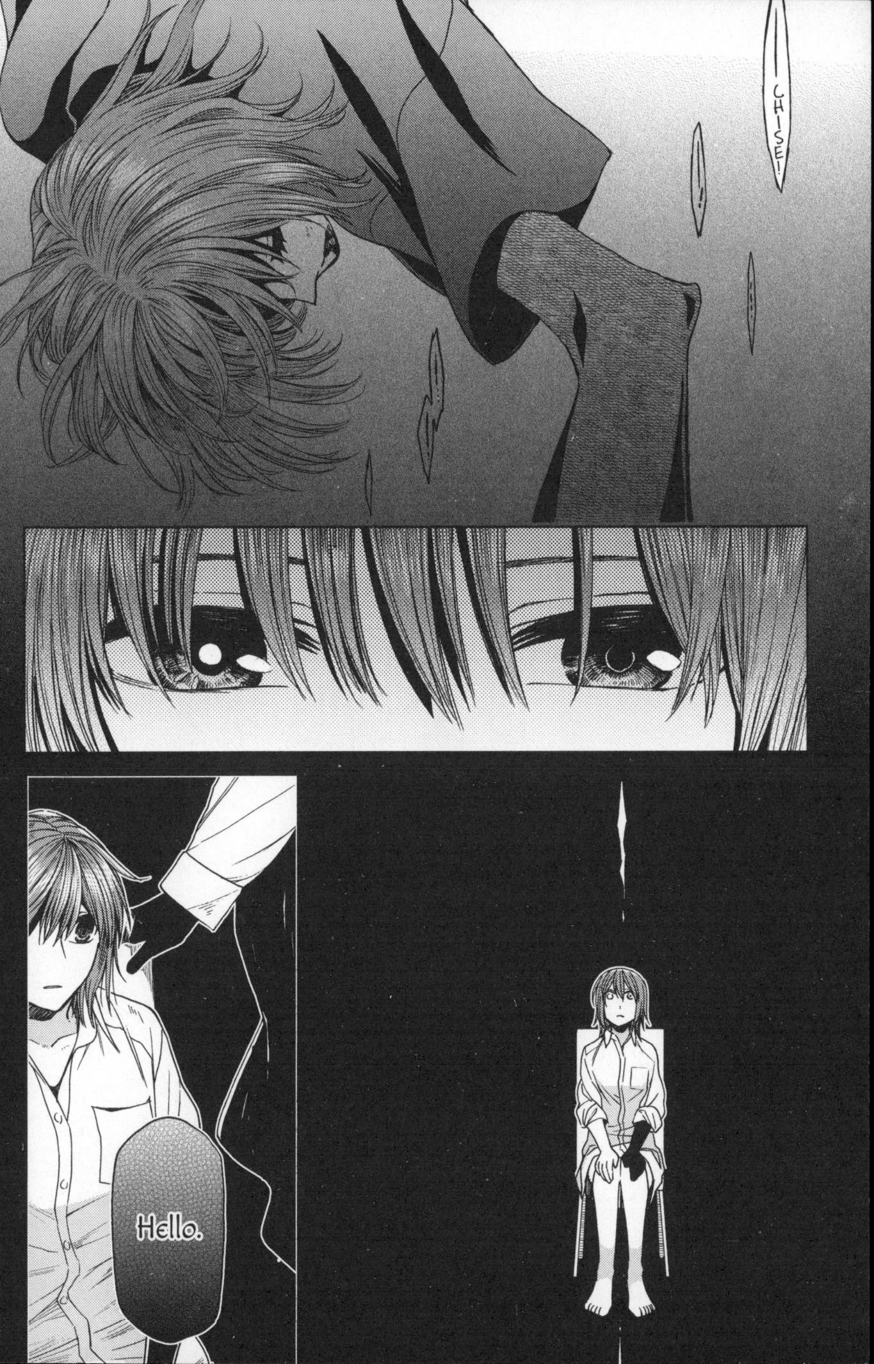
CHISE!
Hello.

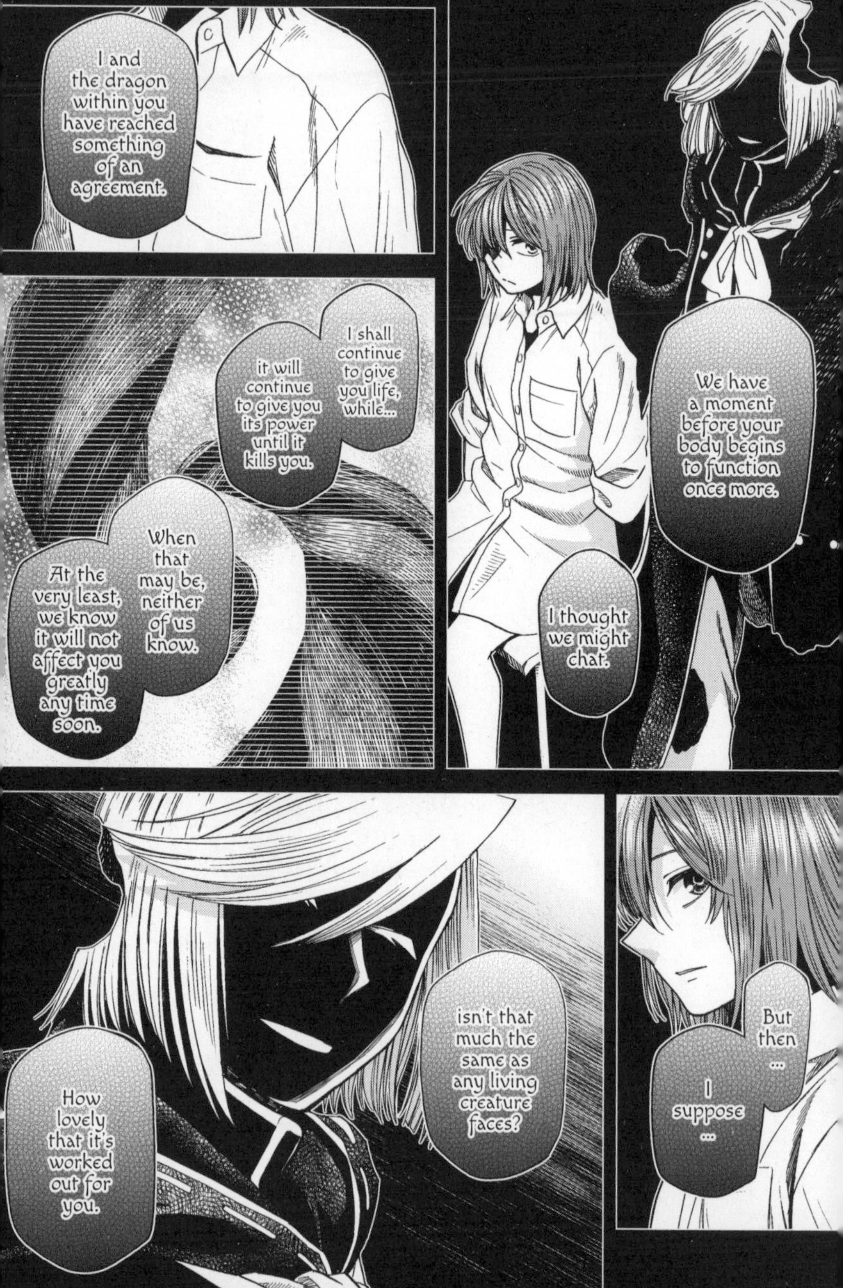
We have a moment before your body begins to function once more.
I thought we might chat.
I and the dragon within you have reached something of an agreement.
I shall continue to give you life, while...
it will continue to give you its power until it kills you.
When that may be, neither of us know.
At the very least, we know it will not affect you greatly any time soon.
But then ...
I suppose ...
isn't that much the same as any living creature faces?
How lovely that it's worked out for you.

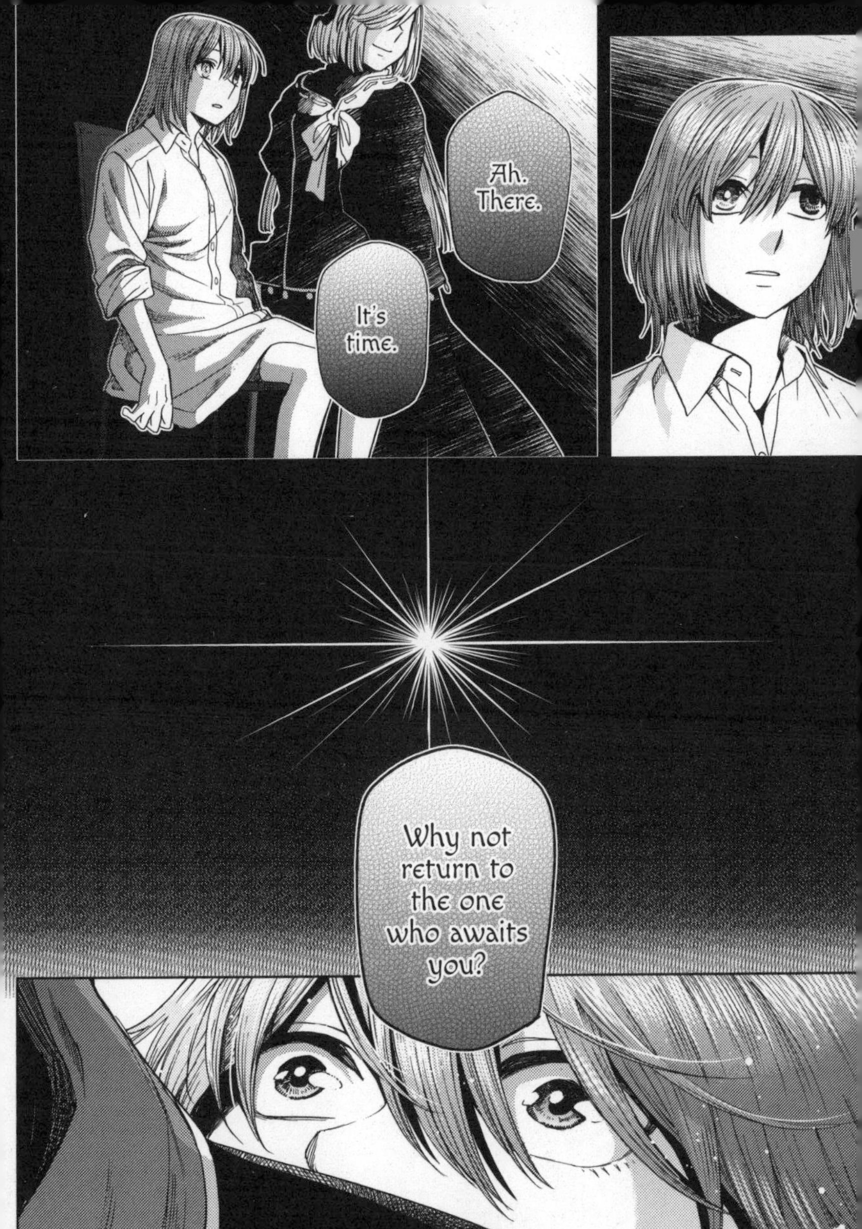
Ah. There.
It's time.
Why not return to the one who awaits you?

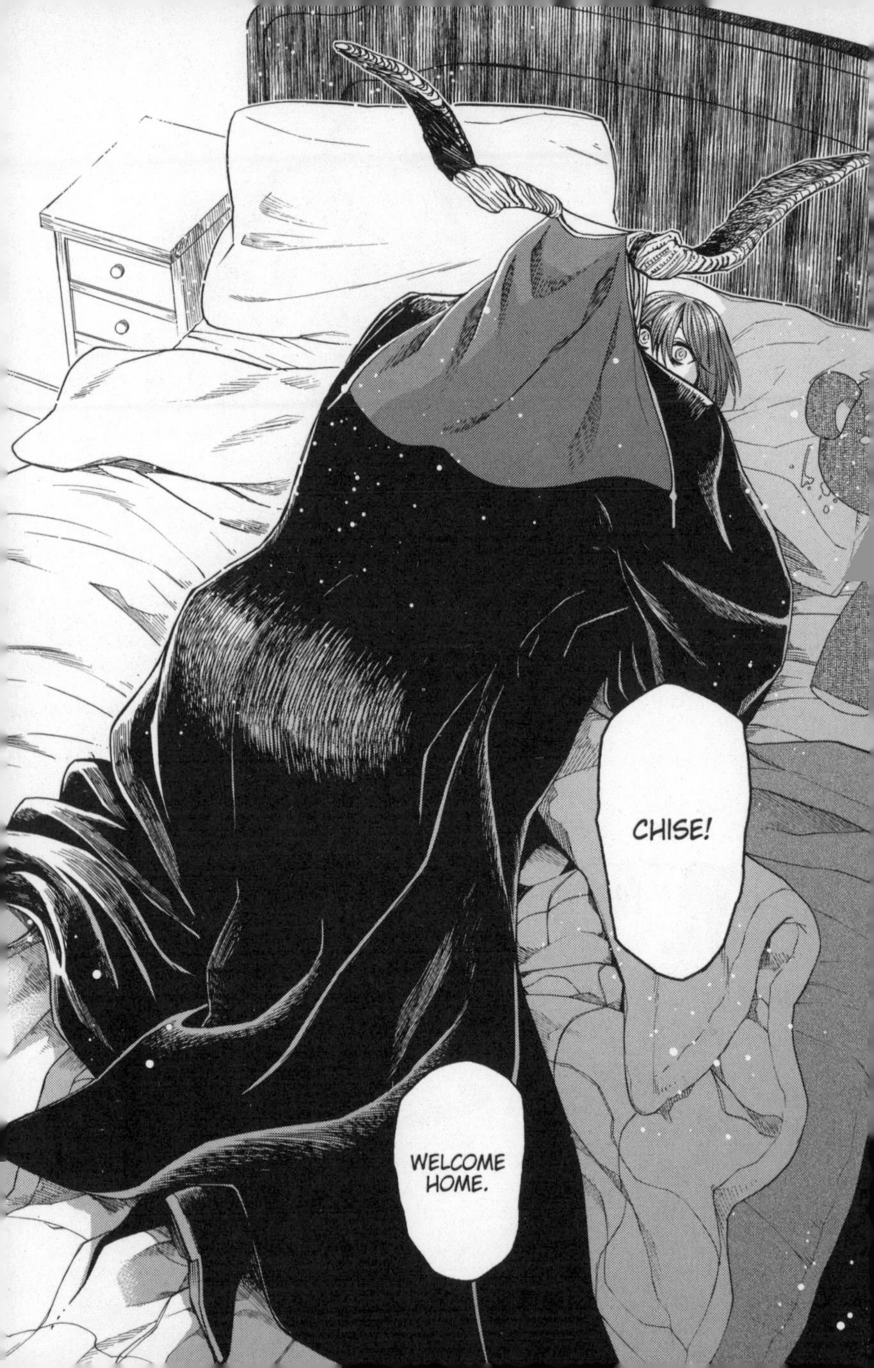
CHISE!
WELCOME HOME.

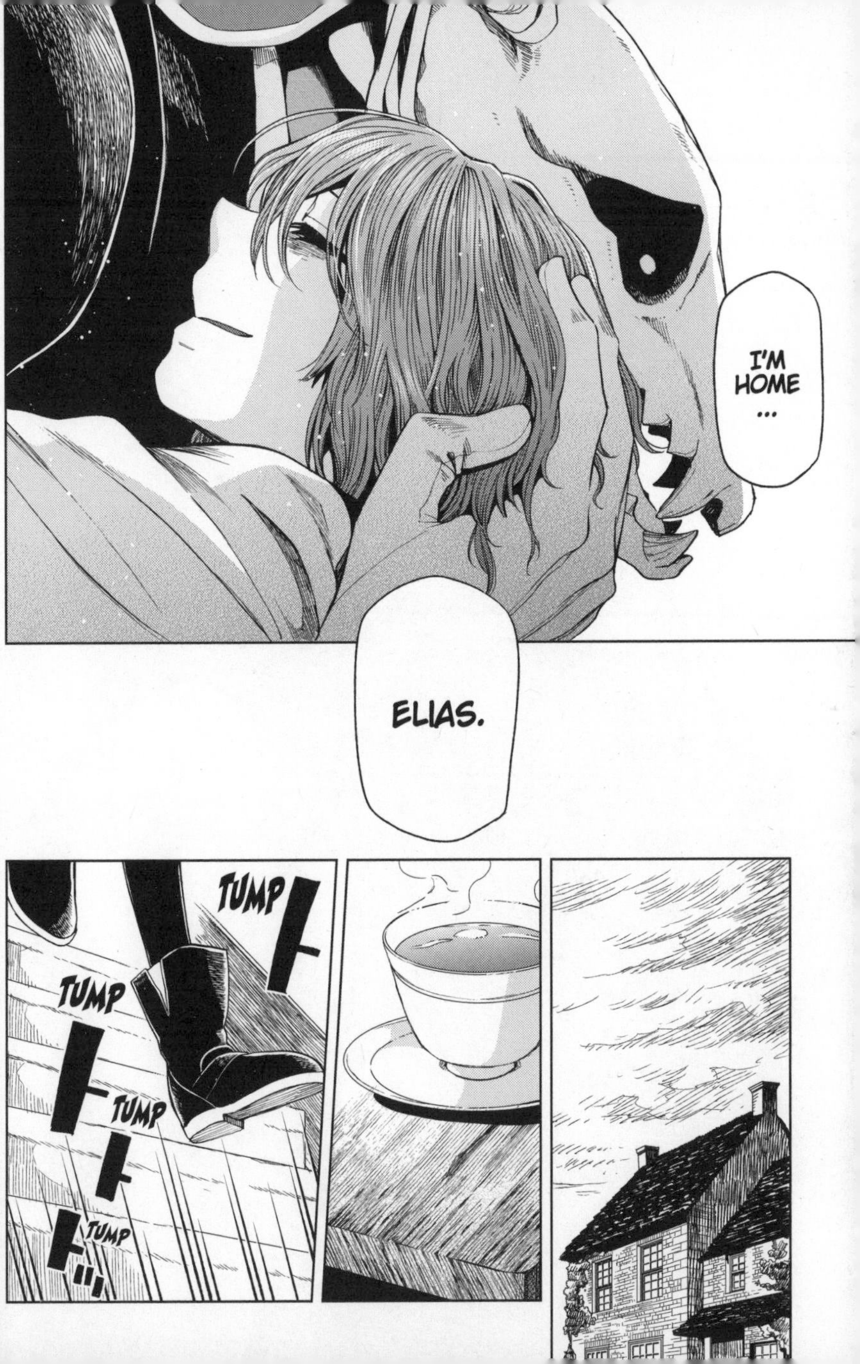
I'M HOME ...
ELIAS.
TUMP
TUMP
TUMP
TUMP

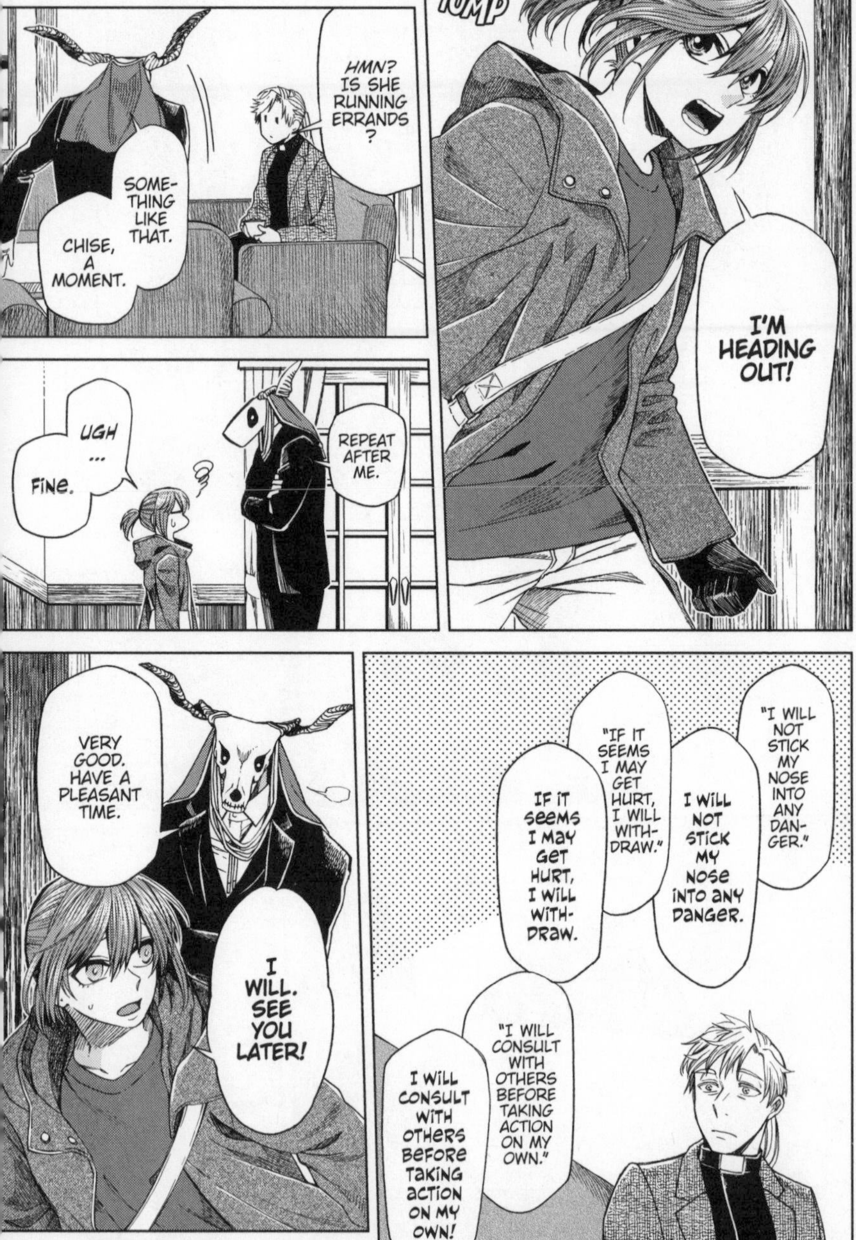
TUMP
I'M HEADING OUT!
HMN? IS SHE RUNNING ERRANDS?
SOMETHING LIKE THAT.
CHISE, A MOMENT.
REPEAT AFTER ME.
UGH... FINE.
"I WILL NOT STICK MY NOSE INTO ANY DANGER."
I WILL NOT STICK MY NOSE INTO ANY DANGER.
"IF IT SEEMS I MAY GET HURT, I WILL WITHDRAW."
IF IT SEEMS I MAY GET HURT, I WILL WITHDRAW.
"I WILL CONSULT WITH OTHERS BEFORE TAKING ACTION ON MY OWN."
I WILL CONSULT WITH OTHERS BEFORE TAKING ACTION ON MY OWN!
VERY GOOD. HAVE A PLEASANT TIME.
I WILL. SEE YOU LATER!

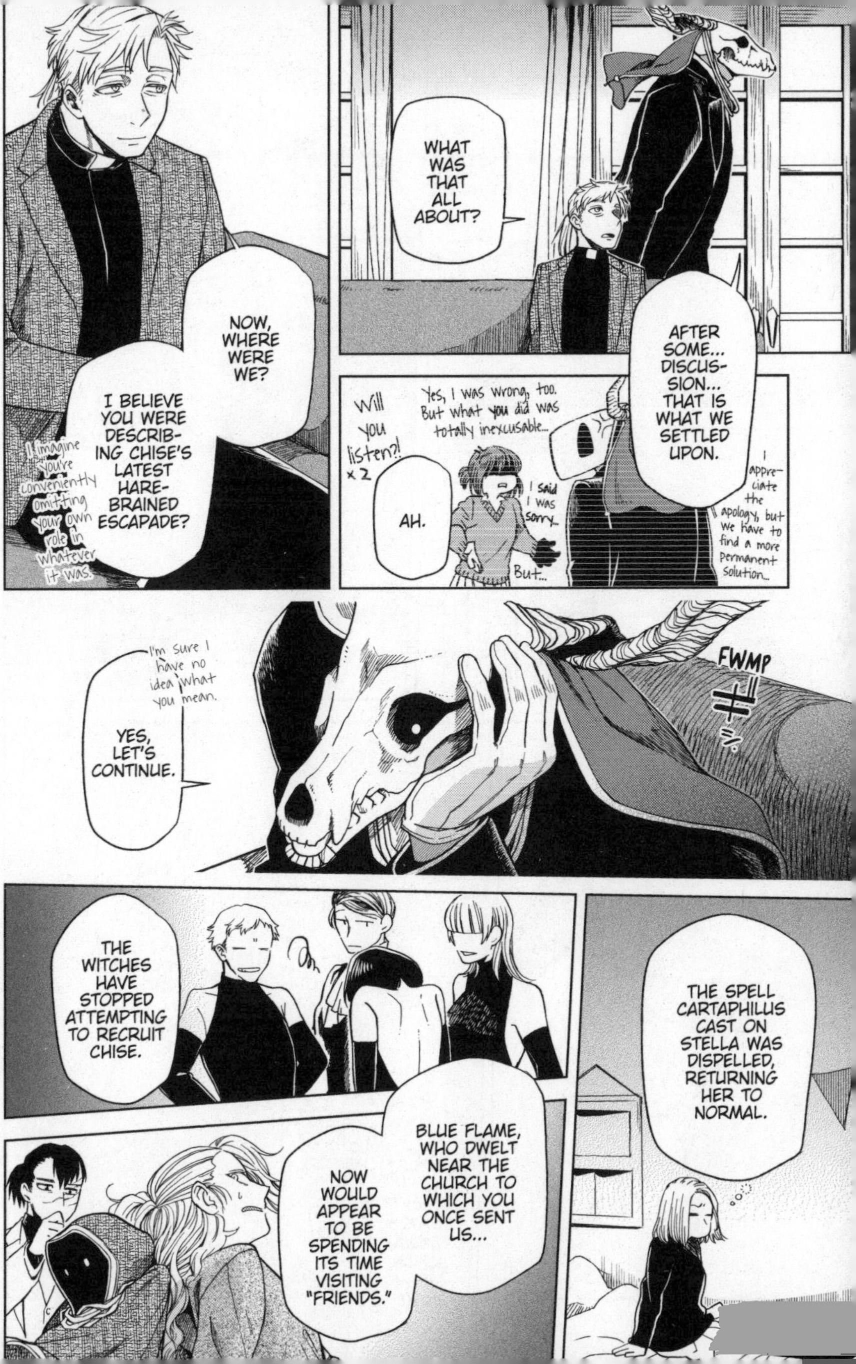

WHAT WAS THAT ALL ABOUT?
AFTER SOME... DISCUSSION... THAT IS WHAT WE SETTLED UPON.
I appreciate the apology, but we have to find a more permanent solution...
Yes, I was wrong, too. But what you did was totally inexcusable...
I said I was sorry...
But...
Will you listen?! x2
AH.
NOW, WHERE WERE WE?
I BELIEVE YOU WERE DESCRIBING CHISE'S LATEST HARE-BRAINED ESCAPADE?
I imagine you're conveniently omitting your own role in whatever it was.
FWMP
I'm sure I have no idea what you mean.
YES, LET'S CONTINUE.
THE SPELL CARTAPHILUS CAST ON STELLA WAS DISPELLED, RETURNING HER TO NORMAL.
THE WITCHES HAVE STOPPED ATTEMPTING TO RECRUIT CHISE.
BLUE FLAME, WHO DWELT NEAR THE CHURCH TO WHICH YOU ONCE SENT US...
NOW WOULD APPEAR TO BE SPENDING ITS TIME VISITING "FRIENDS."

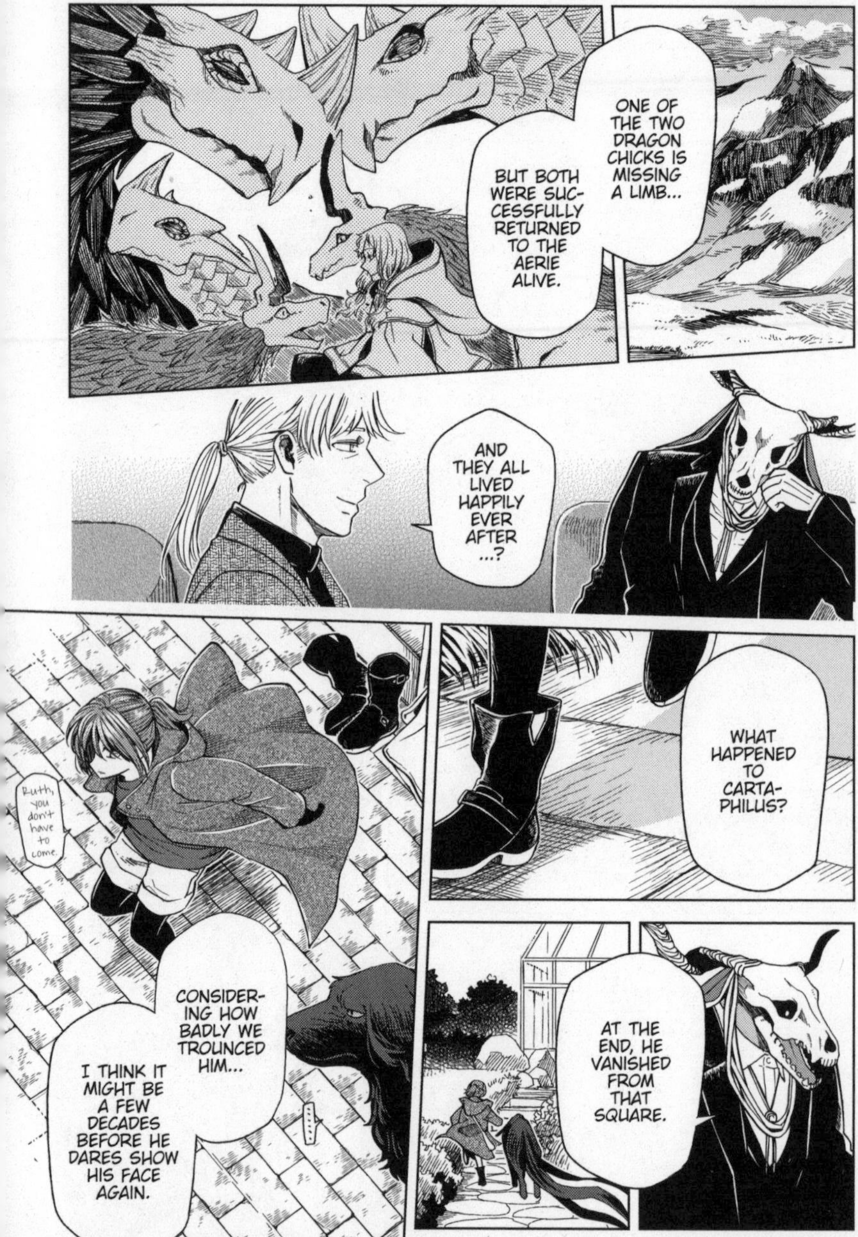
ONE OF THE TWO DRAGON CHICKS IS MISSING A LIMB...
BUT BOTH WERE SUCCESSFULLY RETURNED TO THE AERIE ALIVE.
AND THEY ALL LIVED HAPPILY EVER AFTER ...?
WHAT HAPPENED TO CARTAPHILUS?
AT THE END, HE VANISHED FROM THAT SQUARE.
Ruth, you don't have to come.
CONSIDERING HOW BADLY WE TROUNCED HIM...
I THINK IT MIGHT BE A FEW DECADES BEFORE HE DARES SHOW HIS FACE AGAIN.
......

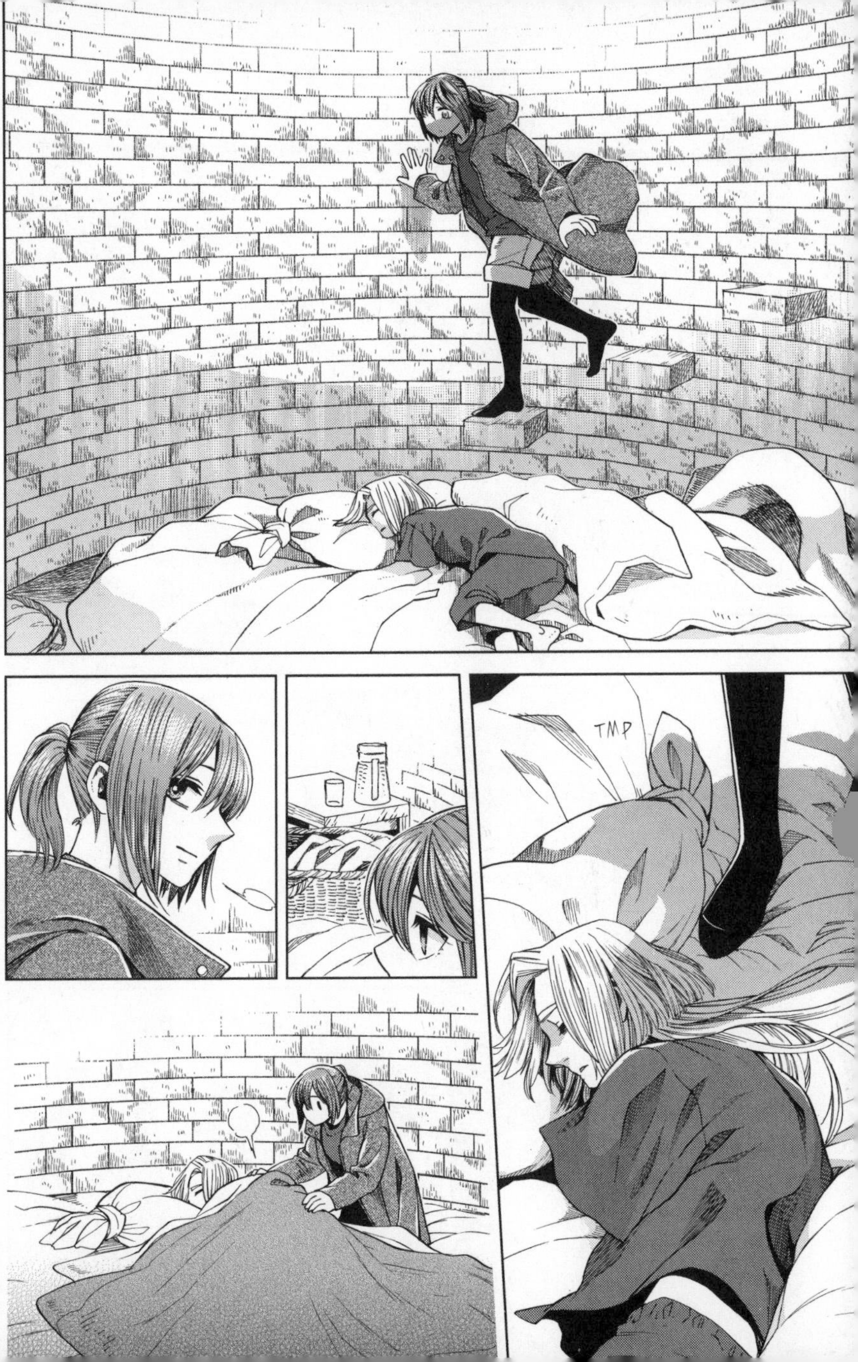
TMP

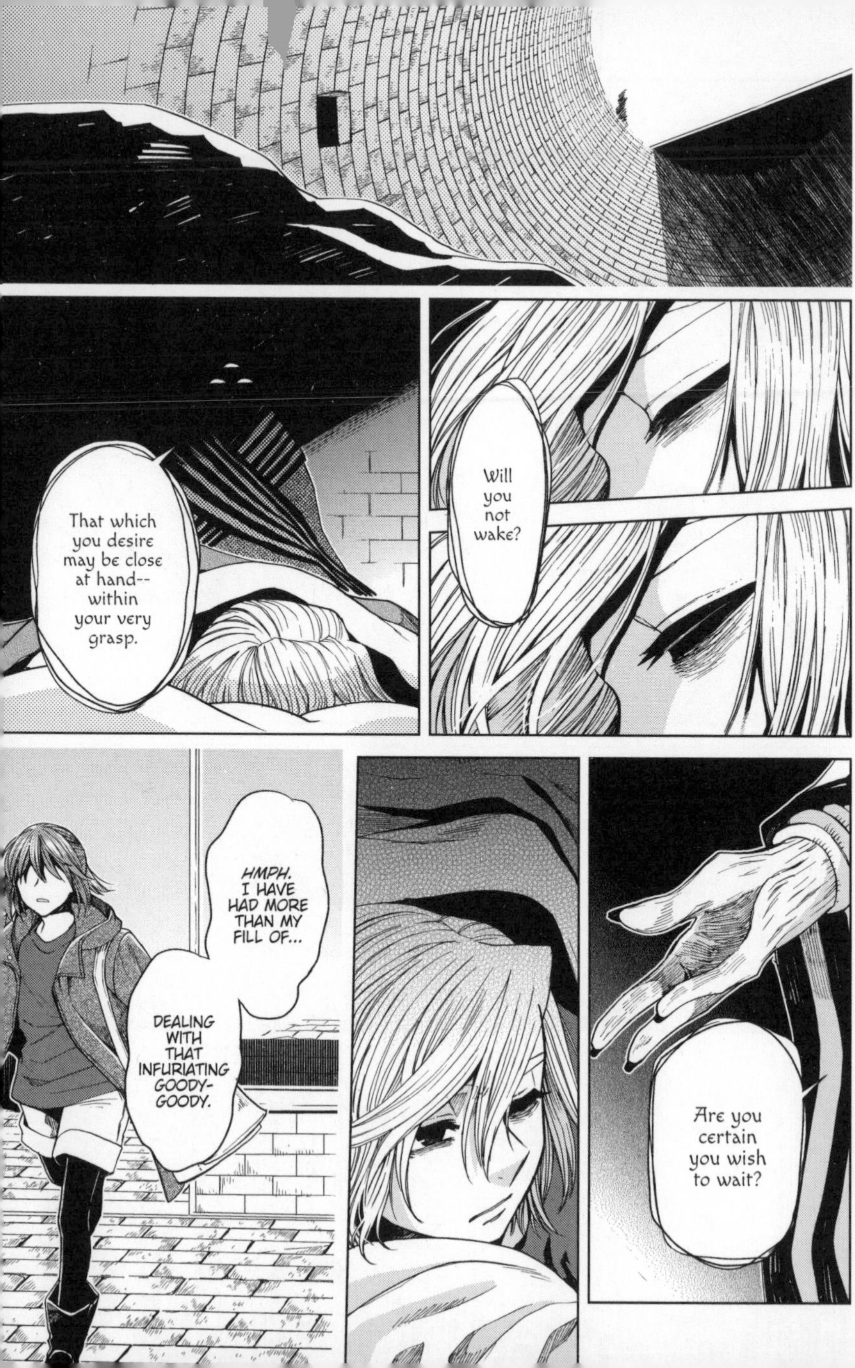
Will you not wake?
That which you desire may be close at hand-- within your very grasp.
Are you certain you wish to wait?
HMPH. I HAVE HAD MORE THAN MY FILL OF...
DEALING WITH THAT INFURIATING GOODY-GOODY.

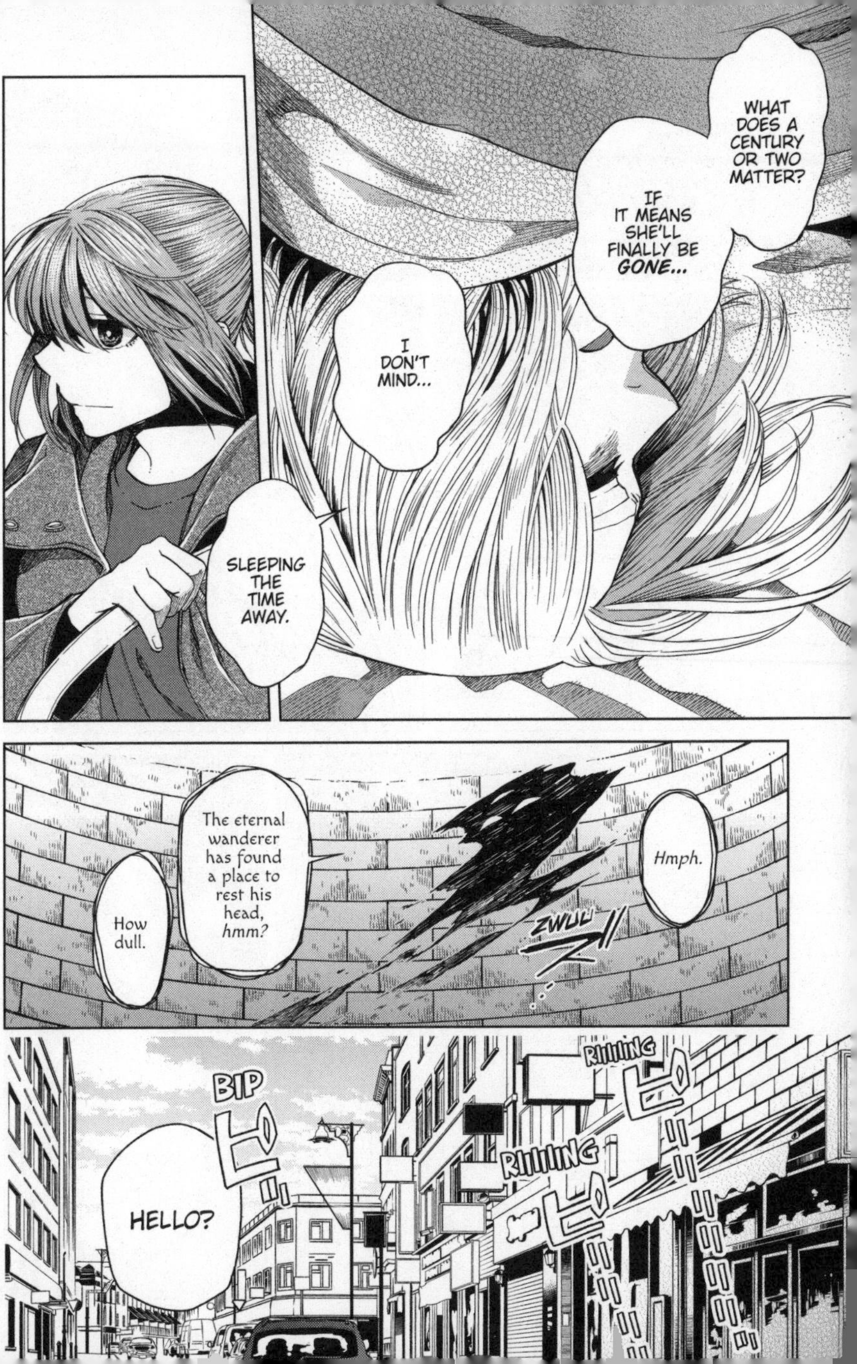
WHAT DOES A CENTURY OR TWO MATTER?
IF IT MEANS SHE'LL FINALLY BE *GONE*...
I DON'T MIND...
SLEEPING THE TIME AWAY.
Hmph.
ZWUU
The eternal wanderer has found a place to rest his head, *hmm?*
How dull.
RIIIING
RIIIING
BIP
HELLO?

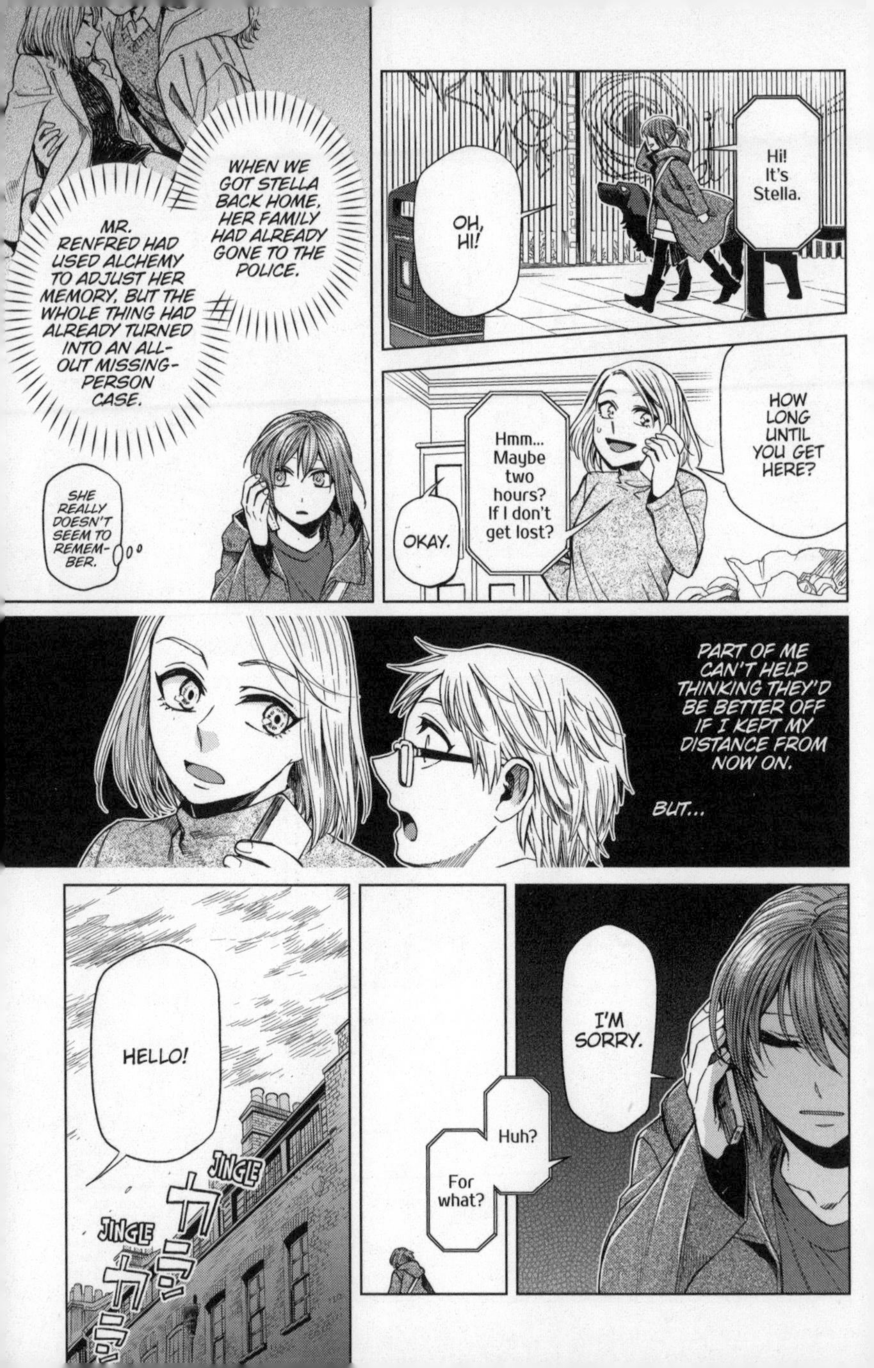
Hi! It's Stella.
OH, HI!
HOW LONG UNTIL YOU GET HERE?
Hmm... Maybe two hours? If I don't get lost?
OKAY.
WHEN WE GOT STELLA BACK HOME, HER FAMILY HAD ALREADY GONE TO THE POLICE.
MR. RENFRED HAD USED ALCHEMY TO ADJUST HER MEMORY, BUT THE WHOLE THING HAD ALREADY TURNED INTO AN ALL-OUT MISSING-PERSON CASE.
SHE REALLY DOESN'T SEEM TO REMEMBER.
PART OF ME CAN'T HELP THINKING THEY'D BE BETTER OFF IF I KEPT MY DISTANCE FROM NOW ON.
BUT...
I'M SORRY.
Huh? For what?
HELLO!
JINGLE
JINGLE

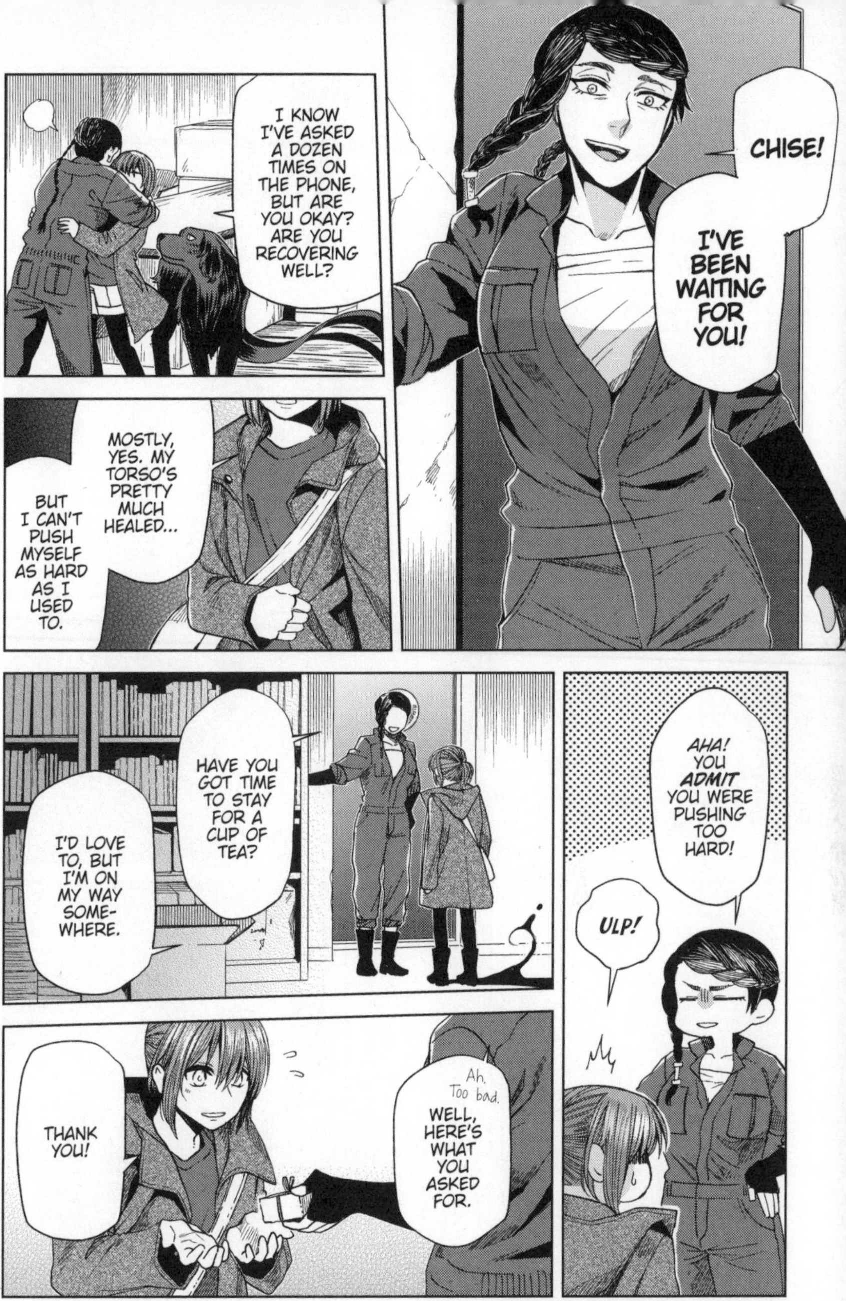
CHISE!
I'VE BEEN WAITING FOR YOU!
I KNOW I'VE ASKED A DOZEN TIMES ON THE PHONE, BUT ARE YOU OKAY? ARE YOU RECOVERING WELL?
MOSTLY, YES. MY TORSO'S PRETTY MUCH HEALED...
BUT I CAN'T PUSH MYSELF AS HARD AS I USED TO.
AHA! YOU *ADMIT* YOU WERE PUSHING TOO HARD!
ULP!
HAVE YOU GOT TIME TO STAY FOR A CUP OF TEA?
I'D LOVE TO, BUT I'M ON MY WAY SOMEWHERE.
Ah. Too bad.
WELL, HERE'S WHAT YOU ASKED FOR.
THANK YOU!

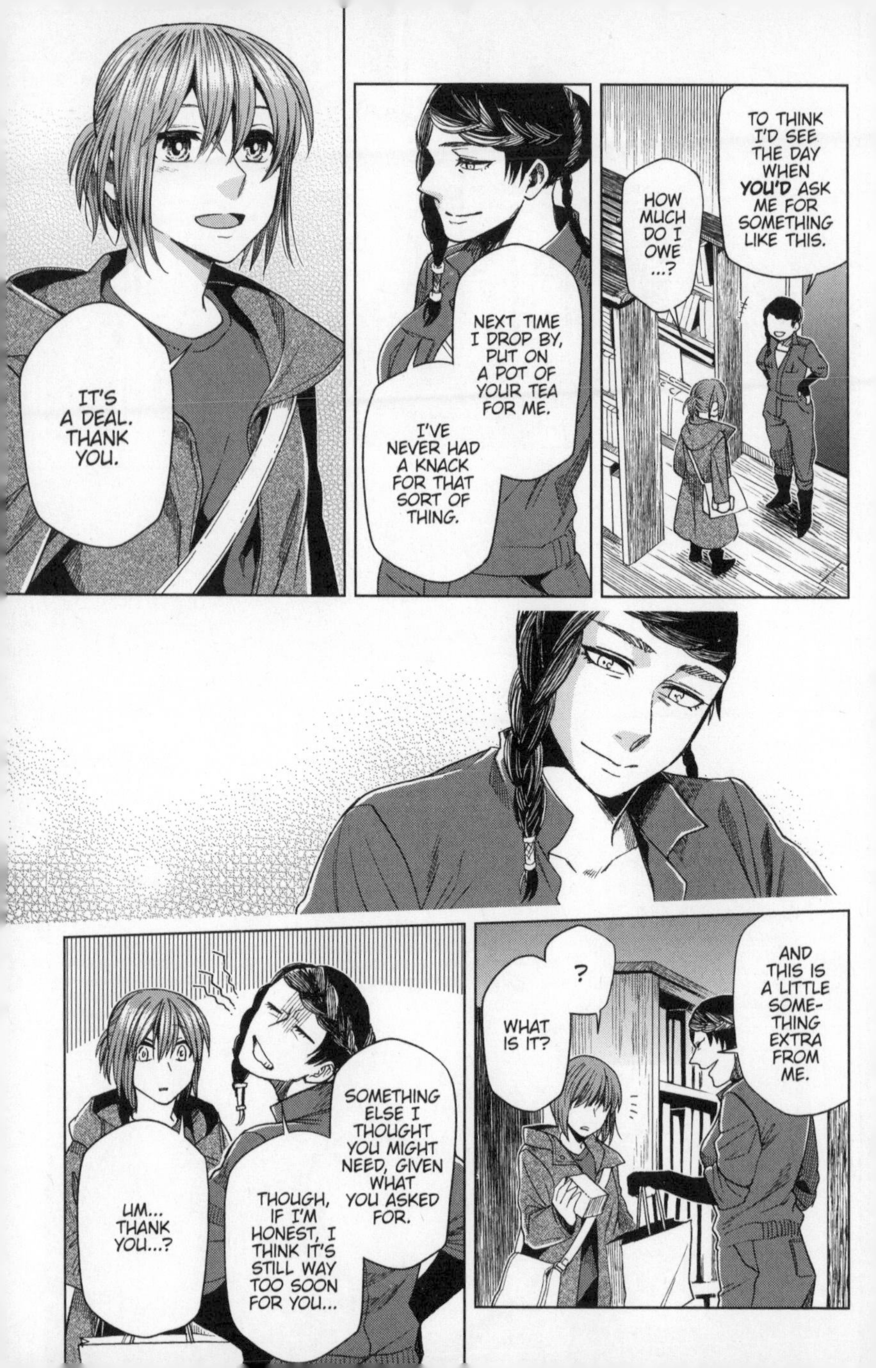
TO THINK I'D SEE THE DAY WHEN **YOU'D** ASK ME FOR SOMETHING LIKE THIS.
HOW MUCH DO I OWE ...?
NEXT TIME I DROP BY, PUT ON A POT OF YOUR TEA FOR ME.
I'VE NEVER HAD A KNACK FOR THAT SORT OF THING.
IT'S A DEAL. THANK YOU.
AND THIS IS A LITTLE SOME-THING EXTRA FROM ME.
?
WHAT IS IT?
SOMETHING ELSE I THOUGHT YOU MIGHT NEED, GIVEN WHAT YOU ASKED FOR.
THOUGH, IF I'M HONEST, I THINK IT'S STILL WAY TOO SOON FOR YOU...
UM... THANK YOU...?

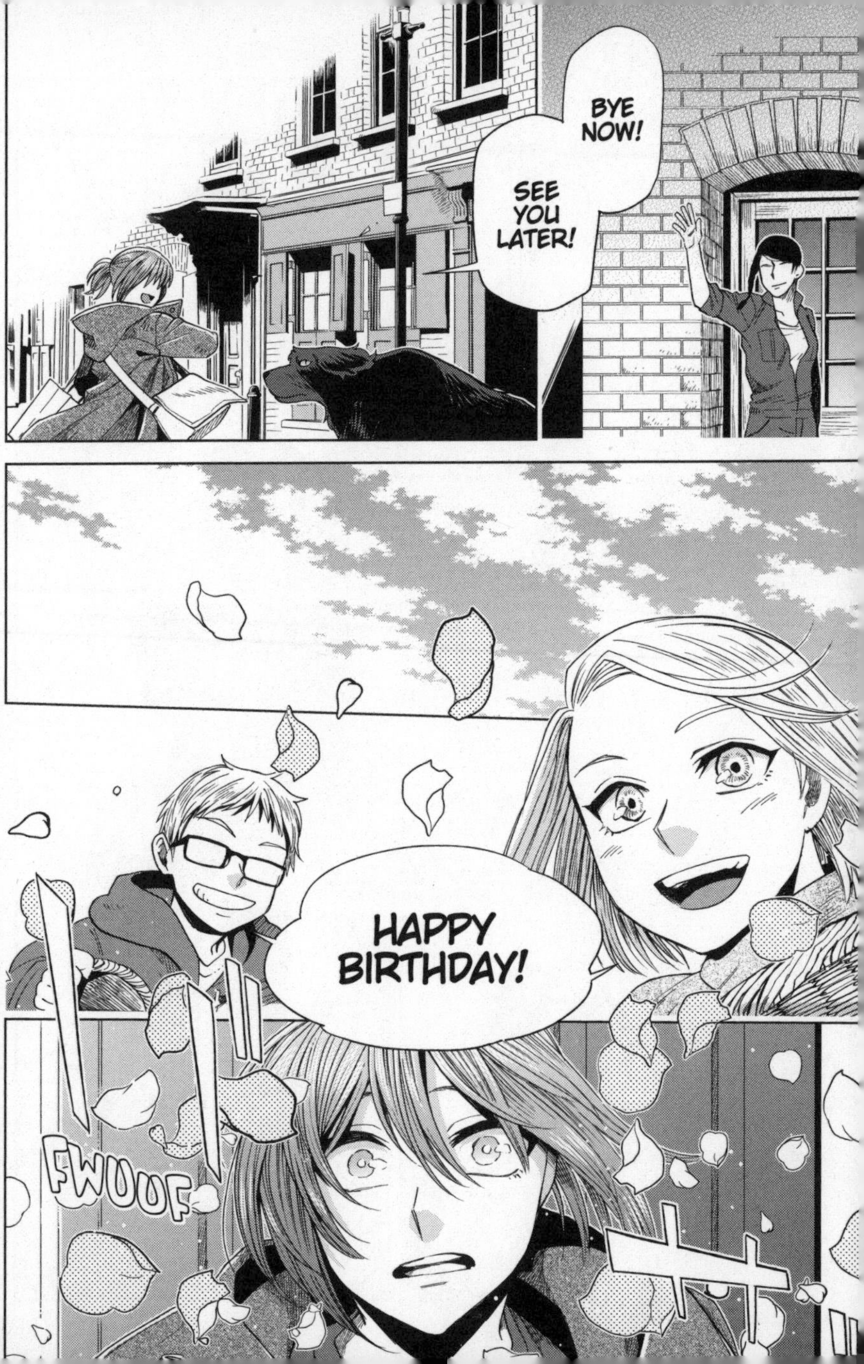
BYE NOW!
SEE YOU LATER!
HAPPY BIRTHDAY!
FWUOF

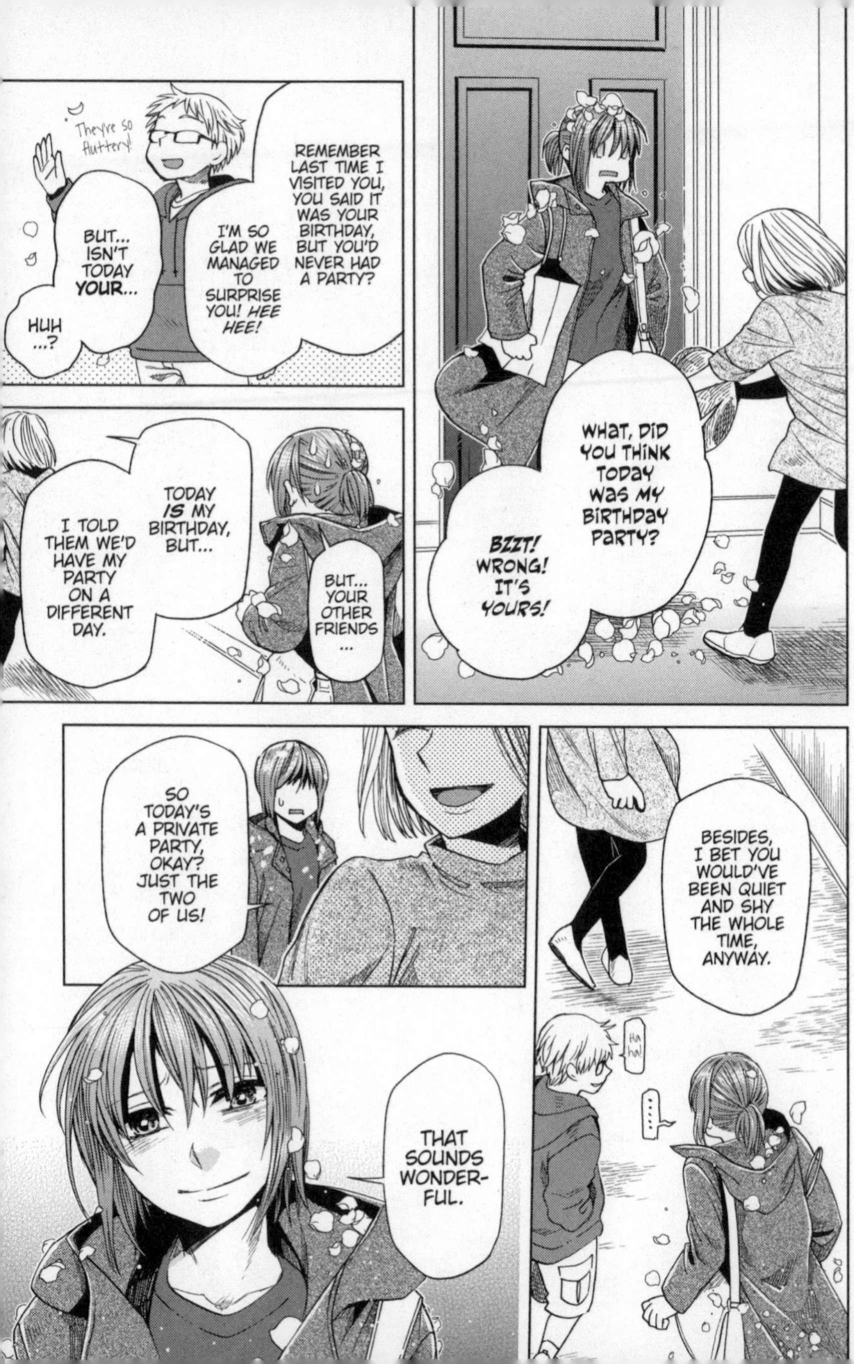
WHAT, DID YOU THINK TODAY WAS MY BIRTHDAY PARTY?
BZZT! WRONG! IT'S YOURS!
REMEMBER LAST TIME I VISITED YOU, YOU SAID IT WAS YOUR BIRTHDAY, BUT YOU'D NEVER HAD A PARTY?
I'M SO GLAD WE MANAGED TO SURPRISE YOU! HEE HEE!
They're so fluttery!
BUT... ISN'T TODAY YOUR...
HUH ...?
BUT... YOUR OTHER FRIENDS ...
TODAY IS MY BIRTHDAY, BUT...
I TOLD THEM WE'D HAVE MY PARTY ON A DIFFERENT DAY.
BESIDES, I BET YOU WOULD'VE BEEN QUIET AND SHY THE WHOLE TIME, ANYWAY.
SO TODAY'S A PRIVATE PARTY, OKAY? JUST THE TWO OF US!
Ha ha!
......
THAT SOUNDS WONDERFUL.

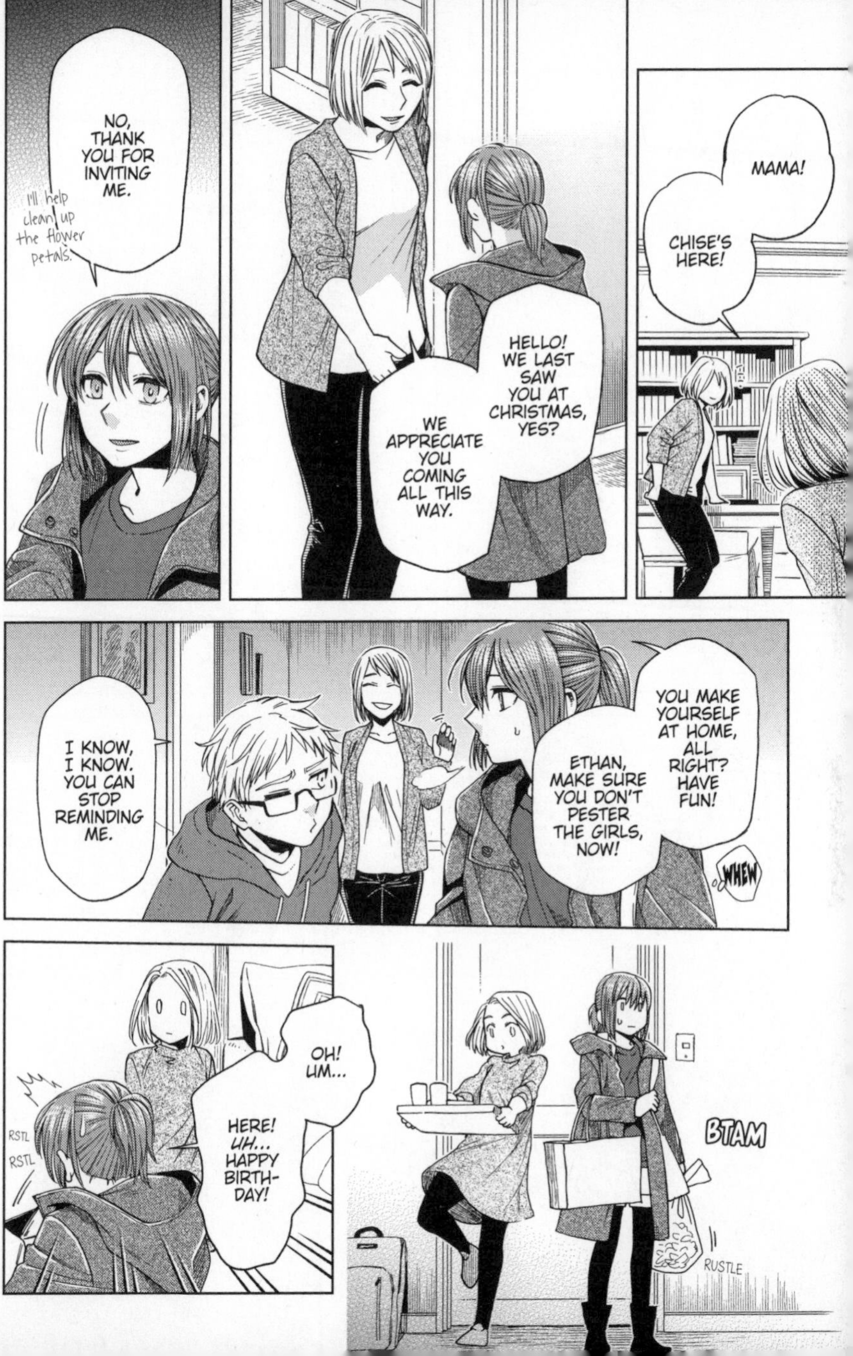
MAMA!
CHISE'S HERE!
HELLO! WE LAST SAW YOU AT CHRISTMAS, YES?
WE APPRECIATE YOU COMING ALL THIS WAY.
NO, THANK YOU FOR INVITING ME.
I'll help clean up the flower petals.
YOU MAKE YOURSELF AT HOME, ALL RIGHT? HAVE FUN!
ETHAN, MAKE SURE YOU DON'T PESTER THE GIRLS, NOW!
WHEW
I KNOW, I KNOW. YOU CAN STOP REMINDING ME.
BTAM
RUSTLE
OH! UM...
HERE! UH... HAPPY BIRTH-DAY!
RSTL
RSTL

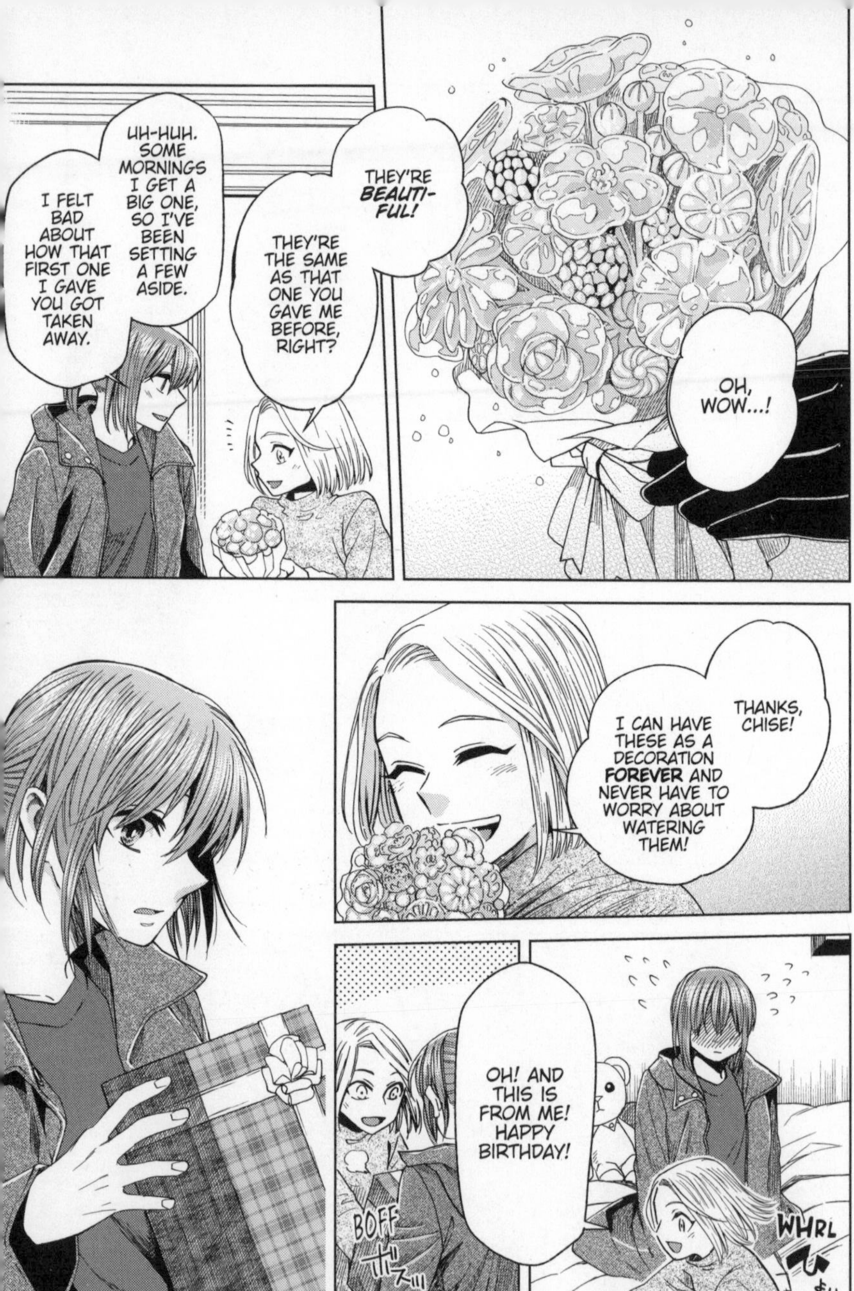
OH, WOW...!
THEY'RE BEAUTIFUL!
THEY'RE THE SAME AS THAT ONE YOU GAVE ME BEFORE, RIGHT?
UH-HUH. SOME MORNINGS I GET A BIG ONE, SO I'VE BEEN SETTING A FEW ASIDE.
I FELT BAD ABOUT HOW THAT FIRST ONE I GAVE YOU GOT TAKEN AWAY.
THANKS, CHISE!
I CAN HAVE THESE AS A DECORATION FOREVER AND NEVER HAVE TO WORRY ABOUT WATERING THEM!
WHRL
OH! AND THIS IS FROM ME! HAPPY BIRTHDAY!
BOFF

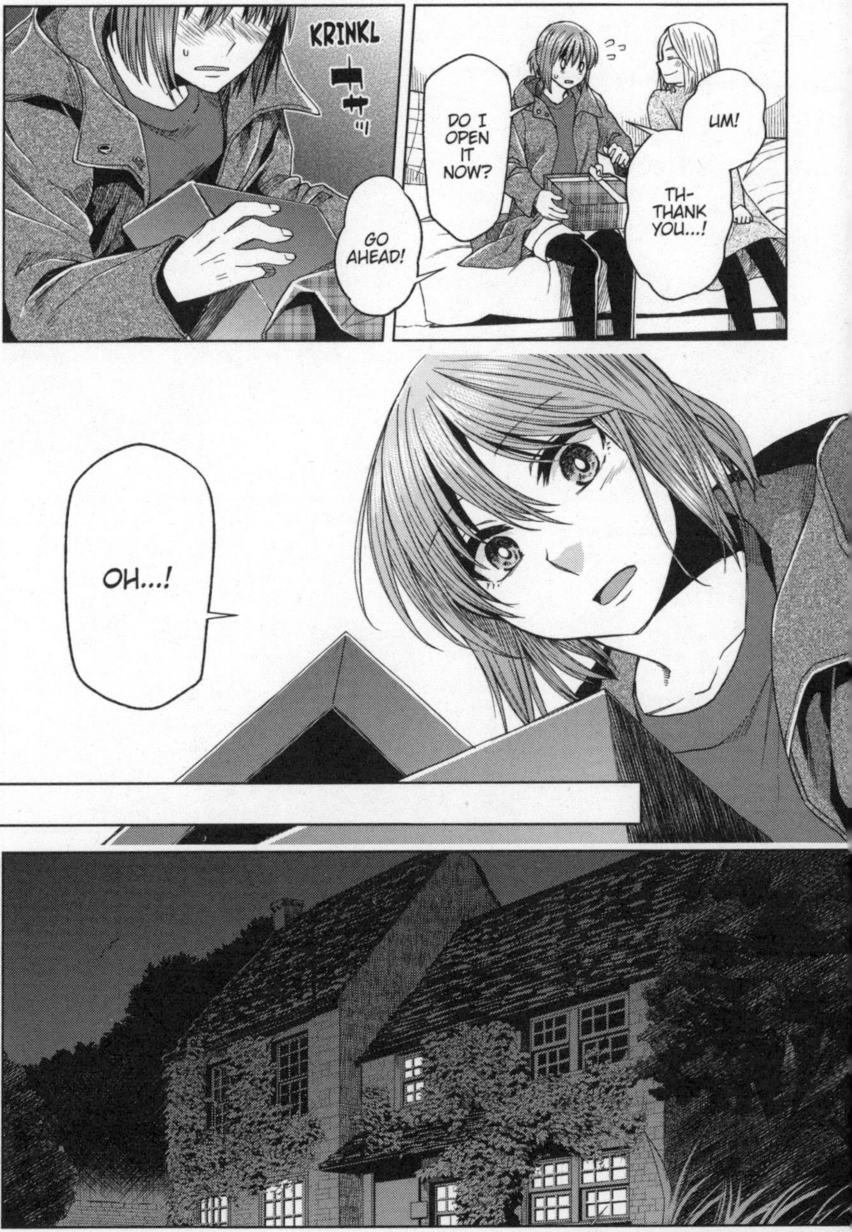
UM!
TH-THANK YOU...!
DO I OPEN IT NOW?
GO AHEAD!
KRINKL
OH...!

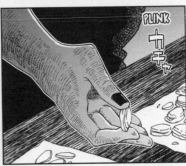

PLINK

ウキャ

RSTL

RSTL

FWISH

RSTL

RSTL

FWISH

FWISH

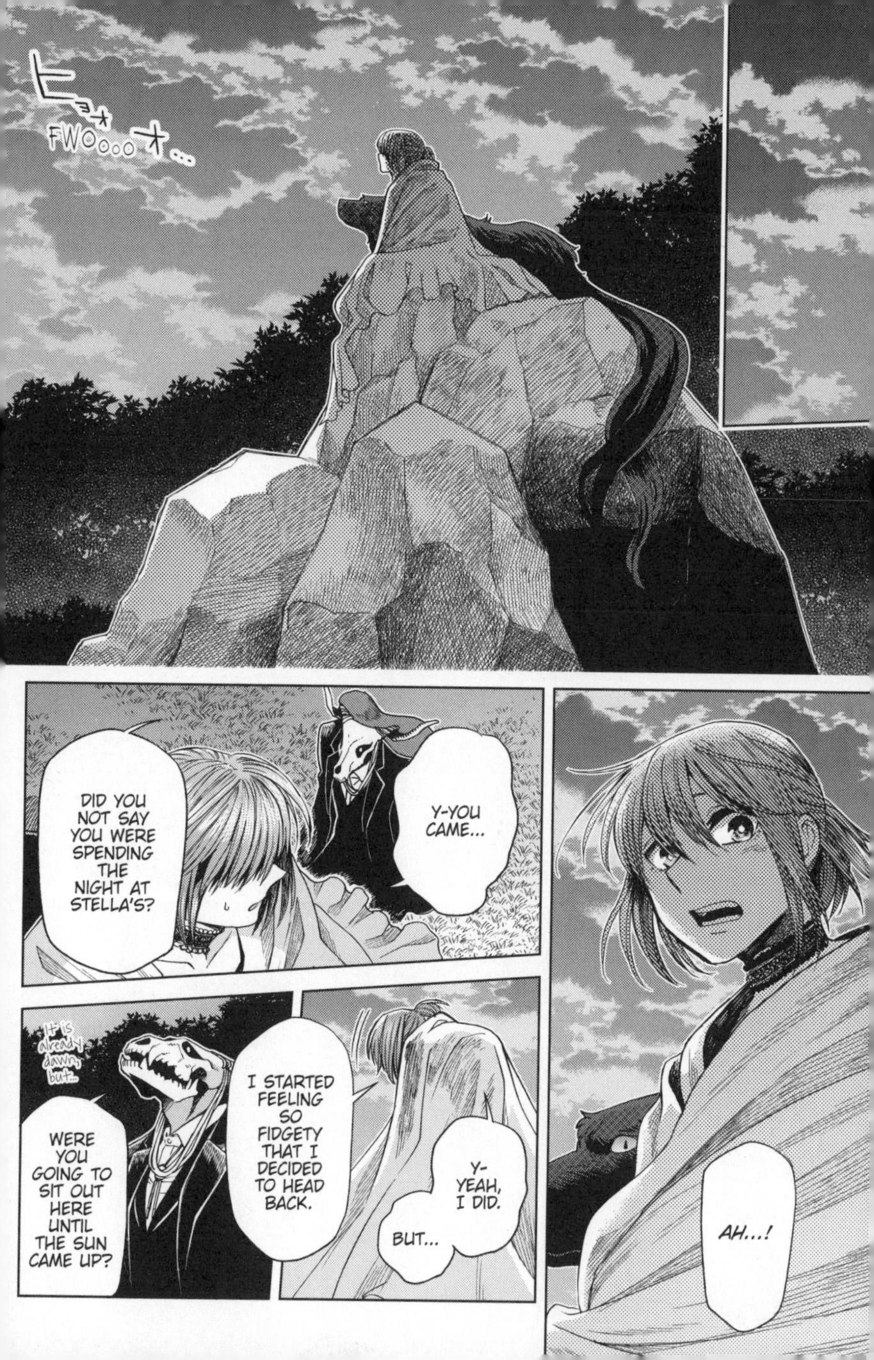
ヒョォ
FWOooo オ...
AH...!
Y-YOU CAME...
DID YOU NOT SAY YOU WERE SPENDING THE NIGHT AT STELLA'S?
Y-YEAH, I DID.
BUT...
I STARTED FEELING SO FIDGETY THAT I DECIDED TO HEAD BACK.
It is already dawn, but...
WERE YOU GOING TO SIT OUT HERE UNTIL THE SUN CAME UP?

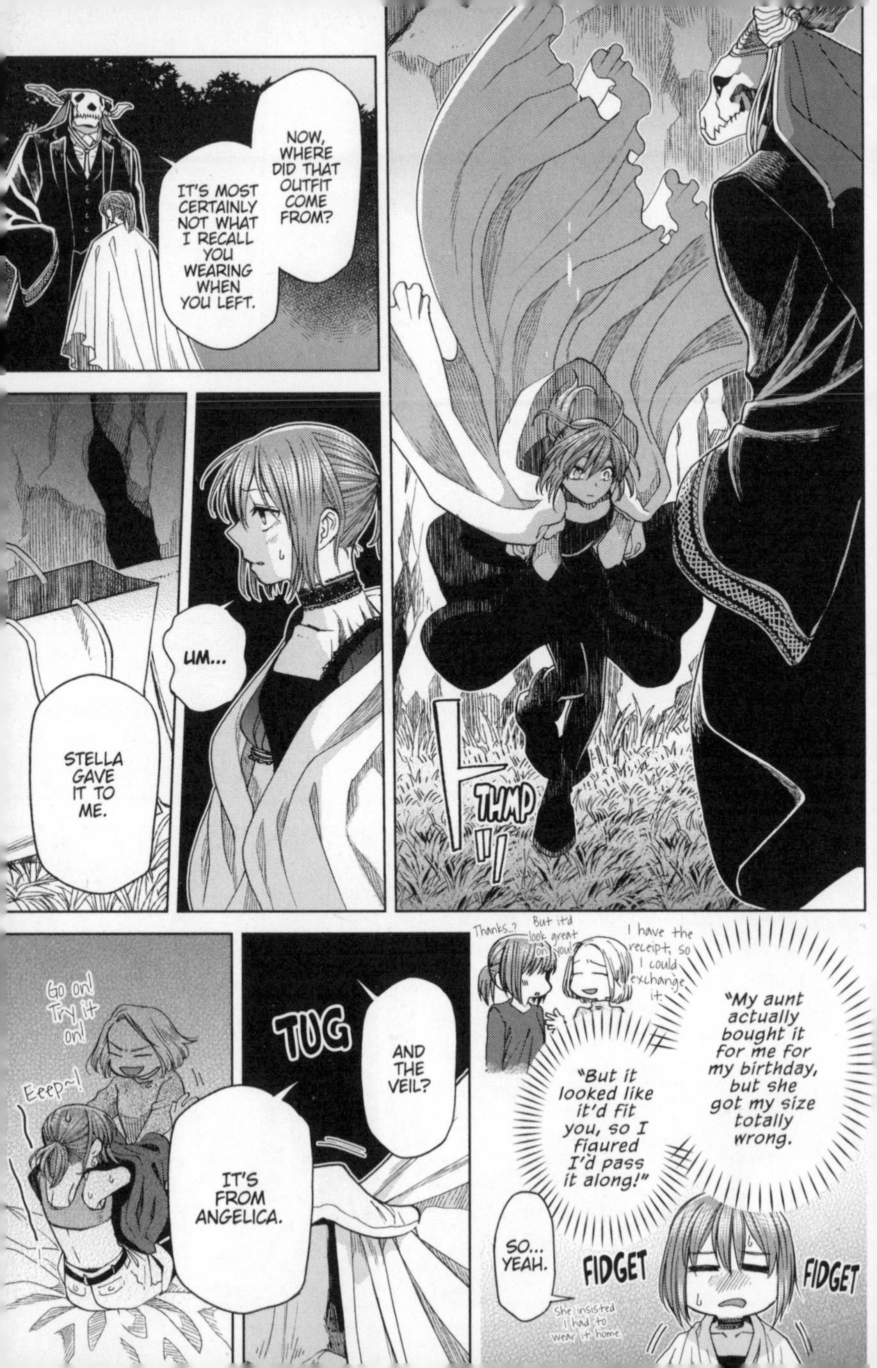
THMP
NOW, WHERE DID THAT OUTFIT COME FROM?
IT'S MOST CERTAINLY NOT WHAT I RECALL YOU WEARING WHEN YOU LEFT.
UM...
STELLA GAVE IT TO ME.
"My aunt actually bought it for me for my birthday, but she got my size totally wrong.
I have the receipt, so I could exchange it.
But it'd look great on you!
Thanks..?
"But it looked like it'd fit you, so I figured I'd pass it along!"
FIDGET
FIDGET
SO... YEAH.
She insisted I had to wear it home.
TUG
AND THE VEIL?
IT'S FROM ANGELICA.
Go on! Try it on!
Eeep~!

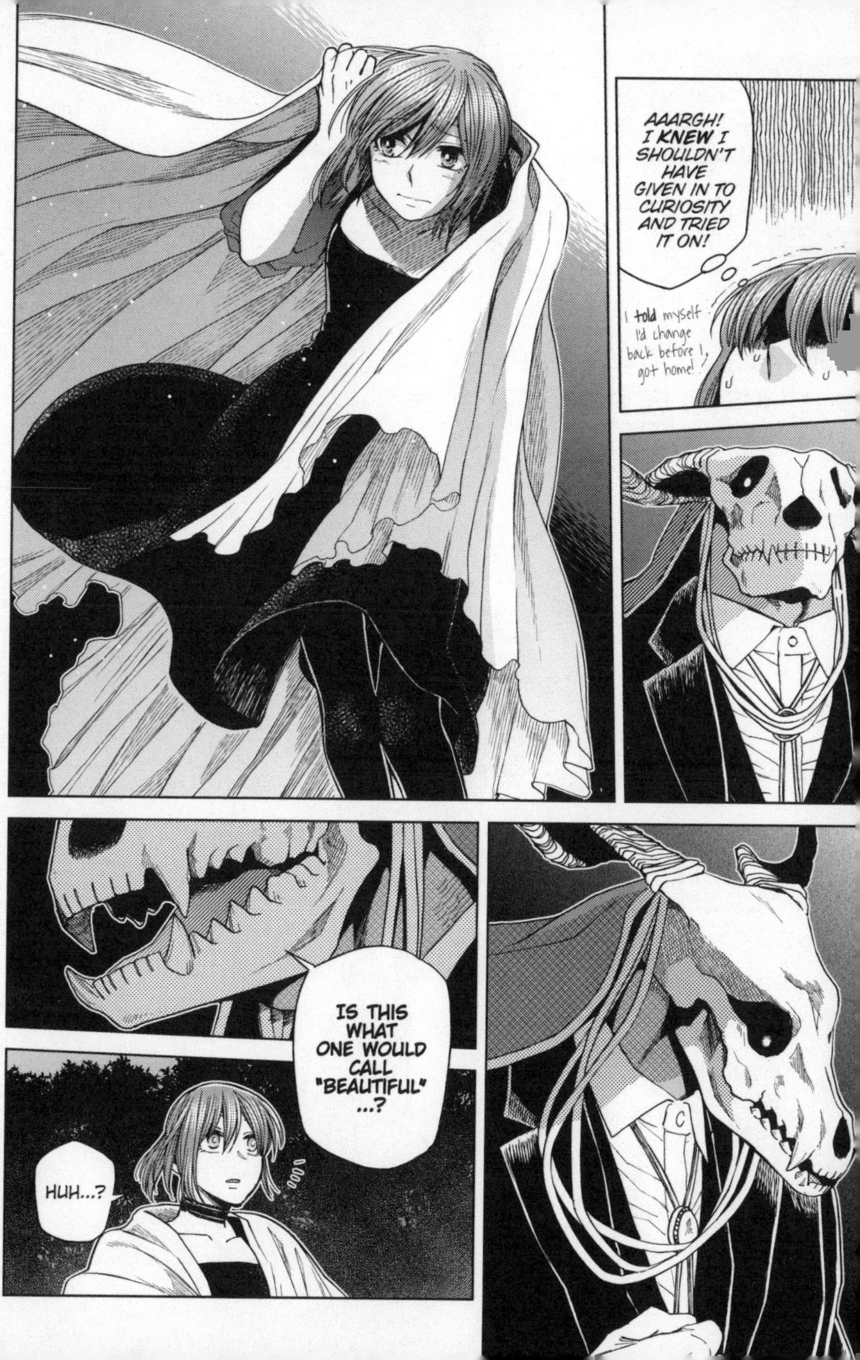
AAARGH! I KNEW I SHOULDN'T HAVE GIVEN IN TO CURIOSITY AND TRIED IT ON!
I told myself I'd change back before I got home!
IS THIS WHAT ONE WOULD CALL "BEAUTIFUL" ...?
HUH...?

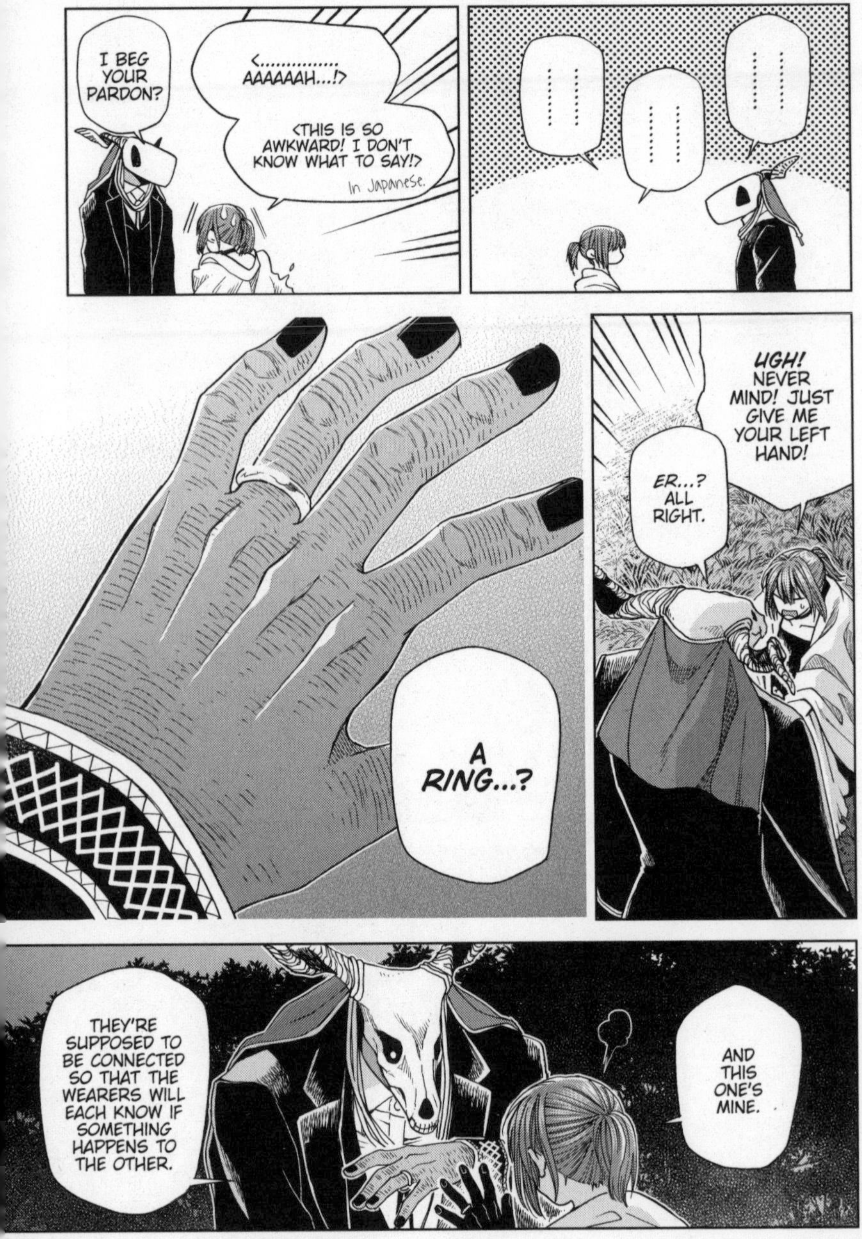
......
......
......
<..............
AAAAAAH...!>
<THIS IS SO AWKWARD! I DON'T KNOW WHAT TO SAY!>
In Japanese.
I BEG YOUR PARDON?
UGH! NEVER MIND! JUST GIVE ME YOUR LEFT HAND!
ER...? ALL RIGHT.
A RING...?
AND THIS ONE'S MINE.
THEY'RE SUPPOSED TO BE CONNECTED SO THAT THE WEARERS WILL EACH KNOW IF SOMETHING HAPPENS TO THE OTHER.

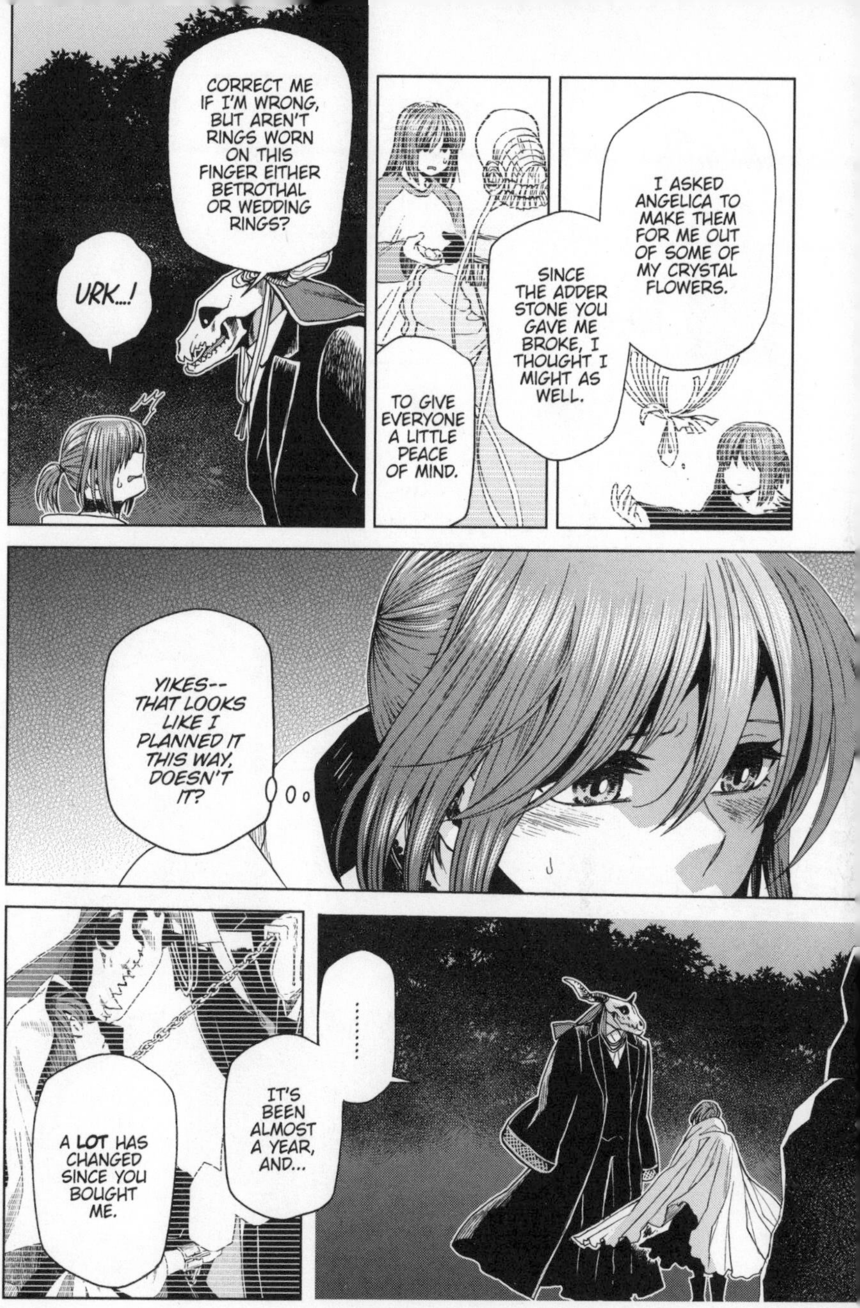
I ASKED ANGELICA TO MAKE THEM FOR ME OUT OF SOME OF MY CRYSTAL FLOWERS.
SINCE THE ADDER STONE YOU GAVE ME BROKE, I THOUGHT I MIGHT AS WELL.
TO GIVE EVERYONE A LITTLE PEACE OF MIND.
CORRECT ME IF I'M WRONG, BUT AREN'T RINGS WORN ON THIS FINGER EITHER BETROTHAL OR WEDDING RINGS?
URK...!
YIKES-- THAT LOOKS LIKE I PLANNED IT THIS WAY, DOESN'T IT?
......
IT'S BEEN ALMOST A YEAR, AND...
A **LOT** HAS CHANGED SINCE YOU BOUGHT ME.

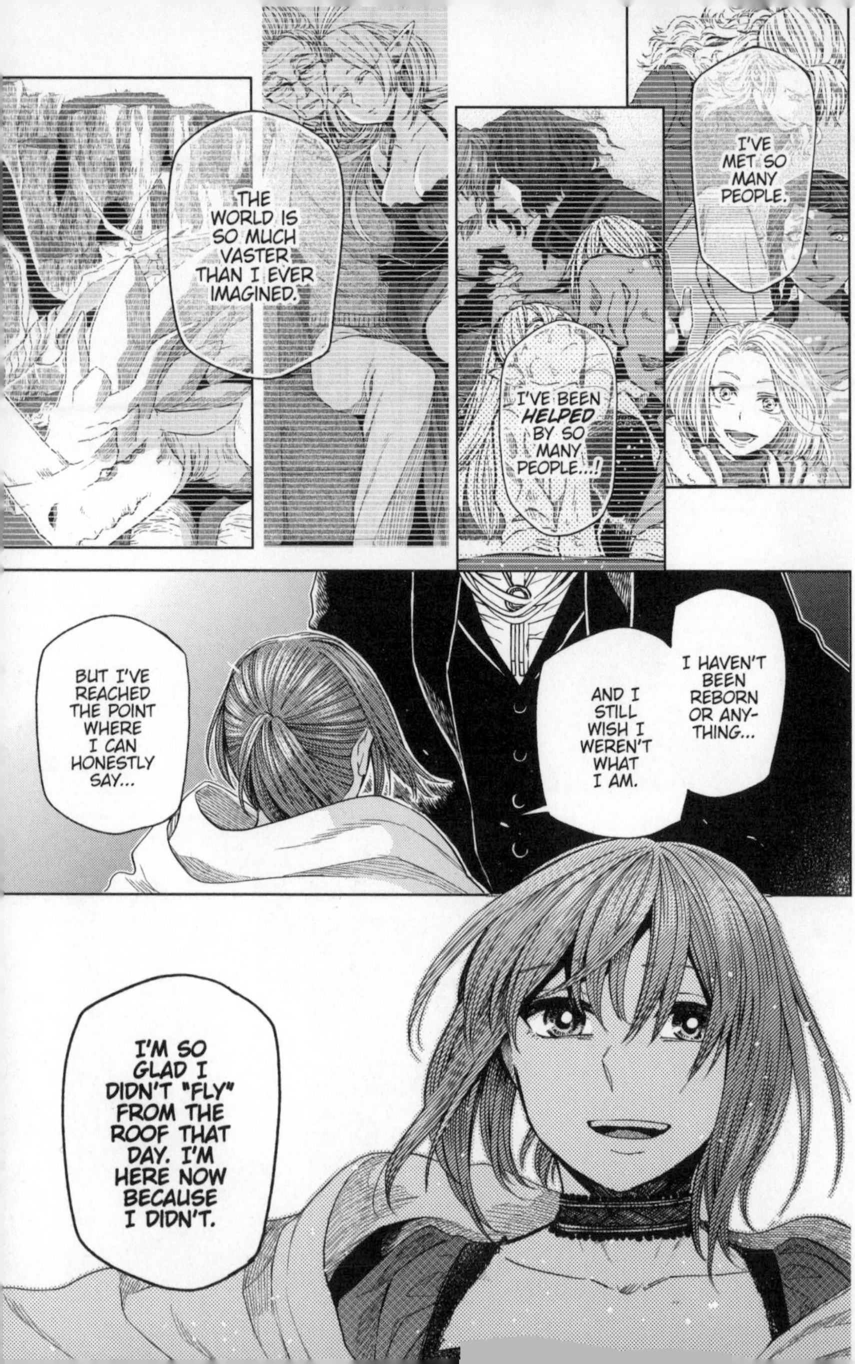
I'VE MET SO MANY PEOPLE.
I'VE BEEN *HELPED* BY SO MANY PEOPLE...!
THE WORLD IS SO MUCH VASTER THAN I EVER IMAGINED.
I HAVEN'T BEEN REBORN OR ANY-THING...
AND I STILL WISH I WEREN'T WHAT I AM.
BUT I'VE REACHED THE POINT WHERE I CAN HONESTLY SAY...
I'M SO GLAD I DIDN'T "FLY" FROM THE ROOF THAT DAY. I'M HERE NOW BECAUSE I DIDN'T.

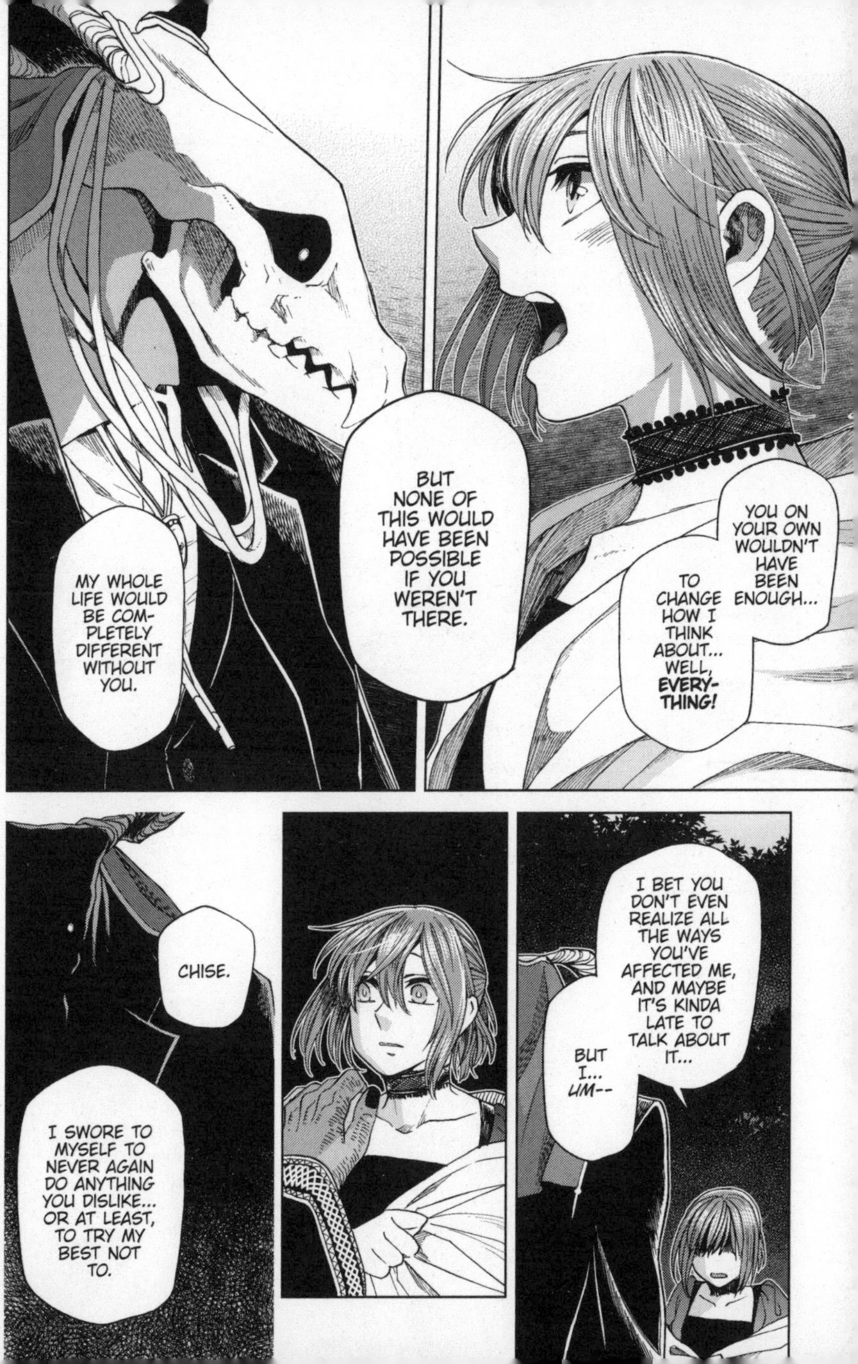
YOU ON YOUR OWN WOULDN'T HAVE BEEN ENOUGH...
TO CHANGE HOW I THINK ABOUT... WELL, **EVERYTHING!**
BUT NONE OF THIS WOULD HAVE BEEN POSSIBLE IF YOU WEREN'T THERE.
MY WHOLE LIFE WOULD BE COMPLETELY DIFFERENT WITHOUT YOU.
I BET YOU DON'T EVEN REALIZE ALL THE WAYS YOU'VE AFFECTED ME, AND MAYBE IT'S KINDA LATE TO TALK ABOUT IT...
BUT I... *UM--*
CHISE.
I SWORE TO MYSELF TO NEVER AGAIN DO ANYTHING YOU DISLIKE... OR AT LEAST, TO TRY MY BEST NOT TO.

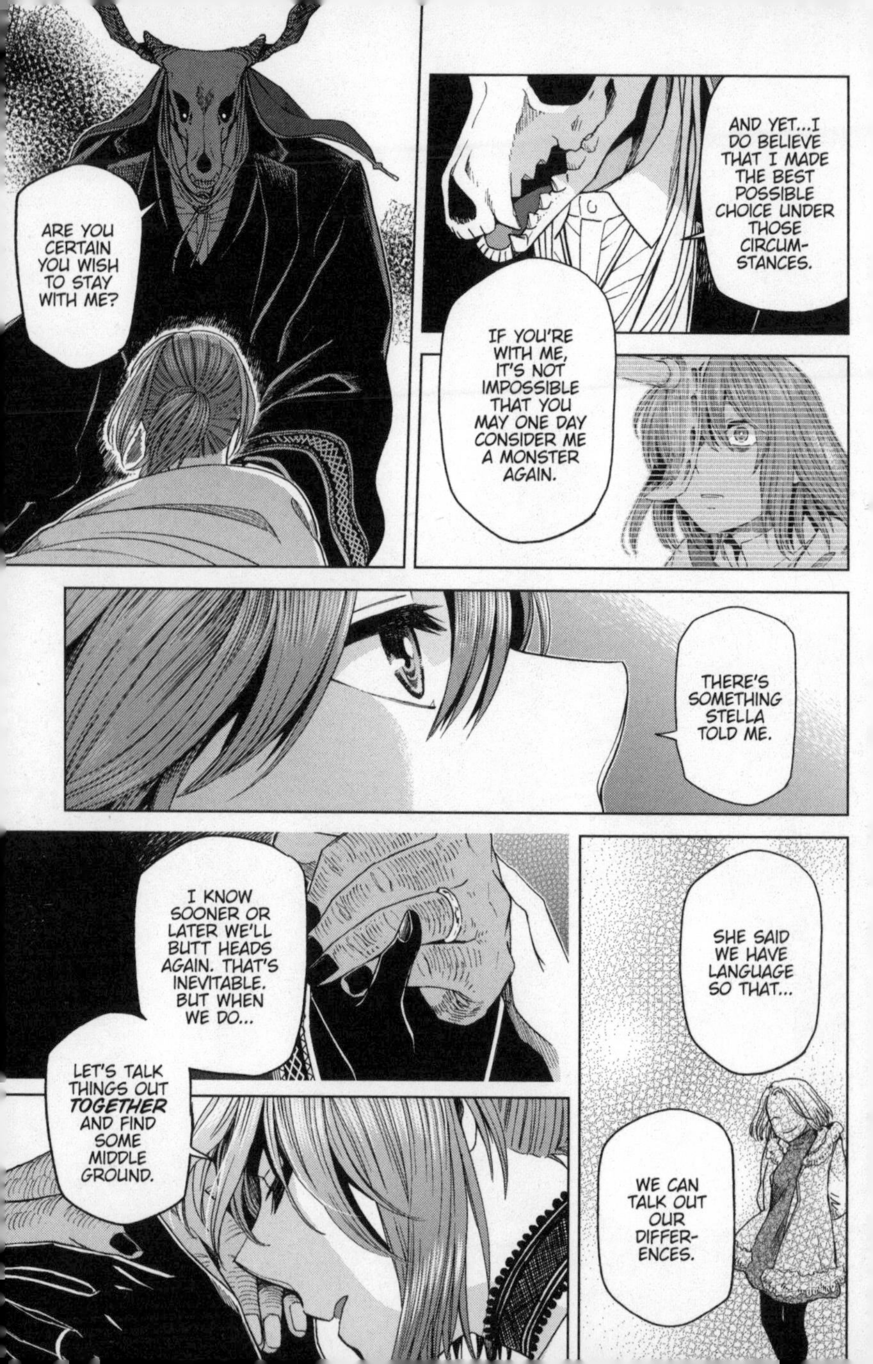
AND YET...I DO BELIEVE THAT I MADE THE BEST POSSIBLE CHOICE UNDER THOSE CIRCUM-STANCES.
IF YOU'RE WITH ME, IT'S NOT IMPOSSIBLE THAT YOU MAY ONE DAY CONSIDER ME A MONSTER AGAIN.
ARE YOU CERTAIN YOU WISH TO STAY WITH ME?
THERE'S SOMETHING STELLA TOLD ME.
SHE SAID WE HAVE LANGUAGE SO THAT...
WE CAN TALK OUT OUR DIFFER-ENCES.
I KNOW SOONER OR LATER WE'LL BUTT HEADS AGAIN. THAT'S INEVITABLE. BUT WHEN WE DO...
LET'S TALK THINGS OUT ***TOGETHER*** AND FIND SOME MIDDLE GROUND.

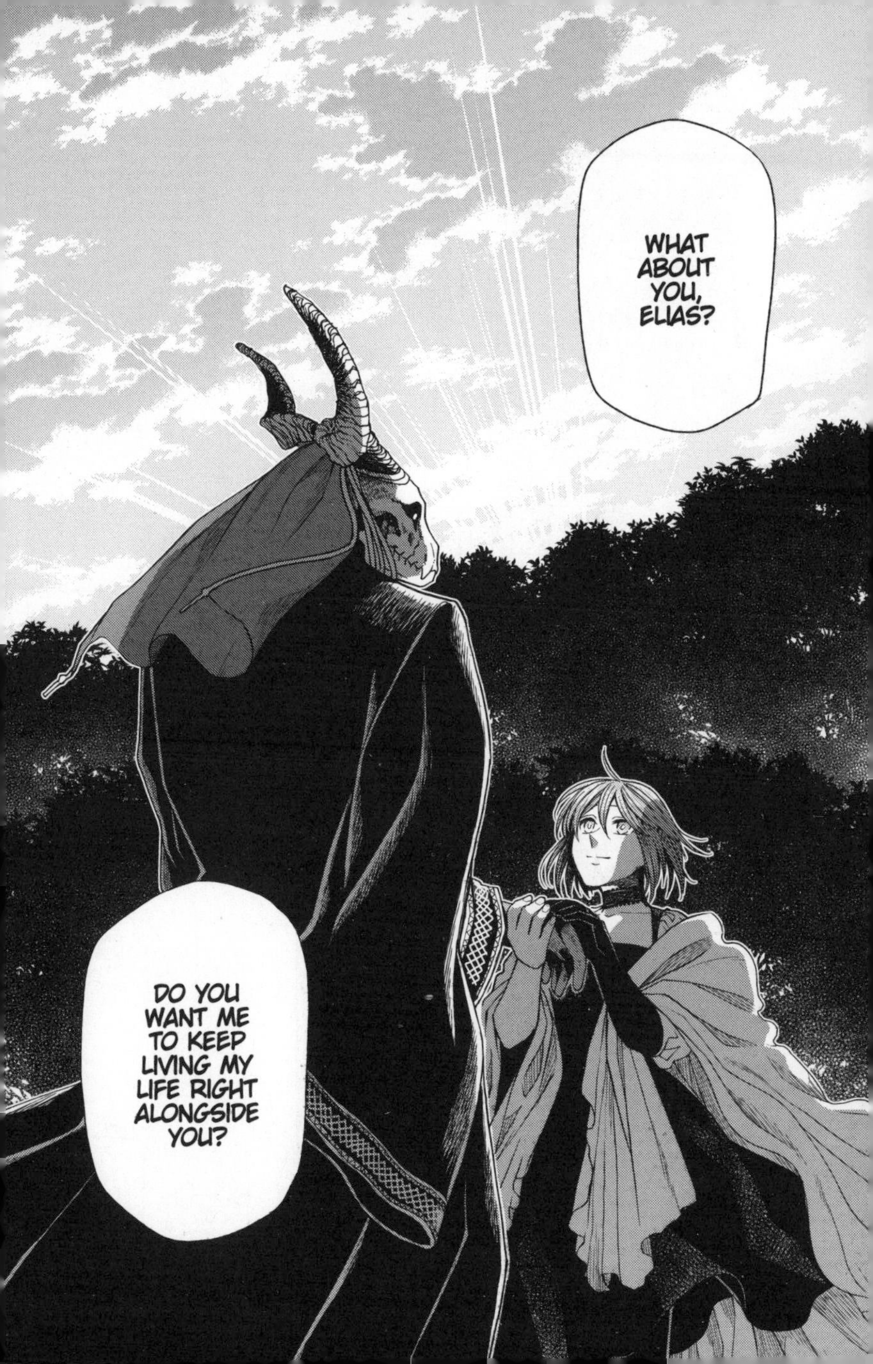
WHAT ABOUT YOU, ELIAS?
DO YOU WANT ME TO KEEP LIVING MY LIFE RIGHT ALONGSIDE YOU?

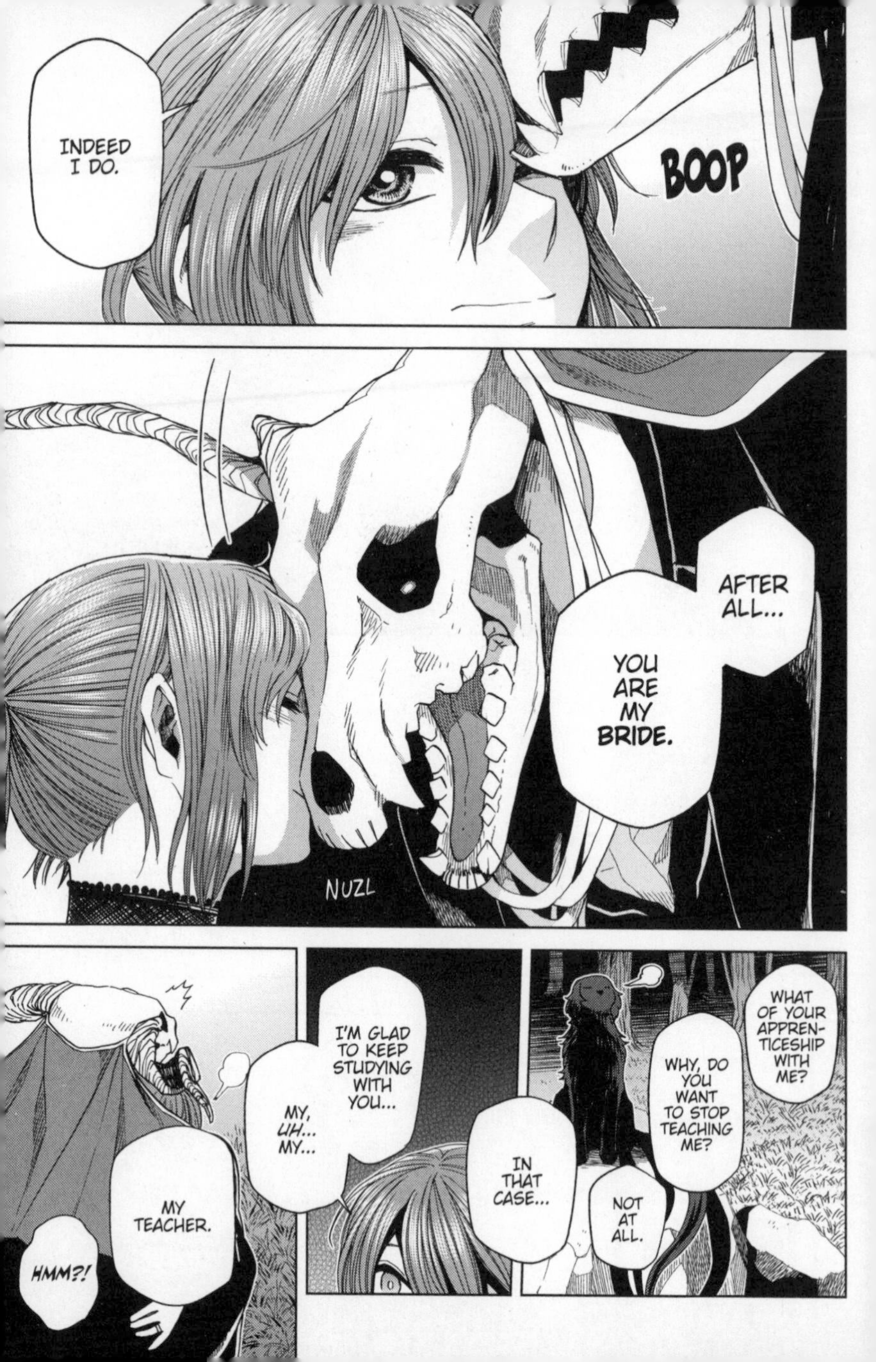
BOOP
INDEED I DO.
AFTER ALL...
YOU ARE MY BRIDE.
NUZL
WHAT OF YOUR APPRENTICESHIP WITH ME?
WHY, DO YOU WANT TO STOP TEACHING ME?
NOT AT ALL.
IN THAT CASE...
I'M GLAD TO KEEP STUDYING WITH YOU...
MY, UH... MY...
MY TEACHER.
HMM?!

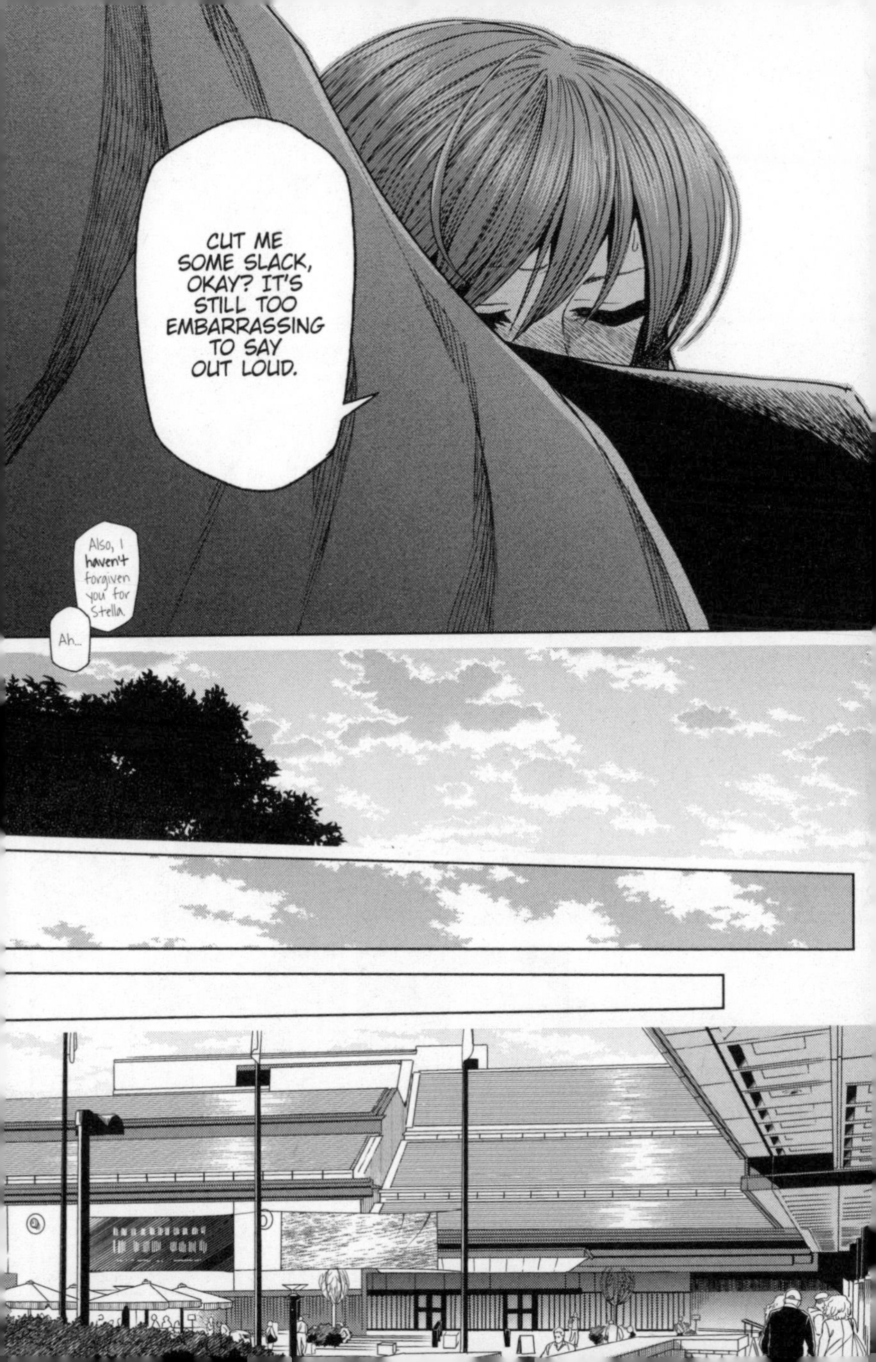
CUT ME SOME SLACK, OKAY? IT'S STILL TOO EMBARRASSING TO SAY OUT LOUD.
Also, I haven't forgiven you for Stella.
Ah...

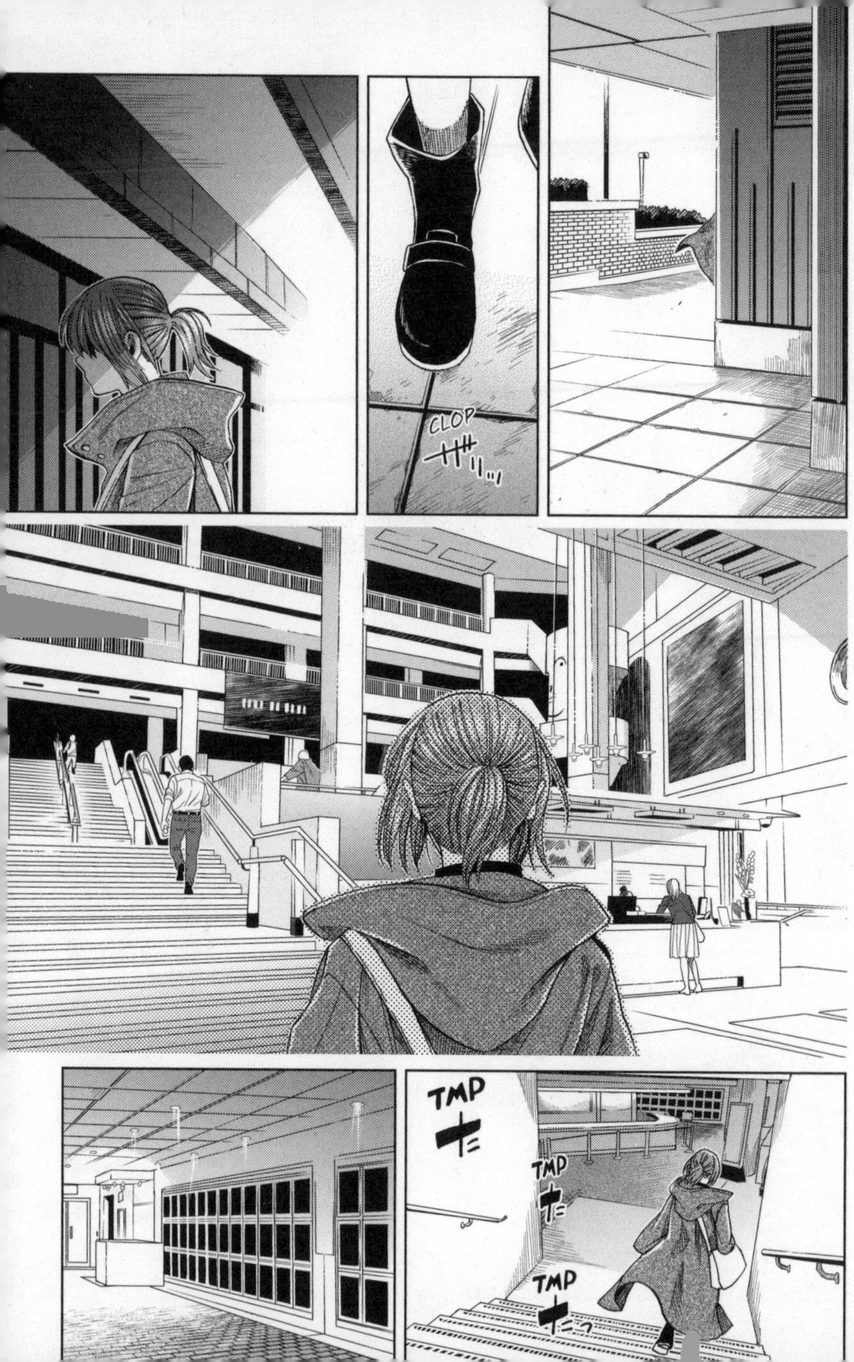
CLOP
TMP
TMP
TMP

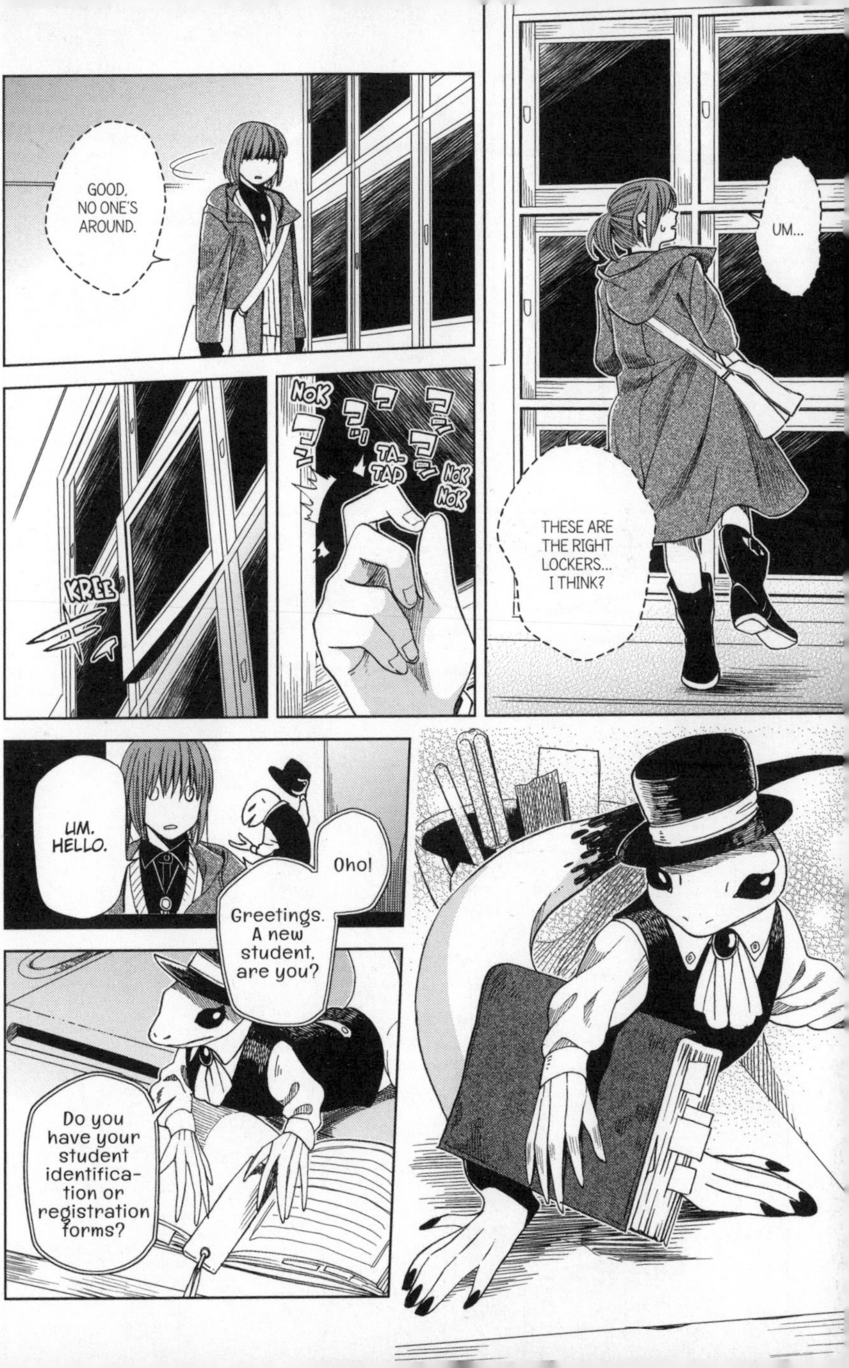
UM...
THESE ARE THE RIGHT LOCKERS... I THINK?
GOOD, NO ONE'S AROUND.
NOK
TA-TAP
NOK NOK
KREE
UM. HELLO.
Oho!
Greetings. A new student, are you?
Do you have your student identification or registration forms?

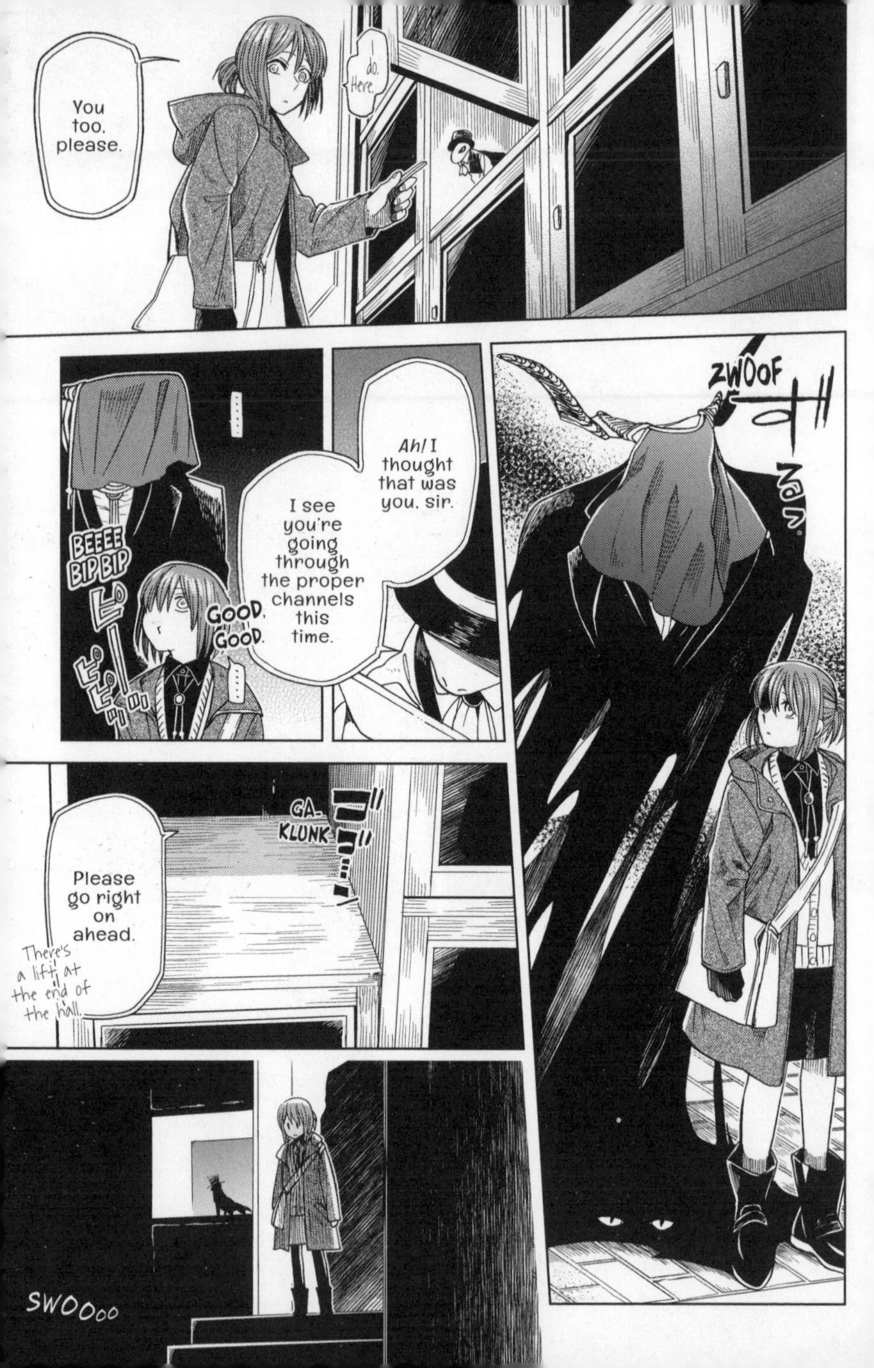
I do. Here.
You too, please.
ZWOOF
Ah! I thought that was you, sir.
I see you're going through the proper channels this time.
...
BEEEE BIP BIP
GOOD, GOOD.
GA-KLUNK
Please go right on ahead.
There's a lift at the end of the hall.
SWOOoo

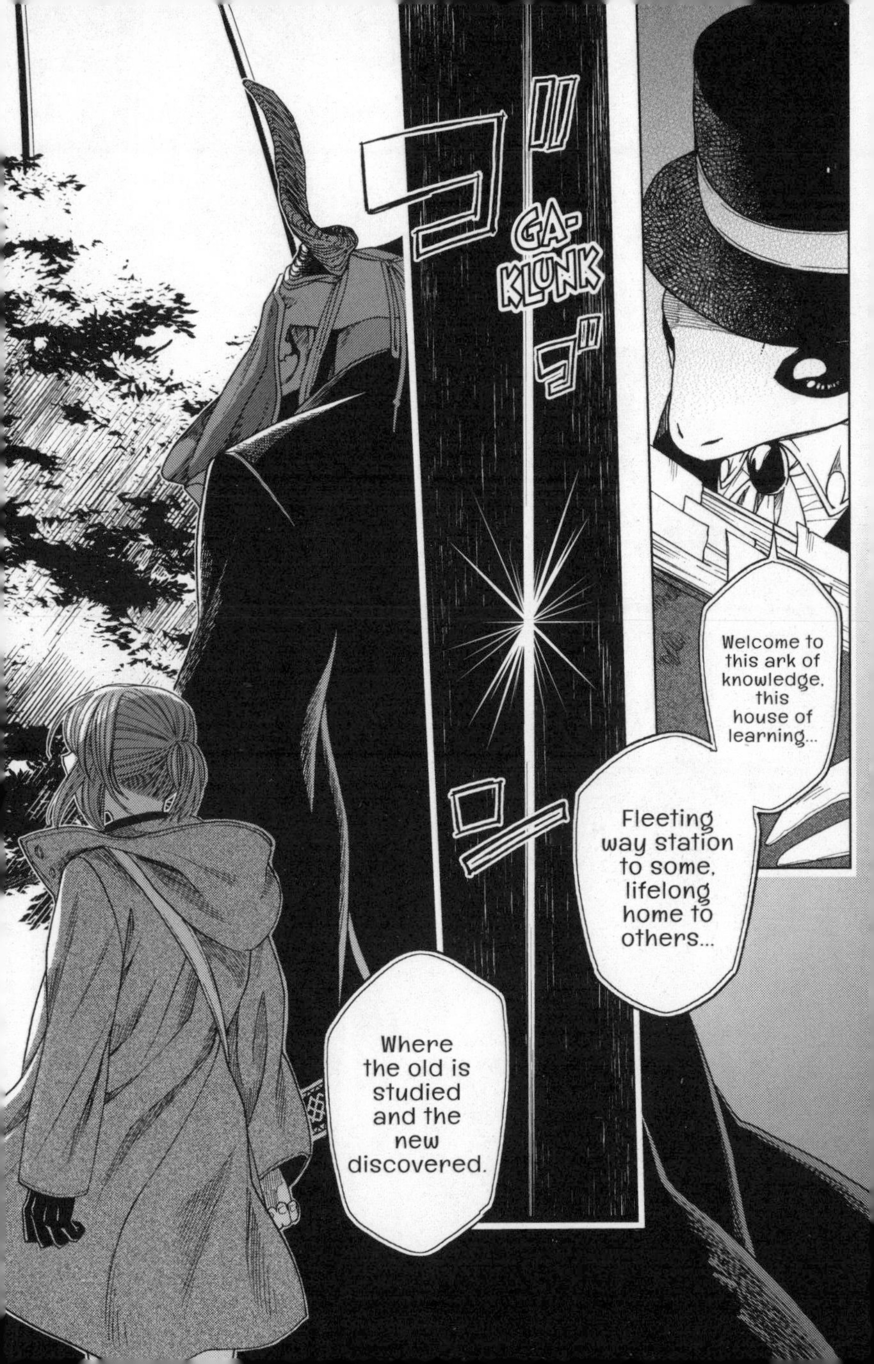
Welcome to this ark of knowledge, this house of learning...
GA-KLUNK
Fleeting way station to some, lifelong home to others...
Where the old is studied and the new discovered.

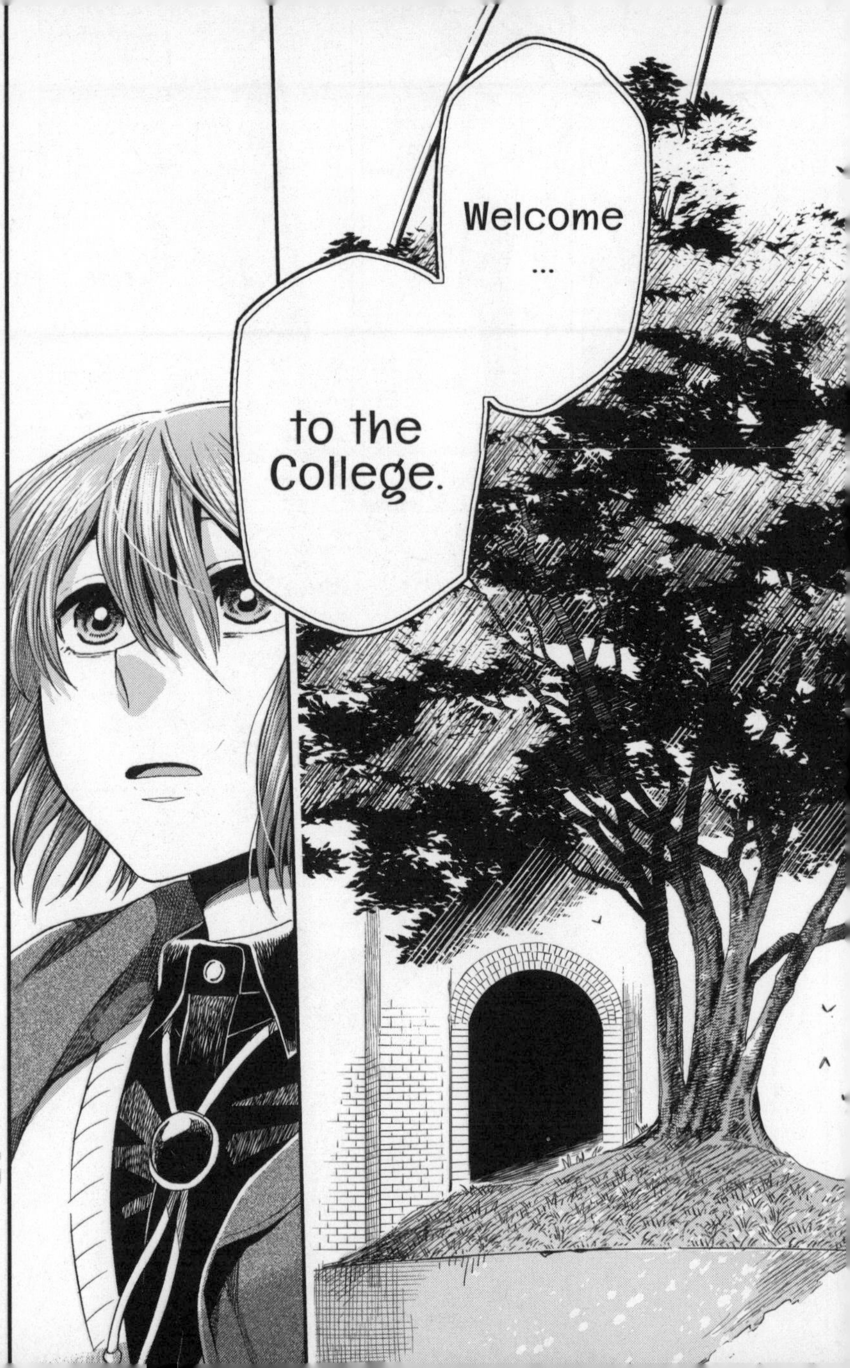
Welcome ... to the College.

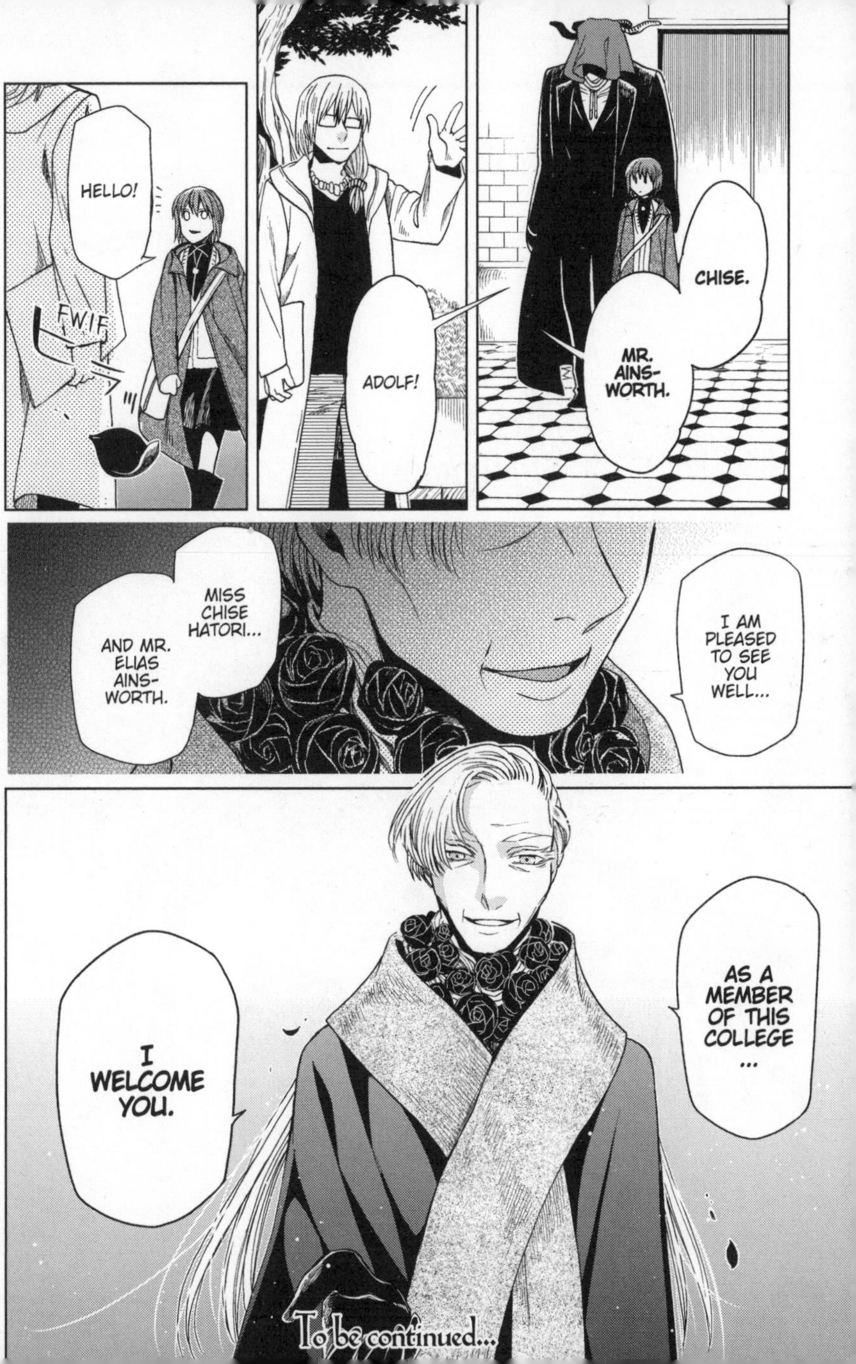
CHISE.
MR. AINS-WORTH.
ADOLF!
HELLO!
FWIF
I AM PLEASED TO SEE YOU WELL...
MISS CHISE HATORI...
AND MR. ELIAS AINS-WORTH.
AS A MEMBER OF THIS COLLEGE ...
I WELCOME YOU.
To be continued...

The Ancient Magus' Bride

enters a new

chapter...

The College Arc Begins!

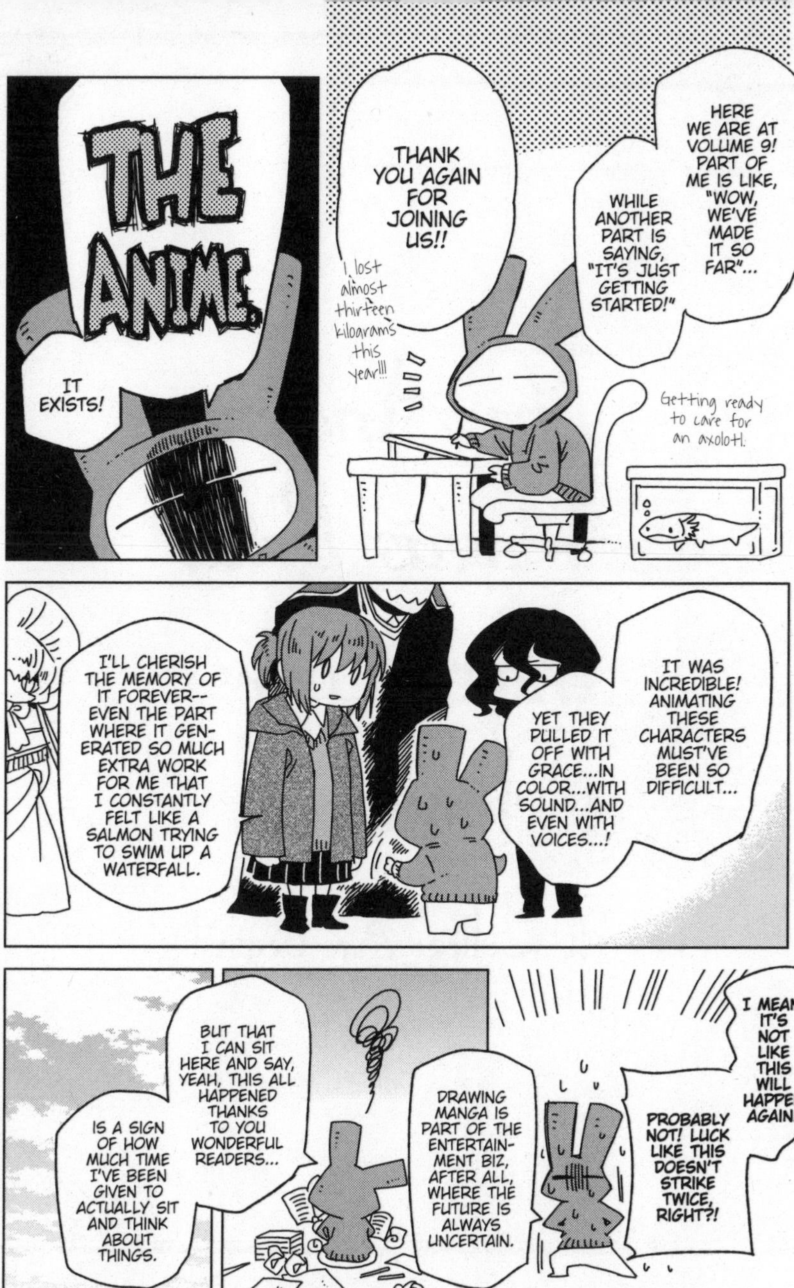
HERE WE ARE AT VOLUME 9! PART OF ME IS LIKE, "WOW, WE'VE MADE IT SO FAR"...
WHILE ANOTHER PART IS SAYING, "IT'S JUST GETTING STARTED!"
THANK YOU AGAIN FOR JOINING US!!
I lost almost thirteen kilograms this year!!!
Getting ready to care for an axolotl.
THE ANIME.
IT EXISTS!
IT WAS INCREDIBLE! ANIMATING THESE CHARACTERS MUST'VE BEEN SO DIFFICULT...
YET THEY PULLED IT OFF WITH GRACE...IN COLOR...WITH SOUND...AND EVEN WITH VOICES...!
I'LL CHERISH THE MEMORY OF IT FOREVER--EVEN THE PART WHERE IT GENERATED SO MUCH EXTRA WORK FOR ME THAT I CONSTANTLY FELT LIKE A SALMON TRYING TO SWIM UP A WATERFALL.
...w!
I MEAN, IT'S NOT LIKE THIS WILL HAPPEN AGAIN!
PROBABLY NOT! LUCK LIKE THIS DOESN'T STRIKE TWICE, RIGHT?!
DRAWING MANGA IS PART OF THE ENTERTAINMENT BIZ, AFTER ALL, WHERE THE FUTURE IS ALWAYS UNCERTAIN.
BUT THAT I CAN SIT HERE AND SAY, YEAH, THIS ALL HAPPENED THANKS TO YOU WONDERFUL READERS...
IS A SIGN OF HOW MUCH TIME I'VE BEEN GIVEN TO ACTUALLY SIT AND THINK ABOUT THINGS.

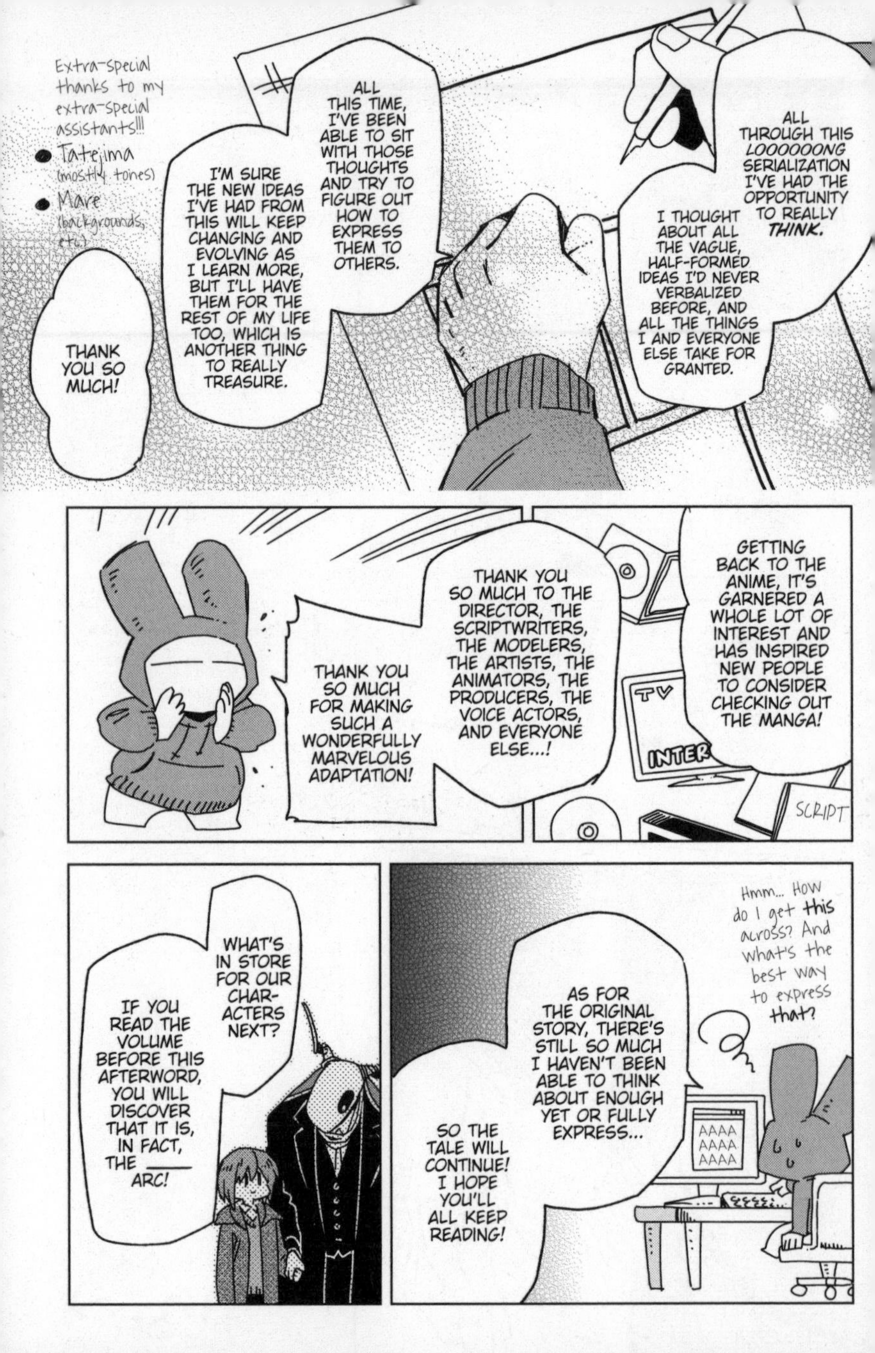
ALL THROUGH THIS LOOOOOONG SERIALIZATION I'VE HAD THE OPPORTUNITY TO REALLY *THINK.*
I THOUGHT ABOUT ALL THE VAGUE, HALF-FORMED IDEAS I'D NEVER VERBALIZED BEFORE, AND ALL THE THINGS I AND EVERYONE ELSE TAKE FOR GRANTED.
ALL THIS TIME, I'VE BEEN ABLE TO SIT WITH THOSE THOUGHTS AND TRY TO FIGURE OUT HOW TO EXPRESS THEM TO OTHERS.
I'M SURE THE NEW IDEAS I'VE HAD FROM THIS WILL KEEP CHANGING AND EVOLVING AS I LEARN MORE, BUT I'LL HAVE THEM FOR THE REST OF MY LIFE TOO, WHICH IS ANOTHER THING TO REALLY TREASURE.
THANK YOU SO MUCH!
Extra-special thanks to my extra-special assistants!!!
● Tatejima (mostly tones)
● Mare (backgrounds, etc.)
GETTING BACK TO THE ANIME, IT'S GARNERED A WHOLE LOT OF INTEREST AND HAS INSPIRED NEW PEOPLE TO CONSIDER CHECKING OUT THE MANGA!
TV
INTER
SCRIPT
THANK YOU SO MUCH TO THE DIRECTOR, THE SCRIPTWRITERS, THE MODELERS, THE ARTISTS, THE ANIMATORS, THE PRODUCERS, THE VOICE ACTORS, AND EVERYONE ELSE...!
THANK YOU SO MUCH FOR MAKING SUCH A WONDERFULLY MARVELOUS ADAPTATION!
Hmm... How do I get **this** across? And what's the best way to express **that**?
AAAA AAAA AAAA
AS FOR THE ORIGINAL STORY, THERE'S STILL SO MUCH I HAVEN'T BEEN ABLE TO THINK ABOUT ENOUGH YET OR FULLY EXPRESS...
SO THE TALE WILL CONTINUE! I HOPE YOU'LL ALL KEEP READING!
WHAT'S IN STORE FOR OUR CHAR-ACTERS NEXT?
IF YOU READ THE VOLUME BEFORE THIS AFTERWORD, YOU WILL DISCOVER THAT IT IS, IN FACT, THE ____ ARC!

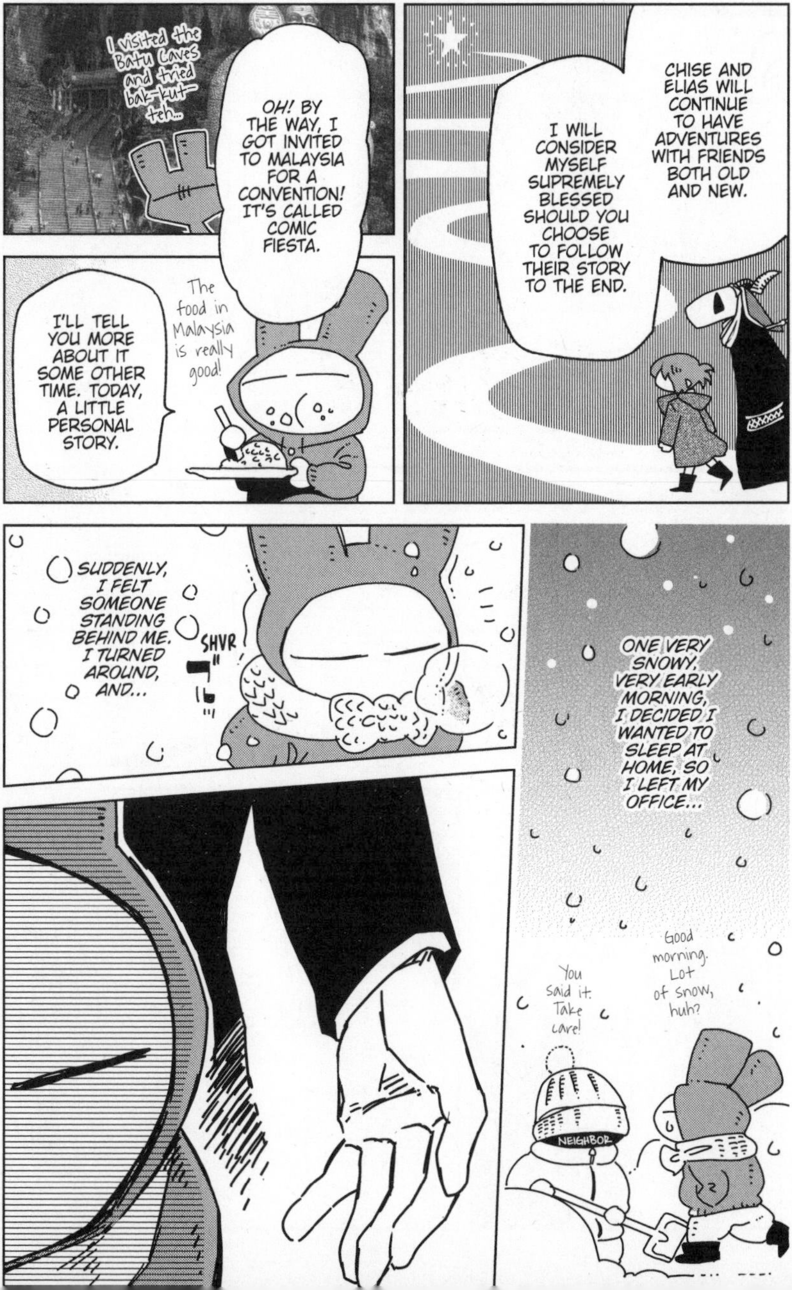

CHISE AND ELIAS WILL CONTINUE TO HAVE ADVENTURES WITH FRIENDS BOTH OLD AND NEW.
I WILL CONSIDER MYSELF SUPREMELY BLESSED SHOULD YOU CHOOSE TO FOLLOW THEIR STORY TO THE END.
OH! BY THE WAY, I GOT INVITED TO MALAYSIA FOR A CONVENTION! IT'S CALLED COMIC FIESTA.
I visited the Batu Caves and tried bak-kut-teh...
The food in Malaysia is really good!
I'LL TELL YOU MORE ABOUT IT SOME OTHER TIME. TODAY, A LITTLE PERSONAL STORY.
ONE VERY SNOWY, VERY EARLY MORNING, I DECIDED I WANTED TO SLEEP AT HOME, SO I LEFT MY OFFICE...
Good morning. Lot of snow, huh?
You said it. Take care!
NEIGHBOR
SUDDENLY, I FELT SOMEONE STANDING BEHIND ME. I TURNED AROUND, AND...
SHVR

※ I got invited to America for conventions not long ago, too! Two of them! I'm so grateful!

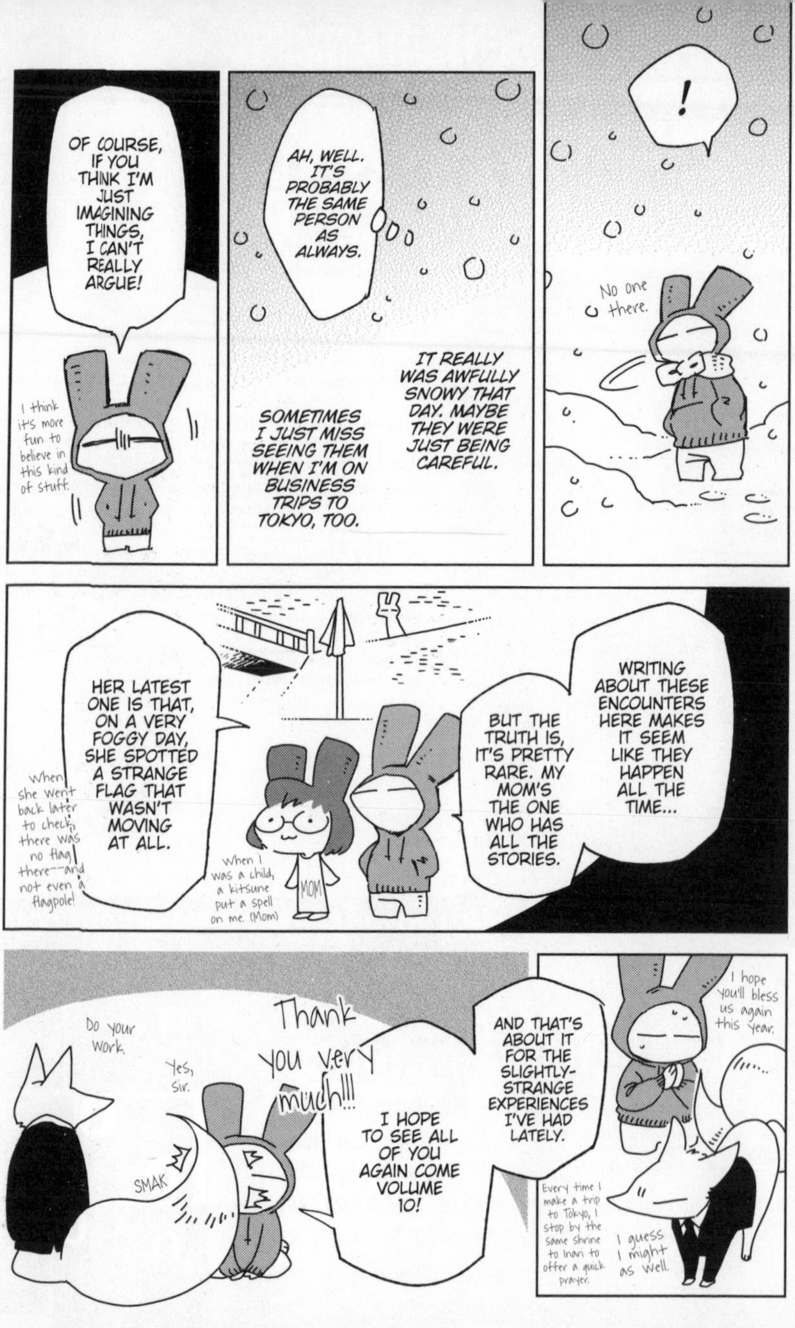
!
No one there.
AH, WELL. IT'S PROBABLY THE SAME PERSON AS ALWAYS.
IT REALLY WAS AWFULLY SNOWY THAT DAY. MAYBE THEY WERE JUST BEING CAREFUL.
SOMETIMES I JUST MISS SEEING THEM WHEN I'M ON BUSINESS TRIPS TO TOKYO, TOO.
OF COURSE, IF YOU THINK I'M JUST IMAGINING THINGS, I CAN'T REALLY ARGUE!
I think it's more fun to believe in this kind of stuff.
WRITING ABOUT THESE ENCOUNTERS HERE MAKES IT SEEM LIKE THEY HAPPEN ALL THE TIME...
BUT THE TRUTH IS, IT'S PRETTY RARE. MY MOM'S THE ONE WHO HAS ALL THE STORIES.
MOM
When I was a child, a kitsune put a spell on me. (Mom)
HER LATEST ONE IS THAT, ON A VERY FOGGY DAY, SHE SPOTTED A STRANGE FLAG THAT WASN'T MOVING AT ALL.
When she went back later to check, there was no flag there--and not even a flagpole!
I hope you'll bless us again this year.
......
AND THAT'S ABOUT IT FOR THE SLIGHTLY-STRANGE EXPERIENCES I'VE HAD LATELY.
Every time I make a trip to Tokyo, I stop by the same shrine to Inari to offer a quick prayer.
I guess I might as well.
Thank you very much!!!
I HOPE TO SEE ALL OF YOU AGAIN COME VOLUME 10!
Do your work.
Yes, sir.
SMAK

SEVEN SEAS ENTERTAINMENT PRESENTS

The Ancient Magus' Bride

VOLUME 9

story and art by KORE YAMAZAKI

TRANSLATION
Adrienne Beck

ADAPTATION
Ysabet Reinhardt MacFarlane

LETTERING AND RETOUCH
Lys Blakeslee

COVER DESIGN
Nicky Lim

PROOFREADER
Shanti Whitesides

ASSISTANT EDITOR
J.P. Sullivan

PRODUCTION ASSISTANT
CK Russell

PRODUCTION MANAGER
Lissa Pattillo

EDITOR-IN-CHIEF
Adam Arnold

PUBLISHER
Jason DeAngelis

THE ANCIENT MAGUS' BRIDE VOL. 9

Originally published in Japan in 2018 by MAG Garden Corporation, Tokyo.
English translation rights arranged through TOHAN CORPORATION, Tokyo.

Seven Seas books may be purchased in bulk for promotional, educational, or business use. Please contact your local bookseller or the Macmillan Corporate and Premium Sales Department at 1-800-221-7945, extension 5442, or by e-mail at MacmillanSpecialMarkets@macmillan.com.

ISBN: 978-1-626928-01-5

Printed in Canada

First Printing: September 2018

10 9 8 7 6 5 4 3 2 1

FOLLOW US ONLINE: ***www.sevenseasentertainment.com***

READING DIRECTIONS

This book reads from ***right to left***, J
If this is your first time reading ma
reading from the top right panel on
take it from there. If you get lost,
numbered diagram here. It may see
first, but you'll get the hang of it! Have fun!!

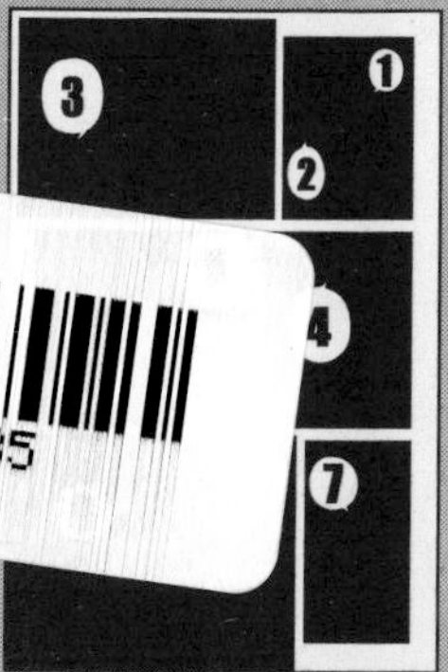
3
1
2
4
7